THE
LIVING
AND THE
DEAD

The Living and the Dead

ROBERT McNAMARA AND FIVE LIVES OF A LOST WAR

PAUL HENDRICKSON

ALFRED A. KNOPF NEW YORK 1996

Grateful acknowledgment is made to the following for permission to print
unpublished material or reprint previously published material:

Georges Borchardt, Inc.: "When the War Is Over," from *The Lice* by W. S. Merwin,
copyright © 1967 by W. S. Merwin (New York: Atheneum). Reprinted by permission of
Georges Borchardt, Inc.   *The Dartmouth:* Excerpts from poem by Alexander Laing (*The
Dartmouth,* November 12, 1965). Reprinted by permission of *The Dartmouth.   New
Directions Publishing Corp.* and *Faber and Faber Limited:* Excerpt from "Hugh Selwyn
Mauberley," from *Personae* by Ezra Pound, copyright © 1926 by Ezra Pound. Rights
outside the United States and Canada administered for *Collected Shorter Poems* by Faber
and Faber Limited, London. Reprinted by permission of New Directions Publishing
Corp. and Faber and Faber Limited.   *Hugh Ogden:* Excerpt from "Chautauqua" by Hugh
Ogden. Reprinted by permission of Hugh Ogden.   *Poetry* and *George Starbuck:* Excerpt
from "Of Late" by George Starbuck (*Poetry,* vol. 109, no. 1, October 1966), copyright ©
1966 by The Modern Poetry Association, copyright © 1966 by Atlantic Monthly Press,
copyright renewed 1994 by George Starbuck. Reprinted by permission of the Editor of
Poetry and George Starbuck.   *Random House, Inc.* and *Faber and Faber Limited:*
Excerpt from "Musée des Beaux Arts," from *W. H. Auden: Collected Poems* by W. H.
Auden, copyright © 1940 and renewed 1968 by W. H. Auden. Rights in the United
Kingdom administered by Faber and Faber Limited, London. Reprinted by permission of
Random House, Inc., and Faber and Faber Limited.   *University Press of New England:*
Excerpt from "At the Executed Murderer's Grave," from *Above the River: The Complete
Poems* by James Wright, copyright © 1990 by Anne Wright. Reprinted by permission of
University Press of New England.   *A. P. Watt Ltd.:* Excerpts from "The Palace," from
Rudyard Kipling's Verse: Inclusive Edition, 1885–1926, by Rudyard Kipling. Reprinted by
permission of A. P. Watt Ltd., on behalf of The National Trust for Places of Historic
Interest or Natural Beauty.   *Anne Morrison Welsh:* Excerpts from unpublished letters
and essays by Norman R. Morrison, and excerpts from unpublished letters and essays by
Anne Morrison Welsh. Printed by permission of Anne Morrison Welsh.

Library of Congress Cataloging-in-Publication Data
Hendrickson, Paul.
The living and the dead: Robert McNamara and
five lives of a lost war / Paul Hendrickson.
p.   cm.
Includes bibliographical references and index.
ISBN 0-679-42761-9 (alk. paper)
1. Vietnamese Conflict, 1961–1975—United States.
2. McNamara, Robert S., 1916–   . I. Title.
DS558.H445 1996
959.704'3373—dc20   96-7445 CIP

Manufactured in the United States of America
Published September 1, 1996
Second Printing, September 1996

FOR MY SONS, MATT AND JOHN

When the war is over
We will be proud of course the air will be
Good for breathing at last
The water will have been improved the salmon
And the silence of heaven will migrate more perfectly
The dead will think the living are worth it we will know
Who we are
And we will all enlist again

—W. S. MERWIN

CONTENTS

x   *Contents*

THE
LIVING
AND THE
DEAD

Many years after, you would spy him now and then on the street—a narrow figure in a tan trench coat hurrying down Connecticut Avenue or across Farragut Square or through the park that cuts in front of the White House. You would see him and start: My God, it's McNamara. The body was still lean and fit, remarkably so, but the face had now aged almost terrifyingly, as if meant to be a window on what lay heaped within. He was a ghost, a ghost of all that had passed and rolled on beneath his country in barely a generation.

ROBERT McNAMARA, 1984, A DECADE AND A HALF AFTER
HE LEFT THE PENTAGON

Prologue

A STORY
OUT OF TIME

SEPTEMBER 29, 1972. The easily recognized and semifatalistic man standing in the lunchroom of the *M.V. Islander* as it crossed Vineyard Sound that rainy Friday evening could not possibly have known—could he?—that a murderous rage was climbing up inside the throat of someone just feet away from him. Certainly, had Robert S. McNamara been aware, he would not have set down his drink on the metal counter, wouldn't have said to his companion, "Excuse me a minute, I'll get this and be right back," would never have turned and followed a short, bearded stranger in tennis shoes out into the darkness. But wouldn't almost anybody have done the same thing? you ask. Probably, although the assailant himself is still puzzled, even in his ambivalence and periodic shame about that night, over how trusting his victim seemed, how willing to comply. It was almost as if McNamara had long been waiting for such a moment and understood implicitly it was now here. Listen:

"He just stopped in the middle of his conversation and nodded and followed me right out. I've never really understood that part of it. I must have been pretty convincing, that's all I can think. I remember he was leaning up against the counter of the snack bar, laughing and talking. . . . He had on these sporty weekend clothes. I don't know, the two of them just seemed above everything around them, maybe that's part of what got to me. Anyway, I walked right up to him and said, 'Mr. McNamara, there's a phone call for you. Please follow me.' I didn't even know what I was going to say. I swear the words just came out. It's not like I told myself, okay, this is it, you're gonna take the guy outside and throw him off the goddamn boat."

The *M.V. Islander*, a serviceable old tub built in 1950 by the Maryland Drydock Company, is a "double-ender" in her design, which means that either end can serve as stern or bow, depending on the direction the boat is headed—to Martha's Vineyard or back to the mainland at Woods Hole, Massachusetts. The lunchroom, which is about the

7

size of a living room, sits up on the ferry's top deck, just behind the
pilothouse. During night crossings, and especially when the weather is
bad, this small, brightly lit area of the vessel is nearly always packed
and noisy, a kind of lantern against the sea's roughness. Nobody pays
much attention to famous faces in the lunchroom; famous faces are a lot
of what Martha's Vineyard is about in the first place. The trip across
Vineyard Sound takes forty-five minutes and covers seven miles of
open water. Mostly it is a boring transit, something you have to put up
with to get from here to there.

   *"I just wanted to confront him on Vietnam. I know it sounds
extremist now. But tell me, what good would screaming in his face have
done? What I felt about Vietnam was a lot deeper than that. I suppose
this arrogance thing came back pretty hard. Here he was, starting out
his long privileged weekend on the Vineyard, stretched out against the
counter like that, talking loud, laughing, obviously enjoying himself a
great deal. It was as if he owned the lousy steamship authority or something. I mean, why isn't he at least sitting down in his car with a ski
mask over his face? I guess I began to feel crazy inside. This won't make
any sense to you, but it may have been his posture as much as anything
that really did it to me."*

   The bearded man in tennis shoes was a twenty-seven-year-old artist
who once had lived on Martha's Vineyard but who lately had been staying in Vermont. That afternoon he and two friends had driven down to
Cape Cod in a red Chevy pickup. Their plan was to catch an evening
ferry over to the island and collect some of the artist's belongings, and
then, in a day or so, head back up north. At the dock in Woods Hole
there'd been a wait, as there often is, and so to pass the time the painter
and his friends had gone into the Lee Side, which is a tavern across the
street from the ferry slip. That's where they had first noticed McNamara. He was standing at the bar with his back partly turned, talking to
the man with whom he would soon board the *Islander.* The sight of the
former secretary of defense under two presidents hadn't seemed to rile
the artist's two friends, at least not in the beginning, although they too
remembered easily enough who he was. "What's the guy doing now?"
one of them said. "Runs the World Bank or something," the artist said.
It was true the artist had been drinking a little more than usual that day.
It was also true things had not been going especially well in his life—
though not badly enough, he ever would have guessed, to ignite half-
conscious impulses of murder in him. Two or three times before, the

artist's drinking had got him in trouble, nothing very serious, maybe a night in a local clink, that's all. He was a nice Catholic kid from Worcester who was trying to be a painter—basically, this was how he liked to think of himself.

"Anyway I led him around by the wheelhouse. He was right behind me. I felt very much in control. I think we were about a mile or two out of Woods Hole. It was very dark. Those can be pretty rough waters out there. Now the pilothouse on the Islander, *if you've ever been on the boat, comes around like this, in a kind of hard oval. There's a very narrow walkway on both sides. You're right at the edge of the ferry. All you've got protecting you from the sea is a four-foot railing with a metal grate in it that runs down to the floor of the deck. That's how he saved himself, you know. He got his hands locked in that damn grillwork of the railing and I couldn't get them loose for anything."*

After he had driven the pickup truck onto the boat, and had secured the gear, the artist had gone upstairs to the main deck to search for his friends, who had already boarded. He found them in the lunchroom. Many things were now roiling in his brain, all sorts of memories and pieces of memories seemed to be rushing back: the way he'd felt, for instance, when his two brothers went to the war and he had ducked it. (One was an officer who had served twice.) And the letters he had gotten from some of his relatives after he had finished art school and was living in Cambridge, letters that said such things as "What's the matter with you?" and "Hey, why does every family have to have a black sheep in it?" There also was a certain McNamara press conference the artist thought he could remember. He'd watched it on TV. They had been bombing heavily in the north then, and someone had asked him whether any bombs were hitting villagers. He had stood up there at the Pentagon with his wooden pointer and his eyeglasses reflecting those weird polygons of light. His answer was so curt and condescending, at least that's how it came across to the artist. He had said something to the effect of, well, one of the obvious things we learned in World War II is that bombs don't always fall where they're supposed to—or this is how the artist remembered it, anyway.

"Have you seen him?" he said to his friends as soon as he entered the lunchroom. "Right over there," one of them said, nodding.

"So we're out there on the walkway now, just the two of us, and he thinks I'm leading him to the pilothouse for his nonexistent phone call, and, well, I just turned on him. I was scared as hell but I think I was

pretty calm, too. I didn't say a word, you know, here's to Rolling Thunder, sir, or, this one's for the Gulf of Tonkin, you lying sack of crap. Nope, nothing like that. I just grabbed him. I got him by the belt and his shirt collar, right below his throat. I had him over, too. He was halfway over the side. He would have gone, another couple seconds. He was just kind of hanging there in the dark, clawing for the railing. I remember he screamed, 'Oh, my God, no.' But only once. Those may have been the only words between us. I'm pretty sure his glasses came off. I suppose the whole thing didn't last a minute. This was a cumulative thing in me, that's what I'm trying to tell you. Actually, I don't think they would have had a prayer of saving him. We were on the back side of the boat, since we were headed toward the island, so there was a good chance he was going to get sucked underneath, and in that case the propeller probably would have gotten him if he hadn't drowned first."

What is running through the mind of an arrogant-seeming man whose flesh has gone ice-white in the dark and whose famous wire spectacles have been knocked to the floor but who has managed somehow to interlock his fingers in the sharp metal grillwork of a ship's railing and hold on with something beyond strength—even as a short, insane bull of a figure beside him keeps jamming at his throat with the heel of his hand, keeps struggling to pry the stuck fingers free and finish off the job?

"He was amazingly strong, I'll give him that. You know, this thing has shown up over the years in a lot of places. It's always part of some larger story, some larger point. I saw it once in the Boston Phoenix. *It was a paragraph or two in either* Time *or* Newsweek. *It was in a* New Republic *article about him. A lady named Anne Simon included it in a book about Martha's Vineyard. The thing is practically folklore in certain quarters of the island. But nobody ever came around to ask me about it. As a consequence they always get it wrong. Almost everything that's ever been written about it is wrong, as a matter of fact. I've seen it said, for instance, that the reason I attacked him was because I was angry that he and his wealthy friends from the mainland had formed a syndicate to buy up property at Jungle Beach, on the south side of the island, and that they were going to try to shut down the nude swimming that goes on out there. Well, let me tell you something, you don't try to throw somebody off a boat in the middle of Vineyard Sound because of that, unless you're really crazy. I'll tell you something else: It's always annoyed me a little bit, the way they say McNamara 'overpowered' his*

assailant. You know, the big Colorado mountain-climber proved too much for the crazed hippie type half his age. Well, he was going, he was over the side, believe me, another couple seconds, I'd say. I guess you'd have to say I'm glad he didn't go, because that would make me a murderer and I'd probably be in prison, wouldn't I? I suppose I kind of regret what I did, but maybe in the context of the sixties and everything else, it makes some sense. I couldn't believe the way he was holding on. I almost like him for that. But anyway, the next thing I knew, somebody had me from behind by the neck, people were spilling out of the lunchroom, the crew was running over. There was a lot of commotion. A guy I knew who worked on the boat started pulling people off me. He got down by my face and said, 'Now, look, don't you dare jump off this boat, okay?' I said, 'Don't worry 'bout that, pal.' "

Everything is calm now. The attacked man retrieves his glasses and smooths his sports clothes and reenters the harsh fluorescent safety of the lunchroom. He cannot stop himself from trembling and so he sits down in a booth against the wall. "Just keep that man away from me," he says to the first mate, who has already radioed ashore to the state police at Oak Bluffs and to the constables at Vineyard Haven. The attacker, meanwhile, is being held outside, a reasonable distance from his victim.

By the time the police come aboard the *Islander*, thirty minutes later, the man in tennis shoes has vanished. His friend from the crew has helped him jump off the back of the boat and disappear into the dark before the gangways are even down. But it doesn't matter, because the president of the World Bank says he has changed his mind and will not press charges after all. He just wants it dropped. Yes, he is sure. So no police report is filed, no arrest warrant is made out. Nothing of the attack shows up in the ship's log for that evening, nor is any kind of note inserted at a later date into the corporate records of the Woods Hole, Martha's Vineyard and Nantucket Steamship Authority. But of course a story like this cannot disappear. People will always talk, and within hours of the incident half a dozen versions have burned across Martha's Vineyard. Two weeks later a brief story goes out over the Associated Press wire ("Ferry Assault on McNamara"), describing the artist as an unidentified man who "had been around the island for some time." Vineyard residents continue to gossip all that autumn as to who exactly the assailant is. Among some of the artist's semiradical friends, and even among his more conventional friends, the consensus seems neatly split: It was a mad thing to have done; or, it was, well, exactly the thing to have done, not that anyone wished the guy dead or anything, no, just a terrible scaring in the wet pitch of an open sea was fine. But no one ever comes up to the artist and says, "Listen, buddy, you ought to be behind bars." People seem to treat him now with a certain curiosity and wary regard.

There is talk the FBI has been around investigating. The attacked man, understandably, finds it difficult to discuss the incident with anyone. McNamara's wife doesn't tell her sister for years, and then Marg only mentions it to Kay in the context of some other outrageous Vietnam-related behaviors. Once, on a visit to California, McNamara lets it be known to the wife of his best man from forty years before that, of all the ugly things that have happened to him in his public life, this one came closest to unhinging him. And yet he says it in a way as to suggest he bears no particular grudge toward the man who did it. And still later, when McNamara is describing that night to one of his old deputies from the Pentagon, Ros Gilpatric, he suddenly stands up and begins clawing smooth high-rise Manhattan office air for an invisible grate. True to character, Robert McNamara tells Gilpatric and others that he will be damned if somebody thinks for two seconds something like this, or anything else, is going to drive him off Martha's Vineyard, a place he has grown to love so much these last several years. No damn way; they can lob all the garbage up on his porch they wish, they can perform lewd acts on the sand down below his house till the tide comes in if they feel like it.

The artist? Well, he lies low for a little while, then slips off the island. But eventually he comes back and resumes his painting. His work gets into some galleries in New York, he marries, he becomes a father, he sets up a studio behind a laundromat in one of the island's smaller towns. In an ironic turn, comedian John Belushi, who has purchased McNamara's house on the Vineyard, even comes by one afternoon to paw through the artist's paintings. The word "counterculture" doesn't seem to fit the artist anymore. One night five or six years after the incident, the artist is sitting in a restaurant in Edgartown, having dinner with friends. He looks up and there, at another table, no more than six feet away, is McNamara. The artist nods, almost imperceptibly. Both men go back to their dinners. Their eye contact has lasted only a second.

"I suppose I think about it every now and then. I've seen him around the island several times, actually. Look, I've got kids, you know,

it's not exactly as if I want this thing on my tombstone. No, I wouldn't say I hate the guy at all. You get a chance at one of these people, right? You're out there. Maybe the chance will never come back. I figure we both paid something that night. He got the message. I seriously doubt it would have happened if it had been practically anybody else from the war standing there, maybe not even old LBJ himself. Nope, it had to be McNamara, at least for me. He became for me, well, something I can't really describe to you. Look, I was a slacker from art school with two brothers who went to Vietnam. I just wanted to do my painting and be left alone and instead I'm being threatened by my local draft board. That was part of it, not all of it. Sure, I had gone to the meetings in Cambridge about leaving for Canada, I was considering doing that. But my mother's brother was an admiral in World War II. He even won the Medal of Honor. A cousin in our family was a major in the Marine Corps. One of my own brothers, the one who went to Vietnam twice, is now a general. There were all these family ghosts in me, that's what I'm trying to say. I saw him there and something happened.

"This thing still comes up in my life. Just the other day I was stepping off my front porch when a woman I'd never seen before yelled out from across the street, with a kind of cackle in her voice, 'Hey, aren't you the guy who tried to throw McNamara off the ferry?' My standard answer is 'Nah, I was just there that night.' Here's something. I went into a bar way up by Canada a few months ago, a place where I used to drink occasionally. Now those guys up there, they don't know Robert McNamara from Kermit the Frog. And one of them sees me coming in the door and calls out, 'Hey, lookie who's here, and Robert Mac-Na-Marry is comin' in right behind on his shoulder.' On his shoulder, the guy said. That's rich."

Part One:

AT THE OPEN NOON
OF HIS PRIDE

A man cannot get rid of himself in favor of an artifi-
*cial personality without punishment. Even the
attempt to do so brings on, in all ordinary cases, unconscious reactions in the form of bad moods, affects, phobias, compulsive ideas, backslidings, vices, etc.*
—The Basic Writings of C. G. Jung

T he personal drama in Harlot's Ghost *revolves
around identity. Specifically, it explores the dilem-
mas of people whose profession compels them to hide
and alter their real identities, to feign beliefs, feelings
and names wholly different from their own. These conflicts . . .*
—from an article in The New York Times Magazine

"*N* ow what I want is Facts. . . . In this life, we want
nothing but Facts, sir; nothing but Facts!*"
—Charles Dickens, Hard Times

A 1955 FAIRLANE VICTORIA, PUT OUT BY FORD DIVISION AT FORD
MOTOR COMPANY. FORD DIVISION HAS A BRAND-NEW LEADER:
ROBERT S. McNAMARA.

IN THE WINTER OF 1955

HIS WIFE WASN'T DRINKING MILK with her cocktails in the hope her stomach might hurt a little less—not then. A man bearing a child hadn't set himself on fire below his Pentagon window— not yet. A wigged-out woman hadn't stolen up behind his seat in an outdoor café in the warming winter sun of Aspen to begin shrieking there was blood on his hands. (He was applying ketchup to his hamburger.) A Viet Cong agent—his name was Nguyen Van Troi—hadn't been found stringing fuses beneath a Saigon bridge he was due to pass over. Odd metaphors and strange turns of phrase weren't seeping from him like moons of dark ink. His pressed white shirts weren't hanging loose at his neck. He wasn't reading Homer late at night in an effort to compose himself. His dyslexic and ulcerated son hadn't been shown in a national newsmagazine with his ropes of long hair and kindly face reading aloud a list of war dead at the San Francisco airport. Reputed members of an organization called the Symbionese Liberation Army hadn't yet stored in a Berkeley garage some crudely drawn but surprisingly detailed descriptions of the interior and exterior of his resort home in Snowmass, along with thumbnail sketches of members of his family. ("WIFE: name unknown to me. She is small, not outstanding in appearance, & probably not aggressive. . . .") He hadn't stood in the Pentagon briefing room in front of his graphs and bar charts to say with perfect seriousness, "So it is fifteen percent of ten percent of thirteen-thirtieths that have been in dispute here. . . ." He hadn't stood on the tarmac at Andrews, at the roll-away steps of his blue-tailed C-135, before winging to a high-level meeting in Honolulu, and told another tangle of lies into a tangle of microphones, made more artfully disingenuous statements to the press boys, this time about the kind of forces—which is to say, combat forces—soon to be shipped to the secretly escalated war. ("No, uh, principally logistical support—arms, munitions, training, assistance.") He hadn't hunched forward in his field fatigues at a news conference in Saigon and said, as though trying to hug himself, and with only the slightest belying stammers, "The military operations have progressed very satisfactorily during the past year. The rate of progress has exceeded our expectations. The pressure on the Viet Cong, measured in terms of the casualties they have suffered, the destruction of their units, the measurable effect on their morale, have all been greater than we anticipated"—when, in fact, the nation's chrome-hard secretary of defense had already given up believing, in private, a long while ago, that the thing was winnable in any military sense. The president of the United States hadn't yelled at him in the cabinet room, "How can I hit them in the nuts? Tell me how I can hit them in the nuts!"—the "them" being little men in black pajamas in a skinny curve of an unfathomable country 10,000 miles distant. He hadn't yet gone to this same president and told him he was afraid of breaking down. The expressions "body count" and "kill ratio" and "pacification" and "incursion" hadn't come into the language in the way snow—to use Orwell's image—falls on an obscene landscape. The casualty figures of U.S. dead and missing and wounded hadn't spumed, like crimson geysers, past the once-unthinkable 100,000 mark. Nor had this man risen at a luncheon in Dean Rusk's private dining room at the State Department (it happened on February 27, 1968, forty-eight hours before he left office) and, without warning, begun coming apart before Rusk and Clark Clifford and Bill Bundy and Walt Rostow and Joe Califano and Harry McPherson, telling them between stifled sobs, between what sounded like small asphyxiating noises, between the bitter rivers of his cursing, that the goddamned Air Force, they're dropping tonnage on Vietnam at a higher rate than ours in Germany in the last part of World War II; we've practically leveled the place, and what's it done, nothing, goddamned nothing, and Christ here's Westmoreland asking for another 205,000 troops. It's madness, can't anybody see, this thing has to be gotten hold of, it's out of control I tell you . . .

No. None of this. Not yet. It all lay waiting in the decades up ahead.

Because in the winter of 1955, Robert Strange McNamara was making cars in Dearborn, Michigan. And his soul seemed his own. And America had barely heard his name.

*   *   *

HE HAD JUST WRITTEN a memo on cooling systems and the new Magic-Aire heaters that stated in its penultimate paragraph: "For purposes of amortizing tools and engineering, a volume of 65,000 units during the next four years has been assumed. Even at this volume, a profit of $48 per unit will be achieved which is a return of 15 percent on sales. The unit cost and profit position is summarized in Exhibit III." Three pages of exhibits followed, with cost-profit summaries and dealer-margin percentiles.

Back in September, as the new models were about to roll off, he had flashed up a slide in a darkened room and said over top of the projector: "As you see, the installation of radios rose from 37 percent to 60 percent. Heater installations increased from 55 percent to 86 percent. And installation rates now amount to 39 percent for Fordomatic, 41 percent for windshield washers, 28 percent for tinted glass, and 90 percent for turn indicators—all items of functional value." The words "functional value" were stressed, because that's his dictum in this tacky manufacturing orb: Don't load the car down with dross and gorp it up with phony selling gimmicks. Real options, real accessories, fellas—that's where the ten-strike is. "Ten-strike" is a favorite expression, although none of the Ford fellas has ever seen or heard of the man in a bowling alley.

Next week he's going to do a memo on the subject of easy-closing doors. It will go three pages, single-spaced, and cover weather-stripping and striker plates and cantilevered sealing mechanisms and also the so-called flipper method of adhering doors to their jambs. Mercifully this new McNamarian missive will be free of the usual blizzard of unit-cost comparisons and wholesale delivered price ratios.

He can tell you about fin treatments on the Fairlane. He knows about torquing of the spring-bolt nuts on the rear axles. (He finds that the rubber pads extrude when torqued to specifications, but his new study hasn't yet determined the degree of improvement obtainable.) He'll quote you until hell won't have it the diameter of wiring harnesses on the ragtop Sunliner. This past Sunday, January 30, maybe you saw it, there was a feature on him in the local paper—it was pegged to the big promotion he's just gotten. Real puffball piece. "New Boss of Ford Division Is a Go-Getter Not Yet 40," the headline said. The automotive reporter for the Detroit *Free Press* did the article. You got the feeling the general readership of Motor City hadn't yet heard much about R. S. McNamara: "A young man not yet 40 is the new vice president and general manager of the huge Ford Division of Ford Motor Company. Robert Strange McNamara, former lieutenant colonel in the Air Force, holder of the Legion of Merit and a Phi Beta Kappa key, came to the top in Wednesday's shuffle of Ford executives. You will see him occasionally hurrying across the campus at Ann Arbor, where he lives, or rushing down the corridors of the Ford Division's warehouselike headquarters in Livonia. He has a purpose in every quick move and a warm, friendly smile. He is clear and direct in speech. And he listens with the attentiveness of a Harvard professor. That's because he was a Harvard professor before joining the Air Force in World War II."

The story didn't report that he grinds his teeth in his sleep—but it's fact. (As yet, this hasn't become such a concern that his spouse will arrange for cap work out of state, both to protect the disappearing enamel and to help relieve his sometimes fierce head pain.) The feature didn't mention there've been several instances of fainting and a condition one might accurately diagnose as Frozen Jaw—but it's fact. (Some at the company have witnessed the bruxism, but few know or have even heard about the faintings, which have struck outside the office, and those who do know have put the phenomenon down to stress and overwork. Because no one at Ford Motor Company would deny how long and stressfully hard Bob McNamara works, sometimes against every bolt of common sense.) Nor did the piece make note of the fact that the just-named head of Ford Division has had at least two close mishaps with company cars, neither very serious, the most recent occurring fourteen months ago late on a Friday night on his way home from the office. (He was assistant head of the division then, but few doubted he would gain the top slot, though maybe they weren't guessing it would happen this soon.) He was not at fault, apparently. The other party—parties, to be exact—apparently had been consuming alcohol. While awaiting the police at the side of the road, the Ford man got out a flashlight and made pencil notes on the back of a three-by-five index card that was printed up with some recent sales figures. On Monday he wrote a 300-word statement, giving the facts as he knew them, writing in a third-person and almost out-of-body way:

> Company Car No. P-1214 was involved in an accident on Willow Run Expressway, Friday, November 20. The accident occurred at approximately 10:30 p.m., at a point on the Express-

way approximately 200 yards south of the entrance to Willow Run Airport. R.S. McNamara, the driver of the Company car, was proceeding toward Ann Arbor at a speed of approximately 53–54 miles per hour when, suddenly, there appeared in front of his car a vehicle, stopped and without lights, perpendicular to the edge of the road. Mr. McNamara applied the brakes as quickly as possible; his car skidded on the wet pavement and eventually crashed into the side of the other car. . . . Mr. McNamara suffered a split chin, which required six or seven stitches, and what appeared to be minor cuts and bruises on the head and body.

The lefty dated and signed the document, as he signs all of his Ford correspondence, "R.S. McNamara," the letters lank as Macanudo cigars, sloped to the right.

He weighs a notch over 170 pounds. He'll be thirty-nine come June 9. He holds his socks up with garters. His thinning, keened-back hair parts two degrees left of center. He wears an accountant's glasses and dark suits that fit him like envelopes. He has thick, hairy, muscular calves, and in an argument with one of the product planning guys or somebody from the styling department who's trying to persuade him to widen a car a fraction of an inch, his trousers will hitch higher and higher until finally what you see, should you glance under the table, are the bobbing cue-ball knees. Because you see, even though R. S. McNamara wishes most everybody in the auto game to think of him as the chilly systems analyst, naked of doubt, the truth is he's strung tighter than a snare drum, and in some areas of the work he's fairly roiling with doubt. Like product. Which is to say automobiles, and the strange impulses that make people purchase them. Not that an outsider would know, not most of the time, what with the body so tight, the voice so driven and sure, speaking, no, intimidating in the exact and quadratical parlance of the mathematician.

"Did I overdo it, Jim? Be sure to tell me all the time, because I know I overdo it," he'll sometimes say to his good friend Jim Wright after a particularly hard product meeting. He and Wright arrived at the company together, nine years ago, fresh from their victories in Statistical Control in the U.S. Army Air Forces, part of a legendary team of ten mustered-out Whiz Kids who had fought the paper war against Hitler and had then come straight into Dearborn and the auto business and begun turning things over here as well with their astringent management principles and fearsome financial controls. Bob McNamara places much trust in Jim Wright, isn't afraid to appear a little vulnerable before him, and perhaps one reason is that both men understand how many galaxies smarter Bob is than Jim. In any case, the two have gotten up a plan: Jim sits close and gives Bob a little knock under the table whenever he starts to overdo it on stress-relieved cylinder heads or how many gallons of antifreeze get produced per hour at the factories in northern Michigan. Another decade from now, affable Jim Wright will be watching the evening news in his Bloomfield Hills living room and suddenly his old friend will come on. It's 1964, and LBJ's defense secretary is touring Southeast Asia in short-sleeved khaki, parading in marketplaces and public squares with a short squat general, arms up over their heads, fingers entwined, the American crying, *Vietnam Muon Nam!* "Long Live Vietnam!" My God, what have they done to our Bob McNamara? is the first thought that will enter Jim Wright's head. (Unfortunately, and unbeknownst to the barnstorming and tin-eared American, Vietnamese is a tricky tonal language, and *Vietnam Muon Nam!* is coming out not "Long Live Vietnam!" but "The southern duck wants to lie down!" Is this why people appear to be snickering at the back of the crowd?)

He's a registered Republican but votes his conscience. He has a membership in a country club though doesn't fool with golf and rarely goes near the place. Every Sunday morning you'll find him with his family in church. He worships with his wife of fourteen years and his three behaved children (ages thirteen to four) in a tawny Gothic building on Washtenaw Avenue in Ann Arbor called First Presbyterian. First Press is what the locals say. He serves on the budget committee for the new wing, and last Thursday evening, in Lewis Parlor, they elected him to the "Fifteen Ruling Elders." One day soon in America, Washtenaw Avenue, if not First Press itself, is going to be part of a vast beachhead of insurrection—or, as one Ann Arbor anarchist will put it, "a total assault on the culture." Hill Street, which is quite close to the church and to his own home, will be filled, as a memoirist of those days will write, with "fringed-leather postadolescents incandescing from acid, anarchy, and the certitude that . . . 'you don't need to get rid of all the honkies, you just rob them of their replacements and let the breed atrophy and die out.'" But by then one of the head iconographic honkies won't be residing in the leafy, cultured, fractured, midwestern college town of Ann Arbor.

Speaking of church and worship: It isn't unknown for the head of Ford Division to call up one of his product underlings at about noon on a Sunday and ask, with little chitchat in front of the question, "Listen, Chalmers, is it possible to fit a power-window motor in the door of that model we're working on as it's presently being designed?"

"No way."

"Good. Because I was thinking about it at church this morning." He'll then say thanks and hang up. The point being, he doesn't want some son of a bitch on Monday trying to get in the way of the design he's ramming through.

He holds $4 tickets for University of Michigan home football games, and enjoys going, unless he has to be at the office or out of town. His friend Herb Estes, owner of the local Ford dealership, got the seats for him. They're deep in Michigan Stadium, which fills up with 101,000 crazed Big Ten fans. "Bob, these tickets aren't very good, they're on the east side, the sun'll be in your eyes the first couple games, best I could do," Estes apologized. "No, no, Herb, they're just fine, I want to sit there, I'll be glad to sit on that side," Bob answered. Heck, the head of Ford Division could have had a pair of fifty-yard-liners delivered to his Tudor door by the university's athletic director on the strength of a phone call, had he wished to jerk that perk. But that would be an abuse of his position. In Ann Arbor they don't experience him that way at all.

For there is already in this very attractive man a deep and rigid and almost schizoid but in any case essentially deceitful code of opposites: opposite beliefs and sensibilities and values and ways of living in and dealing with the world. But somehow the deceit is working, working almost magically. Somehow the figures eater in Babylon (it's one of the hallway names they have for him at Ford) has been able to bifurcate his life between all the beady-eyed and hard-driving things he is by day and all the soft-sided and warmhearted things he seeks to be by night. He has done this as neatly and arbitrarily as you might place a garment on the ground and draw a sword through it. He has done it for a welter of complicated reasons, though mostly for the familiar reasons of ambition and pride. To understand it more clearly than this, you would have to know much about his parental psychic history, and it's too early to pry open those sealed California mysteries. But know this: In his wondrously cost-effective way, he has decided he can make the whole thing work. Know this, too: For all his brains, it's such an idiotic idea: a willed and fierce compartmentalization of who you really are. And yet, owing to will and incredible discipline, he has pulled off this siamesing into the public daytime self and the private nighttime self. But of course huge conflicts are being stored up. Eventually, when he gets enmeshed in an event of unspeakable enormity, the interior cruelties will have no choice but to seek the light. By then they will have grown monstrous as goiters. "High rests on low," says a Chinese proverb, and perhaps this is just a way of saying that houses set against themselves cannot stand forever. But that is trying to tell a sorrowful story in the abstract.

AT TEN MINUTES OF SEVEN every weekday morning—and about three out of four Saturdays, too—a technician exits the front door of the large wood-and-fieldstone Ann Arbor home that's partially hidden by willows and shrubs at 410 Highland Road. He is going off to Dearborn to eat some numbers and the day. *Homo mathematicus.* Now in motion.

Behind him, on the table in the foyer, he has deposited a glass. It has just been drained of orange juice and a raw egg. In the darkened foyer he has just stepped through, there are bookshelves on either side of the door, with volumes by Kant and Toynbee, the economist Barbara Ward, and also the great British philosopher Hume, who argued that human knowledge arises only from sense experience, and that reason is really emotion's slave. In the step-down living room he has just crossed there's a grand piano, and on top of it is a marble chess set with the pieces in their start-up positions: art snuggled up to logic. Beyond the room's leaded-glass windows is the university arboretum, with hillocks and berms and many varieties of birds. Nichols Arboretum slants down to the Huron River, which flows into Lake Erie, which connects by straits and canals and small and large rivers right out to the sea and Europe itself, though it isn't known whether the man ever stops to reflect on such a macrogeographic thought.

Forty to forty-five minutes after pulling out of his inclined driveway, bet on it, he's at his desk. The twice-daily commute is a fraction under thirty-eight miles each way. He's nearly always the first white-collar guy in the shop. No one has ever witnessed him warming up with coffee and the box scores. His new office at division headquarters is utilitarian as a gas station. A meeting with a subordinate on the efficacy of the Kelsey-Hayes power brake vis-à-vis the Bendix Master-vac model might start as early as seven-forty and go expansively to seven-fifty. Call up and ask for ten minutes, and a scheduling officer will say, "Let's make it eight."

The cars his division is putting out, as befits the age and consumer appetites, tend to be as big as boats and loaded to their gunwales with chrome and kitschy sales features—for example, the all-new "Astra-Dial" instrument panel (three circles in the lower center of this year's dash where the heater controls, radio, and clock go). These cars have names like the Crown Victoria, and the Customline Tudor, and the Mainline Fordor, and, oh yes, hot off the line, first time ever, the Thunderbird, a sleek little two-seater boulevard job being marketed as a "personal" car with sports-car overtones. The T-Bird isn't chromey or junk-loaded or ocean-liner-bulky at all. She comes in Raven Black and Thunderbird Blue and Torch Red. She got unveiled a year ago at the Detroit Auto Show, with busty showgirls reclining on her hood and bands blaring and soap bubbles bursting, but the first one actually to carry the nameplate and the crossed checkered flags on the nose cowl didn't roll off the line until this past September. The pride of ownership in this doll seems immense—but how do you quantify that? The answer is, you can't, not really. It's an intangible, an immeasurable. Pencil it in as X.

Sometimes the marketing people will cart a busload of housewives up from Toledo to look at clay models of cars, lavishing them with a big lunch, asking them to fill out questionnaires. R. S. McNamara believes absolutely in this kind of targeted data, though other Ford high-ups think it's full of shit.

The in-house stylist who thought up the name "Thunderbird" won a $250 suit of clothes. Some of the thrown-out offerings were Beaver, Detroiter, Hep Cat, Flag Liner, and Wheelaway, which just goes to show that the price of being right—as the head of Ford Division likes to point out—can sometimes take a little longer. "We've got to think precisely," R. S. McNamara has been known to say to aspirants who wish to be in the place where he's gotten. "The cost of being wrong is very, very high."

The first Bird got sold this past November 12. In the showrooms that week, dealers sealed up their windows with butcher wrap, such was the country's stoked sense of manipulated excitement. "What a mink coat does for a lady, a Thunderbird does for a male," proclaims one of the ads now saturating the airwaves. But you've doubtless figured out what's coming. R. S. McNamara, who didn't have a lot to do with the original designs, is dead against the car; she isn't practical. The market's too small. She'll drain off more important dollars. He intends to turn the Bird into a four-seater. It will take three years to do the squarebird, by the time they get things redesigned and retooled, but his will shall prevail.

When R. S. McNamara of Ford Division ventures into the field, to talk to dealers in Sheboygan, Charlotte, or Chattanooga, he records his notes and observations and direct quotes on the back of anything—an envelope, a piece of loose-leaf—writing almost always in his furious pencil. Later, back at headquarters, his secretary will transcribe this raw data and place it in the Visit-to-Dealer file or the Notes-to-the-Field file. He also has an Unethical-Dealer-Advertising file, and in it he keeps fraudulent attempts to bilk the buying public—such as a cheap come-on that will show up in the Philadelphia *Evening Bulletin* a little later this year for a brand-new "stripped" Ford at an unbelievably low $995. Only trouble, "stripped" means no engine, not even a radiator or a battery. Donald Riegel of Drexel Hill, Pennsylvania, will walk into University Motors at Broad and Christian, see a Ford with no hubcaps and the spare tire gone, lift the hood, and guess what—no engine, either. He'll then pen his disgust to the company headquarters: "When I saw that I had been made a fool of by one of your dealers I decided that I couldn't depend on a Ford product." R. S. McNamara, in complete sympathy, will answer that this is not the way his company does business and later he'll call the perpetrators into Dearborn and threaten to lift their dealership.

"No one holds power very long unless it is invested with moral purpose," he's going to tell some hungry students of the Harvard Business School a few years from now, when he's even higher up at the company, just one notch from the presidency itself. He will outline for the burgeoning managers the "3 dangers which most businessmen face: 1) Self-righteousness. 2) Cynicism—against those he doesn't like: politicians, labor leaders, intellectuals—the very antithesis of morality . . . lack of belief in man. 3) Perfectionism—claiming too much, making too many promises, overcommitments." He'll fly home to Michigan and put the manuscript notes of his talk in the company files.

The numbers. Several years ago, when he was still a streaking corporate financial officer and not invested with any direct responsibility for creating cars consumers would buy, he applied for membership in the Controllers Institute of America. He was asked on the application form for the number of total personnel responsible to him. He stroked in with his pen: "400 directly—4,500 functionally."

Naturally, this is what a lot of the real car guys in the company feel he is and will always be—a bean counter. Your basic comptroller type. Somebody who probably doesn't even like automobiles deep down. "Car guy" is a very hard Michigan animal to define, but this much can be said: He works on 90 percent emotion and intuition and 10 percent logic. He may not even have gone to college. He's probably not articulate. What he loves is moving machines. He has long reconciled himself to the idea he's in the schlock business. He's giving Mr. and Mrs. Front Porch America what they want—or maybe what they're being manipulated to want. To a car guy, these New Age corporate beanies issuing out of B-schools might just as well be manufacturing electric can openers or pie crusts or Muntz TVs (a jaundiced view, of course).

Next year, in a twenty-six-page speech entitled "Mass Producing Variety," the head of Ford Division will present an astute analysis of the electric-appliance industry as a way of demonstrating to his car colleagues the need for a diversity of styles, sizes, and options. Slide five will come on, and R. S. McNamara will say: "The growth in sales volume for these kitchen-range substitutes from 1949 to 1955 is startling: 1) Broiler sales have risen from 260,000 to 1,545,000; 2) automatic coffeemaker sales from 800,000 to 3,675,000; and, 3) sales of deepfat fryers and frypan skillets, two products which were not even available in 1949, have skyrocketed to 4,900,000 units." What the real car guys in that room at the Greenbrier Management Conference in West Virginia will be saying to themselves can't be reported here, not with pinpoint accuracy.

Next year, the head of Ford Division will be pushing hard on safety, too. It's the only choice we have, he'll say over and over, lobbying for a sea change in FMC and industry attitudes. Almost singlehandedly, on the moral urgency of his presentations, R. S. McNamara will have convinced his company for the first time in its history to promote auto safety over performance and horsepower. The fifty-six ad campaigns will be all about dished steering wheels, the breakaway rearview mirror, crashproof door locks, the padded dash—your total "Lifeguard Design" package. But the campaign is going to bomb in the marketplace. It's ahead of its time. The consumers won't respond. Over at General Motors, they'll be snickering: McNamara's selling safety, we're

selling cars. And yet . . . the probity of the man's position is un-
arguable.

By this time next year, too, against every probability, the man will
have cemented a friendship with a marketing-and-sales shark named
Charlie Beacham. The two will be going out on Saturdays to sneak
looks at local Ford dealerships. They'll get a company car and park
across the street from a showroom, not let on to anyone that they're
there. They'll be studying who's going in and who's coming out. The
head of Ford Division, secretly yearning to know more about product,
will be asking this older man—who reports to him—all sorts of questions about sales and marketing and what goes on in people's heads
when they buy an automobile. Because Charlie Beacham seems to
know things about human beings just by feel. He's from McRae, Georgia, and is never without an unlit cigar in his mouth. It takes him an
eternity to get that damn stogie out to say something. Anyway, on these
secret Saturday forays, R. S. McNamara will hop out of the car that's
parked across the street from the dealership, will be walking up and
down, will be jotting down notes in a little book. Then he'll come back
and stick his head in the window and say, "Charlie, I'm saying eight
hundred thousand volume, I'm guessing twelve hundred units a year."
And the older, wiser man will respond to the younger, streaking pupil,
"Okay, Bob, you're doing pretty good here, but, see, your numbers
aren't quite right, because you haven't taken enough of a look at what
the neighborhood is, and besides that I can tell you just from being
parked here that this guy draws from all over the city, and, besides,
Bob, you're underestimating the units to the total volume because you
didn't think about discounts. Christ, I can tell you right off that this guy
gives out one helluva lot of discounts." And on the following Monday
at the office, Beacham will arch his shaggy brows in an exaggerated way
and say to somebody in his great McRae drawl, "Just had this strange,
powerful experience. Been out spyin' on dealers with R. S. McNamara." But there'll be affection in it.

Come this summer, Bob McNamara will take his family camping in
Yosemite National Park. They'll go in at Tuolumne Meadows and spend
six or seven days. He has already written to an old schoolmate in California named Harry Barber to ask if he'll be able to drive them in and
drop them off. The McNamaras will show up at Barber's doorstep in a
rented station wagon acquired at a Ford agency in Oakland. Now can
you imagine the kind of favors a local Ford franchise guy would want

to lay on if he knew that the head of the whole damn division was renting a car from him?

Harry Barber, telling this parable many years hence: "You see, he never let on. That was Bob. Straight arrow all the way."

S O M E T I M E S — when, say, the design for a new gas tank or the engineering prototype on a steel crankshaft has driven up the weight of a car by a quantity he cannot abide—the straight arrow of Ford will lose it bad and fairly shriek at an underling, "But we can't take this kind of weight? Where's your staff on this?" (In truth, these outbursts are rare; he works hard to hold them in.)

Sometimes—when a discussion is droning on—the man won't speak up, but will wait until the first lull, and then come in hard and beautiful with the correct analysis.

Sometimes on Friday evening, when the clock has slipped past six-thirty, he says, "All right, fellas, let's resume at seven-thirty in the morning." For the last thirty minutes, the fellas sitting on the other side of his desk in their rolled-up white sleeves have been sneaking glances at their wristwatches. But he'd missed it.

On a Saturday not long ago, a product planner named Chalmers Goyert was in. Goyert, who's been at the company four years, was there to see the man with the requisite numbers at the minute he'd been asked to be there. R. S. McNamara, who'd come to the office with an open shirt, waved Goyert in. There was a big bandage on the boss's hand. He was on the phone with his wife. "No, no, I'm all right, honey, promise, no, listen, Marg, I'm fine," he said several times. Then he hung up and said to Goyert, "I slammed the car door on my hand and, stupid thing, I fainted. Let's get going."

Sometimes the head of Ford Division seems to set up an issue in "such terms that he'll telegraph his conclusions before the discussions begin." These are Norm Krandall's words. He's a product guy, and a fast-rising one. What he feels, but could never say aloud, is that the new head of Ford Division is a dissembler and a cheat who "puts his analysis and conclusion of a problem in the center of the matrix . . . so that all the variants would be studied. But the fact is, it was loaded up so that it could only come out one way, his way. . . . What you're doing with such a setup is paying respect to the B-school method. But you're using the very device to arrive at your own predetermined set of answers. You're using the device to confirm your own decisions made before any so-called analysis." Norm Krandall's view is a little harsher than most—or maybe he's just being more honest than most.

What the man will not allow, what he's on the record as having contempt for, is the ballooning up of the sides. Stretching the metal, it's called, one of the oldest tricks in the styling game. It gives a different look at small cost and effort. R. S. McNamara cannot abide such dishonest bending-of-the-tin.

You should see his personal expense reports: the same rageful sense of probity and precision. On the road, when he was more junior and would sometimes bunk in with a fellow employee, he was known to take a sheet of paper and write at the top, "Analysis of Hotel Bill." Underneath there would appear long columns: *tip .35; phone .88; lunch .55; shoes .50; suit 1.50; I owe Ed 1.85; Ed owes me .90.* There would be little check marks beside the numbers, as if they'd been gone over for accuracy. The head of Ford Division still files his personal expense reports but bunks alone now.

Incidentally, he enjoys making small sporting bets with colleagues on numerical problems, but it turns out he sometimes has trouble fishing up the sawbuck or the ten-spot on the rare occasions he's proven wrong. ("Besides," a subordinate named Grant Chave will recollect many years from now, with more forgiveness than ruefulness, "Bob was right by the time he got around to your way of thinking.") He also has a habit of appropriating the wit and folksy sayings of some others who are a little more at ease with the common man. "Let's don't nickelplate a crowbar here, fellas," he'll say to the spear carriers, who wouldn't let on for anything.

R. S. McNamara, former corporate beanie, commands something on the order of 55,000 factory workers, not only across Michigan but at Cleveland Engine Plant No. 2, at Buffalo Stamping, at the just-completed Mahwah Assembly in New Jersey. His division alone, he likes to note, has $800 million of company assets, accounting for 75 percent of sales. Ford Division is like a company in itself. (The other FMC car divisions—Mercury, Lincoln, and Continental—account for beans, numerically speaking.) Gigantic, all right, but only a fraction of all he will one day command from a five-sided building with seventeen miles of corridors on the Potomac River. In that edifice there will be something like 30,000 people toiling for him under one roof.

It's a damn thrilling time to be alive. As cultural chronicler William Manchester will later write: "Technological change had never held a greater fascination for Americans. Men talked wonderingly of transistors, those slivers of germanium or silicon no bigger than a shoelace tip. . . . There was nothing inherently wrong with the innovations, though their sheer number was sometimes bewildering: central vacuuming, vinyl flooring, push-button phones, stereo FM sets, washer-dryers, automatic transmissions, drive-in-shopping malls, air-conditioned buses, electric blankets. . . ."

You should see the man at the show, when they're best-balling. Nobody at the company can touch him when it comes to the art of best-balling—and art, more than science, is what it is. The show is held on Thursday afternoons at the styling studio, which is known by some as the dream room. The styling studio is the womb of any automobile company. It's the place where commercial art and sculpture get practiced on a grand scale. There are three floors at Ford's styling studio, filled with clay models and glass prototypes and sheet after sheet of pencil dreams, most of which are going to end up going nowhere. The job of the men in the dream room is to draw ideas for cars, or for parts of cars, at first just whatever crazy fandangle comes to them. A journalist, visiting this place, once wrote: "A magazine picture of a tropical fish may inspire a sketch for a fender, or the nose of a jet fighter may lead to the contour for a hood." That catches it. In the dream room, artistic men with big egos and argyle socks and very sharp pencils work on roll-away stools before great panels of vertical paper.

You're going from first doodles to life-size drawings to small clay models built on wooden armatures to steel or glass prototypes. It's a three-year cycle. In the second year you can make minor changes (hood, grille, taillights), and in the third you can make major changes (all of the metal on the car, with the exception of the roof and doors), and in the fourth year, you're back at zero. In the cornfield, as they say.

At Thursday's show, the supervisors keep restricting the number of alternatives. With each week's review, another set of design possibilities gets eliminated, ratcheted down. R. S. McNamara has never been known to make a midnight visit to the dream room that will produce the brilliant hunch that will revolutionize the automobile business. Fact is, he seems to loathe going over to the design studio.

He arrives first, punctual to the minute. The head designers are out in the lobby to greet him. He takes the stairs three at a time. Everyone knows he hates elevators and desires the exercise of the stairwell. And so these artistic and even flamboyant personalities, not particularly driven to climb floors for the well-being of their hearts, have no choice but to go panting along behind. "Uh, where do I go?" he'll say when he's reached the right floor. "Now what do I look at?" Years from now, a respected designer named Dave Ash will recall: "Once Bob Maguire, who was the chief stylist for the division, and who got along with him, ribbed him a little. He said, 'Bob, how are you always so damn punctual, do you wait in your car or what?' And McNamara just killed him with ice."

You could think of the show as a kind of interface between the client and the properties—properties being the latest ideas the stylists have come up with, and the client being the engineers, the product planners, the sourcing guys, the cost estimators, the production sched-ulers, the assistant managers, and finally the man himself. Maybe thirty or forty items are on the agenda. Maybe twenty or thirty people are in the room, gathered around a sculpture or a larger prototype that's now up on a draped and rotating platform.

He stands there, tabbing on his fingers: *Now look, I want this . . . But I thought you said we could get this grille for . . . Here are the nine reasons why this eye-beam . . .* It's nothing for him to tab through the alphabet to the letter *j*. Who could stand up to it? Some of the product-planning guys are known to carry their figures on five-by-eight cards, so scared are they to be caught with a number down. Years from now, a stylist named Bill Boyer, who's junior but extremely talented (he has much to do with the original two-seater Thunderbird designs), will emit a low whistle and say, not exactly meanly: "He could recite the costs of body parts and estimate what you ought to be able to put a car together for better than anybody on earth. He could remember what a front bumper on the Ford car cost ten years earlier. He was always try-ing to shave pennies by component parts. I can see him talking faster and faster. Once Damon Woods and I went back to the boards and drew a car based on one of his best-ball performances. It physically wouldn't go together. What I'm saying is the parts wouldn't reach. It was a won-derful display, but you couldn't build something from this abstruse, theoretical performance."

In good weather they might decide to study the clays outdoors. There's a different feel outdoors. Sometimes they'll take a clay over to the test track and then get into real automobiles and drive slowly by— just to get the feel. Because feel is so much of it.

One of his favorite words seems to be "handsome." One of his favorite tricks is to say, "Uh, listen, let's take off that side molding, there now, I actually think that looks better, don't you?" Then he'll turn to the product guy and say, "Listen, how much does that save us?"

"A buck and a half."

"Good. Now, let's take off that taillight and put on a smaller one. I really think that looks better, don't you? Don't you think it's more handsome?"

"George, this car doesn't impress me. Just doesn't give me the feeling one gets when he looks at stained-glass windows in a European cathedral," he said one Thursday not long ago to the vice president of styling, George Walker. Walker wears silk suits and heavy cologne and weighs close to 300 pounds and has an effete hairy-looking throw rug in his office. He and R. S. McNamara don't get each other at all.

He seems mad for the idea of "commonality," for an interchangeability of parts—you know, this windshield on that car three years from now. He wants all his people to think in terms of commonalities and five-year projections.

What he's doing, not wrongly, is subjecting fertile imaginations to the disciplines of cost. If you held a harsher view, you'd say he's crushing everyone around him, not unknowingly. Crushing them to the Talmudic certainty of his numerical systems. No wonder it's oil and water between them and him. No wonder the bulk of these stylists and product guys and old hands-on manufacturing types view him as the soulless money idiot who possesses no basic qualifications to judge the aesthetic worth of an automobile. The McNamara problem, as the stylists see it, is that the guy thinks he can come over for the show on Thursday, look at the specs on a four-door, cut them down the middle: Presto, he's got a two-door. Maybe you could do that, but the damn thing would look like it was put together with two-by-fours, with a right triangle and a T square. If R. S. McNamara had his way, the high end of every automobile line would probably be chromeless.

But whiny artists are full of their own biases and repressed animosities. They're in the fruits and nuts department of the car game, a kind of necessary evil to the industrial process.

Sometimes—when someone at the show appears to be mounting a challenge—he'll suddenly stand back and say, "Well, okay, what do you think about it? Let's hear your program." And then he'll nod and drum his fingers on the nearest tabletop, looking so very pained. "In other words, he'd have to take off his mask, in a sense, just to hear this other side" is the way a recipient of one of these scrinched Thursday tabletop-drummings will put it many years hence.

"Mask" is a very good word. Because all they're seeing is half the man. All they're seeing is the consciously preferred self. There's nothing unreal about this self. It's not a veneer, it isn't a facade. It's hard and true. It's the Bob McNamara that's been developed over many years. But the fact is, underneath this highly developed self with its ferocious ambitions lies another self. It too is quite real, is true and hard. You don't tend to think about it or see it very often because what's outside, what's up top, is so incandescent it tends to blind everything in its path. This other Bob McNamara has been kept in a box all day. But the mask is about to be removed and in its place will be a gregarious cosmopolite, consumer of culture, warm human being.

Most Ford high-ups leave Dearborn after work and point their cars east or north—to the two-martini exurbs of Grosse Pointe Farms or Bloomfield Hills. But when the president of Ford Division cuts out, he heads due west, on a four-lane, to a middle-class university burg named for trees.

"Oh Christ, numbers are just a language. Excessive quantification is actually a loose way of thinking," this Bob McNamara has been heard to remark, calm nights, to his burgeoning book-study club and his economic dinner-discussion group. "Shit, I'm really anticomputer, if you want to know."

Harlan Hatcher is a member of the economic dinner-discussion group. He's the university president. He knows Henry Ford II well and has seen firsthand not only the Ann Arbor Bob McNamara but the Dearborn one, too. Many years from now, a very old man, Hatcher will say: "I can still see him sitting over there in his shirtsleeves in the big chair in his living room, just shedding the executive side of himself, discoursing as though he was holding a seminar—the warm philosopher. He needed it. I sort of think it was a restoration for him, he had to have it, that's the way I always looked at it. Here he was sweeping people out of the way by day. And then at night he sails into the harbor of Ann Arbor. Totally different man. Kind of a Jekyll and Hyde thing, it seems."

Ann Arborites have seen this Bob McNamara get teary at his Yeats. Ann Arborites have known this McNamara to recite verses from "The Palace" by Kipling. He has had that poem inside him since he was a brother of Golden Bear, back at Berkeley, in the fomenting thirties. Wrote Kipling: "When I was a King and a Mason—in the open noon of my pride / They sent me a Word from the Darkness—They whispered and put me aside / They said—'The end is forbidden.' They said—'Thy use is fulfilled.' " He'll almost choke at that last part, because now it's night and words are permitted to have their connotative, not just denotative, meanings.

Trying to be loose with himself: "Look here, Ben, I'll bet you five bucks I can throw myself down the stairs and not get hurt. Look, I'll show you. It's all in how you do it. If you roll into your shoulder, and keep yourself loose, it won't hurt a bit," this Bob McNamara was heard to say one night a couple years back at a party, when he wasn't lit like some others, but glowing in a way no one at the office had ever seen him glow.

This McNamara can well up at the memory of mountains—those good times when he and Joe Cooper went hiking up Big Kimshew Creek in the Sierras on semester break. Or when he and Willie Goodwin, Stan Johnson, Vernon Goodin, Bill Hewitt, and some others motored up to Badger Pass in Yosemite, and how they got their bunks and three squares for a dollar at the ranger lodge, and how the view was enough to make granite melt, never mind how they narrowly missed death every time just at the point where Glacier Point Road takes that nasty curve.

This Bob McNamara can get sentimental about old joints in San Francisco named the Sine Aloha and the Tin Angel, which was a dockside saloon where Earl Fatha Hines was jamming and the boccie balls were rolling and some waiter even sang an aria.

This McNamara loves holding hands and walking with his spouse over to a bookstore or Drake's Sandwich Shop for the Big M burger, or to a performance at Hill Auditorium where they might take in a little Mozart by the touring Budapest Quartet. The heart of campus is only six or seven minutes away through the west engineering quad. He doesn't stroll to campus, exactly, but damn if the man doesn't love being on green college quads.

Don't get it wrong, the computer by Dearborn daylight hasn't transmogrified into some unidentifiable night-town species. You'd recognize him in essential ways. This is still the dad who unwraps his Christmas gifts with a sheet of paper and pen beside him so he can record who has given him what—why won't his children follow this advice? This is still the husband who can say to the wife he's mad for: "But, Honey, it's a wasted motion, please don't put it back in." Maybe Margy McNamara has just opened a bill or a letter or a notice for a play from the kids' schools. But the point is, she's unthinkingly begun to return the piece of paper to its envelope. To him it makes no sense to do that.

And yet . . . what is being found here is a heart. What is being glimpsed here is a soul that's been so consciously hemmed in and boundaried all day. Which is perhaps why, in the decades ahead, when so much of R. S. McNamara's life seems ravaged beyond repair, one of his decades-old California pals with whom he went up to Big Kimshew Creek or Badger Pass will fairly grab an interviewer by his shirt collar and say things like this: "No, no, you're getting it wrong, everybody has always got him wrong, you're falling into the same old traps, you never knew the guy like we did, he just couldn't show this part of himself, he had to keep it down, it was the way he coped, it was the way he played it. Shit, man, haven't you come to it by now? Bob McNamara's just the romantic Irishman clamped down on himself."

What his pals won't be able to say, or maybe see, is that he betrayed himself.

IN THE WINTER OF 1955, some other things were going on in America and the world. A British novelist named Graham Greene was completing a parable about innocence and destructiveness in a tiny Southeast Asian nation; the book was called *The Quiet American* and would show up in bookstores in England toward the end of the year. "I never knew a man who had better motives for all the trouble he caused," the burnt-out narrator, Fowler, says of the central character, Pyle, who seems to possess the oddest combination of naïveté and cunning. And on another page, nearly spitting out his contempt for American ideals and idealism, the English-born Fowler says to the Yankee Pyle:

> "You and your like are trying to make a war with the help of people who just aren't interested."
> "They don't want communism."
> "They want enough rice," I said. "They don't want to be shot at. They want one day to be much the same as another. They don't want our white skins around telling them what they want."

But this was just a fiction.

In the winter of 1955, a brigadier general was working in the bowels of the Pentagon; he was a deputy assistant chief of staff, G-1, manpower control, and his name was William C. Westmoreland.

In the winter of 1955, a wispy Asian revolutionary with a spray of whitened chin beard was making appearances in public for the first time in eight years; he was a Communist and a great nationalist. He liked cigarettes and beer and he spoke excellent English and there were moments, as someone later said, when he almost looked like one of those impish Chinese ivory miniatures. His name was Ho Chi Minh. Uncle Ho had been fighting a guerrilla war against the French from his jungle and mountain hideouts, and guess what, he'd now won the damn thing. On New Year's Day 1955, 200,000 worshippers had thronged the squares of a place called Hanoi to get a glimpse, to sing the name.

In the winter of 1955, far from the bifurcated capitals of Saigon and Hanoi, the distinguished foreign-affairs columnist of the New York *Times,* C. L. Sulzberger, wrote under a Paris dateline: "The American Government is now taking over from France responsibility for maintaining independence in rump Indochina." Rump Indochina—where was that precisely? The journalist used this expression on January 17. Four days later, he told his readers how the United States had been officially requested by the wobbly and maladroit premier of South Vietnam (his name was Diem) "to assume full responsibility for assisting the Government of Vietnam in the organization and training of its armed forces." There were a few follow-up news stories.

In the winter of 1955, the Eisenhower administration was tidying up a formal (and much-orchestrated) agreement whereby America would now begin to provide direct military assistance to South Vietnam in the form of advisers, money, and equipment. It was a turning point. Something called the Training Relations and Instruction Mission—which was being folded into the U.S. Military Assistance Advisory Group (MAAG) Indochina—was about to be instituted. The Training Relations and Instruction Mission had come officially into existence on the same day that the new head of Ford Division at Ford Motor Company out in Michigan was writing a memo on Magic-Aire heaters, with the three pages of exhibits and footnotes relating to unit cost and profit position.

Rump Indochina, wherever it was, was not an unheard-of place to America in 1955. There had been some large headlines about Vietnam, especially the spring before, when the arrogant French colonials had met their defeat by Uncle Ho's lowly forces at the small mountain outpost near the Laotian border named Dien Bien Phu. There had even been the possibility then of American military intervention to aid the French, but the crisis had passed. America had not gone to war in Indochina in 1954, after all, although it was a fact that America was financing something like 85 percent of the French colonial struggle against the invaders and insurgents from the north. Supporting the idea of a non-Communist government seemed a noble enough, harmless enough, useful enough idea in the winter of 1955.

After the humiliations of Dien Bien Phu, a conference in Geneva had divided Vietnam into two temporary countries. The division was along the seventeenth parallel, with a Communist government in the north and an anti-Communist regime in the south. General elections were to be held two years thereafter, at which time unification would be achieved. The situation there bore watching. Occasionally one heard and read things about "containment" and "domino theories" and "the Indochina question." At a news conference in 1954 discussing Dien Bien Phu, President Eisenhower had explained: "You have a row of dominoes set up, and you knock over the first one and what will happen to the last one is the certainty that it will go over very quickly."

The fact is, it was possible to trace American dollars and military support missions to Vietnam back to the Truman administration. But the difference now, in the winter of 1955, was that these new American millions and this new dispatching of trainers and advisers were no longer to be funneled through or managed by the French. This time the American mission in Saigon would handle matters on its own and presumably for the better in the part of the world that C. L. Sulzberger had colorfully called rump Indochina. It was clear that the post–World War II French had been bent on their own colonialist, mistaken, and avaricious aims, but America was going into Southeast Asia (in an advisory capacity, you understand) to help a decent people determine their own future. In promising this new aid, Ike wished America to know he was only continuing an earlier president's commitment to freedom for the region.

But really it was all so puny, this news, these distinctions, nothing to thrust itself onto the front page. In the last week of January 1955, what owned the headlines in the New York *Times* was the crisis in the Formosa Strait between the Reds and Taiwan. Not that there weren't other interesting bits and pieces of news inside—the latest redemption notices for the New York, Chicago and St. Louis Railroad. The banker that American Smelting had just added to its board. The splash that perky songbird Gisele MacKenzie made on the Jack Benny program on CBS. In the January 26 edition of the *Times,* in the business section, on page 33, there had been the report, out of the Midwest, that four officials of Ford Motor Company had been elevated to key executive posts by company president Henry Ford II. Robert S. McNamara, one of these raised, looked so handsome and boyish, gazing into the lens with his flat unbroken confidence. There wasn't anything in the paper that day relating to rump Indochina. But the day before, on the twenty-fifth, when the promotions had been announced in Dearborn, there was a four-grapher about Vietnam that spoke of "the rapid expansion of the government's responsibilities as it takes over functions previously exercised by the French." The editors tucked those four graphs next to a display ad for after-Christmas furs.

What you couldn't have known from reading the New York *Times* in the winter of 1955 was that there was a preministerial student at a Presbyterian liberal arts college in Ohio who had been thinking hard about questions of pacifism and conscientious objection. His name was Norm Morrison and he was running on the cross-country squad and recently he had dislocated his shoulder in a game of touch football out front of the dorm and he had also recently begun meeting on Sunday mornings with a little Quaker worship group in the basement of the campus library. Friends of this idealistic and inarticulate young man said he possessed a blunt gift for action. It would be another ten years and nine months before Norman R. Morrison took the lid off the jug and poured the kerosene on his clothes and struck the match and turned himself, though not his baby daughter, into spectacular fire in a raised garden below the window of the nation's war minister.

What you couldn't have known from reading the *Times* in the last week of January 1955 was that there was an eleven-year-old Catholic boy living on a scrubby twenty-acre ranch in the Rincon Hills outside of Tucson. Not long before, he had lost his father. He possessed violent sides and some exquisitely sensitive sides. He liked going out into the morning desert light with his half brother Jerry and lassoing rattlers and then dragging the snakes behind them on their bikes at high speed. This boy, whose name was James Farley, had lived briefly in Germany after World War II. It was there he had been taken by his father to Hitler's bunker. It was there he had begun to wonder if his vocation, like his dad's, wasn't destined to be in the service of his country. The half brother, Jerry, would not end up going to war for his country as a U.S.

Marine in a tiny Southeast Asian nation the way James would; would not end up being pictured in *Life* magazine, the way James would, hiding his face against a trunk in a supply shed at an airfield in I Corps because he had just seen the dying of a comrade down at his shoe tops—at the same synchronistic moment, oddly enough, that policymakers in Washington were redirecting the nature of the entire conflict.

What you couldn't have known from the pages of the *Times* was that there was a fifth-grader outside Pensacola, Florida, a Navy child, who loved more than anything in the world to pretend. Her name was Marlene, and she lived at 755 Mainside Courts. You could say her gift was dreaming. The year before, her long pencil curls had been shorn by her mama and afterward she had cried and cried. After school she'd meet her pals under the oak tree near the air station to play Witches Eggs, or Red Light/Green Light. She had wanted to be a Girl Scout, but her folks had to tell her they couldn't afford the uniform. The thought of growing up to be a nurse hadn't yet struck the perky child, much less any idea of someday going off to war and getting trapped in the middle of a red and torrential thing known as a "push."

What you couldn't have known from the *Times* was that in the same bifurcated nation that a distinguished columnist called rump Indochina, there was a family named Tran. They were nine in number and they lived in a lovely old walled villa in Saigon. Nearby were homes of foreign ministers. Across the alley lived the big-shot director of the Brasserie Glacière de l'Indochine, a giant ice firm. This family, the Trans, were cultured and civilized; also rather quiet, for all their accomplishments. The mother was quite beautiful. The father, who was really a patriarch, had already known a large career as a liberal Vietnamese politician—though greater achievements were to come. At dinner he liked engaging his older kids in debate. He would say things like "Never believe anything the Communists say, and never believe anything the Americans promise. They'll drop us when we're no longer convenient to their cause." It would be two more decades before Tran Van Tuyen, spokesman for human rights in a dirty war, would meet death alone in a forced labor camp of the north, his country having fallen, his dreams having failed, his first wife dead before him, and every one of his children having endured or about to endure some form of torture or degradation or loss at the hands of the victors.

Who could have said in the winter of 1955 that these lives, and others too, would intersect—and sometimes literally—with an exautomaker's life at a kind of sixties bridge of San Luis Rey? That these lives and histories would find circles within circles, make strange arcs within their arcs? Wouldn't the probability of that occurring be something to bet against mathematically? Of course it would. Just as a logical positivist and rational utopian would have said it was nigh on impossible that there could ever one day be sticking up from the Washington earth a gash of glossy black marble with the names of 58,000 Americans on it. In the winter of 1955, glossy black gashes coming out of the Washington earth were not being conjured.

Part Two:

PHOTOGRAPH OF A LIFE, 1916–1960

RIGMA SOCIAL CLUB, PIEDMONT HIGH SCHOOL, 1933. BOB McNAMARA, PRESIDENT, FIRST ROW, FAR RIGHT.

A CONE OF LIGHT

T HINK OF A VERY OLD MAN in dark clothes sitting by the
radio in the parlor of a modest yellow stucco house canted into the
side of an Oakland, California, hill. It is the pit of the Depression, 1933.
This man has small, fine, white hands. He cannot drive a car or nail.
Roses make him sneeze, so he rarely goes into the backyard. He works
across the bay, in San Francisco, at a wholesale shoe concern, and com-
mutes there daily by streetcar and ferry. Sometimes, coming up the hill
from the Trestle Glen trolley stop in the late Oakland afternoons, he
pauses and with great dignity sits down on the curb to get his breath.
Then he raises himself with the aid of his cane or umbrella and continues toward 1036 Annerly Road. Often he passes the evening in the
small downstairs room off the kitchen, saying little. His beloved crank
phonograph is close by (it's in a mahogany case and has a wooden stylus, for perfection of tone), and he'll put on Caruso or Tetrazzini,
though sometimes he just sits and tries to remember the voice of
Adelina Patti, whose birdlike soprano on the San Francisco opera
stages of his youth could make him weep. Often now, he's in bed by
eight o'clock. He has high blood pressure and hardening of the arteries
and sometimes he'll start spurting blood from the nose. (His wife will
tell people after his death that the nosebleeds had become so violent
she had to get the bedroom painted twice—it went all over the walls.)
To most of his son's high school friends—there aren't that many—and
to the kids next door, Mr. Mac is little more than the aged, inward, frail-
looking, and semiforbidding presence sitting in the leather chair in his
necktie and old-man's shoes. But what these youths don't see, could
never know, is that there are the deepest romantic reveries and yearn-

45

ings inside this failing Victorian gentleman. What they have no comprehension of is the heroic journey he's made: out of immigrant Irish bootmaking poverty in the middle of the last century (and on the other side of the continent) to this respectable middle-class East Bay hillside. What they have no appreciation for is the mystery of his cultivation, the unlikelihood of his refinements. What they don't get about Robert James McNamara—who has just under seventy years on his arches and five remaining to him—is that he is the *artist* in shoes. Even now, in his slow sinkings.

Next, think of a far-younger-looking and prone-to-gabbiness woman standing in the kitchen of this same household. She has on her usual apron and matronly dress and sensible low heels and is possibly putting the last touches on another of her famous confections—that, or talking through the raised window to Mrs. Helmer. (When she's on the second floor, she likes talking through a raised window on the other side of the house to Cynthia Lowell's mom.) Her first name is Claranel, and she's spent a fair amount of time in her life tinkering with the spelling and spacing of it—in the way you might write something out in large letters and paste it on a wall, then stand six paces back to regard it. Once her name was Clara Nell. Then it was Claranelle. Then it was Clara Nelle. At some point it shifted to Claranell. A long time ago it was just Clara. These days most people call her Nelle or Nellie. (Her children tend to address her as "Mother.") Her maiden name is Strange, and she's of French and Scotch and some English blood, and she's let it out in conversation that she may be related to Winston Churchill. She comes from Southern Methodists but has switched to Presbyterianism and lately has been eyeing the doctrines of Christian Science. (Up the road she'll flirt with the Unity church.) She is willful, talented, intense, socially pretentious, an absurd embellisher, occasionally daffy, extremely capable, compulsively neat, increasingly eccentric, a monopolizer of all talk. To be plain, the woman's gotten awfully overbearing as she's moved into her late forties. And yet she has a certain native class and taste and goodness and generosity and even sweetness of character—it can't be denied, any more than you could deny how devoted she is to her family and her home. She'll talk your fool head off in this home. It's almost as if she's pumping you for something, anything. One might call her obsessive: The carrot shavings on her fruit salad at Thanksgiving have to be laid on just so, as if by blueprint. Her Sunday table is like a hotel setting. Calories count for nothing with her.

She'll stand over you—say, you're a friend of her son's and have come by with him after school—until you've gagged down the last bite of one of her tarts or puffs or tortes or fluted-edged raspberry pies. You won't find a mote of dust or drop of liquor in here. And what you'll doubtless recall years hence is the furniture polish—the smell and sheen of it. Overall, Mrs. Mac seems a mother driven by little more than huge needs of success for her children, Peggy and Bobby, both of whom are in their teens, but most especially driven by needs of success for her son, who is firstborn and whom she has made the centerpiece of all. She isn't an unintelligent woman, although there's no way she can appreciate fully what she's got on her hands in terms of this adored male child just now beginning to swim to his intellectual surface. Sometimes you get the impression she feels she has married beneath her—nothing she says in so many words. She likes to think she rises from distinguished folk—lawyers and doctors and teachers and post-masters—and it's somewhat true, but there's a large family secret having to do with violence and her own ne'er-do-well father that Nelle S. McNamara is concealing in her ample bosom.

Finally, think of a serious-minded and attractive-looking sixteen-year-old boy bent over a cone of light in the back corner bedroom on the second floor of this morally decent and well-intentioned home. The boy's at the books again. His friend next door, Jimmy Helmer, whose bedroom is opposite his—so close that you could pass something over on about twenty feet of clothesline—often sees him bent this way at 7 p.m., when Jimmy is going out. And bent this way at 1 a.m., when Jimmy is slipping back home. In a few weeks, after school is out, the boy will turn seventeen, ever a year younger than his peer group. (His mother has told friends, and will continue to tell it long after he's a famous American, how Bobby skipped four grades early on, and how she kept him from school until he was eight, because she could do better, and besides he was so sickly, which again is something like the plausible truth, even if the arithmetic and facts don't stack up.) The boy is an Eagle Scout in troop three of the Piedmont Council of the Boy Scouts of America, having earned all of the required merit badges in textiles and pioneering and bird study and civics and so forth in nearly record time. This summer he'll work as a counselor at Camp Wallace Alexander on Spanish Creek up in the Feather River country of the Sierra. This semester, his last in high school, he has been elected president of Rigma, which is a social-service club at Piedmont High, the accent being far

more on the first word than the second. Rigma, spelled backward, stands
for All Men Grow in Righteousness. Shhh, it's a secret. The boys of
Rigma—Roy Jones and Marvin Pomeroy and Charlie Wheeler and
Jimmy Helmer and John Erichson and Russ Raine and Bob McNamara
and the rest—have lately memorialized themselves in sepia at the Nov-
elty Photography Parlor at 1018 Broadway in Oakland. (Of the ten Rig-
mas in the shot, only the one in the first row on the far right seems
spotless and contained.) Sometimes the Rigma gang will drive initiates
up to Mountain View cemetery in Jimmy Helmer's Nash touring car,
make them moo like an elk in moonlight while hanging from the top of
some ornate monument—this sort of thing. The club president goes
along, not exuberantly, but goes along. He was along the night they
siphoned gas out of a state-highway steam shovel by the side of the road
so they could make it back to town from Clear Lake in Helmer's Nash.
He's game, you could say. He's awkward, you could say, at least in social
matters, especially with his own sex, and let's face it, in high school the
social stuff counts more than books. At Piedmont High, one of the better
college-preparatory schools in northern California, the boy not only
leads Rigma but edits the Clan-O-Log yearbook and is a member of Boys'
Council and Board of Control. He also goes out with Hallie Booth and
Annalee Whitmore, both of whom are lookers. Hallie owns all the
teenage male hearts of Piedmont High. He has escorted her to dances at
big-band affairs at the Mark Hopkins Hotel across the bay. (This might
surprise you, but he's known to be quite light on the dance floor. On the
way over to San Francisco on the ferry, the word is he won't take nips at
anything but fruit juice while the others are swilling rotgut from silver
flasks hidden in their vests.) All these things said, it remains a fact: The
boy is self-conscious and a little awkward socially, especially among
other males in a peer group. This fall he plans to enroll in college, and
again these same social awkwardnesses and overcompensating mechanisms with his own gender will reassert themselves. He has decided
he'll study economics at Cal. He has begun to think he was born to the
uses of the scientific method, that it's something in his character. Didn't
old Christian "Doc" Niemann give him a straight 1 in Chem II in second
semester last year? Yes, he did. A straight 1 means you made an A on
every test in every grading period. Doc Niemann entered the mark like
this, in blue ink in a marbleized cardboard copybook manufactured by
Webster Publishing Company, St. Louis, Missouri: "McNamara, Chem II,
1,1,1,1. Final: 1. Lab book: 1."

*   *   *

R O B E R T   M C N A M A R A   was born—at 5:45 a.m. on June 9, 1916, in a San Francisco hospital—into what was almost a three-generational family: a father old enough to be a grandfather, a mother more than two decades younger than her husband and vastly different in personality and preoccupations. The father, who gave much to his son's character (and much more than has been paid attention to by previous McNamara chroniclers), was closed-off and of another time, trying as best he could to parent children as an old man, an old man whom nobody seems ever to have witnessed tossing a ball to his children or getting down on the floor to roughhouse. "He might have," a man named Dick Quigley, who was a close family friend of the McNamaras, told me. "But I never saw it. And I was over there pretty much with my own dad." (McNamara's sister, Peggy McNamara Slaymaker, verified this.) When Robert McNamara was at Berkeley, there were those classmates and FIGI fraternity brothers who would have sworn his dad wasn't alive—they'd never seen or even heard about him. It was the mother in central view. Much later, when his father had been dead for decades, McNamara would often seem a little pained to tell friends his dad had spent his working life in shoes. "If you watch his face, he seems embarrassed sometimes when his family comes up, and there is this kind of jerky twitching motion. . . . He's quite protective of himself, there and elsewhere," a woman named Mary Joe Goodwin, the (now deceased) wife of one of his closest college friends, told me. At the point she said it, she'd known him for forty-five years, and it was evident she loved him a lot—but she didn't hesitate to talk of the twitching. The first time we discussed McNamara and his parents, Goodwin used the word "diffident," and it seemed right. And yet what also seems right is that the son would always hold inside of him many more tender, unresolved, conflictual feelings about his father than he ever would about his mother. At least partly this must be because he and his mother were always too much alike—a basis for despising each other, finally. Washington socialite Joan Braden—who in the mid-1980s was to emerge as McNamara's much-gossiped-about paramour and traveling companion (she was married and the mother of many children; he was the grieving widower in flight from his past)—confirmed that McNamara once sat beside her and cried openly and even startlingly at a production of *Death of a Salesman.* McNamara's father wasn't Willy Loman, lugging his pasteboard suitcase toward oblivion. But something in that performance made a closeted man in a darkened hall erupt.

Basically, the father of the Oakland hillside couldn't touch, no matter what emotional currents were volting through. "Peggy, is that your *skin?*" R. J. McNamara once said to his teenage daughter as she crossed the living room with the back of her blouse accidentally out. Six decades later, Peggy Slaymaker could recall the exact aghast tonal quality of the question.

Robert James McNamara, the late San Francisco shoe traveler, seems to have been fair, moral, strict, proud, proper, accomplished, fussy, brainy, crotchety, and almost totally lacking in humor. But most especially he was cultivated, even dandified—almost foppishly so at times—in the way many fin-de-siècle gentlemen of gaslit San Francisco were cultivated and even foppified. San Francisco, queen city of the instant West. San Francisco, Bay Area bohemia where silver kings and railroad barons and painted ladies of flexible virtue, as they were called by the local populace, strode the Golden Gate night.

Robert McNamara's father was a man of commerce and the world—with a squishy side. Robert McNamara's father was an up-from-shanty Irishman—who'd spent years prissifying himself. Robert McNamara's father was a Pacific Coast footwear salesman—who kept a pair of patent-leather dancing shoes with a black bow on the toes in an upstairs closet. No one in his family had ever actually seen him *in* these shoes, according to his daughter.

"My father was always rather vague about his age and background," Peggy Slaymaker told me. That qualifies as understatement. On his 1938 death certificate—filled out by his wife the day after he died—R. J. McNamara's date of birth was wrong, the number of years he had lived in California was wrong, the name of his father was wrong. However, Nelle got her husband's birthplace correct: Massachusetts. Nelle wrote down James for her husband's father. But that man's name had been Jeremiah. James had been one of her husband's brothers. "James, James?" Peggy said as the two of us looked at the mistakes on the certificate. "You mean my father had a brother named James?"

If the emotionally boxed father was the businessman with artistic predilections, a lot of which tended to come out at night, then the stay-at-home and not-overly-intelligent mother was a kind of breathtaking driver and crusher—who nonetheless nurtured and supported her children in ways her spouse never could. Think of her as the mannish force of nature, with the feminine class. Once you entered 1036 Annerly, it was Nelle McNamara's show. She wished to be supreme, and mostly was. And yet she didn't hold purse strings, and apparently knew little about her husband's financial affairs. In a sense there were two Nelle McNamaras, a minimum of two, in Robert McNamara's life: the early-good, albeit excruciatingly purposeful Nelle; and the late-bad Nelle, who grew selfish and small and ended up alienating almost everyone around her, most especially her son and daughter. (When Nelle McNamara died, at Christmas in 1964, at seventy-nine, which was two and a half decades after her husband died, the secretary of defense was on a skiing holiday in Aspen. He flew to Oakland in a military transport from Grand Junction, Colorado, then clattered into First Presbyterian Church on Broadway in ski clothing. At the service, friends of the family were struck by the lack of any outward emotion in either child.)

McNamara's parents seem to have been not only polar opposites but almost comically contradictory in their own natures. In a sense the first offspring of this union came out a double hybrid, a contradiction of their contradictions. It was as if the atom had split and then split some more. The single-mindedness is from the homebound mother, yes. But the serious quiet and not-small achievements of the salesman-aesthete father have a greater place than has been previously understood. On both sides there were things submerged, and things precise. Both parents contributed to the crucial feeling side of things. It's as if Mrs. Mac's intensity got harnessed to Mr. Mac's brain, and what issued was this brilliant, brittle, overengineered son who became, well, a machine, at least by daylight. This brilliant, brittle, overengineered son who would never be able to comprehend, much less reconcile, the lifelong interplay of parental opposites inside him.

And yet . . . all of that sounds far too deterministic and reductionist, not to say arrogant, in the classic McNamarian way. Because just as with any life, there had to have been 10,000 other known and unknown and partially revealed and microscopically small contributory factors and events and turns and triumphs—quite apart from whatever life he knew with his parents—that helped create the inordinately complex being Robert S. McNamara became.

THE ARTIST IN SHOES. Consider a photograph. A small man, maybe five foot six or five foot seven, with a high collar and plastered hair, is leaning back on a rococo table in a turn-of-the-century photo parlor. If the pose and the subject weren't so determinedly serious, you'd want to say they are hilarious: Cleopatra in pince-nez and three-piece suit semireclined on the burnished Frisco tabletop. The subject can't carry the moment off—but wants to. He's propping himself with his right arm. His hands look as if they're about to be swallowed by the enormous cuffs of his starched shirt. On the fourth finger of his left hand, which is resting on his pants leg, just below his crotch, are two rings. One looks like a thick wedding band (although it can't be, since he's an Irish bachelor at this point), and the other looks like a thin ring of gold with three stones on it. "Oh, my, he's wearing two rings, isn't he?" Peggy Slaymaker said to me the first time she produced this wonderful old album print. She put her hand up to her mouth and the sentence seemed to flap out somewhere between a gasp and a laugh.

Poems are hard to read, and music can be hard to hear, and long-ago lives can seem impossible to know. He was in thrall to ocean crossings and lounging robes. He owned a profusion of stickpins. One of his monogrammed walking sticks had an elk's head for a handle, carved from ivory, smooth as scrimshaw; the piece sported huge antlers and a fierce flying eye. (There was also a carved clock on the handle, with the hands showing five minutes to twelve.) On the beach in Santa Cruz he would emerge from a changing cabinet before his wife and small children in this terribly embarrassing black bathing gown. He had a soft chin and delicate lips and he detested loose shoes in the way Miniver Cheevy, in Edwin Arlington Robinson's poem, eyed a khaki suit with loathing. His own brand of dress shoe was Stacy-Adams. They were "high shoes," and their soft calflike leather pulled up so tight over his instep that you couldn't see a crease. They were like the finest gloves on the hand of a woman.

"Peg, play me something sweet at the piano," he'd say, nights, slack in his leather chair, eyes closed, swaying.

He had a fine tenor voice and there are stories that in his youth he'd performed in Bay Area light-opera companies. (I could find no record of it.) For years he resisted the Colonial Cafeteria in downtown Oakland—too informal, he thought, taking food on a tray, how awful—but once he'd actually been *exposed* to the place, he found he liked it so much that he wished to institute it as a Sunday-evening ritual with the Quigley family. His eating habits were famously persnickety: Once, toward the end of his life, after he'd become sales manager of a large San Francisco wholesaler named Buckingham & Hecht and was traveling in Oregon with one of his salesmen, he sent back prunes. "But these prunes are much too wrinkled," he told the startled waitress.

His daughter says that she never remembers him coming through the front door that he didn't stop, lift his hat, and buss his wife. A peck, nothing passionate. But there was tenderness in it.

He never got past eighth grade; the factory got him instead. His best suits were always custom-made and he felt that a gentleman never left home without a hat. Perhaps this severe attention to dress was the most direct means a man knew of communicating his vision, his soul. Perhaps it was a way of saying: *And think what I could have done had I had your opportunities.* "Now, Fred, did the tailor get this coat right?" he'd say to his best friend, Fred Quigley, sheathing the lapels of a newly tailored jacket between his thumbs and forefingers. It was a rhetorical question. The best friend would kid: "For God's sake, Bob, stand up straight, you'll be old before your time." He wasn't old all of his life, but on the other hand the twentieth century must have seemed such a rude intruder. It's as if when the century made its turn, so did Robert James.

"I remember the way Uncle Bob smoked," Dick Quigley (son of Fred) told me. "There was this great curvy elegance to it. He'd blow smoke at the ceiling, he'd talk through the puffs." I brought up the penchant for glitter, knowing how Quigley admired him. "I know, I know," he said. "So odd on a man." Fred Quigley and R. J. McNamara were both commercial shoe travelers, and the two knew and confided in each other for something like half a century. Fred's firm was Cahn, Nickleburg; R. J.'s was Williams-Marvin, at least for the bulk of his career. Fred was the first to fall to matrimony; not long after, the other confirmed Irish bachelor took the plunge.

When Dick Quigley was a teenager growing up in the mid-twenties, R. J. McNamara would come over to the Quigley house on Sunday morning when Nelle had taken young Bobby and Peggy to First Presbyterian. Dick would sit near his father and watch the two men tilt smoke ceilingward and tell shoe tales. After a time Uncle Bob would take out his watch and say, "Well, Fred, Nelle and the children will be home by now, I'd best get along in your machine." And Fred or Fred's son Dick would drive him home. R. J. McNamara tended to speak of cars as "machines." He preferred sailing vessels. Once a year he went by steamship to see his two sisters in Honolulu. On the *Lurline,* jewel of the Matson lines, he was reputed to know the captain personally and receive nightly invitations to his table. His daughter has shown me passenger manifests of his crossings, printed on special cards and illustrated with palm trees and ladies in gay hats: "Sailing from Honolulu, Hawaii. Voyage 49 Homeward. Mr. R. J. McNamara."

Once a year he'd repair to a sanitarium up in the wine country. It was known by Bay Area Victorians as "the water cure." If you wished to try archery at St. Helena, there were white-uniformed boys to hold the quiver. If you wanted the vapors of the steam cabinet, there were burly figures in chalky shoes and starched trousers to help you step into the thing. Sometimes Nelle came up to St. Helena on a train for the second week of Rob's stay (she liked calling her husband Rob), but a rural spa run by the Seventh-Day Adventists in the pines and madrones of Napa was not her idea of the sublime.

It isn't known where all these first-cabin tastes and sensibilities came from, but we do know that Robert James McNamara's life opened during the Civil War in an unlettered New England shoemaking poverty and closed in a steel hospital bed in the room off the kitchen on the Oakland hillside at about the moment Hitler was starting to overrun Europe. So much in between—between October 4, 1863, and November 4, 1938— seems lost.

The core family legend is that the first of this line to spy the new world, Jeremiah McNamara—which is to say, R.J.'s father and Robert McNamara's grandfather—fled County Cork in the midst of the potato famine, stepping out in the exact middle of the nineteenth century onto the rickety wharves of East Boston. The paterfamilias—whom Nelle and her son were never to know—entered the shoe trade sometime after 1850 in a little south-of-Boston town named Stoughton where Paul Revere had cast cannon for the Revolutionary War. Not quite two decades later, in the early months of 1868, after the birth of his fourth son, Jeremiah and his wife, Margaret (she was a Purcell from Ireland who'd also fled the famine), took his family to the promises of California. The family myth is that one part of the trek was made on muleback across the Isthmus of Panama. Robert James, the secondborn, would have been about four and a half on that trip. San Francisco, a place, as someone has said, with a genius for geography, sunny in January but foggy in July, had gone from an infestment of wild rabbits and sand fleas barely twenty years before to a city pressing on a population of 150,000, tenth in the nation. It was as if it never had time to be a village before it was forced by gold and other circumstances to be a city. The immigrant Irish were coming in multitudes to this quick dream at the edge of the continent. By the 1880s, the Irish and their children would account for nearly a third of San Francisco's population.

By October 1, 1868, the three-word listing "Jeremiah McNamara, laborer" was on the worker rolls of San Francisco. Jeremiah and his increasing brood (four more children were to be born in California) were lodged in a flat on Howard Street, in the south-of-Market district, in a ward heavily concentrated with Irish, though not quite an ethnic ghetto. In the next several years the patriarch treed boots and shoes in at least four Bay Area factories. He took to delivering milk. He went back to shoes. He moved to the other side of the Bay. His older sons joined him at the bootmaking bench. The few surviving photographs of Robert McNamara's paternal grandfather present a short bulky man with thick wrists and a wide face and the smallest little black spindly glasses that don't quite curl over the back of his ears. Jeremiah lived to see eight years of the twentieth century.

But Robert James, the one who rose: In 1880, at the age of seventeen, the second son was in Ira M. Wentworth's Boot & Shoe Manufactory in Berkeley. Over the next sixty years this mysterious dandy was to progress from a cutter at a shoemaking bench, to a commercial traveler, to a secretary at a central office of a wholesaler, to a sales manager of a subsidiary firm, and finally, at the age of sixty-four, in 1927, eleven years before his death, to a sales manager of a parent company that was the largest manufacturer of footwear on the Pacific Coast. (That was Buckingham & Hecht.) He held this job almost literally until the day he died. Financial pressures were part of it, but so too must have been duty, drive, determination, sense of self.

Peggy Slaymaker once said to me, "We never thought of ourselves as coming from . . . *laborers.*" There seemed something so hurt in it, confused.

By 1891 R. J. McNamara was a man in a coat and tie and boater hat riding up the coast of California and through the San Joaquin Valley with a plywood trunk that held either left shoes or right shoes but never pairs. (A pair took up too much room; the traveler working an adjacent territory carried the mate to yours.) It was the nineties of San Francisco and R. J. McNamara, the opera lover with the watch fob and handlebar, was offering lines, just as his own son, in the middle of the next century, would offer lines for Ford Motor Company.

One day about thirteen years into the new century, R. J. McNamara, still living at home and helping out in the usual way of the unmarried Irish, came into the home offices of the Williams-Marvin firm at Bush and Battery streets in San Francisco and saw a full-bodied girl with short dark hair and a wide firm mouth. She was a new secretary. (Although she wasn't *his* secretary, as Nelle would always say in later years—travelers didn't have secretaries.) The two courted. On June 29,

1914, this couple went to City Hall to fill out an affidavit for a marriage license. One pictures them, the reined-in older man and the talky younger woman with the infectious features of a Sears, Roebuck catalogue girl, sitting close on the wicker-back seats of a streetcar clanging down Market Street. The newspapers are full of dispatches about the assassination in Yugoslavia of an Austrian archduke by a Serbian nationalist. Colonel Roosevelt is trying for the presidency again. At City Hall, the intended fill out their forms. In answer to "age at last birthday," the shoe traveler strokes in forty-eight. He's really three months shy of turning fifty-one. The next morning, at St. Mary's Catholic Cathedral, he weds the twenty-nine-year-old moonfaced girl named Nellie Strange. (She's given twenty-eight on the affidavit for her age.) It's a private ceremony, below the communion rail, not at the altar itself, because the marriage is "mixed." The groom's faith is shaky, but he has bowed to all of those old deep atavistic Irish pressures to get married properly, by a priest, in a house of God. In the cathedral's book of record, in Latin, the words "dispensation given" are entered. On this same morning, June 30, 1914, a two-line notice about the marriage license appears in the *Chronicle.* But it gets balled up.

HER PATH to that cathedral wedding rail was heroic too. But first, a glimpse of her character, as recorded in her own handsome penmanship. The book is called *The Record of Our Baby Boy,* and it was begun in the summer of 1916, right after the blessed event at Mt. Zion Hospital. The word "record" is accurate—the documentarian seems bent on noting her newborn's every third breath and burp. Sometimes the record is kept in the voice of the infant, although more often it's in the voice of Nelle. It's full of gentle scold and the sweet petulance and also the kind of suffocating precision for which the baby boy himself would one day know his own cravings.

She clocks his weight: "8 and $^{11}/_{16}$ pounds"; "9 and ¼ pounds"; "11 and $^{9}/_{16}$ pounds;" "12 and $^{3}/_{16}$ pounds." She seizes on teeth, recording the date and location of each arrival and the moment when all sixteen are in. ("Two uppers are showing this morning—a birthday gift to mother"—February 23, 1917, he's at eight months and fourteen days.) She kisses his foot (it's September 3, 1916, and he's been in the air of the world three months), and rejoices in how he laughs out loud. Come November she's whispering in his ear ("Do you love mother?") and imagining what he's saying back.

She's chronicling every *first:* first haircut; first smile; first visit to a portrait studio ("At 1:40 this afternoon a Taxi called to take us to Terkelson & Henry's, on Market Street near 8th Street, S.F., Cal. . . ."); first shoes ("They are tan kid with white buttons and brown silk tassels—how proud he is of them! Daddy brought them up from Williams-Marvin Company—size #3, some *foot!*"); first toy; first word: "Am very sorry I cannot write 'Daddy' in that space. It is certainly no fault of your mother's that it is not there, as I have said 'Da-da-da' to you constantly since birth, but, 'what's the use?' "

She calls him Little Man. She calls him Little Robert. She strolls him in a pram to nearby Golden Gate Park, and the pram has large wire wheels and a wicker hood. She takes him visiting at her mother's place, which is just around the corner. She prays with him, taking up his voice: "Our Father-Mother God, loving me. Guard me while I sleep, guide my little feet." You get the loneliness when her spouse is out of town. You get the disappointments: "June 9th—1917—Auntie Rene brought over a cake today, but Bob was out in his buggy. A very quiet day for Bob's first birthday. Never mind, wait until next year!"

Consider a photograph—rather two photographs, one of which has been pasted into the book of record, and both of which seem to have been taken within moments of each other. It's a summer Sunday in San Francisco and there are hydrangeas blooming at 804 Balboa Street. The new father has come out into the sunlight in a necktie and a checkered robe, the rope cincture of which is knotted loosely at his middle. As the picture is snapped, he isn't looking into the camera but instead is peering down through his round glasses at the sunbonneted package in his arms. It's as if he's trying to fathom what his life now means. The mother has also come outdoors in her robe, and it too is gathered modestly about her plump frame. Standing just to the rear of her spouse, she has set her left hand lightly on his elbow and is now inching up over his shoulder to get a peek at her baby. A joyful smile is breaking on her wide firm mouth. The photograph is later entered on page nine of the book of record above the words "First Picture." Below it Nelle writes: "July 9, 1916—One month."

But the *second* picture, the one that didn't get pasted in: Rob and Nelle are still outdoors, standing in front of the hydrangeas. Baby Boy has been taken away, or at least out of the frame of the viewfinder. Nelle is seated in a chair. And it's her expression that nearly jolts. What the camera has caught now is not the chubby-cheeked schoolgirl but the hard set of the thirty-one-year-old woman's mouth. She looks squarely into the sun.

The crusher with class. She once assailed her son-in-law (that is, Peggy Slaymaker's husband) for not coming down with the flu; everybody else in the family got it, why didn't he? You must not care enough about them, is the suggestion that was made. That was fairly late in her life. But much earlier, she once leaned across the front seat of an automobile and said to an Oakland traffic cop, "Now look here, officer, this young man is driving very carefully, and what's more he's driving me to a funeral of a close relative, and I don't know why you've stopped us, we certainly weren't speeding, what could you have been thinking, but in any case we're going to be late now and I think you'd better let us go." The cop jerked his head back out of the window. Yes, ma'am, he said. And Joe Cooper—one of Robert McNamara's econ classmates from Cal who'd volunteered to drive Nelle to the funeral that day—wheeled off, the moment sealed inside him.

The force of nature: She used to tell her children about how she survived the great San Francisco earthquake of 1906. She was twenty-one and had just come in from a date, and the stairs moved in her mother's house, and the house collapsed beneath her, and none of them could get out at first. Nelle ended up across the bay in her nightgown, sleeping on a cot in a gym at Berkeley. No damn earthquake was going to defeat her.

She used to say she would have gone to Stanford, just like her brother the doctor, and maybe on a scholarship, and done pretty well, had she not come down with a case of amnesia. Some kind of truth must reside here. "Oh well, Mother used to say these things," author Deborah Shapley quotes McNamara as saying—in regard to the amnesia bit—in her 1993 biography, *Promise and Power.* But the fact is that Nelle Strange didn't graduate from high school until she was two months shy of her twenty-first birthday. She earned a diploma from Girls' High in San Francisco in December 1905. Her oddly bare transcript has the word "accepted" after several courses and there's a note attached that she withdrew in 1902 because of illness. The nature of the illness isn't stated, but Peggy Slaymaker believes it was typhoid. A stream of moves and a bout of typhoid must have had a lot to do with the lateness of the graduation, but not everything, because there was at least one other thing that had to have played a large role. And that was the family rupture eight years before, the family violence and subsequent divorce of her parents when Nelle was twelve—in a rural California community—that she could never bring herself to speak of, not even to her own daughter, at least until she was an old woman in a Peninsula nursing home, suffering from a twisted colon and arthritis and plenty of rage. And even then Nelle McNamara found herself only able to speak to her daughter of a "separation between mother and daddy when I was a little girl, this decision to live apart that we never really understood." Nelle understood it, all right, just couldn't say it. Until I showed her court documents, Peggy Slaymaker had never known of an actual divorce of her grandparents, much less of the violence that had prompted it. Nelle was prone to stretch and twist anything.

"Dick, look how much money he makes working at Ford, why, he could get them beautiful clothes, and he makes Marg get all their things at Sears," she once said to Dick Quigley, after McNamara had been named head of Ford Division and was making very few visits to see her. (When she traveled to Michigan to see him, she decided her five-year-old grandson should have his mouth washed out with soap.) After McNamara had made group vice president of cars and trucks in Dearborn, she told the Quigleys, in a whisper, "Well, it's all under cover, but Bob's in charge of this great new car, the Edsel. He and Marg are driving one down to Carmel for the weekend." Well, something like that. Actually, he despised the Edsel, the car being so antithetical to his Puritan tastes, and he was maneuvering from the moment it came out to shut it down.

She seems never to have forgotten a birthday, an anniversary, a distant friend's promotion or engagement. On the other hand, she could perceive a slight from anybody. Over the years she was to fall out with her brother the doctor (among other things, she hated his wife and kept both of them from coming to her son's wedding); with her sister-in-law the artist (whom she saw as greedy, pretentious and manipulative, and always trying to take little Bobby and Peggy away from Protestantism and back to Catholicism); with her sister the milliner; with her sister the math teacher; with her own children after they were grown and no longer as needy for her as she wished. In college, but especially in the years after, the older of these two tended to stalk from the room whenever his mother started in. The younger, around whom all constellations did not revolve, seems to have been far more forgiving, understanding.

One day at Peggy Slaymaker's, her easygoing and engaging husband—whom people call "Slay"—suddenly said to me, "No question, you know, Bob cut his mother off, cut her out of his life, had to, at the end." And Peggy, who was in the other room fixing a perfect impromptu lunch, came in and said, "Slay, not really, no, he didn't cut her off. I mean, not financially." And her husband said, "No, of course not, not financially, that's true, he was very generous."

In the yellowing clip files marked "McNamara" in the Oakland *Tribune* library, there is a memo dated January 17, 1964. A *Tribune* reporter wrote a note to himself and his editor after he'd spoken to Nelle McNamara—by phone, it appears—in a convalescent hospital. This was eleven months before Nelle died. She was ill with diverticulitis and other ailments. This was after her son, who'd been in Washington three years, had placed her in a rest home, had generously paid $18,000 up front to give his mother a lifetime residency and round-the-clock care. Between the lines of the reporter's memo, you can sense an old woman's anger and hurt: She'd been paid for, put away.

The memo: "Mrs. R. J. McNamara (Claranel), mother of Defense Secretary Robert S. McNamara, is in Sharon Heights Convalescent Hospital, Menlo Park, with rheumatic arthritis. Taken there from Sequoia Guest (retirement) home, her residence. Says it is 'very doubtful' if the fast-paced schedule of her son will allow him to stop and see her. She says she has seen him only once since he took the Washington post, and then only for one and a half hours. 'I'm just so sorry . . . and I know he is too,' she said."

Nelle McNamara would have been far too classy and concerned with appearances not to have appended that last sentence to her fury.

In the mid-1980s, the following Nelle story was still passing around the East Bay, obtainable from certain old biddies sitting under Oakland hair dryers: At the 1938 probate hearing of R. S. McNamara's will (five days after he died), a judge said, "Mrs. McNamara, how long have you and your husband been separated?" The will had a provision in it that $2,000 was to go to Robert James's maiden sister in Hawaii. Her name was McNamara too, but stories being stories and gossip being gossip, this apparently is how word began to travel that moneys had been left to "another woman." It was rubbish, of course. The deceased had left everything except that $2,000 to his wife and children.

Peggy Slaymaker seemed terror-struck when I asked if her mother could have been the source of what the judge supposedly asked. She couldn't conceive of her mother spreading that kind of talk. Embarrassment alone would have precluded it.

That seems true. And yet the following is also true: Nelle was "shocked" (her daughter's word) when this same highly disliked maiden sister-in-law, Mary Gertrude McNamara, ended up marrying the Dole pineapple executive to whom her younger sister had earlier been married. Nelle thought that was close to incestuous. Robert James was long dead by the time this happened, which may have made a widow's gossip about it easier.

Maybe one reason Nelle grew to despise her sisters-in-law on her husband's side is that her husband always used to send them money—although it isn't clear if Nelle ever knew in his lifetime. "Oh, they were taken care of for years by my father," Peggy Slaymaker told me, and let it go.

Another story about money: Dick Quigley told me that Nelle had to borrow $8,000 from the Quigley family after R. J. McNamara's death so she could get through the probating period. The astute businessman-husband had failed to make adequate provisions. Quigley said his father was glad to loan it to Nelle; the McNamaras were almost a part of their own family. But Nelle must have been pretty embarrassed to ask. Asking other people for money wouldn't have been something in this woman's character.

What was in character was pushing herself and her children, especially her firstborn, beyond a point that was healthy. Was there any malevolence in the pushing? The answer to that seems a loud no. In Henry L. Trewhitt's early McNamara biography (it was published three years after he was gone from the Defense Department and is called *McNamara: His Ordeal in the Pentagon*), this sentence appears: "One Piedmont teacher recalled the mother's saying years later that Bob felt she had pushed him too hard, and that Bob had told his mother so." In Deborah Shapley's much later biography of McNamara, she quotes McNamara as saying: ". . . the pressure on me was unbelievable. If I got an A minus, the question was, 'Why didn't you get an A?' " Almost all of McNamara's elementary, high-school, and college teachers are dead now. But more than a decade ago I sat in the living room of Anna Lee Guest Mallory in Leisure World in Laguna Hills, California. She had taught him history and civics. (It was easy for her to remember how lovely and neat the pupil's copybooks always were.) I told Mallory that Henry Trewhitt was fairly certain that she'd been the one who told him about Nelle's eventual admission of the pushing. "It may have been me that his mother said that to, I can't recall," she said. "It also may have been Miss Lane, who taught him English. But it sort of sounds right. I can tell you this, though. All she wanted was for Bob to succeed. She wanted everything for those kids."

Many have echoed that. "Nelle was for that kid like you wouldn't believe," one of McNamara's fraternity brothers at Cal told me, but then tacked on, "I got the impression he wasn't all that grateful to her." The president of McNamara's fraternity, Carson Magill, could instantly remember Claranel McNamara: a wonderful and likable little bird of a woman with a big personality and much sweetness. "She wasn't a pain in the ass. I would have known. I had to deal with some pain-in-the-ass mothers in the Mothers Club, which was a regular part of the fraternity." At a minimum, I'd question the description "birdlike." In almost every picture I've seen, Nelle looks stolid as Churchill. The arms are large, the ankles heavy. Her husband was spare as she was stumpy. Peggy Slaymaker told me her mother never got fat until she had children, and then the weight seemed to fall on her all at once.

But *why* would Nelle have so badly wanted her children to succeed? Some of it would have had to do with wanting them to have opportunities and comforts she'd been denied—any mother's wish. But heightened needs for respectability must surely come into play, too. I once asked Peggy Slaymaker if she felt her mother was a "driven" person—and why. The question was going to make her uncomfortable, and I knew it, but I asked anyway. I didn't really get an answer, so I changed directions and asked which parent she felt was the larger influence. I already knew the answer. Peggy, a redhead still very attractive and marvelously organized, said: "All I can say is what a remarkable person my mother was. Without a car, without knowing how to drive, she was determined to get me to every lesson and activity she could. I took sewing classes at eleven with adults. I was at the California College of Arts and Crafts on Saturday. I had swimming lessons at the Y. I was at Prather's Dancing School. She'd take us to the city on Saturday. We'd go over on the ferry. My brother had bands on his teeth, and he'd have to get them checked. We'd sometimes meet my father, because he often worked on Saturdays. I can tell you she got my brother to a lot more lessons and activities than she got me to." There was no rancor in the words.

I asked Peggy what might have attracted her mother and father to each other. She said that perhaps her mother felt she was getting older and she wouldn't be married at all if she didn't do it pretty soon.

Another time Nelle's daughter told me, "My parents didn't have a very loving relationship." She meant loving in the context of physical love. What seems fair to say here about two long-dead people is that their twenty-four-year marriage had a good deal of respect in it, a lot more respect than ardor.

What also seems fair to say is that Nelle may have *needed* to marry a dignified, moral, and restrained older man to whom she could give respect if not her passion; a dignified and restrained older man with whom she could feel safe. And why? Because of all the unsafe and destabilizing things she'd come from in her childhood. And viewed from that perspective, Claranel Strange's passage to adulthood, marriage, and parenthood, like her husband's passage, begins to bump up large. It begins to seem courageous. What you suddenly sense in her life is both an emotional bruising and the will to cover it up and go on—a theme that would have great repetitions in this family. As with so much else about her son's life, the answers to the important riddles seem knotted in the psychic past.

Story of a secret: Robert McNamara's maternal grandfather—that is, Nelle's father—was a hard-luck Missouri dirt farmer named William Miller Strange who went West to Sutter County, California, with his wife and children and in-laws in 1881. Bill Strange was big-chested and wore suspenders and western hats and he was descended from a man who was even larger: six-foot-six Gideon Elijah May Strange. (McNamara gets his height and angularity from his maternal side, not least from his Old Testament–sounding great-grandfather, who, in pictures, has piercing eyes and a foot-long white beard.) The cutworm had damaged the fruit trees the year that Strange and family left Missouri for greener Pacific fields. The outlaw Cole Younger was in federal prison owing to a botched bank raid up at Northfield, Minnesota, and had already confessed to a Christian temperance lady: "Circumstances make men what they are. If it had not been for the war I might have been something, but as it is, I am what I am." Jesse James, another Missouri son, hadn't yet been shot in the back by the coward Robert Ford.

In Yuba City, California, which is near the western foothills of the Sierra, up past Sacramento, the last child of Bill and Martha Strange was born. She was christened Clara Nell. In the next decade a marriage of twenty-seven years tore itself apart. One March day in 1896 Strange, who was nearing fifty, struck his daughter Ida, "within sight of other children" (the court documents state), knocking her "across the room and onto the floor." The baby of the family, Nelle, had turned eleven three weeks before.

Three months later, Strange threatened to "beat out the brains" of his eldest daughter, Bessie, and maybe some of the brains of the younger ones too. Strange's wife, Martha Elizabeth, was a tiny woman of delicate nerves. These threats and outbursts, often in the middle of the night, broke her sleep and drove her to her bed for days on end. Were they prompted by alcohol? The documents don't say, nor is anything really suggested about *his* side of events. The rampages went on. On May 4, 1897—according to testimony of Superior Court Case No. 735—Strange was heard by neighbors bellowing, "The damn thing is lying up there in bed." Two days later, the man was allegedly out of his head again. Neighbors went to their windows and tried not to be alarmed.

Legal action was initiated. The Sutter County *Farmer* ran a report: "Mrs. Elizabeth Strange last Tuesday filed papers in the Superior Court of the County asking that a divorce be granted her from her husband, W.M. Strange, on the grounds of extreme cruelty. . . . They have resided in Yuba City for the past twelve years or more and the proceedings commenced are somewhat of a shock to this community." The community, which was churchgoing and tight, consisted of many of Martha Strange's own people. She was a Phipps, who'd married a Strange, and some of her people, who'd come from Missouri, were respected business and civic leaders of Yuba City. A brother had been appointed postmaster; her father lived in a huge house that would eventually become the Sutter Hotel. There were lawyers in the clan.

The divorce was granted in four days. The only community property consisted of some household furniture, one cow, a couple dozen chickens. The delicate-nerved Martha Strange and her five children packed their belongings and left town. They turned up on the coast, in Palo Alto, where Martha's son Shelby took pharmaceutical courses at the new private university of Stanford and where Martha herself ran a boardinghouse. Over the next two decades, at uncounted locations around the bay, the divorced woman, whose health was never good, found it difficult to state the truth of her marital history—at least if registries, directories, tax forms, and other such documents are any proof. Sometimes she gave her name as "Mrs. M.E. Strange." Other times she declared herself a widow. (On the 1910 federal census, she was able to state her true status—"divorced"—although numerous San Francisco directories and registers continued to describe her as "the widow of W.M. Strange.") She and her children moved from a flat on Broadway to one on Larkin to one on Filbert to one on Waller and then to one on Haight—all in seven years. Her boy Shelby became a doctor and was eventually placed in charge of the Southern Pacific Emergency Hospital. (His med-school thesis was on oxygen anesthesia, and he presented a "method of overcoming rigidity.") Her daughter Bessie rose high in the San Francisco school system. Her youngest, Nellie (one imagines her as slightly pampered and fussed over, no matter what the financial hardships), finished secondary school very late and then sometime afterward went to work as a secretary for a shoe wholesaler in the city. There she met an Irish shoe traveler named McNamara, married him, relocated around the Bay with him, bore two children by him, and, then, in 1924, when her somewhat sickly firstborn was eight, moved into a yellow stucco house canted into an Oakland hill. Thanks to the obsessiveness with which she kept a baby diary, it's possible to follow all of the changes of address of those early years—the four months and twenty-nine days between September 1917 and February 1918, for instance, when Nelle and Rob and the little man were boarding at Mrs. Knollins. Baby Boy was a year and a half. His sister, Peggy, wasn't on earth yet. Bobby's sinus and bronchitis problems hadn't surfaced yet. Mrs. Knollins lent ornaments for the Christmas tree.

Later, after the family had moved to 1036 Annerly (it was the only home a shoe traveler would ever own, and he got it when he was sixty-one), William Miller Strange, the Missouri bad seed, came for an occasional Sunday afternoon visit to the house where things were always in their place and behavior was proper and liquor not seen, much less consumed. Bill Strange was old then. His youngest daughter had stayed in occasional contact, had not cut him completely from her life, as had his other children. (This fact alone seems to say a lot about an impossible woman's native instincts for decency and generosity.) He'd drifted in and out of jobs and locales and states in the intervening years: dissolving partnerships; working as an inspector on a levee; losing $6 and some clothing in a robbery in the Harkey Tract north of Yuba City; going back to the Midwest to be with his father, Gideon, who'd topped ninety. In Carrollton, Missouri, Bill Strange, Gid's only son, came into a little dough.

Once, on a visit to Nelle's, he sat out in the backyard on a wobbly chair with a glass of cider; the chair crashed under his weight. The maternal grandpa liked putting up on his knee his granddaughter Peggy and his grandson Bobby—a precocious child with bands on his teeth. He liked telling stories about life out in the wild Missouri during the War Between the States, when the border country had been all aflame with steel and ambuscade and slaughter. The shame of his past never came up. The secrets had been kept.

THAT SERIOUS-MINDED and attractive boy with the high ideals studying under the cone of light in the back-corner bedroom went to college in the fall of 1933, and this is how he went: down Annerly to Harvard; a little bit on Lake Shore; to Boulevard Way; to Grand Avenue; to Pleasant Valley, which wound around to Broadway; a right on Broadway past St. Mary's Cemetery (his grandfather Jeremiah lay just on the other side of the fence); up to Brick Hill; left at the Claremont Hotel; down Domingo and into the huge hillside neoclassical campus of the state university that had redwoods and a clear stream running through its middle; that had 3,000 students in the freshman class; that had perfervid socialists and young Communists holding meetings and rallies almost every night of the year; that had wizards of a coming atomic Armageddon named J. Robert Oppenheimer and E. O. Lawrence wrestling with something called quantum mechanics. It was a short ride, about twenty minutes, to a different world. It must have been intoxicating as hell. And it was accomplished in a black Ford roadster with green wire wheels that his father had bought for him. His father from another age, who didn't drive.

Every day the son would take this combination of northerly back streets and main roads out of Oakland into the steeper, lusher hills of Berkeley. He'd leave at about twenty-two minutes to eight, often in morning fog, having downed at the front door the glass of orange juice with an egg in it that was handed to him by his mother. Already, he liked timing things close. His friend Vernon Goodin, who lived a block and a half over, rode with him, at least for most of that first year. They'd become pals while they were finishing at Piedmont High. Both were from Depression families, though Goodin's family had lost much more. That afternoon they'd wind back through the East Bay hills to Annerly Road, to what is still called—a little inaccurately—Lower Piedmont. Sometimes the good son would go down to Lake Shore and Trestle Glen in the car to wait for his father, give him a lift home from the trolley stop. After supper he'd be bent over his cone of light.

One of the themes of Robert McNamara's early life is a pattern of *almosts*. Which is to say: He grew up in a not-broke but hardly cushy middle-class thirties family, next to some kids whose families were upper-class and exquisitely cushy. Almost literally next door: The boundary line between what was considered Piedmont and what was considered Oakland ran through the east side of the McNamara yard. What this meant, among other things, was that Nelle and Rob's gifted child was entitled to attend Piedmont schools, which were considered much superior to the Oakland schools. Piedmont, California, was and is a Grosse Pointe and Larchmont of the East Bay. It was and is an isthmus of white wealth bordering the larger and far poorer black metropolis. It's 1.8 square miles of privilege, looking down (in more ways than one) on a city that is trying hard to keep from rotting. In the Depression, Oakland wasn't rotting, although the distinction between the two towns was nearly as marked. The higher you climbed on the twisting streets of Piedmont, the cooler the air on your skin, the finer the view of the sea, the grander the Tudors and Mediterraneans with their red-tile roofs and jacket-and-tie gardeners. Piedmonters at the top were steamship and supermarket and coffee barons. Up there nearly every millionaire had a Chinese manservant living in the basement or in one of the back rooms. Up there the Depression was an inconvenience. Today the groomed gardeners of Piedmont wear muffs on their ears to shut out the noise of their power trimmers. The community's population is roughly what it was—10,000. The tax base remains residential— there's almost no tawdry retail, never has been. Retail's for Oakland.

Lower Annerly Road—which is really the city of Oakland, at least the McNamara part of the street—was and is a transition zone of houses set close together with well-tended yards. It's not quite one place or the other. You can still stand on the walk at 1036 Annerly and look upward to raw class advantage.

So: McNamara went to Piedmont; he was never of Piedmont. He once said, "As a boy my home was in Oakland, California, but I went to school in Piedmont, where the rich kids lived. Those children didn't have anything I wanted my children to have." He earned twenty-six A's and seven B's at Piedmont High; that's the legacy he wanted for his children.

All of McNamara's early life—really, his first forty-four years, right up until the moment in December 1960 when he stood on a snow-shoveled stoop at the Georgetown home of an excessively privileged president-elect and accepted a too-hasty offer to join a New Frontier—reveals a theme of almosts: He went to Harvard for graduate school, but in a sense the wrong Harvard, the one across the river, in Boston, where the doctors were doctors of commercial science and not thought to be academic enough. He went through Ford Motor Company in the fifties like a missile, but let's face it, a Ford was still largely a chintzy old Ford in the fifties. No wonder he seemed to fall into such a swoon in those first days and nights of Camelot, practicing the twist in his bedroom mirror. He was on the inside. The late Eric Sevareid of CBS News once told me that so many of those eager New Frontiersmen—the Bundys, the Rostows, Salinger, Arthur Schlesinger, Jr., Stew Udall, not least Robert S. McNamara—seemed to be behaving as though they'd never had any *fun*.

The barely seventeen-year-old college freshman who lived on the outside edge of Piedmont would have liked to enroll at Stanford University, down on the Peninsula, which stood for a certain pedigree his family never had. But the school where his parents could afford to send him was Berkeley, the hometown university, which happened to be emerging just then as a world-class institution—half jockdom and beery fratville, half scholar's paradise. An Irishman's luck, that, at a fee of $52 a year. You could walk the campus and almost get high on the menthol of the eucalyptus trees.

He was going to study the sciences, especially economics, which would become the bridge to all of his systems. But he would study philosophy too, not some airy, unreal philosophy, but an applied, hardheaded, practical-based philosophy that could nonetheless conceive of utopias for mankind. And ethics, yes, he was interested in ethics. Moral and Civil Polity was the ethics course he would most enjoy in the coming four years. It was taught by a man named George Plimpton Adams, who posed questions developed from items in the day's newspaper about "conflict of obligation." Plimpton taught his ethics courses as moral philosophy: Upon what grounds do you make a rational decision?

He would take Jacob Lowenberg's famous course in Hegel. Hume might have thought the mind a bundle of sensations, but Hegel viewed man in terms of reason—the play of human history as the unfolding of reason.

He went FIGI, which is to say Phi Gamma Delta. They weren't his kind, to put it mildly. FIGI wasn't a bad frat, it just didn't have the class of the Betas or the Alpha Delts or the Zetes. The FIGIs were sort of small-town and wild. They had come for the party, which often enough was in their basement, known as the Figi Islander Room. The FIGIs were Leroy V. Traynham, a big sincere rancher; Judd Madden, whose father was president of a bank in Dixon, California; Reggie Kittrelle, who got potted out of his mind and jumped into the (drained) swimming pool at the Fairmont Hotel in San Francisco and thus went around the rest of the term in plaster of Paris; and Speed Bennett (Harlo Ulysses Bennett, Jr., was the full label), who could get any girl on campus, and who played football but never took it half-serious, and who could strip off his clothes on Saturday night and stomp on them and then get back into them and look like a Brooks Brothers ad. Later, Speed would drink himself to death.

McNamara pledged FIGI because they got hold of him early, rushed him ahead of the more likely houses, and the socially unsure boy said yes. He was in a new environment and he needed to make quick decisions about the next four years. Fraternity life was crucial to your standing. It was unthinkable not to go Greek. The better houses tried to rush you while you were still in high school, especially if you were a local. They would get your name and take you out on an all-day yacht.

The day dog of 1036 Annerly always showed up at the house for the Monday-night meetings and dinners. He would come down on Saturday mornings to help clean up the place. He would park his little polished car in the FIGI driveway on Bancroft Way and go off to classes with those economics and philosophy tomes under his arm. In FIGI group photographs, McNamara is usually the one in the second row, in the cardigan and white bucks, looking glum.

But he stayed a FIGI all through Berkeley. There must have been times when it was brutal for him. But it was in character to stay. He would remain friends with a few FIGIs—like Phil Pierpont, who went on to corporate life—for several years after college. But the Berkeley friends who were to become his lasting friends—Willard Goodwin, Harry Barber, Joe Cooper, Bill Hewitt, Wally Haas, Stan Johnson, and, of course, Vern Goodin—were all in the classier fraternities. Sooner than later the bad-fit FIGI would cross-pollinate.

"Everybody knew he was so damn smart, we respected Bob for that," FIGI president Carson Magill told me. "It was as if we all had said to ourselves, 'You don't have to be like us, Bob, because we know you're so damn bright.' " Magill added: "The one or two times I doubled with him, I got mighty thirsty."

Bill Bricca, another FIGI: "I'll tell you what it was: He was missing a feeling he was anybody. As soon as he got a sense of that, that turned him on. He was like a guy who came to a cocktail party ten drinks behind. . . . You just sort of passed him. . . . He never seemed to enjoy it. It wasn't that he was unpopular, he was a nonentity, in a sense."

Years afterward, when he was high up at Ford and Carson Magill was a successful and content San Francisco advertising man, a local Ford guy for the Bay region went to Dearborn for a meeting. He said to McNamara: "I bring you greetings from an old fraternity brother back in California."

"Yeah, who's that?"

"Carson Magill."

"Oh, that's nice." The subject was dropped. A year later, when McNamara became president of Ford, Magill wrote him a note. No response. A couple of months into the New Frontier, Magill wrote him another note. Nothing. Call it the phenomenon of seeking your own kind. Call it twitching on your past.

HE JOINED THE CAMPUS Y and enlisted in humanitarian projects. The Y was run by Harry Kingman, a beloved Cal figure who had played two seasons of baseball in the New York Yankees organization. Kingman had a way of motivating young men to think of serving other men.

He went out for crew and made stroke on the second freshman boat. This was no little thing. The Golden Bears were a Pacific Coast rowing power; they had represented the United States at the 1928 and 1932 Olympics. Their coach was Ky Ebright, the Little Admiral. He wore specs and a bashed hat and a big Cal sweater and looked almost like a cartoon. He was a tough and profane cookie who would bounce you right out of the rowing house, you gave him any lip. Of McNamara, Ebright once recalled, "He was a good kid, tenacious. But he wasn't big enough. . . . He couldn't beat out the bigger fellows." In a university oral history, the coach noted again that McNamara was too light: "He wasn't very big so decided to go out for manager in the following year." Many years later, having just arrived in Washington, McNamara would revise his crew history a smidge: "I liked the sport except for those last damned 200 strokes. But I had to give it up as a sophomore. I didn't have the time." He told this to a sportswriter for the Washington *Post* who didn't think to check the veracity of it and who'd been sent over to the Pentagon to do a short feature on the trim new defense chief of the athletically conscious New Frontier.

Getting an assistant managership of crew in your sophomore year was not without its own prestige. But it also meant you got to pick up a lot of jockstraps—which the 155-pounder gamely did.

He took economics from Malcolm Davisson. On the day I spoke to Davisson he was an old man with a blue poplin jacket zippered to his throat, sitting in a near-darkened Berkeley room against a pulled curtain. "I'm cold," he said. But as we talked, a memory welled up warm. "He had something different, some breadth of intellectual curiosity that was different from his friend Vernon Goodin. I could tell it." McNamara has singled out Davisson's classes in recollections of Berkeley. He has told chroniclers that after Davisson he started to think and talk quantitatively—a consciously chosen style, an identity, to wear like a coat.

The year he became a manager of crew, he recorded eleven A's and one B. Decades after, sentences like these would show up in any journalism morgue drawer marked "McNamara": "San Francisco-born, Bob McNamara was a sophomore Phi Beta Kappa at the University of California." (That's from *Time* magazine, the week after he made the Kennedy cabinet.) Phi Beta Kappa is the national honor society for upperclassmen—so how do you get in as a soph? The answer is that Nelle's overstriving son was the beneficiary of a quirk. And the further answer is that he didn't get in as a soph but, rather, got elected as a soph. In the thirties, the local chapter at Cal permitted standout underclassmen to be elected in their second year, and invested at the beginning of their third. McNamara was voted in for what he achieved as a sophomore, which was remarkable by any standard, but he wasn't initiated until November 6, 1935, as a first-term junior. A few years later, the Berkeley chapter began to conform with the national charter. But still: eleven A's and a B in his second year. A feat. He was on a rising plane. He was opening.

Which in a way could be said of San Francisco itself. The Bay Bridge, nearly finished, was about to narrow the gap between cosmopolitan San Francisco and hometown Oakland. The Golden Gate Bridge was also nearing completion. (When the rust-colored marvel opened on May 27, 1937, 18,000 people stood at the barriers for the 6 a.m. walk across; McNamara wasn't one of them.) And flight: sleek-hulled, four-engine Pan Am China Clippers were now lifting out of San Francisco Bay, able to fly 3,200 miles nonstop at 130 miles per hour.

You could get to Hawaii from San Francisco in eighteen hours: an astonishing statistic.

He must have been absorbing bundles of sensations, not all of them ordered or rational. The school president, Robert Gordon Sproul, and the provost, Monroe E. Deutsch, are known to have had a large effect. In a sense they were the animus and anima of Cal; in a rougher sense, they were Nelle and Robert James, writ academic. Sproul, with his outsized personality, was insistent on turning Berkeley into one of the great public institutions, on a par with Ann Arbor. The dream had long been to create on the rim of the Pacific a center of world learning. (In the thirties, the University of California still largely meant Berkeley. UCLA, to the south, was still "the Westwood branch" in many minds.) Sproul was the engineer with a lowly undergraduate degree who had worked himself up through the business side of the university. He had the greatest speaking voice on the West Coast—so it was opined. "The Family California" is the way he thought of his statewide university. He'd boom you a "hello!" with a big wave from halfway across campus. He was FDR, lugging his enormous briefcase to his office in California Hall, stopping to address you by first name. He could hand you an award and hype it, greatest thing that had ever happened. He was astute politically and liked power and knew all the levers of coercion. But his provost, Deutsch, was a soft, poetic, learned man with a cane—a classics scholar much loved by the students. Sproul could lead the cheers on campus before a big game with Stanford; Deutsch could soothe a riled faculty. Deutsch was Sproul's link to the Ph.D. network, though Sproul wasn't cowed by anybody with a lofty degree.

Sproul's secretary, Agnes Robb, who served him for decades, told me how McNamara, when he was a senior, came into the president's office one day, telling Sproul how he should run the university. McNamara was chairman of the student affairs committee by then, he was warden of the premier secret society Golden Bear, he was Phi Beta Kappa. After he left, Sproul shook his head, laughed out loud. But he seems to have liked McNamara a lot.

Golden Bear and its members and the high university administrators held their meetings in a redwood lodge in Faculty Glade. It was there that Provost Deutsch sometimes stood and recited verses from Kipling's "The Palace"—and made the warden dab at his eyes. Getting elected warden (that is, president) of Golden Bear was a high honor, but the election didn't rest on popularity; rather, on your intelligence and commitment to the values of the university. McNamara's best friend and co-commuter, Vern Goodin, was far more popular; he possessed almost effortless social skills. (In yearbook pictures he's always the one laughing and throwing back his head.) Vernon became president of the sophomore class, and after college married Marion Sproul, the president's daughter. He has lived his life in the Bay Area and for many years was a San Francisco litigator. A decade ago, he and his wife told me much about McNamara. Marion dated McNamara several times in college. "He once took me to a big dance. Everything was very proper—the corsage with the note in it. We survived."

I asked Vernon if it was apparent that his best friend was the smartest guy in the room. "He didn't seem so much smarter," Vernon said. "Although I did look over once and see Bob with a one-page bluebook answer while the rest of us were filling up page after page. That worried me."

The one-page blue-booker didn't earn highest honors in econ (his friend Joe Cooper did), and he narrowly missed getting a Rhodes scholarship. The provost had written a strong letter in his behalf ("I have found him always honorable and straightforward in his dealings, courageously ready to set forth his opinions although without bumptiousness"), but the Rhodes committee chose Bruce Waybur, a farm boy from Sacramento. At the judging Waybur gave a hog call. Maybe that took the judges over the top in his favor.

In March of his senior year, McNamara wrote a note: "Dear Dr. Deutsch: As I intend to start graduate work in September at the Harvard Graduate School of Business Administration I should like to apply for the Charles Mills Gayley Fellowship. At this time I feel I should mention that I am also applying for a scholarship to be awarded by the San Francisco Harvard Alumni Club." He'd already gone to Vern Goodin's father and been turned down on a request for a personal loan for grad school. Next he went to his own father. Robert James asked him to make out a budget. The son did. He said he felt he could do it all—the $600 tuition, the cross-country travel, the room and board—for $3,000. His father sat down and wrote the check. Vern Goodin was stunned that McNamara's dad could do that.

That summer, the summer of '37, the Bay Area boy went out to sea again, this time with his Berkeley classmate Willard Goodwin. They went as ordinary seamen on the SS *President Hoover,* cruise ship of the Dollar Lines, finest liner in the Pacific. (How in the world did Nelle ever let him go on these sailing adventures? He had also gone in the summer of '35.) San Francisco has always been a city connected to the world by ships, and McNamara was making his own lifelong connection to the sea. He would end up loving the mountains even more, but in the summer before he went East to grad school, he and Goodwin lined up at the hiring hall during their two weeks of finals and got a listing aboard the *P. Hoover Maru,* as they liked calling it. *Maru* is Japanese for "steamship." They threw off lines, scrubbed decks. Theirs was the dogwatch, midnight to four. Sometimes the cooks brought down the "black pan" from the first-class kitchen—leftovers of lobster and caviar and filet mignon.

The two hands were on the *Hoover* when a fighter-bomber in the Chinese air force mistakenly attacked the boat while it lay at anchor at the mouth of the Yangtze River. The pilot thought the *Hoover* was a Japanese troopship. War was beginning in the Pacific, and the Japanese had attacked Shanghai. The U.S. ship, and these two sailors, were smack in a Sino-Japanese shooting war. A steward on the ship was killed. It made all the papers back home. There is a story that the sailor from Annerly Road had to be yanked down below during the attack— he was trying to get photographs.

A month earlier, this sailor had written a letter to classmates Harry Barber and Joe Cooper, who had begun their careers in the real world and were now rooming together in a fleabag hotel in San Francisco's North Beach district. In pen and ink, on *Hoover* stationery, McNamara wrote: "On a few occasions the night sky has been cloudless and at such times an almost full moon and millions of stars have presented a spectacular and moving sight."

Before going to sleep one night, he said to his fellow Eagle Scout, who would be entering Johns Hopkins medical school in the fall, and who had just bought himself a shiny Zeiss microscope in a Hong Kong bazaar: "Willie, you know, I kind of envy you going into medicine, because that means you know exactly what you're going to do. You know that you're going to be taking care of people and you're going to be helping people. I'd like to do that, too, but I'd like to do it on a big scale." Goodwin thought his friend was done. But the mildly troubled ordinary seaman lobbed one more sentence across the bow of the dark. "I'd like to do it on a big scale, on a worldwide scale, what I want to do." He meant "big" in terms of serving global humankind, or at least this is what Willard Goodwin would always believe in the years afterward when so many in the world seemed to view Bob McNamara as an arrogant, bad, and dissembling person.

I ONCE PASSED a lovely evening at the home of E. T. Grether and his wife, both of whom were eighty-six and had spent nearly twin lifetimes at the university. I sat on a sofa in a Berkeley brown-shingle that was tawny with lamp glow and memories of the thirties: when a country was coming out of Depression, on the cusp of war, an era of great romanticism but also fear, a time for hardheaded liberals like Robert S. McNamara. Many Cal people told me that if I really wanted to get a feel for the history and values of the school, I must go see E. T. Grether and his wife.

Toward the end of the night, this kindly old man and his mate revealed their feelings about McNamara and Vietnam. I could see they were struggling with it. Their slant on it, they said, was that here was this bright, idealistic Cal boy who ends up head of this great big thing, Ford Motor. And who then serves two presidents of the U.S. And who goes on to run the World Bank. "And, and, he just seemed to desert something, lose some ideals he had blossomed with here," Grether said. "I mean, he was one of Harry Kingman's boys. How could he have stayed in the war that long, how could he have been for it at all, really?" There was something very sad in it, and on the way home I was mindful of cautionary tales: Whom the gods would destroy, they must first give too many gifts.

ROBERT McNAMARA, HARVARD UNIVERSITY, GRADUATE SCHOOL
OF BUSINESS ADMINISTRATION, 1937.

ALL MEN GROW
IN RIGHTEOUSNESS

STOP-TIME.

August 13, 1940.

The benedict, as one of the papers will call him in the morning, is in a snap-brim fedora and a double-breasted suit; his bride's got on a brown wool coat and a corsage of orchids that's big enough to pot. Look at their grins. They're very happy. They were hitched barely two hours ago over in Alameda by the Reverend Sumner Walters. And now, following their car chase across the Bay Bridge and a tangy dockside reception, the new and charmed Mr. and Mrs. Robert S. McNamara are arm in arm at the rail of a 20,000-ton honeymoon liner that's moving off like a glacier in evening light from Pier 35 in San Francisco.

It's a Tuesday evening, just past six o'clock. Two people are steaming out of California for good, although perhaps they have only suspicions of it.

In tomorrow's *Examiner,* there'll be this:

> A wedding reception on the Embarcadero was the gay and unusual program yesterday for the new Mr. and Mrs. Robert McNamara. Married at 4 o'clock in Christ Church in Alameda, the former Margaret Craig and her bridegroom dispensed with a formal gathering before they sailed at 6 aboard the Washington. Since guests were not allowed on the New York–bound liner, friends said their congratulations and farewells at the pier. The newlyweds are going to Boston to make their home, while Mr. McNamara takes up duties on the faculty of the Harvard School of Business Administration.

You wouldn't have to wait for the paperboy to know the last part. Because for three weeks now, which is about as long as the wedding plans have been known, Nelle McNamara has been telling neighbors and friends: "The president of Harvard just won't leave Bob alone. He's made a special trip out here to see him. I guess Bob's going to have to leave his great job at Price, Waterhouse." Nelle told the Quigley family that, and they nodded, not particularly knowing the degree to which Bob loathed his great job of the past ten months in the San Francisco bureau of the famous accounting firm, even as he was excelling at it. (It was the B-School dean at Harvard who tendered the offer to come back and join the faculty, and he didn't make a trip to Oakland.)

"MR. AND MRS. ROBERT MCNAMARA ARE SAILING THROUGH THE CANAL" is the way one daily will headline a small story a day or so from now. "NO TIME FOR COMEDY—OR A RECEPTION" is the way another local rag will write it up. Don't get the wrong impression—these are all small headlines tucked into the women's pages. But still.

Down on the two-tiered wooden dock, forty or fifty teary people are waving, leaning out of windows, blowing kisses, shouting things that can't be heard. Nelle is one of these dim receding figures (she came in a hat today that looked put on with a hammer, but on the other hand there's an elegant black veil across her face), and so too is sister Peggy, as well as Vern Goodin, best man. Vern got on board a little while ago with the maid of honor to short-sheet the honeymooners' bed and to string a banner across their doorway. You'd have thought Vern was the one getting married and steaming through the Golden Gate, so fidgety was he, so thrilled for Bob.

The former Margy Craig wore a printed silk dress to her altar this afternoon, the hell with a wedding gown, and besides, there wouldn't have been any time to change afterward. She's an Alpha Phi from Cal who's been working at an athletic club in the city and teaching at a high school in her hometown, which is only across the estuary from Oakland. She was a phys-ed major in college and anybody will tell you she's warm, outgoing, unaffected, prankish, a sort of pluperfectly decent person. Not a phony bone in her. A small-town girl from the East Bay, essentially. "Cutup" is one of her names. Others know her as "Muggs." Muggs doesn't own smashing looks or brains, she's got something better: soulfulness. It's true her pals from the sorority have been asking themselves how in hell Margy—who'll do the hula and sing "Little Grass Shack" on demand—could have fallen, and so fast, for a guy who may have gorgeous manners and all and is brainy as hell but who still seems a bit of a stiff, to be charitable about it. But then they don't really know the guy, do they?

At the reception a little while ago, two stewards from the liner stood behind a table covered with a white cloth and poured the champagne. Even Nelle, who doesn't drink, raised a glass. "Take care of my little girl," Tom Craig (he's in the insurance game) said to his new and bespectacled son-in-law. And the son-in-law, who looked a million, with a big flower in his lapel, said, "Oh, I will, I will." Everybody laughed, because it sounded scripted. The bride's father likes Bob fine, but along with everybody else he's been taken aback by the speed of this thing. T. J. Craig already despises Nelle, for the woman's monopolizing. But never mind that on a night like this.

The honeymooners weren't even dating four months ago. In May Bob took Margy skiing up at Lassen Park and apparently that's where it happened. At dockside, guests were saying how they guessed Bob McNamara fell headlong in love at the sight of Margaret McKinstry Craig of Alameda on skis up in the springtime mountains. (One of the things people consistently miss is the degree to which this sober man is bowled over by romance and fascinated by women.) Joe Cooper was along when they went to Lassen Park, and he noted that the couple in the back were getting awfully lovey. Once Bob makes up his mind, bar the door, Katy. The man of action—who, it's a fact, had been more than ready to quit his job and go back East to join the Harvard faculty—had soon decided Margy Craig was the one and that he wouldn't go without her.

He popped the question long-distance. She was traveling with her mom and aunt on a prior-planned vacation. Had a devil of a time finding her, but he did. He proposed as she stood on her toes in a YWCA pay-phone booth in Baltimore. (She's only a nudge over five feet three, weighs a hundred.) "Will you marry me?" he shouted. "Yes," she shouted back. One of these days the benedict is going to go get a look at that damn lovely Baltimore YWCA phone booth—so he's promised himself.

After she had told him yes, Margy had sent Bob a Western Union from Red Wing, Minnesota. (She was making her way back to the Bay Area and realized how little time there would be to prepare for the wedding.) "MUST ORDER ENGRAVED WEDDING INVITATIONS NOW—WHAT IS YOUR MIDDLE NAME?" she'd cabled. "STRANGE," he'd wired back, always happy to economize. "NO MATTER IF IT IS STRANGE," she answered, "WHAT IS IT?"

Somehow he had missed her charms in the Berkeley years. They had known each other from the first week of freshman year, but only casually. Margy had gone out with Vern Goodin a few times, and Bob and Margy had worked together on some campus humanitarian projects at Harry Kingman's Y. But he hadn't seemed to take any real romantic notice. Since Cal, they hadn't managed to bump into each other—for one thing, Bob had been in Boston for two of those three years, recording some of the highest grades in the history of the B-School, which again was one of the things being talked of at dockside in terms of the unknowable ways of Cupid: uncommon smarts going for average ones.

The true gen on why they never fell in love until just weeks ago is this: Bob had been too stuck on Hallie, Hallie Booth, the beautiful Piedmont girl with the green eyes and the thin black line around the rims, but also with the mysterious stiffening disease rising in her arms and shoulders. Hallie Booth isn't among these forty or fifty well-wishers at Pier 35 tonight, growing tinier in the distance, throwing good-byes across the foamy wake. No, Hallie Booth is in her parents' home, deeply hurt at the way Bob McNamara swerved away from her and went in another direction once she'd told him she couldn't marry him. It's almost as if Bob had been waiting to hear her no, wanting to hear it, as if honor and loyalty and duty made him stay.

Ask anybody: Hallie Booth is a lot of the reason why Bob McNamara came back to California last year after finishing Harvard. Hallie's sister, Jean—the two are extremely close—had read some of Bob's letters from Boston, saying things like, "Now this will be our budget when we're married." That kind of love letter may not have thrilled Hallie, but there isn't any question she loved him. Hallie Booth was the most popular girl at Piedmont High. She was thought to be one of the finest girls at Cal. She had gone out with other boys in college, fancied them all in a way, but she and Bob McNamara were special. And yet at some point this past winter, after he had come back to the Bay and was living under Nelle's roof, Hallie had said no. And it seemed right after this that he'd made a swerve, lit the new match.

Hallie Booth's hands have begun to gnarl, her walk is limped, she has trouble cutting her meat, she can't play tennis anymore; she had once been a tennis champion, with her red ankle socks and smart little backhand. She's a devout Christian Scientist, and her folks are too, and so stories abound locally that she isn't taking nearly enough medicines or seeing the right doctors to fight the stiffening, which is said to be some strain of rheumatoid arthritis. "I don't want Bob marrying that girl!" Nelle told friends on more than one occasion this past year, which only infuriated her son. And tonight that same son, in his snap-brim fedora and big grin and with the huge orchid in his lapel, is pulling out of California with Margy Craig of Alameda at his side. And Hallie, the girl with the green eyes and the thin black line around the rims who'll be dead within six years of this moment, is stunned.

Within six years of this moment, following a world war during which he'll have made undeniable contributions, former lieutenant colonel Robert McNamara of Stat Control in the Army Air Forces will have conquered his own sudden stiffening illness, as will his wife, an illness called poliomyelitis, from which he'll have made a far speedier recovery than his spouse. And after this recovery he will have gone right on, burned right on, to his industrial conquests.

ONE WAY TO READ Robert McNamara's life is longitudinally: His paternal ancestry travels from east to west, but his own history moves in the reverse direction. You could say it took two generations and ninety years for the famine-fleeing McNamaras to get from the wharves of East Boston to the junior faculty of the Harvard Business School—a distance of only a few miles—but that a continent had to be criss-crossed in between. When twenty-two-year-old Jeremiah McNamara of Ireland, first of the line, stepped out into the New World (the best evidence is that he came in steerage on a British bark named the *Urania,* sailing from Cork, landing in May 1850), he also stepped out into an event of history: the industrial revolution. This revolution had to do with the saving of labor and the wonders of mass production but also with the control of how fast people worked, how much they were paid, when they rested; things speaking more to mechanical time than to human time; cost-effectiveness, if you will, although surely no one in the bootmaking trade in nineteenth-century New England had dreamed that awful term.

Almost exactly nine decades later, in the late summer of 1940, on the eve of U.S. entry into global war, Jeremiah's just-wed descendant—who didn't have to toil with his hands—sailed out of San Francisco on his honeymoon, bound for the East Coast of America via the Canal route. California-bred Robert McNamara was duplicating, only in the opposite direction and with a lot more comfort, the trip his forebears had made to the Pacific Coast in 1868. The grandson of Jeremiah and the son of Robert James was about to take up his proud $1,800-a-year faculty position at the part of Harvard that's situated directly across the Charles River from Cambridge—the one whose mailing address is Soldiers Field, Boston. He had been appointed an instructor in accountancy at a ripe twenty-four. However, in later years it seems he had either forgotten or upgraded his initial faculty rank, because what you consistently find in old McNamara résumés and biographical summaries are sentences such as this one: "In 1940 he returned to Harvard to become Assistant Professor of Business Administration." (That's on his résumé from the mid-1980s.) The same words appear on a 1956 press release from Ford Motor Company's Ford Division. *Who's Who in America* for 1954–1955 has the Harvard history listed like that, as does the bio summary that the secretary of defense–designate provided to members of Congress before his appointment hearings in early 1961. Actually, the youthful and excelling B-School accounting instructor didn't make assistant professor of business administration until he'd been on the Harvard faculty for almost two years—in July 1942.

Sailing off to a new academic life through the Panama Canal with a good woman at your side had to have been a large moment for Jeremiah's grandson, and for all that figuratively flowed behind. But it wasn't the pivotal moment in terms of who he became. That moment was three years before, in 1937, when history tilted eastward the first time, not in a professor's gown but in a student's twill suit, and when— as it happens—another revolution was unwittingly stepped into by another sort of emigrant. This revolution had a pretty prosaic name: control accounting. But like a lot of things that sound prosaic, its consequences turned out to be profound. That word "control," tagged on to the word "accounting," amounted to the spirit of the age on the Boston side of the Charles in the late thirties—at least in the accounting sector of the MBA program. Henry James once wrote of the impact on him of the painter John La Farge: "He opened up . . . prospects and possibilities that made the future flush and swarm." For Robert McNamara, the future began to flush and swarm about the third week of September 1937, when he unpacked his bags at the campus that's a handsome and self-contained clot of Georgian-styled brick buildings, with its own dining halls and dormitories and library, constructed on what had once been Boston tidal flats. The reclaimed land was and is just across the Anderson Bridge from Harvard College and the Harvard Yard and Harvard Square, where all the important cultural life of the university lay.

The hot heart of the revolution the student stepped into was this: Numbers need not just be something in the rearview mirror; they can soothsay the future. Numbers need not be merely for establishing historical record—the home ground of traditional cost accountants—but for planning, for forecasting, for quantitatively analyzing, for segregating the trouble spots and identifying the upcoming trends, for abstracting and projecting and predicting.

Such a disarming idea: numbers for management instead of numbers for audit. Think of it this way: Historical numbers—that is, bookkeeping numbers—clarify what's past. Those are useful numbers, but they are essentially reactive. They are not inventive or creative. They are the numbers of a financial statement. What they do is impose order on something that by definition is already over. But numbers for management, numbers for forecast, ah, what they will do is put high beams on what's up ahead, out beyond the windshield. These are an activist's numbers. These are the tools of a rationalist, and if used well, they can be made not only to read the future but even to help fashion it, create it. And the power of that idea might candle the world.

In the old order, numbers supplied record; in the new, numbers could provide . . . choices. Of course you'd have to be careful. It could all shade off into a lack of truth if you were overconfident of your abilities or not respectful enough of the human factor, the pride factor.

"What do you want the numbers for? What are you going to do with them? Are you looking for relevant costs or do you want a financial statement?" one of McNamara's teachers used to say. His name was Ross G. Walker, and he probably had the largest influence on the MBA candidate's thinking. People called him Johnny Walker. He didn't have an advanced degree, just a lowly A.B. He was a kind of philosopher of numbers, a warm, sweet man who loved to play golf and fraternize with the troops and even seemed a little mystical about the idea of long columns, and the secrets they contained. He liked saying things like, "We are now engaged in the job of keeping the body bolts tight in the cost chassis." Or, "Figures and human nature sleep in the same bed even though they do not like each other." Johnny Walker is remembered for having a certain humility in connection with the figures he adored. His was not the technical arrogance that overcomes people when they see what they can do with their minds.

Another teacher who seems to have imparted much, but wasn't nearly as philosophical, was a feisty, moral, moody, and dapper little Englishman named Thomas H. Sanders. He had been trained at the

University of Birmingham. Three years before the student arrived he had written a book called *Cost Accounting for Control*. In 1938, when McNamara was about halfway through the program, Sanders published *A Statement of Accounting Principles*. When McNamara returned to Harvard in 1940, he worked as Sanders's assistant and represented him at faculty meetings. Of the two, Walker and Sanders, the latter seems to have been more of a bookkeeper in his soul—but he was part of the revolution with the prosaic name.

This reversal in thought—that numbers could look ahead instead of behind—had taken seed in the early years of the century, under the Du Ponts of Delaware, both in their own gunpowder company and later at General Motors. A man named Donaldson Brown, who was a self-taught accountant, incessant smoker, and ex-electrical-parts salesman, made a seminal contribution to theories of control. Ultimately he would be recognized as the architect of the decentralized system of financial control at both E. I. du Pont de Nemours & Company and the close-to-shipwrecked GM of the early twenties. In February, March, and April of 1924, in a magazine called *Management and Administration*, Brown—who by then had moved to Michigan and was vice president of finance at the car company—published a series of articles under the general title "Pricing Policy in Relation to Financial Control." Three years later there was another heavy-going exposition by Brown titled "Decentralized Operations and Responsibilities with Coordinated Control." With the Du Pont family working to protect its Detroit investment, and with a 130-pound, vividly blue-eyed, self-made millionaire named Alfred Pritchard Sloan, Jr., turning the gears, GM was able to leap between the two world wars from a nearly bankrupt 12 percent share of the market to a 52 percent share and near-supremacy: the biggest company on earth. What Silent Sam Sloan did, standing on Donaldson Brown's shoulders, was to initiate a system of divisional autonomy. Each division was equipped with a self-contained organization that had authority over manufacturing, sales, and finance—but with everything subject to control from headquarters. The moral for students of business was this: It was the accounting people, not the square-handed machinists or the essentially shallow marketing and sales staffs, who rescued the company. And they did it on the stallion of their numbers, riding the word "control."

It's a word that must have tolled in the Oakland student like a bell from somewhere back beyond. As biographer Deborah Shapley has accurately written, "Even the name of this new field suited McNamara's emerging personality. At different times and in different applications, it has been termed *financial control, management control, statistical control, or control accounting.* In all variants, the word that had the most meaning for the stiff, cautious McNamara was *control.*" That sounds harsh, and isn't.

After GM, Harvard took hold of control and burnished all its parts and moved the revolution along through the thirties. It got taught to incoming acolytes through the case method. Professors like Johnny Walker and Tom Sanders would use great swing-over charts crammed with details, and as a case progressed they would reveal additional information about it. One of the key features of the case method was the call for a specific course of action. The case method, indeed the B-School itself, was never built on the idea of knowledge for knowledge's sake but on enabling its acolytes to find a program, a course, a remedy. Knowledge for knowledge's sake—that was across the river. Over here the view was micro, not macro; vertical, not lateral.

Long after McNamara was gone from Harvard, the case method of instruction, not to say the theologies of control accounting, would come in for some specific harsh criticism by educators as being far too delimiting and devoid of human feeling. But by the time McNamara and some fellow accounting majors got to Soldiers Field, it was thought to be pretty much a science, the idea you could take somebody and school him in the modern principles and then put him into almost any business institution or system imaginable and be confident he'd be able to run it like a clockwork orange on the strength of two twin-towered concepts: planning and control. The only problem with this is that a revolutionary named Ho Chi Minh never went to the Harvard Business School.

Years removed from B-school, when he was very high up at Ford, one slot from the company presidency (having earned in the year just prior a combined salary and bonuses of $410,833), McNamara sat in his office on a winter day and talked to three interviewers about the words "planning" and "control." The interviewers were working with scholar Allan Nevins on an authorized three-volume history of Ford. McNamara told them how his Planning and Control Division (he'd uppercased it) was a unique operation. They had developed a whole new conception of the controller's function. In the past the controller had merely recorded what had happened, but now the controller planned and projected happenings. McNamara told the researchers that his finance staff rarely used the "actual accounted data." His finance staff dealt with abstractions to indicate the trends. He talked about cost centers and budget centers and profit centers—the whole megillah of decentralized governing and systems analysis and control accounting. In that January 1960 interview at Ford World Headquarters, the group vice president of cars and trucks traced in two or three paragraphs the development of control in the twentieth century—how the baton passed from the Du Ponts in the teens, to General Motors in the twenties, to the Harvard faculty in the thirties, to Ford in the late forties and fifties. McNamara gave credit to his old teachers, Ross Walker and Tom Sanders, but also to a man named Edmund Learned.

Learned was the only one of the three who was still alive by the time I found a copy of that Nevins interview. He had taught marketing and accounting courses at Harvard and was known for saying, especially in the postwar years, "Listen, *feelings* are facts." In the middle and late forties, when McNamara was already heading for the automotive highlands, Learned was instrumental in bringing some human-relations and social-psychology courses into the curriculum—qualitative stuff. There was a course called Administrative Practices, in which the ideal manager is thought of as the person who can integrate feelings with logic. Learned also had a long career as a consultant to the Air Force. On the day in 1985 I sat down with him, he was eighty-five and seemed wise, not slavish to ideologies or systems. Some of his memory was foggy, but the heart was intact. I asked what it was the student possessed. Well, he said, sounding a little mystical, of course it was the drive, the ambition, the relentless work, the tremendous focusing ability. "But you know, I almost got the feeling he was ingesting these systems as if he'd somehow known them all before, in another consciousness. . . ." We drifted to Vietnam. Learned sighed. "He was overconfident of his abilities to go over there and get the facts. He acted on the wrong facts."

HE WANTED TO ROOM ALONE. He took a third-floor single in the middle of Gallatin, between the C and D wings. The cans were down the hall. His space was small and narrow and looked out onto a courtyard with two trees. It was almost monastic. Wally Haas and Bill Hewitt, who had also come East from Cal to train at the Harvard control altar, were on the same floor. They had been fraternity brothers at Berkeley and decided to room together. Most nights a study group assembled in their sitting room. The faculty encouraged group study— heads beavered on a case until it got cracked. Usually four first-year students assembled nightly in the Haas-Hewitt sitting room, the most crucial member being the occupant of CD-39. Sometimes they would light a fire and then get going. The other fire, they couldn't put out. "We'd get to the foothills of the Sierra with him, then he'd take off for the mountains," remembered Haas, a little ruefully. (Haas would one day become head of Levi Strauss & Company, the family business.)

And yet . . . there's paradox here as everywhere. Strong evidence exists that no matter the rate of ingestion; no matter the way the scales were dropping; no matter how he seems to have grasped the true implications of the revolution before him, McNamara had basic questions about whether he wished to be in this life at all: too greedy, not humanistic enough. This was the yin to the yang, the secret man. His father was in a moneyed world. Medicine and law would have cost too much and besides it was too late to switch now. He was on this path, he'd stay on it: This seems to be where he was.

He had been enrolled a month when he wrote a letter to President Sproul back in Berkeley: "Although the policy of this school appears to be one of piling more work on the students than they can possibly do, the material is interesting and I heartily approve of the general atmosphere which the Dean expressed very well when he said, 'It is no sin to make a profit.' " He said he was homesick for California and its warm temperatures. Four months later, in a letter to Provost Deutsch: "Although the work here has proved very interesting, I sometimes think that the faculty places too much emphasis on the chase for the almighty dollar."

Typed papers, between ten and twenty pages in length, were due in "the slot" every Saturday night at nine o'clock. The slot was a metal box in the hall of Baker Library, and they took it away at nine on the dot. The slot would draw crowds of onlookers who would cheer for those who had to sprint down the hall of Baker with a paper over their head. Nobody remembers ever seeing the occupant of CD-39 racing to the slot.

He liked turning on the radio to hear Benny Goodman after three hours in the study group. On Saturday night he liked going to a joint down near Faneuil Hall where you could get a fat lobster for a buck. He was eager to get up into New Hampshire's mountains to sample eastern skiing. Soon he intended to take the train down to New York to attend the Metropolitan Opera, so he could write to his dad about it. At the top of every week he'd pay his $10.50 for twenty-one meals in the dining hall.

Suppose you put a nickel in a pay phone—how much ends up in surplus on a balance sheet? Suppose you're the president of Otis Elevator—what would occupy the main portion of your thinking? Think about it, pilgrim. Energy costs money. Answer: reduction of weight. These were B-School problems. (One of his classmates was John D. MacDonald. He'd become a managerial washout—and a great mystery novelist.)

By the end of that first term he was first man. Mrs. Marion Hoyle McCleary, the registrar, wrote a letter to the Berkeley provost: "Dear Dr. Deutsch: I am giving you below a statement of the record of Mr. Robert S. McNamara for the first half of this year. . . . As you will note, Mr. McNamara's record has been very good; in fact, for this half year he has stood at the head of his class of 500 students." She gave the grades for six courses, which included Business Problem Analysis, Business Statistics, Accounting Principles, Industrial Management. After every course, there was one word: "distinction."

As the registrar was writing, the student was working on a second-term business economics paper that sought to estimate the next year's Harvard football team home-gate receipts. He put it on onion-skin paper. He decided that the main element of the control problem was "the elasticity of demand" above and below a certain price line. He analyzed price changes over prior seasons, the quality of teams, position on the schedule, degree of prosperity in a given year, weather conditions. And then he wrote: "As these factors are so important, and because their effects are in most instances immeasurable, I believe that more depends on the judgment of the estimator, tempered by past experience, than on a rigid statistical analysis (which would be based on untenable assumptions) of the data given." He was taking in a revolution, but by the evidence of this sentence the student seemed to have a healthy respect for subjectivity—then.

The next month, April, another letter, this one to Harry Barber and Joe Cooper, who were back in North Beach with their real jobs: "I am anxious to hear how both of you are progressing and how you feel about business in general. With little practical knowledge of it, the more & more I study the more I think it is a pretty mercenary sort of thing affording one little opportunity to be of use to society in general and forcing one to subordinate broad social ends to one's own personal aims." Twice in this letter he spoke about his doldrums.

The control acolyte with the leak of doubts also talked about how he and Bill Hewitt and Stan Johnson (who was at Harvard Law) had borrowed Wally Haas's car and gone down to Baltimore to see Willie Goodwin at Johns Hopkins Medical. The westerners were sticking together. In Baltimore, Willie had disguised them as interns and gotten them into the surgery theaters. They watched bone replacements and intestinal operations. There were metal pans on the hexagonal tile floors—in case you had to vomit. After two days they left Hopkins and drove another hour south to Washington to see their government at work.

School out, he and Hewitt and Goodwin (whom they picked up in Baltimore) drove across the continent via the southern states in Wally Haas's Plymouth coupe. In Arkansas they peeled off their shirts and sat by the side of the road and slurped watermelon. In New Orleans they posed on the sidewalk in the Quarter with a dummy of Jean Laffite. McNamara—hair slicked, sleeves of white shirt rolled, wearing white bucks and argyle socks—stuck his arm in the dummy's arm. But he couldn't quite bring the picture off.

In Arizona they sat on a stone bench on the rim of the Grand Canyon and watched the sun disappear. McNamara's hair was sticking up. His hands were folded in his lap. The picture was snapped from the rear. What you sense is a melancholy ascetic in the face of nature's hugeness.

Now it was his second year, 1938–1939, and it was more of the same—only it wasn't. Early in the term came word his father had died. Robert James McNamara stopped breathing at 2:15 a.m. on November 4, 1938—or so Nelle registered as the time on the death certificate the following day, which was also the day she put him in the ground. It isn't known when the son found out about the death, or how much he'd been alerted that it was coming. What is known is that at the burial there was also a priest, and friends sat on folding chairs amid poinsettias.

The principal causes of death were listed as angina pectoris and bronchial pneumonia, with arteriosclerosis as a contributory cause. But it was the onset of the pneumonia that took R. J. McNamara off. The old man had held his job at Buckingham & Hecht almost until the last, even though his health had been failing for a long while. In those last days Nelle brought in a hospital bed and set it up downstairs, close to the mahogany-cased phonograph with the wooden stylus that had its own small fame in the Annerly Road neighborhood—as gleaming as a new deep freeze. In those last days Nelle sat in the other downstairs room and listened to her husband's breathing. Vern Goodin came over to keep her company. He was in law school at Berkeley. (One of his classmates was a bright, solidly built Georgian named Dean Rusk.) Once Nelle whispered to Vern, "Did you ever hear the death rattle?" She brought him up close. The blinds were pulled. The breathing was a wet, racking sound.

Nelle spoke several times on the phone to Charley O'Brien, a good Catholic who had long been on her husband's sales force. Robert James had given up his faith long ago and there would be no funeral Mass or sanctified ground to place him in, but still Nelle wanted to get some kind of spiritual feeling into the mortuary service. She said she knew this was what her husband would want. O'Brien said he would see what he could arrange. He asked Nelle about the children. "Now we don't want to disturb Bob, he's in school, he has his hands full, it's so far away, and we'll just have the funeral service immediately, Bob can't do anything about it anyway," she said to O'Brien, or so recalls O'Brien's daughter, Estelle, who was a young woman living at home. She remembers her father being taken aback by this resoluteness. It was the only practical way, Nelle had said. What's come is come.

In the weeks and months after the funeral, O'Brien was to drive Nelle many times to Mountain View Cemetery, grove 285, plot 65, so that she could sit on a portable stool and talk—impractically, you'd say—to the headstone of the beloved Irish infidel. In his soul the lapsed Roman Catholic had been an artist, at least an artiste. In his soul the infidel had had great emotions, but it was as if he could only find a place for them in *things*.

The estate was modest: odd parcels of land in and around Oakland; seven shares in the Soundview Pulp Company; three $1,000 bonds from the Imperial Irrigation District. You can look up the probate papers, filed away in a drawer in the Alameda County Court House, and be struck by several sentences: "Petitioner further alleges that she intends to, and will, pay out of her own funds the legacy in the amount of $2,000 due Mary Gertrude McNamara, sister of said decedent, for the reason that it would be a serious loss to the said estate to sell any further assets at the present time. . . ." And this: "And it appearing further that petitioner's first name is spelled 'Claranell' in said last will and testament of said decedent, whereas petitioner's first name is 'Claranel,' and that Claranell Strange McNamara and Claranel Strange McNamara are one and the same person." Even her husband—who made out the will early in 1938—was confounded as to which spelling his wife was currently using.

I once tried, haltingly, to bring up the quick burial to Peggy Slaymaker. "Well, you see, my mother just thought we shouldn't come home [Peggy was at the University of Colorado in Boulder] because it was November and the weather was bad," she said. A short while later Peggy said, "In later years, I saw it as a mistake." Her brother has never said publicly what he felt.

Peggy and her brother did get to Oakland afterward, though exactly when isn't clear. It has been stated or implied in many places that McNamara went back to California to attend his father's funeral and to help his mother with her affairs. The truth looks grainier. It seems the grad student went across the country around Thanksgiving and stayed a week or more. It can't be said what anger or confusion or regret or sadness may have been in him on that trip, or what he felt on his return to his classwork, which may have interested him even less. In a letter once, I did get McNamara to say this much: "My memory regarding my trip home after my father's death is very hazy. While at Harvard I don't believe I realized Dad's death was imminent. Therefore, I believe you are probably correct: it would have been impossible for me to return home in time for the funeral. My main purpose in flying to California was to be with my mother." (I'm pretty certain he took the train.)

It has been stated or implied in many places that grief from his father's death is why McNamara didn't earn his MBA with honors. For half a century it has been part of Soldiers Field lore that the student who was perhaps the smartest in the history of the B-School messed up on his orals. That part's true.

McNamara went before the three-man committee, and did poorly, and two of the three voted against him. He ended up with neither a "high distinction" nor a "distinction." You couldn't earn honors unless you took an oral examination—and only the highest candidates were entitled to apply. You would get your MBA without doing orals, but there would be no chance for a prize.

The head of his committee was Edmund Learned. The other two, Windsor Hosmer and "Tiger" Lewis, are long dead. Learned told me he was certain that grief was the reason McNamara fell down. He said that his dad had just died the week before. "He didn't flunk, he just didn't do well. I couldn't get the committee to take into account the father's death." But the examinations weren't held the week after the student came back—which isn't to say that grief and other emotions weren't still roiling in him later in the year.

I was once speaking to one of McNamara's Harvard classmates, Robert McVie, about how out ahead of everybody else McNamara was, when he interrupted: "But not the second year. Because he had this girl back in California who began to stiffen up from arthritis and this was bothering him a lot." That a classmate knew and remembered this caught me by surprise. Some in the class of '39 told me that they've always believed the failure to get honors was due to dwindling interest. Others have other theories. But the closest version of the truth may be this: McNamara fell down out of grief and boredom, but also arrogance. Two B-School alums, one of whom was junior faculty then, and the other, who served on the faculty for his entire career, told me that Professor Hosmer, whom McNamara didn't like, and vice versa, asked him a control question. McNamara gave an answer.

"You want to try again?" Hosmer said.

"Nope."

"Excuse me. Would you like to try again?"

"Nope."

After he went out, Hosmer supposedly threw down a pencil and said, "That's it. The guy is arrogant."

HE HAD ALREADY SIGNED UP to go to work for Price, Waterhouse in California in the fall. There was to be one summer of freedom. McNamara and six fellow B-Schoolers spent June, July, and August seeing Europe out of a Ford woody. They bought the secondhand station wagon in New York and shipped it with them aboard the *Vulcania,* a liner of Italian registry. After a seventeen-day crossing (the many ports of call were fine by them, since meals came with the tickets), the grads landed in Italy and unloaded the woody and then carted themselves through eight or nine countries in a torn summer. Bob McVie, not Bob McNamara, kept the books on the car—the cost came to something less than two cents per mile for each traveler. The woody was a three-seater, and they drove with the back down, suitcases stacked to the ceiling. Each man, one suitcase. Each man, one suit. They used cartons of baking soda—as fumigators. They used boxes of Enos Fruit Salts—as laxative.

In Algiers, the tourists bought fezzes. In Capri, the seven chartered a boat and went out to a big rock and swam naked. In Switzerland, they loaded up on discount German marks and lined them inside the tail-light covers of the car before crossing the border. In Germany they watched movements of goose-stepping troops, heard menacing voices on speakers in the squares. In the Austrian Alps, a young man in a trench coat and a knapsack stared moodily down the Tyrolean Glacier. McNamara "kept us up to pace on the cathedrals and monuments," remembered Richard Hodgson.

One night in Paris they went to a girlie club at 32 rue Blondel. The house talent had nothing on but their panties and smiles, and they descended on this table of scrubbed Americans. "I can see him there yet," says Bob McVie. "Here's this exquisite bare-breasted tart named Monique, swaying on Bob's lap, having a saucy old time. He's holding her rather delicately at the waist. His eyes are closed and he's swaying with the music."

The group split up toward the end. McNamara and Rich Hodgson, also from the Bay Area, arrived in Genoa. The start of war in Europe was only hours away. The two had their tickets and about $6. They had already shipped a case of books to the dock. Only now their boat had been canceled and the piers of Genoa were clogged with Americans try-ing to get passage. The two Californians were standing around out front of the American consulate office when a woman from Albuquerque handed them fifty bucks of lira—didn't need it, she said. They took a room over a bar at the dock so they could watch for boats. The *President Monroe* came in, a Dollar Line freighter. There was a bo'sun aboard who knew McNamara from his merchant seaman days in college. "Well, we don't need crew, but I guess we could use you as waiters," he said. McNamara and Hodgson waited tables all the way back—seven in the morning until ten at night, no breaks, glad to get it. At night, exhausted, down below, McNamara would talk of Hallie Booth. "I remember all that summer Bob writing to her, talking about her, wanting to marry her," Hodgson recalled.

At home Hodgson went to work for Standard Oil of California; McNamara for Price, Waterhouse. He started on October 2, 1939, and resigned on July 31, 1940, two weeks before he got married—but not to Hallie Booth. His office was in the Balfour building, in the same district where his father's had been. They paid him a little more than $30 a week. Walter Baird, who was at the firm in those years, remembered that McNamara was extremely diligent and earned rave evaluations. Baird, who later became the partner-in-charge of the San Francisco branch, went out with McNamara on two-week assignments—say, running adding-machine tapes at a client's offices to figure out how many fifty-five-gallon steel bells for oil storage had been produced in the past year. They'd take their half-hour lunch and go back to the counting. "He hated that job," Peggy Slaymaker told me. Maybe the San Francisco branch didn't understand the hot heart of control.

I have seen a photograph of a Christmas or Thanksgiving table of 1939 at 1036 Annerly Road; the diners look somber beyond somber. Nelle's son seems to have set up the picture and then come around to the table to join his arc of diminished family.

Spring came and his old econ classmate Joe Cooper began teaching him fly-casting in the backyard. Nights, the auditor would go over to Arbor Road, a ten-minute walk, and listen to Bing Crosby records at Hallie's. Richard Hodgson said he could remember going over there with him to meet Hallie's parents. He and McNamara double-dated some. They lost track of each other for a little while, and the next thing Rich Hodgson knew his friend Bob was marrying Margy Craig.

Jean Booth Mitchell, Hallie's only sister: "They were engaged, though not formal or a public announcement. But she definitely had something of his, a ring from his fraternity, maybe." In all the years since, McNamara has rarely said the name "Hallie Booth." It's as if the words dropped down a well along with so much else. So what did happen? "She loved Bob, but not enough to marry him. That's what I think," Jean Mitchell told me. But hadn't he been gallant enough to ask her to marry him, despite her illness, despite what Nelle or anyone would have to say about it? Or was he on a path and didn't know how to get off, until he'd been gotten off?

No matter the stiffening, Hallie could still get around. Once there had been a double-date picnic: Hallie and Jean; and Jean's boyfriend, Bob Mitchell, and Bob McNamara. "My future husband, Bob Mitchell, began telling an off-color joke at this picnic," Jean told me. "It was about the 'pee in swimming being silent.' I didn't get it. I kept saying, 'But there's no letter *p* in swimming.' The color was hugely rising in Bob McNamara." Years later, long after Hallie was dead, Bob McNamara would say he couldn't place Jean Booth. A mutual friend had delivered a message to America's defense secretary. Nope, couldn't recall.

Somewhere in here he told his mother he was thinking about applying to medical school. "My mother was furious," Peggy Slaymaker remembered, and then seemed to regret having said it. Nelle told him to buckle down. There wouldn't be the money to advance him for med school.

Then Nelle's son met—rather, saw in a new curve of light—the girl from Alameda.

It's incorrect to say, as some have, that Robert McNamara never experienced early failure and disappointment. He didn't get highest econ honors at Cal. He didn't land a Rhodes. He didn't graduate from Harvard with honors. He got turned down by the doomed Piedmont girl. What's accurate to say is that Robert McNamara always seemed gifted, for a long time anyway, with the ability to turn things around, so that you'd tend to forget his failures.

He and Margy dated furiously. They went to Edy's on Shattuck for ice cream in the half-moon wood booths. They went to movies at the Grand Lake, where the organist rode his instrument up out of the floor to entertain before the start of the feature. They went on picnics and Margy brought along kippered herring, which he loved, and which thus led to the name "Kip." One weekend he left her in Alameda and went up to the mountains to fish with Cooper. They had already been skiing in the mountains. Nearly all he could talk of to Joe was his new love. The two fishermen perched on rocks and dangled flies smaller than a thumbnail into icy Sierra pools. They didn't bother with waders, went right in in their shorts and tennis shoes. Joe had been a fly fisherman nearly all his life and had a second sense about fast, dark water. From his trout journal of June 22, 1940: "Moon: Just a little past full. Weather: warm, clear still. Bob hooked a nice trout in the 24 and ½-inch pool and cursed beautifully when he lost it. His fishing is improving nicely. Dad had stopped at the dam and Bob and I left the impassable pool a little after 5. We ran most of the way from there back to the road. My total: 4. Dad: 5. Bob: 0." The nascent trouter must have been too moonstruck to bring to net something as beautiful and wild as a Sierra rainbow.

Back in Oakland came Dean Wallace Donham's offer. It was as if Harvard had been floated down like a paper plane.

THE BENEDICT and his bride arrived at Soldiers Field on September 15, 1940. The moon was full and pearly. (The previous June, a skinny and erotic and good-time Harvard man nicknamed Mattress Jack Kennedy had graduated from the campus across the river.) They unpacked their few things in a faculty unit in Morris House. He seemed almost giddy to be showing Margy around. Their apartment had a fire-place and bay windows and was a minute's walk to his classroom, just one quad away from where he'd lived in the monastic CD-39 three years before. The place had a cubbyhole kitchen—almost a galley. Soon Margy took a photograph of her husband in an apron, cleaning pots and pans. Soon she got him sleepy-eyed in his robe, and pasted the picture in her honeymoon book, and wrote underneath: "Do come to breakfast."

They discovered a restaurant called Hartwell Farms. It was in Lex-ington, Massachusetts. They would go out on a Saturday night with Myles Mace and his wife, another faculty couple who were quickly becoming good friends of the McNamaras. Mace was a large Min-nesotan, five years older, who, like the Californian, also felt seduced by all that the East Coast and academic life had to offer. At Hartwell Farms you could have the Saturday special for sixty-five cents—as many plates of chicken à la king as you could get down. Scrubbed wooden tables, fine old New England atmosphere. They dined there that first Thanksgiving. FDR had just won his third term, with 27 million votes to Wendell Wilkie's 22 million. But in a straw poll at the B-School, the votes went much the other way: ninety-eight faculty for Wilkie, three for Roosevelt. McNamara was one of the three dissenters but kept it to himself for a long time.

There was a new selective service law. Some 16 million men between the ages of twenty-one and thirty-five were registering for the draft. Secretary of War Stimson had picked the first number (158) in the lottery on October 29, 1940, thereby placing a funny word in the lexi-con: "draft." The Germans had overrun Luxembourg, the Netherlands, and Belgium. France had fallen. Hitler's U-boats had been sinking Allied ships almost at will. Britain was under blitz. Congress had already appropriated $4 billion for a two-ocean Navy.

The legend is that he started keeping a card file of jokes suitable for any teaching occasion; jotted on each card was the date the joke was tried, and the reaction, such as: "Goats-Ghosts. Laughter."

In January Professor Sanders's assistant wrote out the questions for the final exam in industrial accounting. Question two was about aver-age cost and standard cost and whether the company under discussion (Wright and Burwood) should adopt a policy of first-in-first-out or last-in-first-out for smoothing of profits. On a small yellow sheet, Sanders penned: "Mr. McNamara, this is ok except: Question IV goes a little more into standard costs than I think we covered in first half year.

Could you write another form of question?" He did, and the word "controlling" was in it.

He and Margy liked getting together with other junior faculty. The men would play Ponca City Baseball Poker. Threes and nines were wild, as were deuces and aces. Jack McLean, another faculty brain, from Ponca City, Oklahoma, invented the game. The wives would make supper in the other room. The poker pots were small, nobody won much money, nobody had any money. People loved Margy. It was her freshness, her unacademic-ness. But they didn't dislike him. "That power, that ambitiousness, that clawing and arrogance: you never saw any of that around here with Bob, really," remembered a marketing teacher named Harry Hansen, several years older. He remembered McNamara striding to work almost at first light, having downed his juice and raw egg.

One of McNamara's old students told me that what *he* could chiefly remember was the teacher's sensitivity to and patience for those who didn't get control right off.

In the summer of '41, the McNamaras and the Hansens found the money to rent a cabin together on Whitton Pond in New Hampshire. Harry Hansen had a camera and took pictures of Bob in his swimsuit down on the dock, stuffing a hot dog into his mouth. Margy, beside him, was very pregnant. She went off a board and made a watermelon-splash. Bob and Harry swam out to the middle of the lake and hung on to a log. Hansen: "It was easy. I was four years ahead of him, but it was easy." Long after, when Harry Hansen was being honored by the B-School for more than a half century of service, he wrote to his forties faculty friend Bob McNamara and asked if he'd be able to come. The answer was no. No elaboration.

By their second faculty year, the couple was renting across the river, in Cambridge, at 81 Brattle Street. Was it too insular and tight at Soldiers Field? Did they wish to get more to the center of things? They found a microscopically small apartment in a nice old clapboard house almost on the Radcliffe Yard. They owned a couple of worn easy chairs, a big stand-up radio with the speaker in the middle, a bookcase, a lamp on a wrought-iron stand, a throw rug, a clock that had wooden spokes like a ship's wheel. They did the dishes in the bathtub.

He taught a case involving the Brettle Lane Cement Company. The case had been used by others ahead of him. He wrote at the bottom of the typed text: "Suggestions for changing the case. 1) Make it more interesting 2) Point out areas in which controllable expenses existed 3) Outline organization 4) Ask students to question the departmentalization for a) product casting b) control." Control.

Except that there seemed very little control. Christmas, Vern Goodin came. One night Margy and Vern stayed up late. They stuffed a turkey atop some newspapers and talked about where the world was taking them. Pearl Harbor had been attacked; FDR had spoken of infamy through the wood-and-fabric speaker on their console radio. Two months earlier Bob and Margy's first child had been born. "Little Margy," they were calling her. Now it was the holidays, and Congress had declared war, and the color of America was turning khaki brown, and the best man from their wedding was visiting, and were they supposed to be happy? The instructor, twenty-five, married sixteen months, sat on the arm of his worn easy chair in his Cambridge flat and put his arm around his wife and looked down at his baby daughter while his best friend from home clicked the shutter. Beside them, a skinny tree glittered with tinsel. In a way it was like a photograph taken outdoors in San Francisco on July 9, 1916: the Victorian father in the cinctured bathrobe looking down at the sunbonneted month-old baby boy in his arms, trying to understand what his life meant.

Because all bets were off. The B-School would soon become a statistical school for Army Air Forces officer candidates. Control accounting in the groves of Soldiers Field was about to transmute from the religion of profits and loss into a system—no, a cause—that could help generals bring order to flying hours, gasoline consumption, replacement parts, tonnage, the overhaul of a B-24 Liberator, the readiness of a B-17 crew waiting at its aerodrome in England. Or as a professor named Throop Smith would title a Harvard memoir, the B-School was now going to go to work "Putting Bombs on a Business Basis."

It was about five months after Pearl Harbor—close to the first week of May 1942—when the dean called about a dozen of his young and most draftable faculty to a meeting. McNamara was present, as were Myles Mace and Harry Hansen. The group sat at a conference table. There was a man on the other side. The dean said, "I want you to meet Lieutenant Thornton."

Tex Thornton, who held his cigarette in a holder and had suave hair and a Texas charm oozing from his pores, said, "Mr. Lovett and General Arnold sent me up here to see if we can't work out a plan to teach Air Force officer candidates to be statistical-control officers." Mr. Lovett was

Robert A. Lovett, banker from Wall Street and assistant secretary of war for Air. General Arnold was H. H. Arnold, commanding general of the Army Air Forces. And Charles Bates Thornton was a twenty-eight-year-old articulator of dreams, not least his own, who had come to Washington eight years previously and had rousted about in several government bureaus, but was now traveling in the eye of the patriotic task: finding a means to systematize the largest Air Force on earth. "In forty-five minutes," Hap Arnold is claimed to have once said, "I was given $1,500,000,000 and told to get an Air Force." In that same figurative forty-five minutes, lowly Lieutenant Tex Thornton, who had his own bootstrap flair for numbers, had schemed himself an office right next door to Assistant Secretary Lovett. By the war's end this same man, no longer a second lieutenant but a full colonel, would be running sixty-six Stat Control bases and units around the world, with 3,000 officers and 15,000 backup personnel—an electronic brain within the monster. The brain would have the largest private-wire teletype operation in the world. The brain would operate from the basement of the Pentagon—and also from Wright Field in Ohio—and would feature a Strangelovian and antediluvian clanking array of computers and vacuum tubes and adding machines and calculators, some of which had been borrowed from insurance companies. Stat Control would be thought by some to be a little like the Russian commissar—its own shadowy types at most every station, level, and place, enforcing the purity of the regs.

Myles Mace: "What I'd always heard, true or not, was that before the war General Arnold knew his airplanes, every one, by the names painted on the side. . . . His memory was great for strategy and tactics but he didn't know how many airplanes he now had, or what air crews, or bombardier training schools. Later it would all be called management information systems."

Harry Hansen: "I've always wondered if the experience in the Air Force is really where the numbers reliance began—not Harvard. Question: Does the idea of Stat Control work better for the Air Force in the first place? You can count bombs and pilots, but how do you judge the cost-effectiveness of a battalion? Besides which, this huge thing known as the Army Air Forces was starting up from nothing, with all the incredible potential for waste. How do you get control of it? Well, numbers are right there to grab hold of, and they work so well."

That May day in the dean's office, Tex Thornton told the teachers that he hoped a statistical training school could be up and running within several weeks. Thornton said the group should get on a train and come to Washington for a look around. "When?" they said. "Tonight," he said. So that evening the profs, led by Professor Ed Learned, who was the only senior faculty man among them, boarded the *Federal*. They left Boston at eleven, arrived in the capital at seven the next morning. The war had really begun.

Mace: "Basically, we had no option but to go. We knew all the regular classes were going to be curtailed, maybe suspended outright. But beyond all this there was an interest and a need to help out, and even to get into the war in some way. But my God, not to go to boot camp or carry a rifle or any of that nonsense."

On June 8, 1942, the Army Air Forces Statistical Control Officers School was up and running with an initial class of 165 OCS candidates. Almost overnight Soldiers Field began to resemble a military academy. Platoons marched by in formation on the way to class. Rifles were stacked outside Baker Library. Snappy tunes were sung by the "Singing Statisticians," or so the legend.

Over the next few months, in addition to teaching control to student officers, instructors McNamara and Mace, still civilians, drafted the first AAF regulation requiring all units to report on the condition of their aircraft on a daily basis. It was the famous Form 110, the Daily Airplane Status and Location Report. Mace: "What we did was set up a control system to keep count of airplanes. We went down to Washington and worked in the Munitions Building—I think on Constitution Avenue. We sat down with pads of papers. I wrote one reg, Bob another. We said, 'Now, if we wanted to do this. . . .' We learned how parts are numbered. We traded ideas back and forth on paper. We learned how to make an airplane inventory system—on the wing. We were unafraid to try."

And eventually they wanted more. "Here was the question," said Mace. "Do we want to sit out the war teaching OCS guys—or do we want to get in? Do we want to spend the war at Soldiers Field in Boston, or are we going to try to get into uniform?" So in late 1942, the two teachers went to Tex Thornton in Washington and asked about the chances of getting a direct commission and working as officers in Stat Control. But the War Department was no longer giving statesiders direct commissions. A plan was worked out whereby they would be sent to England as special consultants to the Eighth Air Force. They would be paid $25 a day, plus a per diem. If the luck was running, they might be able to stiff-arm officers' school, don't even bring up basic training.

They left for Europe on a Pan Am Clipper on February 2, 1943. (Thornton had secured first-class tickets.) The first stop was Bermuda. They laid over and headed for the Azores. The plane came in at dusk over the Tagus River in Lisbon. That evening the Clipper's fifteen passengers dined at the Avis Hotel restaurant, one of Lisbon's finest. Huge meal, cigars, liqueurs all around. McNamara and Mace didn't even smoke—but sure, they'd have a cigar. Then the bill came. They choked, but somebody else paid. The luck was running.

In Teddington, outside London, they found their billets at Mrs. Bealey's. She gave them a freezing room upstairs, twin beds. There was a "geezer" (gas heater) and you could punch a shilling into it to get one tubful of not exactly hot water. Every morning the bone-cold consultants would get up at six. The younger of the two didn't fool with breakfast—he wished to get right over to work. Besides, breakfast was sprouts, powdered eggs, and Spam—forget that. Mace and McNamara would rush into clothes and ride bicycles over to the command of General Ira Eaker's Eighth, which was trying to pound Hitler from the air.

They were consultants for about three weeks, then went to see the A-1. He was personnel. His name was Pulsifer. They asked about commissions. The A-1 said he could make them immediate second lieutenants. No, no, we need to be captains. Well, you'll have to see General Eaker.

Mace: "Bob had strong black hair combed straight back. We went into the men's room and combed my graying hair forward and tried to make it glisten. 'Sir,' we said to the general, 'we need to be made captains because some of our students in the Statistical Control unit here would be captains and it wouldn't work if we were only lieutenants.' "

Eaker, who could be stiff-necked, said to McNamara, "How old are you?" McNamara: "You mean to my nearest birthday, sir?" Okay, okay. But Eaker told them they'd have to study for an indoctrination test. (They knew nothing of military protocol.) They went out of his office and the indoctrination man said, "Here's a book, come back in two weeks." They came back in two days. "Ask us something." Their impatience and brilliance and hubris, not to say the cause itself, had vaulted them past all convention.

Colonel Pulsifer, the A-1, handed McNamara a piece of paper: "The Secretary of War has directed the Commanding General to inform you that the President has appointed and commissioned you a temporary

Captain in the Army of the United States effective 12 March, 1943." He signed it in his slanty hand.

According to Mace, they never took a day off. Mace: "The problem of the whole thing was this: the officers with their B-17s and overworked crews are trying to win a damn war, keep the Führer out of London, and here's two guys coming along with more reports to bother them. We'd say, 'No, no, you'll have a guy here who will be telling you every day the condition of your crews. Don't you see how valuable that is?' "

There was a restaurant, Simpsons, that Captain McNamara loved; marvelous place, huge portions. One night he took Mace and a crew of fellow officers there. But Simpsons was blacked out, and they had to eat with little flashlights.

It was as if the paper war he was fighting was his alone to win. "In all that time I never once saw a drop in his energy level," Mace remembered. "Bob could never be devious, circuitous. There were no half-truths."

Dusty Porterfield arrived. He'd been in one of their first OCS stat classes back at Harvard. He'd made captain too in the regular man's Army; in fact, he'd been commissioned before them. And here he was trying to boss them around. "Go fly a kite, Dusty," McNamara said. "Captain McNamara, I'm your superior officer. I'm of a mind to rack you back," Porterfield said. McNamara stood up. "I don't give a damn who you think you're superior to." Mace got between them.

After nine months in England they sent McNamara to Salina, Kansas, and the Twentieth Bomber Command. (Mace went back to Washington.) Salina was the home of the B-29 Superfortress program, a potent weapon to help close the war. He stayed six months in the "zone of the interior," as the posting was described on his record, then flew with a Superfortress crew on April 9, 1944, to the China-Burma-India theater. His promotion to major became effective the following day. He stayed in that rank for just four months and one day before they handed him a lieutenant-colonelship. In India the statistician coordinated the flow of matériel for flights over the Hump—Army Air Corps vernacular for the Himalayas. For this feat of analysis, they would pin the Legion of Merit on him.

Harry Hansen (whose own Air Force control contributions were in the areas of personnel systematizing): "Let us suppose you're in Stat Control in these several theaters of the war. You solve all these problems. People depend on you. You get a lot of authority. The Air Force is so poorly run. How do you get your first handle on everything? With numbers. And by the way, let us suppose that after this you go into the Ford Company, which in a way is even more poorly run? How do you solve? With numbers. And after this do you have a religious belief about them?"

You can get a sense of the newfound power by two sentences that appear on the official "Summary of Military Occupations" of the teacher on war leave: "Organized, directed, and operated statistical control system in 8th and 20th Air Forces. Directed Statistical Control System of ATSC [Air Technical Service Command] supervising directly 1,700 employees and having direct or technical supervision over 5,000 employees."

In July 1944, the second McNamara child, another daughter, came. By the time her father got back from India, Kathleen McNamara was three months old. The four McNamaras now moved into a small apartment in Arlington, Virginia. For the next nine months the officer worked out of Stat Control headquarters in the bottom of the Pentagon where he got to know Tex Thornton at firing range. His performance also came to the attention of the assistant secretary of war for Air. This would be an important fact some years hence. The legend about Serial No. 0885931 is that he was so scrupulous about the order to conserve paper that he did his figurings on the cardboard backs of writing tablets.

There was to be one more assignment in uniform—at the Air Technical Service Command at Wright Field in Ohio. He would oversee systems that would help wind down the war. He was to go in as head of the Wright Field Stat Control unit. Victory in Europe had already come. His appointment became effective on July 22, 1945. Which is just about when the polio struck.

From an AAF regional hospital in Dayton, a downed man wired his recently married sister in Murfreesboro, Tennessee: HELP. CAN YOU COME IMMEDIATELY? He didn't use the word "polio."

Polio is a virus that attacks the spinal cord. It's an inflammation of gray matter (polios) of the myelin sheath. In the beginning you think you've caught the flu: aches, sore throat, high fever. But what the disease is trying to do is paralyze you by killing off motor-nerve cells that control muscles. Some polio survivors end up tight, rigid, emotionally constrained. What if you are this way to begin with? Beating polio can also make a person reflective, spiritual, softer, appreciative of the subtler things. It's all qualitative; no precise conclusion can be drawn from the scientific data. An estimated 500,000 Americans in this century were infected by the polio virus—and about 300,000 survived, maybe half of them making a full recovery. There were polio epidemics in the late thirties, in the forties, and in the early fifties, before the development of the Salk and Sabin vaccines made the disease something that now sounds quaint. Two of the survivors of the summer 1945 scourge were Bob and Margy McNamara, who came down with the virus within about a week of each other. On V-J Day they were in bed.

There is no doubt his case was much lighter than hers. At first the doctors thought he had a strain of malaria, something he had brought back from overseas. Talking about his polio is something McNamara has generally shied from. The one chance I had to bring it up, he shrugged and said he had been down only four or five weeks. I tried to obtain records, and couldn't.

No matter the lightness of his case, it is my judgment that McNamara's polio has been treated too lightly by biographers. I once spent an afternoon talking to two doctors at the University of Michigan Medical Center who have done much work with polio survivors—noting, for instance, how overstriving they can become once they are back on their feet. What if you are overstriving to begin with? "If you're young, you get wiped out physically. So if you survive, you count on using your mind, you're not sure whether your body can be counted on from there on out. You live with a certain amount of hidden dread," said Frederick Maynard, then the director of the university's post-polio clinic. "There's an emotional hidden pain there," he said. His colleague, William Waring, agreed, but turned the idea of something concealed on its other side: "If you've won a war, and you've triumphed over polio, wouldn't this really tend to give you a confidence and a hubris? There's a physical hubris I've noticed, a physical need for post-polio patients to push themselves beyond the average thresholds of pain."

Is it possible the will to recover is so strong that in some cases it seems almost to petrify the emotions?

The case of polio McNamara has always wished to recount—sometimes crying about it—is his wife's. How at first Margy had been told she would never lift an arm or leg again. How she had refused to hear this news and fought her way back, muscle by muscle. How, in that Baltimore children's ward where they had taken her, people would come to visit and find her encased in plaster, with her right arm sticking straight up in a kind of goofy salute, but with her spirit so alive. And how those paralytic children were everywhere around her, and how she would talk to them, encourage them, send out for candy and other treats.

Vern Goodin and his wife, Marion, came close to crying the time they told me what it was like going to see Margy McNamara at Children's Hospital in Baltimore. "Everything seemed so dark for them," Vern said, and it made me think suddenly that probably no one is capable of understanding the kind of fear they felt.

When the Ohio wire for help arrived in Tennessee, Peggy McNamara Slaymaker was with her husband, who was in the Army and awaiting orders. Peggy dropped everything and went to Dayton to care for her brother's daughters. Little Margy was almost four, Kathleen was one. Peggy's husband arrived to lend a hand. They moved Bob and Margy's things into a new apartment (the McNamaras had been living temporarily with another military family), and then worked to find a nurse and sitter for the children. Some weeks later Margy was transferred from the base hospital at Wright Field to the larger rehabilitation unit in Maryland. Meanwhile McNamara, back on his feet, arranged a transfer to the Pentagon. By this time Peggy's husband had received orders to Lincoln, Nebraska. Later that fall, with the hospital bills mounting, with Margy's prognosis for recovery still in doubt, Lieutenant Colonel McNamara decided his daughters should be farmed out—Little Margy going to Nelle in California, Kathy to Margy's folks, who were in Toronto. (T. J. Craig's insurance company had transferred him temporarily to Canada.) The plan was that Bob would bring his older child to Nebraska and then Peggy and her husband would accompany the little girl on to Oakland. Peggy Slaymaker believes it was in early December 1945 that her brother showed up in Lincoln with Little Margy and a suitcase of her dolls and clothes—and some surprising news. "Slay," he said, "I've had a wonderful opportunity. I'm going to work for Henry Ford II in Michigan."

He told them how Tex Thornton from Stat Control had come up with this brilliant, cockamamie scheme of selling himself and nine other Stat Control officers as a kind of postwar management package to industry. And twenty-eight-year-old Henry Ford II, who was now running his grandfather's company, had bit on Tex Thornton's telegram. The officers had gone out to Dearborn and met Henry II himself. Peggy's brother related that day in Lincoln how at first he had resisted Tex

Thornton's idea, didn't want to be part of any postwar management package, no, the only thing he wished was to get back to his classes and his students at Soldiers Field. "But you see, I have to go into business," he told his sister and brother-in-law. "The best Harvard can offer me is $5,000, and what with all the expenses of Marg, there's no other way. I'm worried. I have to make more. I've got to go."

You could say the reason a whiz kid from the Air Force named McNamara began working at Ford Motor Company on January 31, 1946, was simple fate—but is fate ever simple? (He went in at ten grand, and the salary shot up from there.) It's foolish to believe Harvard and teaching ever could have held him. He would have become dean of the B-School, he would have gone across the river to a vice-presidency, and it would have been up and out from there. Who knows, maybe he would have ended up in some future presidential administration as a secretary of commerce. But these are the might-have-beens, and McNamara, for one, has always despised the might-have-beens. A war had given the first test of the truth of his numbers. He had been close to battle, but from a slide-rule, adding-machine angle. He had never really gotten involved with product, which is to say dying and screaming. And yet that war had provided hints of beyond—not enough, you'd say. He was almost thirty now, a family man. In postwar rise, in Henry Ford's Dearborn, there would be the next great test of the truth of his numbers. It was as if the Creator were designing for him the perfect second-test application. And because he was such a competitive animal—Nelle's son, after all, on the other side of V-E and V-J Day—there would be no other way but to go in there like a goddamned jackhammer, straight to the company presidency itself. At which point, having won the prize, fifteen years hence, he would be ready to abandon it. Or at least this is what any close content analysis of a few frigid days in December 1960 would make a rational man conclude.

ALTHOUGH GREAT CLAIMS would later be made about how intensive and thorough their selection process had been, the truth is that the president's top headhunters made up their minds to get him on the team before they personally knew him. Unconditional offers for crucial posts were extended to a man the president-elect had never met, didn't know, except by the word of others, except by what he could read in the vaunted New Frontier "talent search" files. (By the way, where are those files? Nobody seems to know.) Once the actual seduc-

tion process began, it took them six days, a Wednesday to a Tuesday—
and it might have taken a day less, had there not been the snowstorm.

On the Wednesday in question—Pearl Harbor Day—the president-
elect's emissary and top headhunter (who also was his brother-in-law)
flew to Michigan on a commercial airliner, hailed a cab, pulled up to
Ford World Headquarters, got a pass from the lobby guard, rode to the
twelfth floor, and proceeded to drop his offer—actually two offers,
first Treasury, secondarily Defense—on Robert McNamara's desktop.
Thump. Maybe the sound of it was something like a fat wallet hitting
mahogany, only what was in the wallet wasn't money. McNamara had
plenty of that. According to both participants, the rather critical question of an interview with the president-elect didn't even arise in the
conversation until after the auto executive seemed to be wavering a tad
on the possibility of the second offer. (He'd said no straightaway to the
first.) Only then did the dangler of dangerous opportunities, R. Sargent
Shriver, sensing the advantage, begin suggesting that the least Mr. Mc-
Namara might do was make a quick trip to Washington to turn down his
brother-in-law in person. But it was employed as a wedge, not presented as a contingency or condition—and the principals themselves
say so, although they'd say a lot of other things, too, these many years
later, trying to explain it in the unreckless and contextual light that sanitized history likes.

But wait a minute, why should there have been any stated or
implied contingencies? Wasn't he just the kind of humane technocrat
they sought for the team? Hadn't they convinced themselves ahead of
time that every qualification was nearly perfect: Republican, but not
very; titan of automobiles who devoured books like Pierre Teilhard de
Chardin's *The Phenomenon of Man*? Hadn't every secret recommenda-
tion and personal scouting report been over the top? They weren't concerned with ideologies or political preferences, they needed people
who could get things done: "action intellectuals," as campaign chronicler Theodore H. White was soon to name them. What they were looking for were lean swift lines. It was almost a government priesthood
they had in mind for this yeasty new time in the life of the nation. If
these secular priests could be witty and talk dirty on occasion, that was
fine. One thing was sure: The candidates for Jack's team could not be
boring.

In a sense it's so simple to understand from their side: He represented all those gear-meshed parts, those hot assembly-line chasms.

They needed a kind of god from a machine, and here *he* was almost literally from a Michigan machine.

But taking it chronologically, or perhaps as a kind of print newsreel between December 7, 1960, and December 13, 1960:

In a Dearborn glass tower, a man with a swell new office and swell new salary arrived at his office and said to his secretary, "Okay, Virginia, let's go down the list of calls. What looks really important?"

"Well, there's one here from a Mr. Robert Kennedy."

(In 1984 McNamara went over the sequence of events in detail with me. As he told how the Kennedys got him, a warmth came into the room. He even put his feet up. Later I discovered he had a number of things wrong. A tiny example: He said the call from Bobby Kennedy was after lunch. It's only the way memory plays tricks. The call came in midmorning. In the spring of 1995, when McNamara published his own memoir, and included the story of how the Kennedys snatched him out of the presidency of Ford, he got that insignificant detail right—but, surprisingly, he had some other and more basic things wrong, including the date he spoke to Sargent Shriver in Dearborn and the date he met John Kennedy in Washington.)

The company president was forty-four years old. He was earning something like $500,000 a year. His small moral car, the Falcon, was the fastest-selling automobile on earth. Twenty-eight days earlier, Henry Ford II had given him the job he had been lunging toward for the past decade and a half. And before the afternoon was out, the mountain he was sitting on would start to feel small and balmy.

He took the secretary's note and went into his office and closed the door. Although he was to claim in later years that he had been caught totally off guard, it wasn't precisely so: He was aware people from Washington had been making inquiries about him, although it's fair to say he had no idea how badly they suddenly wanted him, and what big offers they were going to make.

He dialed the number on the sheet and the younger brother came on the line. "My brother, the president-elect, would like you to see our brother-in-law, Sargent Shriver."

All right, let's get up something next week.

"No, I mean this afternoon. He will fly out to Dearborn today. What would be convenient for you?"

About four o'clock would be convenient.

McNamara's secretary, Virginia Marshall, penciled the name "Mr. Shriber" in the appointment book.

That same day, Pearl Harbor Day, the other new president, the one who'd beaten Richard Nixon by the razor's edge of votes, was in a suite at the Carlyle Hotel in New York City. There was a meeting scheduled with the secretary-general of the United Nations, and there was also to be a news conference to introduce his third cabinet appointee—Stewart Udall of Arizona for Interior—during which somebody from the press would ask again when the country might expect to hear something about secretary of state. Kennedy would nearly snap his reply: "The office is very important, as is Treasury, as is Defense. Whoever is selected for those jobs, their judgment will affect the lives of all Americans." (The president-elect would manage to squeeze in a little Christmas shopping, going out a side door of the Carlyle and down to Tiffany's to look at jewels, to Sulka's to finger ties. His wife was still in a maternity suite at Georgetown University Hospital, about to bring home their new son.)

The big-game hunter from the East arrived. Shriver told me that he thinks he played his first card within a minute or two of entering McNamara's office. Did he even have his coat off?

"Not interested and not qualified," McNamara said, but went right on to describe what Treasury would entail. "He laid it out just as if he were conducting a seminar," Shriver told me.

Next card. This time the change in the quarry's attitude was instructive. What Shriver recalls is that McNamara began computing on a tablet what it would cost to leave Ford. There were many zeroes in the figure. But it wasn't the money. "I've already got more money than anyone in the history of the McNamara family," he said. Money wasn't important to him, he had never really lived up to his income, not even to a third of it, he didn't think it healthy to have such wealth. Still, the offer had to be out of the question. And really, he wasn't qualified to be secretary of defense. His experiences in the military had been a long time ago. Except he said one more thing: "Well, after all, I've only been president for a month. It's not as if they'd be losing someone who'd been here for a long time in this job."

Shriver left after obtaining a promise from McNamara to meet Kennedy in the next few days. Purely a matter of courtesy—this is the way it was left. The president went next door to the chairman's office. But Henry Ford II had departed on a flight to the East Coast. McNamara called flight services and told them to put a company plane on standby. He caught up with Ford in Manhattan later in the evening—he felt a little silly chasing across the country like this, no matter the importance of things—and asked him to ignore whatever news reports he might hear (the Detroit papers had already caught a whiff of the story, and a Ford spokesman was confirming that, yes, Sargent Shriver, of the Kennedy family, had been in town), because while it was true he had discussed the president's cabinet, he categorically wasn't leaving the company. Flattered but uninterested.

(There are some who insist that Henry Ford II knew about Sarge Shriver from the instant he stepped into the lobby of the Glass House but that Ford believed the offer was only Treasury and wasn't worried.)

This was Wednesday. The next morning, December 8, Shriver, back in Washington, got a call on the private listing he had given McNamara the day before. "Look," said the voice on the other end, "I'm already here in the East. Why should I go home and then come back in a couple of days? I could meet your brother-in-law today. I'll go to the Ford suite at the Shoreham Hotel and wait for you to call." Shriver, a little startled, said he'd see what he could put together. Possibly that evening.

Stop the reel again. How had they gotten his name in the first place? What had prompted this rush, *their* gall? As with everything McNamarian, the explanation is tentacled, but in essence it sifts down to Robert A. Lovett, investment banker from Brown Brothers Harriman. Lovett, World War II assistant secretary of war for Air, knew the work of that war whiz from Stat Control and had been following the conscientious young man's rise ever since.

On December 1, Lovett, the ailing establishment hero whose service to the Republic went back to FDR, had come to lunch at Kennedy's Georgetown home. Lovett, who suffered from bleeding ulcers, turned the young man down on taking any New Frontier job he wished—State, Defense, Treasury. But in this same luncheon, he sang the name of Robert S. McNamara. He'd sung it a couple of days earlier, too, to Clark Clifford, who had been sent up to Wall Street to massage Lovett on Kennedy's behalf. Lovett had told Clifford in New York that the young fellow at the Ford company was "the pick of the litter." Clifford remembered the phrase.

While it's quite true and should be emphasized that at least four or five others in the Kennedy transition organization—including Shriver, Harris Wofford, and Adam Yarmolinsky—already had McNamara's name, and were much impressed, and had begun acquiring files and making the calls, it was only *after* the December 1 meeting between Kennedy and Lovett at 3307 N Street in Georgetown that the president-elect himself seemed to swerve across three lanes of asphalt. That's when the McNamara idea lit like a halogen bulb.

Shriver told me he's pretty sure he brought up the name to Kennedy right after the election, when he saw a story on McNamara in the New York *Times*. (It was on his elevation to the company presidency.) But at that point, early November, there had been no propulsive energy, no rage to go, not from Jack. At that point it was mostly: Okay, Sarge, look into it. Adam Yarmolinsky, who ended up working for McNamara at the Pentagon, and who had actually met him in the flesh in Michigan (first in 1955, then again in 1959), explained this powerful last-minute thirst in the innermost Kennedy circles as a kind of proof for the theory of simultaneous invention. Suddenly, everywhere they turned, there was the name, glistening, beckoning: McNamara. No question, they had to have him.

Shriver told me that he and Kennedy got together on the night before his Wednesday flight against fury. They looked at the files again. They still weren't quite sure which job was right, Treasury or Defense. They spoke again the next day, just before Shriver boarded. That one was an airport pay-phone call. "Jack," the brother-in-law said, trying to control his trembling emotions, "I want to go out there today and instantaneously get this guy's attention."

"What do you mean?" Jack said.

"Jack, if you really want to get this man, would you authorize me to make him an unprecedented offer?"

Which is how a twofer came about on the afternoon of the seventh.

In a 1984 Camelot talk to some students at Southern Methodist University, Shriver said: "Try to imagine that situation. McNamara didn't know me. I didn't know McNamara. . . . Kennedy did not know McNamara. Neither did anyone in Kennedy's family or among his friends. But we, in the talent-hunt headquarters, had convinced ourselves, and, of course, President Kennedy, that McNamara was one of the brightest, toughest, quickest, most thoughtful, and patriotic men in America."

It was all true, although some other things were also true.

THURSDAY, DECEMBER 8, 1960, 8 P.M.: The patriot is being spirited down the dogleg alley and around the back and up to the little wooden gate at the rear of the redbrick three-story Federal house. Minutes later two Irishmen, a year apart in age, elected to their presidencies within twenty-four hours of each other, are sitting facing a fire, first room off the left as you come in from the front. Caroline's toy donkey stands in the corner. Out on the icy stoop, the press boys are decked out in everything from goose-shooting mackinaws to chesterfields with silk mufflers.

Earlier today, out in Hollywood, Frank Sinatra, who has been making plans for "the biggest one-night gross in the history of show business," was asked by a reporter: Who appointed you to head the inaugural gala? "The gang in Washington, including Jack," the singer said.

This afternoon's editions of the Detroit *News* are reporting it's Treasury, but what do they know, those hinterlanders.

The two seem to hit it off extremely well. Far from being dissuaded by McNamara's resistance, Kennedy is stimulated. To McNamara's statement that he isn't qualified, Kennedy famously rejoins that he knows of no school for presidents, either. The meeting lasts about an hour; the industrialist finds himself coming under a kind of spell he's rarely, if ever, experienced. "Wouldn't you think about it over the weekend and talk to me Monday?" JFK says. "We'll meet again Monday."

Later, sometime after nine, convinced now that Treasury is all wrong, Kennedy slips out to the home of Douglas Dillon to talk about that post, while McNamara goes for beef stew at the home of Eugene Zuckert. Zuckert is a Washington attorney and old friend who had been on the Harvard faculty of the forties. (He'll become secretary of the Air Force under Secretary McNamara.) At Gene Zuckert's house, there's little talk of Treasury, it's all Defense and it's exciting as hell, although it's true McNamara seems racked with worry about leaving Henry Ford II in the lurch.

Newsweek is already scrambling toward a McNamara cover for Monday's issue. Jim Jones, the magazine's bureau chief in Michigan, is in his office in downtown Detroit. It's very late, probably about eleven now. The phone rings. It's Ben Bradlee, chief of the Washington bureau of the magazine, who's also a neighbor and friend of the president-elect's. Jones is trying to pull copy together from his anemic McNamara file. He thinks the offer is Treasury. "It ain't Treasury, Jimmy baby," Bradlee tells him with the kind of conviction that can come only from the horse's mouth, residing a couple doors down. *Newsweek* will beat the pants off *Time* on this one, thanks to Bradlee.

Friday, December 9: McNamara flies back to Michigan, but not before having met for two hours at the Pentagon with Tom Gates, incumbent secretary of defense. (There's a belief in some quarters that Kennedy will ask Ike's man to stay on for a year or so, but that one's gone.) That evening, home, McNamara is in his study. He's by the window. It's snowing heavily—so he would remember later. In fact, there's barely any snow on the ground in the entire lower peninsula of Michigan, although it's true a big storm is said to be brewing for later in the weekend. But this tiny weather fact has relevance in terms of a call about to be made.

"I think I'll call the president-elect," he tells his wife. "I'll tell him that I'm writing a letter and that the letter stipulates that the only possible way I could be interested was if I could appoint all the senior people in my department solely on the basis of merit. And that I would have to be a working secretary, not a social secretary."

He dials Washington. But Kennedy has left for Palm Beach. (He has decamped the capital at 3:20 p.m. on Friday in twenty-seven-degree weather, aboard his private Convair, the *Caroline;* when he arrives at his family's winter estate four hours later, it's a delightful seventy.) The candidate reaches him in Florida. He tells him about the big snowstorm in Michigan. "Mr. President-elect," he says, "I've been thinking and I want to write this letter and I can have it there Monday."

"Hell, Bob," JFK said, "if it's snowing in Michigan, it's probably snowing in Washington, too. I probably won't be able to get back there till Tuesday myself. Just bring the letter with you Tuesday."

Roswell Gilpatric, a Manhattan attorney and eastern blueblood who became McNamara's deputy secretary at the Pentagon, told me that McNamara's letter had this at the bottom: "Accepted and agreed to, ———— John F. Kennedy." Gilpatric, a McNamara loyalist (now deceased), said Kennedy once showed it to him, yukking. According to Gilpatric, Kennedy kept the letter for a while, then pitched it.

But why the snowstorm bit at all, and when, exactly, was the call to Florida made? According to Deborah Shapley's 1993 biography, McNamara told Kennedy it was snowing heavily in Michigan to avoid meeting him again, the implication being that he intended to remain at Ford. In Shapley's phrase, it was a tactically useful fib to a president-elect. Yet Kennedy pulled an end run: Hey, Bob, just bring it with you on Tuesday. In 1984, when I interviewed him at length for the Washington *Post,* and as he set about in one of our sessions reconstructing the sequence of events, McNamara told me how he'd stood at the window on that Friday evening after he got back, just as it started to snow heav-

ily, just before he decided to call Kennedy about the letter with the stip-
ulating conditions. A long time later, after I'd published a three-part
McNamara series in the *Post,* it occurred to me to check the weather. I
discovered there had been no snow at all that Friday in lower Michigan, and only skiffs of white that Saturday ("not enough to worry about
galoshes" is how the local paper put it). In 1995, when he published his
own book, two years after Shapley's book had appeared and accused
him of a bald—though admittedly trivial—lie to a president-elect,
McNamara wrote that he had placed the call to Palm Beach on *Sunday.*
He wrote that it was really snowing hard that day. But the fact is, it
hardly snowed on Sunday, either. It's checkable. The big snowstorm
skirted lower Michigan and went brawling on toward the East Coast. In
the wrap-up provided by Monday morning's Detroit *Free Press:* Michigan had caught only "the northern fringe of the storm, winding up with
less than an inch. . . . The snow then diminished to flurries." In the
Midwest an inch wouldn't have grounded anybody from anything.

Back to the reel: Saturday, December 10: The Washington *Post* has
slapped the developing McNamara story on the front page. It's Defense,
not Treasury. And in the New York *Times:* "Mr. McNamara, a contem-
porary at Harvard of Senator Kennedy, has been mentioned publicly in
Cabinet speculation only for the last forty-eight hours." The auto man,
just a day or so ago far back in the pack of possibles, is the hottest name
in the country. Who is this guy? What does he like for breakfast? News
editors are screaming to their troops: "Get color. Get color."

That night, Saturday, the Bob McNamaras go to dinner at the home
of the Bob Dunhams. Dunham is in the executive personnel department
at Ford. The two Ford guys stay up until 2 a.m. "You go down there
with those senators and congressmen and they'll tear you apart," Dunham says. "I'm tougher than you think," McNamara says. "And besides,
how do you say no to the president?" It is pretty clear to Dunham he has
already made up his mind.

Sunday, December 11: The McNamaras go across the driveway for
cocktails at Charles and Kitty Sawyer's house. Oddly relaxed, McNamara leans back and says, "You know, the shape of the front bumper of
the Ford next year doesn't seem very important to me right now." This
remark will find its way into the press and not be admired in the upper
levels of the Glass House at FMC.

Monday, December 12: Robert McNamara is on the cover of *Newsweek.* A charcoal line drawing was all the art department had time for.

The legends above and beneath: "Kennedy's Great Task. Picking the Very Best. Ford's McNamara: Wanted on the New Frontier."

A blizzard is dumping twenty inches on the Middle Atlantic states. Washington is getting slammed with eight inches.

Tuesday, December 13, 2:22 p.m.: The Secret Service once again brings him around the block and down the alley. Out front the press is mad with the rumor he has already accepted. Cables from news cameras run into the Kennedy cellar. There's a stenotypist, fingers purple from the cold. A flatfoot in a long blue coat pacing back and forth. A newsman with a scarf tied around his head, holding a copy of that day's *Star:* "RECORD COLD TONIGHT, SLIGHT RISE TOMORROW."

The agents let him out of the car and he trots up the narrow back steps and there sit JFK and Bobby side by side on a love seat. "Mr. President, I've written this letter," he says. He repeats that he doesn't think he's qualified, but that he's ready to accept if the conditions in the letter can be met.

"Let's have a look," Kennedy says.

He reads the letter, passes it to his brother. Bobby reads it and passes it back. "What do you think, Bobby?" the older brother says. "Fine," the younger one answers.

"Well, then, what the hell, let's go out front and announce it," Kennedy says, already scribbling notes on a yellow pad. (Bobby Kennedy would later tell an oral historian that his brother was flabbergasted at the letter; but, sly fox, he passed it over unblinking.)

The Universal newsreel that will flicker in movie theaters and at military installations later this week presents two men in front of a crowd. They are standing beneath a fan window and between two electric lamps on either side of a Georgian door. Kennedy has emerged first, grinning, with that little quick set-piece gesture in which he brushes his left hand past the middle button that fastens his suit jacket. He's hatless and coatless. His tie is blown. With a shooting motion, he says something to the scribe on his left: the great man talking to the peon.

Announcer Ed Herlihy, in that charged voice-over delivery common to all newsreels: "Robert McNamara, who was recently named president of the Ford Motor Company and who gives up potential earnings of $3 million . . ." Herlihy pronounces it "Mac-Na-Mer-Ra," triphammering it, with the accent on the third syllable. Country hasn't gotten onto it yet.

Why is his face so melancholy? His head is tilted to the right. Kennedy introduces him. His frosting breath, the cement grin, and now the stabbing voice: "I accept my full duties with the Defense Department with a tremendous sense of challenge, with full confidence in the ability of President-elect Kennedy to lead this nation forward at a time and in circumstances that demand the best that every citizen has to offer."

THE FIND WITH A MIND — as the pundits at *Time* magazine put it—went home and started packing. Within a week of being named, after hundreds of calls around the country, he had compiled names on little white rubber-banded index cards of some of those he would ask to help him turn Defense upside down. The talent he was to assemble there—Vance and Califano and Harold Brown and Gilpatric and Paul Ignatius and Nitze and Yarmolinsky and so many others—would amount to his own best and brightest, his own cabinet within a cabinet. It was as if Kennedy's magic for finding the right stuff had passed to him in smaller portion, with his own charm and genius drawing people to him in the way the moon will suck at the sea. And David Halberstam would one day write in *The Best and the Brightest:* "He was intelligent, forceful, courageous, decent, everything, in fact, but wise."

Before the Defense-designate flew home on December 13, he stopped in the dimming Washington light to see lawyer Clark Clifford. Kennedy had said it would be a good idea to have a chat about his Ford stock. Clifford, recalling: "One thing I remember, he had a small notebook. And he was making copious notes. I hadn't seen any of the others doing this. He hardly stopped the whole time we talked. He was all business. A serious man. Stayed right on the point."

In Oakland, Nelle McNamara was stopped by a reporter for a quickie quote. Of the tremendous financial sacrifice, she said: "He has done things like this all his life. For instance, when he was in graduate school in Harvard he tore up all the checks I sent him. I knew he was having a hard time getting along with the salary he was getting, but he never cashed a check I sent him."

The day after he was named, Walter Lippmann opined on editorial pages: "It has been, of course, a fascinating game to speculate about who would be tapped. But it is easy to take our own curiosity too seriously, and to assume that from the names of the men who are chosen, as compared with the men who are not chosen, we can read the future policies of the United States."

That same day, December 14, 1960, the newly resigned president of the company held a press conference in the auditorium at Ford World Headquarters. He had already disposed of all 24,250 shares of his stock (worth $65 a share). A reporter asked why he didn't wait a little while—you know, try to spread it over two tax years. "I don't want any question in anyone's mind about conflict of interest," he said. A reporter asked why he chose Defense over Treasury. Because the Defense job "was the one which was made as a firm offer," he said. A reporter asked how many times he'd met with the president-elect before accepting the job. Three times, he said. Both the Detroit *Free Press* and the Detroit *News* took him at his word: three meetings with the president-elect in the past six days. It was a plausibly and defensibly correct answer. (There had been the weekend phone call to Palm Beach, and that was a meeting, sort of.) And why a need to manipulate the truth at all? Who knows, but possibly for this reason: By the day after, back in Michigan, no matter how thrilled he was, the bridegroom was nonetheless feeling a little self-conscious at the speed with which his marriage had been made.

At roughly the same hour on December 14 that he was telling the Detroit media he had met with Kennedy three times, Marg McNamara was entertaining a society reporter in her Ann Arbor home. She served coffee. "I decided I might as well get it over with," she said. What was "it"? The hard and glinting thing she could sense was now coming in? She told the reporter she wasn't really pounding her pillow worrying about her new life in Washington. "One thing I do very well is sleep," she said.

And so he was in, it was done. Myths to the contrary, it was a triumph of Kennedy style over substance, of brass over painstaking deliberation. Both men had leaped toward something, each for his reasons. You might say the whole thing was done like a shoddy car, except this is probably being too hard: Momentous decisions in every presidential administration seem to get carried off with the same combination of the subjective and the impersonal, of the careful and the ill-considered. Government is the art of the possible, the practicable. I once talked about this with presidential scholar Richard Neustadt of Harvard. He, too, had been involved in the Kennedy presidential transition, as a consultant and influential memorandum writer, though not directly concerned with the picking of McNamara. "Dangerous?" he said, echoing the word I'd used. "Sure, but it's the way the system works." Besides, he was the perfect technocrat for the job they had in mind—getting hold of the mammoth Pentagon, finding a way to manage and systematize the place. No one would ever do it better.

Several years later, a high-ranking official in the State Department who knew a lot about Southeast Asia, who had recently returned from there, sat down in the secretary of defense's office and screwed up his courage and said to the new and utterly assured man behind the nine-foot desk, "But, sir, you're trying to stick a Ford engine in a Vietnamese oxcart."

Possibly, he answered, adding, "We can do it."

Part Three:

DIED SOME, PRO PATRIA, 1965 IN AMERICA

*D*ied some, pro patria, non "dulce" non "et decor" . . .
walked eye-deep in hell
believing in old men's lies, then unbelieving
came home, home to a lie,
home to many deceits,
home to old lies and new infamy;
usury age-old and age-thick
and liars in public places.

— Ezra Pound, from "Hugh Selwyn Mauberley"

*N*SAM-328, *as the document came to be known, spelled*
out Johnson's recent military decisions: the two additional
Marine battalions to Phubai and Danang; the increase in
logistical forces preparatory to larger ground deployments;
and the all-important change in troop mission, from
base security to active combat. With these decisions, LBJ
had carried the United States, unmistakably, across the line
from advisory support to war in Vietnam.

— Brian VanDeMark, Into the Quagmire

LANCE CORPORAL JAMES C. FARLEY,
DANANG AIRFIELD, MARCH 31, 1965.

ANOTHER RIDE WITH
YANKEE PAPA 13

WHAT IF YOU CAME to his door many years later and told him that while he was hiding his face against a box in Vietnam, some men on the other side of the world were getting set to hatch one of their more pernicious mistakes, not to say lies, about the war? How would that information make anything different?

CASTRO VALLEY, CALIFORNIA. The tense of modern times.

His face lights. A man with a wrecked back is getting up from a straight-backed vinyl chair in a sunny East Bay kitchen. His Irish-born wife's at work, his little boy's at Montessori. Just the two of us this morning, as it was for most of yesterday, and the day before that. "I still have it," he says. "It's out by the back door. Wanna see it? C'mon."

It's hanging from the doorjamb above a utility sink. The sheath is finely cracked. The leather has a dull reddish gleam, like burls on the trunks of trees, like seats in old Jaguars. In a snap-latch pocket is a whetstone. Former lance corporal James C. Farley, United States Marine Corps, recipient of the Silver Star, crew chief on a long-ago chopper called Yankee Papa 13, reaches over and lifts out his combat-survival knife.

He's resting it in his palm. "Oh yeah," he says, "it's been with me the whole time, ever since I went to Vietnam in 'sixty-five. You were supposed to turn it in, but they didn't enforce it, not really. The back side of it is serrated, for scaling fish, or whatever. See, it's very soft steel. The idea was you'd keep sharpening it whenever you had time, so you could get it like a razor. Here."

It's heavy as a rock. It feels perfectly balanced. The blade is long and fat and silvery. At the butt of the grooved handle are two drilled holes and a pair of leather ties. The ties are braided, making me think this is how someone once spent a few hours of downtime on the flight line or in those old adobe-walled French barracks they lived in a mile or so from the Danang airstrip. "The idea of these ties was so you could lash the butt to a stick and make a spear if you needed to," he says. He means: if you got lost. If the bird went down in some dense green place.

I hand it back. He starts to return it to the sheath. But he doesn't quite do that. He holds the knife several inches above the holster, which is still hanging from a nail on the doorjamb. Now he lets it fall. It goes in with a thunk. He lifts it out again, suspends it, lets it drop. *Thunk.* Lifts it out again, lets it fall. *Thunk.*

"See how clean it goes in?"

I try. *Thunk.* But in a way it's as if I've left the room, as if Jim Farley has been lifted to another zone, coptering through the Yankee Papas of his mind.

"I've used it for trimming trees," he says. "For planting. It's my gardening tool."

A crinkle in his watery eyes. "I converted my sword to a plowshare."

A fifty-year-old-Marine-no-more with a gnarled, handsome face; an authentic American hero who doesn't guess he is; a second-chance dad who's got a child's bright yellow paste-on banana sticker adhered to the shoulder of his Levi's shirt, laughs hoarsely. Half of it is nicotine cough. But the other half, I'm certain, is relief. Relief that we've slipped away again from what we were edging toward all morning. Which is a photograph in a wrinkly magazine. The picture and the magazine are in the kitchen, sitting on the table. And we're out here. For now we don't have to talk about this old outsize black-and-white photo of Jim Farley in *Life* magazine in the just-spring of 1965. We can take turns thunking a beautifully balanced gardening tool into its leather case.

IN THE LONG-AGO just-spring of 1965, the Vietnam War transformed itself: from the nice little one-column firefight a lot of folks thought it was going to be a few years earlier into a huge Americanized conflict. In the beginning the transforming was done covertly. But some secrets get increasingly hard to keep. Consider a statistic: At the end of 1964, right after Lyndon Johnson was elected to his only full term as president, there were 23,000 American military personnel in South Vietnam; a year later there were 184,000. Robert McNamara once said with emotional if not historical precision that all the errors in Vietnam had been committed by the spring of '65; after that, there seemed no way out.

Nineteen sixty-five is when American combat troops were sent to Vietnam. They were sent to deny victory to the hated and deeply feared Communists, to save some fantasized Southeast Asian dominoes from tumbling. It's true that those initial ground forces that splashed ashore weren't thought of as part of some secret government plan for a massive buildup or all-out American ground offensive. And yet in another sense, the sense any right-thinking person should have felt deep inside him, they were the camel's nose under the tent. (Years later, one of the policymakers would employ this image ruefully.) What should have been recognized from the start was that it was in for a dime, in for a dollar. The first land forces were committed, so many followed.

Prior to 1965, Americans had served as advisers to the South Vietnamese, sometimes not advising at all but actively joining the government troops—the "ARVN" is how American soldiers referred to the South Vietnamese army—in trying to beat back the infiltrating Vietcong and their allies in the north. Not that this active joining was terribly well known in America. To America in the just-spring of '65, in places like Baxter, Arkansas, and Kettering, Ohio, Vietnam was still largely somebody else's fight, even if there was now evening news of bombing runs on hard-to-pronounce names. Even if there had been U.S. "reprisals" for overt and brazen enemy "aggressions"—such as the attack on the American barracks at Pleiku in the central highlands (the Vietcong killed eight GIs) or the Gulf of Tonkin incident of the previous summer, surrounding which the muddiness and general craftiness on the part of the policymakers could fill a book and still not get to the way they had provoked it and used it to their own ends and for their own devices.

In the main, though, and in Washington decision-making, the idea still intact at the beginning of 1965 was that the million-footed and all-powerful U.S. military machine should continue in a secondary, logistical, mentoring, hovering, advising, supporting, hectoring role. From the first arrival of advising Americans in 1950, when the French were riding the Southeast Asian tiger, this had been the mission: to aid and train the South Vietnamese in their own war against the Communists. And then all that changed. It changed because the advisory and hectoring effort was judged to have flubbed, flubbed miserably. The thing was slipping from their grasp. So America was taking over. In for a dime, in for a dollar.

Of all the president's steadfast civilian policymakers, in the late winter and spring and early summer of '65, none was pushing or urging or jamming to go harder toward the big war or arguing his case in closed-door meetings more forcefully or brilliantly than the secretary of defense: a man with an intolerance for drift, a man who appeared, on his top side, to have no doubt whatever. This fact becomes clear when one studies the endless river of white declassified paper from 1965, which is the key year among Vietnam years in any effort to decode why and how something could have gone so grievously wrong. In *The Best and the Brightest,* David Halberstam wrote: "There are, in the annals of Vietnam, thousands and thousands of memos and documents, as *The Pentagon Papers* would later show . . . they were at best small markers of a long and complicated and sad trail." Columbia University history professor Henry F. Graff wrote in *The New York Times Magazine* just as some of the back-channel decisions of early-summer '65 were being made: "No full answers can ever be constructed out of the documents alone because the process of deciding is intangible and evanescent." He interviewed McNamara on June 9 at the Pentagon for his piece. The secretary sat on the other side of the desk and said, no, they weren't moving in the direction of a large land war. But Graff was only a professor acting as a journalist, and lying in the name of national good almost didn't count. It wasn't sport, exactly. But you wouldn't have lost sleep.

Vietnam is our great myth now. It has superseded every other twentieth-century fable we have. More than 43 million Americans lost someone in Vietnam; more than 100,000 veterans have died prematurely since the war—which is not quite twice the number of names on the wall. What makes Vietnam so terrible a tragedy and so fine a myth is its impenetrability. It is a puzzle without pieces, a riddle without rhyme.

Was there a turning point, a Rubicon moment, an identifiable divide in those January-to-July biblical waters? I don't think so. The closer version of Vietnam's truth, of Vietnam's riddle, as a generation of scholars and historians have attempted to show, is that there were many divides, many turning points, many Rubicons, many shifts and switchbacks and box canyons; and that the war, and America's falling into it, was really a series of incremental steps, each mistake building on the last. Bombs led to troops and troops led to the full-scale ground conflict—in essence, that's what happened. The wrongful path got chosen in 1965—then there was no exit. An "inexorable movement from bombs to troops" is the way LBJ biographer-historian Doris Kearns Goodwin has described the early part of that year. In a funny way the inexorableness now seems seamless in its folly. This is the real riddle of Vietnam. How could they *not* have seen?

With all the above acknowledged, there are still some large moments, key crossings. And suppose, in that long and sad and winding and evanescent springtime paper trail, the following was true, not in a literary or figurative sense, but in an actual one, nearly a literal one:

That when you were coming back from your gone-wrong "support" mission in that blasted rice paddy up from Tam Ky and climbing out of your shot-up ship and walking into that supply shack and throwing down a Dixie cup of water and then moving over to a corner to sprawl and cry in very unleatherneck fashion, pushing your forehead down into the edge of a trunk—that *there,* almost literally, the aforesaid devious men in their secured Washington rooms were devising a blunder, not to say a lie, amid so many blunders and lies and stealthy miscalculations, that would take them directly if unwittingly not only into the wider U.S. ground war and all the escalations of the weeks and months to follow, but straight into their own eventual destruction as well.

Suppose it was true.

And suppose this error, not to say lie, could be identified by an official-sounding name: NSAM No. 328. (NSAM stands for National Security Action Memorandum.) Such a powerful coincidence.

A Jungian would think of it as a "synchronicity."

And to think, that morning, in the muggy Danang sunshine, knowing nothing of that, you had sauntered to your flying machine with your dungaree hat on cockeyed, with your expandable Timex slid halfway up your forearm, with your .38-caliber service revolver and your combat-survival knife holstered at your bony hips: one good-looking, big-eared, indestructible by-God United States Marine, ready for the fray.

"I was always embarrassed by the words sacred, glorious, and sacrifice and the expression in vain," Ernest Hemingway wrote in a famous passage about a retreat from a place called Caporetto. "We had heard them, sometimes standing in the rain almost out of earshot, so that only the shouted words came through, and had read them, on proclamations that were slapped up by billposters over other proclamations, now for a long time, and I had seen nothing sacred, and the things that were glorious had no glory and the sacrifices were like the stockyards at Chicago if nothing was done with the meat except to bury it. There were many words that you could not stand to hear and finally only the names of places had dignity."

Quick cut. A man with a bad back in a sunny noonday California kitchen stubs a filtered cigarette into a metal tray. In Vietnam, the cigarettes weren't filtered, and they didn't have names like Benson & Hedges, and they got sucked and bitten down to the tune of four and five packs a day. This is one midlife hedge against younger unhealthy habits. Jim Farley stands up. A somewhat widened-out man, in whom you can still see the lanky indestructible self, isn't going to the garage to get a jungle knife, he's going over to the sink for another cup of coffee. He takes it black and as strong as he can get it. I wonder how many cups he's had today. Farley's sister Marilyn, who's a nurse in Tucson, and who was a nun named Sister Maura in a convent in New Orleans when her older brother appeared in a big *Life* photo spread, told me it was nothing for the two of them to drink thirty-six cups of coffee a day. Every day. That was later in the sixties, after Jim had gotten back and Marilyn had come home and the two were living in Tucson in a little two-bedroom house that Jim had bought, both released from something, both trying to make it in another world.

Jim Farley's uncle, a man named Walter Roberts, who is dead now but was a kind of surrogate and much-beloved father to him, especially after Vietnam, was once quoted in *People* magazine as saying in regard to the postwar jumpiness: "He was nervous as a cat on a slick rock." His nephew was living at the Aggie House at the University of Arizona and was taking mining engineering and elementary ed and explosives and opera and was generally drinking his brains out on weekends and also working part-time as a stunt man at a cowboy movie lot in Old Tucson. The splintered vet on the GI Bill liked that work. It let him put on a black hat and a pearl-handled six-shooter and go flying backward through the breakaway banisters on the second floor of dance halls. He worked on one called *Heaven with a Gun.*

In that same updating feature story in *People* magazine (it was published in 1985, on the ten-year anniversary of the fall of Saigon, two decades after he'd been in *Life,* and was titled "Where Are They Now?"), Jim Farley's younger brother, Dave, who was also a Marine, but in a later part of the war, and who also has inside him great tunnels of decency and darkness, was quoted as saying: "Sometimes, Jim will be telling a story and he gets this look on his face like another idea has come into his head. He will be thinking about Vietnam, and he will pause. The story will cease for a moment, and then he will go on again."

We're going on again now—unsheathing memories from all the tight-fitting cases.

The coffee pot is only five or six feet away from where he's sitting. But even in the short distance, I see the pain. It's a concealed pain that's not concealed at all. Farley has had five major back surgeries in a twelve-year span. He's got steel bars inside him that run from his ribs down to his hips. He's been classified by the insurance companies as permanently disabled, as having reached his "maximum medical improvement," and if you ask on the wrong day he'll tell you that each of his surgeries has been more ruinous and shitty than the last. Vietnam didn't give him his wrecked back—a series of deteriorating disks and some bad luck and a freak fall down a set of stairs in the engine room of a ship a few years ago did. But still: There are times when he wonders if all of his spine troubles didn't really begin when he was spending so many hours bent over inside his wind-rocked bird.

Which was made out of magnesium. Magnesium is a highly flammable element that burns with brilliant white flame. Earlier, with odd affection, Farley told me why helicopters of his time in Vietnam were built of magnesium. Something light seemed to come into him. "It's lighter than aluminum, designed to fly, strong as hell," he said. "Those old UH-34D Sikorskys were firetraps. Actually, they were great helicopters, unless you crashed. Then it was good-bye."

"Death trap?" I'd said. "Oh, yeah," he'd answered. "I mean, it's instant fire. You've got the light weight, the tensile strength, and instant fire. We burned superhigh octane av [aviation] gas. It carried, let's see, about 3,000 pounds of fuel. The tanks were right under the belly."

The light weight, the tensile strength, the instant fire. Tomorrow, talking again of the UH-34D, which some called the Sea Horse, and which marines called the Shuddering Shithouse, I'll hear the same affection. He'll be talking of the way spent shell casings from the mounted machine guns used to snap off the interior walls of the cabin, off the side of your helmet, getting down your shirt. Those M-60 machine guns fired 750 rounds a minute, and the floor of the bird could pile up almost ankle-deep in cartridge links. You'd arrange your ammo belts so that they'd play nicely out of the box and through your weapon—didn't want the damn gun jamming.

"The sound level in there had to be 150 decibels, easy. We flew with the doors open. Without a helmet it would have been unbearable. You'd have to get right up to the ear of somebody and scream in it to be heard. Those old nine-cylinder radial engines were straight pipes, no muffler. The ship was just skin and bone." A few minutes later he says with the same affection: "Oh, yeah. She was an old workhorse. Very forgiving aircraft. You could beat the hell out of her and she'd survive."

A six-foot-three, natively quick noncom, who weighed a skin-and-bone 155 when he went into the corps, is bracing himself with his knee against a lower cabinet. Sunlight is bouncing off the sill beyond him. He's had hell beaten out of him and he's survived. It's a comfortable, attractive yellow house canted into the side of an East Bay hill, just below Oakland.

Hidden in the blades of the Swiss Army knife in his pocket is a white plastic toothpick. After lunch he'll get it out and work his teeth.

He's got a bristly mustache, and it's yellow in the middle, from the years of nicotine and coffee. Running down the middle of his stomach is a red ridge. There is another going up his backside. He's got twin pulpy surgical scars down the sides of his legs. They form a Y, splitting from his crotch.

He has already taken off and hung up in a closet the harness contraption he wears for four hours a day and which fires therapeutic messages to his spinal column. The signals get transmitted via a pulsating metallic magnet pack that's positioned at his belly button. For someone in such physical pain, Jim Farley is determinedly mobile. But there's always a price. The way he'll hunch forward and move his fist down toward his crotch. The way he'll cross his leg and insert his finger in the cuff of his pants and then tug on it lightly as he talks—as if trying to establish the right counterforce. The way he'll put his left hand over his right and lightly hold his wrist—as if feeling for a pulse. What he's really doing, I think, is trying to shift something around inside.

Last night I watched him get down on the floor to try and fuse the pieces of a blue plastic train track. He'd leveraged himself out of an easy chair and down onto the carpet because three-year-old Matthew Farley had importuned, "Daddy, you fix my train?" I watched him sustain himself on all fours with his knuckles. He'd hung over the kid like an oversize and loving mantis. "Uh, let's see here, son," he'd said, biting into his cigarette, his knuckles going white against the floor.

Oh, yes: the banana sticker. That came from Matthew. He's an excellent napper. The other day, they were teaching him how to pour from a plastic pitcher. He was great at that, too. So his Montessori teachers rewarded him with a sticker in the shape of a banana—which he came home with and pasted on his dad. The dad's been wearing it ever since. "He told me I was a good boy and it had to stay there," he says in the singsong voice of a child.

I didn't make it out to California this trip in time to see the decorating ceremony. But I rode over to the school yesterday afternoon to help collect Matthew. I watched the blond kid tear out of the building hell-bent-for-Montezuma toward the man in the paint-smeared jeans and black Reeboks padded with their extra foam. In other corners of the yard, mother-and-child reunions were taking place. The mother of this child was still at her accounting-office job in San Francisco.

So the dad caught the kid and raised him up with a palpable pride. Hang time. Screw pain. Farley was wearing his banana medal. In 1966, in Cherry Point, North Carolina, the commandant of the Marines pinned a medal on Lance Corporal James C. Farley—it was for heroism in Vietnam. I had witnessed this small scene at school and thought of the way John F. Kennedy climbed out of presidential helicopters on the White House lawn and bent down in his not-very-concealed pain to receive, though not lift up, little John-John. Don't bring up the myths of John F. Kennedy to Jim Farley, not unless you want to be whumped and spattered with his cursing, the way the mortars used to whump and spatter, turning nights to days. "Yeah, that chickenshit back-stabbing mother-you-know-what, leaving them there on the beach like that. That's when my relationship ended with him, when he did that at the Bay of Pigs. Right then and there. I have no use for this Kennedy myth bullshit, okay?"

Okay. Don't bring up Jane Fonda, either, who once went to Hanoi and consorted with the enemy, at least in Farley's view. "I hate that fucking bitch," he says in his loud gravelly voice, as though daring me to contradict the statement.

"My wife says I have two faults," Jim Farley says. " 'One, you exaggerate. And number two, you're always black-and-white, that's the only way you can see things.'

"Oh, I'm hotheaded, all right," Jim Farley says. "I'm still hotheaded. I can be hotheaded as hell.

"I hate people," Jim Farley says. "I hate crowds. I hate San Francisco. I'm antisocial, really. Well, I'm okay one-on-one."

Anyway, we had picked up Matthew and driven back here. You should have seen how he drove. He slumped himself into his late-model gas hog and rode the pedal not quite to the metal; a need for speed, even with the child who means everything riding behind you. There was a time after Vietnam when the decorated vet had a five-bay repair garage at the corner of Swan and Speedway in Tucson, but what he was doing, more than fixing other people's cars, was souping up stock rods. He would work on them all night and try to come to the job in the morning. "Dirt track, full-bodied," he grins. He wrecked one or two on that Tucson dirt.

All morning long we've been sitting in these straight chairs in this sunny California kitchen tripping over the names of some of the places that had dignity: Chu Lai. Phu Lam. Monkey Mountain. Hoi An. Quang Nam. Phu Bai. Quang Tin. Ba Gia. Khe Tre. They are only exotic sounds to me. All morning we've been sitting here getting closer and closer to a picture in a wrinkly magazine I've brought with me from Washington and that's now sitting on the table before us. But we lift off to something else.

There are twenty-odd pictures of Jim Farley in the *Life* on the table. They're all powerful. Farley's on the cover, too. But the photograph I've turned the magazine open to is the one on page 34C. It's the last image in a long photo-text essay titled "One Ride with Yankee Papa 13." It's the picture that conveys everything about war and the unprepared men who inevitably get caught up inside them. No text, just a top-to-bottom photograph of a bony Marine whose face you can't see. What you can see is a wristwatch going up an arm, a service revolver at a hip, an open mouth hanging at the rim of a box. In the foreground, stenciled on another box, as if to transmit a signal: the word "Valuables."

It's too awkward for us to talk about this picture, even after several visits and many hours of talk. What I want to tell Jim Farley, and can't, not yet, is how long I've admired him and wished to know him, just for this photograph—but that sounds sappy as I silently form the words. I saw the picture for the first time thirty years ago, when I was living another kind of life, and not in the service of my country.

We lift off, turn away. It was this way when I came out here last time. We're more comfortable with each other now. We've had some long late-night cross-country phone calls. He's confided things off the record. But still we don't discuss the picture. Not that his other stories and subjects aren't interesting, they're plenty interesting, even if a lot of them seem to come out in code. For instance: He had begun telling me last time of a sister-in-law he once picked up and threw across the room. He said, "I got in an argument with her at Dave's. I thought she was wrecking his life. I just got up and did it, and she kind of fell in a heap. I said, 'That's it,' and walked out and about two weeks later Dave and she filed for a divorce." The image I had was of something folding softly into a wall, like a sack of grain.

For instance: He had begun talking of how he once left Idaho in the broad daylight at a hundred miles an hour driving a forty-six-passenger school bus with beds and a kitchen and racing engines in it and also a big luggage rack up on the top that whistled like hell. The law of Ada County was hot on his behind. He was trying to make the Oregon border. He said it laughing. "A hundred miles an hour?" I said, doubting it.

"Everything's relative. Depends on which you want more." He didn't specify. I didn't ask more. He went on to say he had gone up to Idaho from Arizona with his then wife (his second) because he thought maybe he could make life work better up there. There was a lot more I wanted to hear, was hoping he would bring up into light, but he wasn't willing, not then.

He had begun talking of a California hydraulics company he'd co-owned in the eighties, and how they were trying to live on accounts receivable, and how he took it into bankruptcy. "I guess maybe that's one reason I grew the beard," he said.

"I don't follow," I said. "Trying to hide from the creditors," he said. The art of the laconic, of the possibly stretched.

But this isn't stretched: I have seen pictures of Jim Farley in the after-blur of Vietnam, before he found his way, in which the wild beard and the wilder hair and the puffed-out face of a man trying to hide from creditors seemed the least of the disguises. The real disguise was in his eyes. He looked locked—which is how he looked to me on the cover of *Life* magazine in the just-spring of 1965. In the *Life* cover photo, unlike the one on page 34C, you could see his narrow boyish face. He was half-turning from his mounted machine gun in the doorway of his cartridge-littered ship, and down below was a smoky patchwork of earth, and at his feet was a helmeted human form that looked limp as a straw dummy. This human form had black blotches on its sleeves and pants legs. The cover caption said: "With a Brave Crew in a Deadly Fight. Viet Cong Zero in on Vulnerable U.S. Copters."

One of the first things Jim Farley and I talked about on my first visit to Castro Valley was how much he liked singing, especially opera.

"Opera?" I said. I didn't get it. Marines aren't into opera. "You mean you took a course in it?" "No, singing," he said. "On a stage. Russian bass. I think I still have some old programs. But I stopped."

"Why?" I said. "Well, I got a pretty bad case of stage fright one time. After that, I sort of said the hell with it." In a later conversation, he filled this in a little: "I got thrown to the wolves. I was in the wrong place at the wrong time. I forgot all my lines and couldn't sing a note, basically. I haven't sung since then. Oh, I might hum a few notes now and then. But I make it a point not to sing."

Wrong place at the wrong time. Thrown to the wolves. As his brother Dave said to *People* magazine in the mid-eighties, Jim will be talking about one thing and then get this funny look. As if the quick intelligence were stun-gunned.

The rhythms of your heart, the Yankee Papas of his mind. He's got the coffee and he takes up the chair opposite the opened magazine. He positions himself so that he's half turned from it. I can see it over his shoulder. It's there, lying flat, big as *Life,* his long-ago, unletherneck self.

And it's as if he now says: Okay.

What he really says is, "It embarrassed me for years."

And I say, "You mean because you're crying like that?"

He clears his throat, nods. "I guess because, well, it's not what a Marine is supposed to do. I guess it still bothers me, you want to know."

"But wouldn't anybody have felt the same thing if they'd gone through what you'd gone through that day?"

"Well, okay, I think anybody would feel it. But I guess it depends on how you show it."

"You mean that you didn't hold it in?"

He nods again. "Yes." Then: "That's right. That I didn't hold it in."

Earlier today I watched a recovering Marine with a banana sticker on his shoulder reach into the pocket of his Levi's shirt and take out a white plastic pill box. There were green oblong painkillers and round orange painkillers and some other painkillers in there whose color and shape I couldn't tell. He popped one—maybe more than one. The medicine was in his fist, so all I could really see was someone cocking his head toward the ceiling and bringing his rough hand up to his mouth and putting something in—the way I've dropped in airline peanuts a hundred times. I asked what it was.

"Voltaren," he said. "It works better than some others."

Some days, Jim Farley says, he takes 4,000 to 5,000 milligrams of Tylenol on top of his anti-inflammatories.

When I first got here, he said with no detectable irony, "See, this is nerve injury and there's no healing timetable." This morning he said, sans any double meaning I could tell: "Some of it is getting accustomed to it. Your brain ignores it. And then it gets better a little too. So."

THIS IS ABOUT SYNCHRONICITY, which *The American Heritage Dictionary of the English Language* defines as the "coincidence of events that seem to be meaningfully related, conceived in the theory of Carl Jung as an explanatory principle on the same order as causality." This is about walking eye-deep in hell. This is about not holding it in. About revealing your softer, other, un-Marine side. About not knowing what *they* were doing while you were just trying to stay alive. About believing in old men's lies, and then unbelieving, and then coming home, home to a lie, home to many deceits and some new infamies and big liars in public places. Call it dying some, Danang. And dying some after, stateside, *non dulce,* not *et decor.* But can all of the after-dying be put on Vietnam? No, the truth must reside somewhere in the middle. I've come to think that a lot of Jim Farley's after-dying, before he found himself, might have happened anyway. Some of it he brought on himself. The harder truth here might be that a boy—which is all Farley was when he went to Vietnam, never mind that he was also a hugely brave man—was the lost boy long before he climbed inside the flammable fur of YP-13. And that fact has to do, from all I can figure, with the father taken from him when he was eight.

YP-13. This is what was lettered on the stub green nose of Farley's bird. He wasn't the pilot or copilot, he was the crew chief, he was the door gunner belted into the belly of the beast, the one whose job among other jobs was to soften up the LZ with rounds of M-60 ammo when they were bringing in and discharging a fresh load of ARVN troops to slay the brotherly enemy. That's how they spoke of it, "prepping the zone."

YP-13. Yankee Papa 13. Such an unlucky number. The ride was so long ago. And the ride will never be over.

But in another way, this is also a story *about* a story: Which is to say, a now-famous photo-text essay that appeared synchronously in *Life* magazine in the just-spring of 1965, and that was shot in documentary black-and-white by a great and courageous British combat photographer named Larry Burrows, who later lost his life shooting the soldierly face of the Vietnam War. Part of the documentary effect of "One Ride with Yankee Papa 13," as a photo critic said later, came from the inexorable progress of the illustrations: What had started out so sunny on a Danang morning ended fourteen pages later in the corner of a shed. Jim Farley is the central figure in Larry Burrows's essay, which tries to tell what happened to an American helicopter squadron on a particular day, so early in a war, before America really knew it was in a war, during a troop-ferrying mission that didn't turn out to be routine.

It was at just the moment, in the larger context, when Vietnam was transforming itself from the ARVN's conflict into the big Americanized war. The policymakers on their Potomacs of power insisted that it wasn't happening, and they would try to keep up this lie for months. And you could say that Larry Burrows's pictures in *Life* of Jim Farley's suffering were giving the lie to it all.

The pictures were made on March 31, 1965, and the magazine containing them was dated April 16, 1965, and one might also say with a fair degree of historical accuracy that in the linear distance between those two points the nature of our whole involvement in Vietnam shifted, went across the river and into some trees. Inexorably.

But hold that. There's something more important to tell first: what Jim Farley experienced that day.

He experienced one comrade dying at his shoe tops, and he failed—in his mind—to save another comrade who had been shot in the face and was slumped over the controls in the cockpit of a downed sister ship about sixty feet from his own helicopter. That man had to be left behind for the buzzards and the Cong, or so believed a twenty-one-year-old lance corporal from Arizona who had never seen violent human death.

The Marine who died at Farley's feet en route home was an officer named James E. Magel. He was from LeMay, Missouri, and he had just turned twenty-five. Farley knew him pretty well. They had sat in a few bars together stateside. Lieutenant Magel had a dumpy beat-up motorcycle and he was overweight for a Marine and he tended to get ribbed about it by the guys. There's always one in a group. There was something a little immature about Jim Magel, something soft. He liked to garden and had wonderful abilities with flowers and landscaping. No matter how hard he tried, he was never going to be the kind of soldier who goes into whorehouses or cocktail lounges after work and bites the heads off chickens—but maybe that kind of John Wayne Marine is mostly Hollywood caricature anyway. What's true is that he loved being in the corps. Almost everybody I've talked to has made that point, even as they may have been telling me other things.

A lance corporal couldn't save him from dying on the floor of Yankee Papa 13. Nobody could have saved Lieutenant Magel that day, although what does that change in the mind of Jim Farley?

"After he was dead, I moved away from his head," he says, meaning that his panicked mouth-to-mouth resuscitation efforts were in vain, to use two words Hemingway had contempt for.

"After he was dead, Larry asked me to cover his face," he says, Larry being Larry Burrows of *Life,* who kept firing off the rolls while the bleeding and bullet-pocked ship shook violently in the wind, trying to make it home.

Magel was the copilot of a bird lettered YP-3. He'd been rescued along with another Marine, Sergeant Billie Owens. The two had run toward Yankee Papa 13 through the man-high elephant grass. Just before reaching the doorway of Farley's copter, Magel, who had already been hit, seemed to trip and fall. This is what Farley recalls.

"How far away was he?"

The odd, hoarse, stuttering laugh. "Oh, maybe as far as that car across the street—about twenty feet."

There is some dispute about the next sequence of events. But what Farley remembers is that he hopped out and got Magel into his arms and was pulling and dragging and cursing and carrying him the short distance to the doorway. Which is when the lieutenant may have gotten cut into again. Which is when the officer's body may have been a shield for the enlisted man's.

Farley: "What I remember is he seemed to stumble as if he'd tripped. He kind of slumped in my arms."

Once he had been pushed inside the copter up onto the floor behind the mounted machine guns, Jim Magel may have got it again, through the open doorway. The details aren't clear.

Though this is: After Yankee Papa 13 was aloft and free of enemy fire, Farley and others in the cabin began unzipping Magel's flight suit and flak jacket. They removed his helmet. "Soon as we got him open and saw the blood coming out of his mouth, we knew," he says. The major wound was under the right armpit. Bright strings of blood, like red yarn, were running from Magel's nose and mouth.

"Not so much, really."

Magel was looking at Farley like a child. His eyes were sliding under his forehead. Farley was trying to bandage the armpit wound. The wind from the doorway kept whipping the roll of gauze out of his hands and across the dying man's face. If Jim Magel was trying to say something to Farley and the others in the cabin, one of whom was the photographer from Time Inc., they couldn't hear: The roar of the rotors and the typhooning wind were drowning it out.

Several days later, the photographer wrote in his notes: "A glazed look came into the eyes and he was dead. Nobody spoke for a few seconds."

All the Yankee Papas (seventeen went out) that were assigned to Helicopter Marine Medium Squadron 163 were bleeding and bullet-pocked and trembling violently in the wind that day, trying to make it home. Many of the ships had gone into the landing zone three times, each trip becoming bloodier than the last. YP-7 took eighteen hits. YP-6 took seven hits. YP-13 took ten hits, one of which was in its throttle and another in the box that stabilizes the controls. When the chopper Farley was in got back to base, somebody noticed that the throttle had been hanging in the air by a strand or two.

The irony of it, if this word can be used, is that the Marine helo pilots and gunnery crews of HMM-163 were only the backup and support force. They were the transport. It wasn't their fight. Yes, they had gone in "hot" (meaning they were firing at anything that moved), but their principal assigned mission was to ferry 465 troops of the Fifth Airborne Battalion of the South Vietnamese army to the battle zone. It was the paratrooping ARVNs who were supposed to leap from the Yankee Papas and search out and destroy the enemy in the tall grasses. The job of the Americans was to drop off the ARVNs and provide fire cover and get out of there as quickly as possible. But fate didn't follow the script. Because when the Yankee Papas of 163 thunked into a mapped-out series of connecting rice paddies between two hamlets, they came on an enemy that was dug in and waiting behind tree lines and stone walls. The Americans and their cargo were like fat ducks that had set down on the placid-seeming pond. As one of the Americans later wrote in an unpublished family memoir, there they were "sitting high in the middle of a war" in their thin-skinned cages between smoking tree lines. The LZ became the AZ: ambush zone. Death zone.

The battle got reported on the front page of the New York *Times*.

As the squadron's commanding officer wrote in his after-action report: "All crewmen this strike earn battlestar on wings." In the command chronology, which is a kind of official narrative summary of events, there is this Marine prose: "All a/c received intense small arms and auto wpns fire during approach and retirement. . . . Intelligence reports for sqdn briefing fm 2nd Div indicated enemy situation was estimated to be 2 VC main force companies armed with small arms, auto wpns, possible 30 and 50 cal MG. . . . After Action Reports and pilots' debriefing indicate strong possibility of VC trap."

I have spoken to a number of old officers and enlisted men from Squadron 163. One of them told me: "Whenever I need four numbers, the numbers I always leap to are 3165."

Under Point 7 of the command chronology, a Marine desk officer crisply wrote: "On 31 March, a mass casualty situation was declared at this dispensary as a result of enemy ground fire taken by the helicopters of HMM-163 while on a sortie in the area of Viet An. All told, there were seventeen personnel wounded, six of whom were immediately evacuated to the 8th Army Field Hospital in Nha Trang after being initially treated at the Field Hospital, C Med Bn. . . ." The report goes on. Sometimes only the names of the places have dignity.

Quick cut.

"He said I had a baby-looking face. 'You're thin, you look good, you're sort of all-American. You know, big ears, short hair. Yeah, you're the one I want.' " Jim Farley's talking about Larry Burrows, and why the photographer wanted to feature him. He says Burrows liked the unluckiness of the number painted on the nose and side panels.

"It was a puncture wound, and they don't bleed," he says. He means Magel. "I think what basically killed him is he drowned in his own blood."

After it was clear the lieutenant was dead, Farley began cursing and crying. They were still ten or fifteen minutes out of Danang. At first he tried shielding his face from the others in the cabin and then pretty soon he didn't give a shit. Let the violent bear it away, all of it. A farewell to arms, at least in the freeze-frame of those instants, which Larry Burrows of *Life,* both ruthless and humane in his art, kept catching between his crosshairs. Documentary photography: things as they piteously are. The hungry eye, ravenous to stop time in a rectangle. Two weeks later, published pictures of those instants would flatfoot a *Life*-reading nation. Back then *Life* had a nearly religious power.

And yet it's only half the story. There's an earlier part, which again was caught on strips of celluloid and published in that same issue of *Life*. It's this: Back when Yankee Papa 13 was still in the raking crossfires of the LZ, Lance Corporal Farley had tried to save an officer named Dale Eddy. Lieutenant Eddy was from Columbus, Indiana. He was six years older than Farley and had a brush cut and a big goofy easygoing Marine grin. Back home, his wife was carrying their first child. Eddy was the commander of YP-3, the same ship from which copilot Magel and gunner Billie Owens had escaped. The pilot of Farley's copter, sensing something wrong, had put down close to YP-3 and yelled to Farley on the intercom system, "See what you can do for that other pilot." So Farley jumped out and sprinted the twenty or so yards through fire and the rice paddy and climbed up the outside of the sister ship and stood in a foothold with his back to the enemy and cut the rotors and tried to rouse Eddy to life.

The six-foot, 190-pound commander of the ship wouldn't move. Leaning in from the outside, Farley could see the blood. He could see the bullet hole in the commander's neck, which was the point of exit. He struggled to lift the dead-weight flyer through the cockpit window. He couldn't. After a minute or two, Farley gave up and jumped down and ran back through the grass and the fire to his own helicopter, where Lieutenant Magel lay dying and Sergeant Owens lay wounded. It took them maybe thirty seconds to get out of enemy range.

It was at this point, when they were out of range, that the crew chief began trying to bandage Magel and give mouth-to-mouth. (Sergeant Owens's wounds were far less critical.) But what Farley didn't know, as he bent over Magel, was that Lieutenant Eddy was still alive back in the LZ, he wasn't a KIA, he didn't get left for the buzzards and the Cong, he was going to get to see that unnamed child his wife was carrying for him stateside. Because unknown to Farley and the others inside YP-13, Eddy and a comrade from that ship would be rescued by another crew. That crew would take a tremendous chance, and several of its members would later be decorated for bravery, with the pilot of the ship winning the Navy Cross. But the only thing Lance Corporal Farley knew, in the Yankee Papas of his terrified mind, as his own ship shook and the wind whipped the gauze out of his hands, was that he had just had two chances—and blown them both: He couldn't get Lieutenant Eddy free, he couldn't stop Lieutenant Magel from dying in front of him on the way to safety. And so it was a little later, after they were on the ground at home base, after Magel's body had been removed on a litter, that a crew chief of a bird with an unlucky numeral went into a supply room and threw down a cup of water and found a trunk next to another trunk with the word "Valuables" stenciled on it: the last shot, no words, and in time, an icon shot from the bad war.

Quick cut.

"I ran right across their line of fire," he's saying. He is speaking of his attempt to get Eddy out of YP-3. (Larry Burrows, insanely or ingeniously, probably parts of both, had sprinted after him with several cameras swinging from his neck.)

"Did you pray?"

"No."

"No time?"

"No. And no inclination to, either."

The first time Jim Farley and I met, he said: "I wanted to be a professional soldier. And I probably would have been if it hadn't been for Vietnam. Vietnam wrecked it." The same day he said, "I wanted to go to Vietnam because it was the ideal. You know. As the old saying goes, no sense being a Marine unless they're going to send you to the fight." I asked him if he has ever felt used and exploited by people in the media—people of my ilk. "Well, there is probably a lot of that," he said. "A pretty fair amount." I asked him if he felt that way about Larry Burrows. "My God, no," he said. "Larry had big balls. Larry was just there getting the story. Larry would do anything. The story was everything to Larry."

BUT BACK OUT of that LZ. And erase strings of bright yarn running from a pudgy lieutenant's nose and mouth. Seventeen months earlier, on a morning in early fall 1963, America's lean secretary of defense, with a zippered briefcase under his arm, with General Maxwell Taylor at his side, leaned forward on a sofa in the White House and reported to the president of the United States, who was a foot or two away in a Kennedy rocker (and here I'll take up the words of the text of an official White House statement), "their judgment that the major part of the United States military task can be completed by the end of 1965, although there may be a continuing requirement for a limited number of United States training personnel." What's more, 1,000 boys would be home by Christmas.

Same moment, on the opposite coast of America, an obscure Marine helo unit—obscure even to the American military machine—

was re-forming itself, which is to say undergoing an official transfer of flag from its previous commander. This helo unit would be training hard over the next year in anticipation of a rumored deployment to Vietnam.

In JFK's office, Max Taylor and Bob McNamara, having returned overnight from their ten-day inspection tour of Southeast Asia, delivered crisp judgments, and the next day these judgments made top of the fold in the New York *Times,* right side of the page. The date was October 3, 1963. (The left side of the *Times,* top of the fold, was saved for Sandy Koufax, who had just struck out a record fifteen batters in the first game of the World Series.)

The one-column headline: "VIETNAM VICTORY BY THE END OF '65 ENVISAGED BY U.S." It was as if the cock were already crowing. It was as if the ashes were already in their mouths. Many predictions about Vietnam would come back to haunt the Vietnam policymakers in the next several years, but these words would roost high. Never mind that the actual conclusions of the full McNamara-Taylor report to JFK were "riddled with contradictions and compromises," as author Stanley Karnow would show many years later. Never mind that "two separate attitudes were contained in one report, badly bastardized," as David Halberstam would write. Never mind that "the announcement of the 'Bring-the-boys-home-by-1965' flavor would destroy whatever credibility [the report] had," as ex–White House aide Chester Cooper would write in one of the best and most underrated books in the roomful of books about Vietnam, *The Lost Crusade.* Never mind that there were back-stage plots and counterplots having to do with the actual White House wording of the report for official dissemination. Because what America read in a headline on October 3, 1963, were the flat words *done by '65.* As Halberstam would later write: "The programs were going very well, the shooting war was fine, 1,000 Americans would be out by Christmas, and the whole American commitment would be finished by the end of 1965. . . . A lie had become a truth, and the policymakers were trapped in it."

This was seven weeks before Kennedy died in Dallas. This was when Vietnam was a blip on the far screen. This was when a West Coast chopper squadron nicknamed the Ridge Runners was mustering its new members at Marine Corps Air Facility in Santa Ana, California. They were from places like Idalou, Texas, and Cuba City, Wisconsin, and Tucson, Arizona. The one from Tucson had been a leatherneck for three years. He had gotten into the corps with his mother's signature, since he was under age and the eldest son.

The secretary and the general got their photos on the front page of the *Times* on October 3. They said their "timetable" for final victory ("If, by victory, we mean the reduction of the insurgency to something little more than sporadic banditry in outlying districts") was the end of 1964 in all but the IV Corps region, and victory there sometime in 1965. Provided, that is, there could be political stability in the country.

It turns out that in October 1963, the policymakers were passively promoting a political coup in Saigon. The president of South Vietnam was a man named Diem. He was a weak tyrant who had once been regarded as America's friend and ally. But that was past. Shortly, he was to be slain by his own, and America would forever be complicit in it. In for a dime, in for a dollar.

On the West Coast, HMM-163 was set to begin simulations of jungle and mountain-helicopter work in places named Yuma and Goat's Island and Twentynine Palms.

Okay, go forward another fourteen months. It's December 1964. At MCAF El Toro, in Orange County, the gunners and pilots of 163, having passed their Operational Readiness Test with an outstanding grade, are boarding a four-engine turbo-prop C-130 transport. They'll be traveling through the night, refueling in Hawaii, crossing the international dateline, destination Okinawa, which is the first stage on their journey to war. They're due to arrive in Okinawa on Sunday, December 6. In America, it will still be Saturday. Which is the same day, in the East Room of the White House, President Johnson has chosen to decorate the first Medal of Honor winner of the Vietnam War, Roger Donlon. Oddly, LBJ stops in the middle of his prepared remarks and, nodding at the secretary of defense, says to the assembled: "This man represents to me in our civilian life what Captain Donlon represents in the military life, the very best in America." It's an off-the-cuff tribute. It's the Johnson treatment. The secretary, as ramrod as the decorated war hero, gets out a husky, "Thank you, Mr. President." And later that Saturday night—which is Sunday in Okinawa, when some helo leathernecks have disgorged with their duffels—LBJ tells Turner Catledge, managing editor of the New York *Times,* in a private conversation that, yes, there will be some cabinet changes soon, but no way Bob McNamara, he's the most valuable they've got. "He's the best man in this country," Johnson says. After the seance, Catledge, who's in town for the annual Gridiron

Dinner, writes himself a confidential memo: "During the conversation, Johnson was jumping up, and walking around. Two or three times he'd walk over and stand directly above me, waving his arms as he talked. He would take a book from a bookcase on one side of the room and move it over to the other. He opened and shut the door two or three times. He jumped up at one time and said: 'I got to have a drink.' All he ordered was orange juice."

Who could serve this man?

Bring it ahead another two months and two weeks: February 17, 1965. A helo unit is getting its first glimpse of a red-dust place named Danang. Same day, the head of America's military establishment, who once ran an auto company, is writing a memo to the chairman of the Joint Chiefs on the subject of productivity—or, more accurately, the lack thereof. (*The Pentagon Papers* will eventually publish this memo under a heading titled "McNamara's Concern Over Cost-Ineffectiveness of Strikes.") The secretary has just received some disturbing bomb-damage-assessment reports. He presides over a budget of close to $50 billion. He controls more than $150 billion worth of missiles, planes, ships, tanks, and real estate around the world. He oversees 2.7 million men and women in uniform (and another million civilians), and what he wants, evidence the memo, is more bang for his buck.

The night before departing Okinawa, the Marines of 163, a sliver of all the secretary controls, toss themselves a party: two coolers of iced beer in a big tent, and then a touch football game, officers against the enlisted. It's touch football in name only. An officer, who likes photography, takes a color slide of an enlisted kid sticking his head up from the rim of the ice tubs. Some of the beer splashes out. What a waste of good brewski. Lieutenant John Hax, who frames the shot, doesn't know Lance Corporal James C. Farley, Jr., in any close way, but he thinks of him, as he squeezes on the trigger, as a nice kid, callow kid, green, lots of heart, enthusiastic, sucked into this great goddamn roiling inevitability, as they all are.

The men of 163 have been told by their squadron commander, Colonel Norm Ewers, that they will be doing logistical and tactical support work. They will resupply ARVN patrols, haul prisoners, pick up medevacs, carry tons of rice and bullets and cows and chickens to outlying districts—whatever's needed. They're not supposed to be in the center of the fight—they're backup. In his diary, on embarking for Danang, Lieutenant Hax, who took the picture of the kid from Tucson above the rim of beer, writes: ". . . we may well be wasted in a forlorn, hopeless, and unsupported fight, but still be acting in the national interest." Besides the squadron commander, only two men from 163 have ever been to war.

It's 1,200 nautical miles and a couple hours from Okinawa to Danang. The 250 Marines are bunched in rows of canvas seats stretched over aluminum tubing. "Hey, there it is," somebody shouts when the C-130 comes into the final approach at the airstrip. The earth is so red. It looks like finely powdered dust, the dust of the moon. These soldiers who have been jouncing on hard canvas seats, and who have made it in-country ahead of the death and casualty curve, are forty-two days from what will come to be engraved in their squadron history as "Black Wednesday."

HE'S TALKING OF the soldier-father who died at Christmastime 1951, in Middlesboro, Kentucky, home on leave. He'd given snatches of it earlier, always shy of a whole narrative. Once he'd said, "If I hadn't woke him up for breakfast, he would have died in his sleep. . . . He was under the quilts and blankets, it was Christmastime." Another time he'd said, "For years and years after, it was impossible for me to hear someone playing taps on a bugle." Another time he'd said, when I'd pressed, "It left a big soft spot, no question about that."

We're in the living room. In the hallway there's a collage of photographs, which his sister Marilyn put together. In one frame, a thin-spectacled man, angular face, physically slight, stands next to a bigger-boned woman. You can tell she bears the emotional and gravitational weight of the family. It's the wedding day of June Roberts and James C. Farley. He's a Catholic, she's Southern Baptist. She has converted for the man she loves.

In another frame of the collage there's a picture of a man and a boy on the post at Fort Knox, Kentucky. On the back it says, "1948, 1st Lieutenant James C. Farley Sr. and son Junior." Next to it another picture of a father posing with all three of his children: Dave, Marilyn, Jim. The eldest, almost eight, is in a coat and tie and buzz cut and is looking up with something like adoration. The father looks to be in his early forties. On the back: "Taken 13 May '51, probably one of last pictures of 1st Lt. James C. Farley Sr. with his children as he died Dec. 19, 1951."

Junior, recounting the engraved Kentucky death: "He came in the evening before on a Greyhound—about three or four in the afternoon.

We were all lined up to play with him, but he had this terribly bad headache. He played with us a little that night, I guess, talking about putting the tree up and Christmas gifts."

The next morning, the nineteenth, James leaped out of bed. He wanted to play with his dad. He knew he wouldn't have him home very long.

Farley: " 'I'm cold,' he said. 'I want a blanket.' Then he told me he was hot. Then he said, 'Get your mama.' "

The doctor came. "I remember him walking in the room, and he knew instantly what it was." It was a cerebral hemorrhage. "I remember him giving him a shot. He said, 'This is all I can do for him.' "

Adding: "A lot of his officer buddies came to the funeral. That little town of Middlesboro didn't know what was happening for a few days."

"Shitty Christmas?"

"I don't even remember it."

THAT DAY. 3165. They'd been in-country not quite six weeks.

"Nice clear sunny day," he says. "Let's see, we had reveille about 5:30 or six o'clock. . . . We knew we had a mission going out. It was going to be a pretty good-sized effort. There might be some trouble."

Larry Burrows got a picture of the crew chief going to his copter, lugging two M-60s. Those machine guns looked like snakes. Farley was grinning. "Hey, Farley," a sergeant called, "you won't need all that ammo for this one."

"Hell, who can tell, Sarge?" Burrows wrote that down in his notes.

Years later, Lieutenant John Hax, a kind of unofficial historian of the squadron, would write: "On this day Bruce Shirk gave the intelligence brief as usual, and from what he said we suspected that this one would be different. The neighborhood we were entering was most of the reason because it was a VC stronghold of long standing. . . . Just exactly what else was known about our strike zone to cause us to feel differently about that mission I can't remember, but I know that we did even before we climbed into our aircraft."

There had been a rumor they'd get fixed-wing air support from the Seventh Fleet. The fixed-wing boys don't come in to give you a hand unless there's something potentially big out there—say, a VC main-force company, maybe two. At any rate the fixed-wing cover didn't materialize. What the ships of 163 were going to have as protection were the Fangs: seven U.S. Army Bell UH-1 Huey gunships. These were lighter, smaller, more maneuverable helicopters than UH-34 transport choppers. The Fangs had machine guns and rocket pods dangling off their pylons. Their job was to get in early and hose the area down.

Just before 0800 hours, the squadron pilots and their copilots came out of the briefing room and headed toward the line shack to sign for their allotted aircraft. The helo officers rotated in and out of different ships, but the crew chiefs and gunners—who were enlisted men—tended to stay with the same bird. Yankee Papa 13 would be skippered this mission by Captain Peter Vogel. He was from Nebraska, and liked the stock market, and Jim Farley and some others weren't so crazy about him, but Vogel knew how to get the job done. He'd help you out if you got in a jam. Marines don't leave their people behind.

Liftoff was just after eight. The sun was bright and the clouds were sitting low on the mountains—too low. Couple minutes out of Danang came a command on the intercom: "We have to turn back." Shit.

Back at the airstrip, the crews played poker in the shade of the ships. The crew chief of YP-13, who didn't like cards, decided he'd go over his bird again. He found a kinked fuel line.

There were other delays, the usual hurry up and wait, but by ten the weather was good enough. Kick the tire, light the fire, let's go: Once you're in the go mode, nothing's worse than sitting on the edge of things. The temperature was in the nineties now. Good breezes once the Shuddering Shithouses were up.

They headed southeast, flying in formation, 1,500 feet in a column of vees, each four-plane division in a loose cruising formation. As John Hax later wrote: "What sticks is the fact that we were all in a somewhat brittle state." The Hueys were out ahead and there were also two maintenance choppers from another squadron in the flight. At Tam Ky, the provincial capital, they loaded on as many ARVNs as they could fit into each helicopter. The squadron commander grouped once more with his pilots. They put maps on the ground and squatted over them. Mounting his ship, Colonel Ewers called over to the photographer from Time Inc., "We may well have something for you today, Larry."

Nine ARVNs, seated crosslegged, were in Farley's bird, plus the photographer, plus a blond, baby-faced, twenty-year-old gunner named Wayne L. Hoilien. He was a Wisconsin farm boy and looked even more like a kid than Farley. The day before, Larry Burrows had taken the two into town for some background pictures at the markets and bazaars: jarheads on liberty. In truth, the Arizona jarhead hadn't been to town much at all. He'd stay at the barracks when the guys were going in to find whorehouses. In town, day before the mission, Burrows got Farley holding the hand of a little pajama-striped Vietnamese girl. The crew chief wore civvies: high-water pants and a polo shirt. He might have been in the Peace Corps.

The zone was ten miles to the northwest, flying time about eight minutes out of Tam Ky. It was a green valley between two medium-size mountain ranges. Colonel Ewers was in the lead transport helicopter with a Vietnamese intelligence officer. The first Fang flew low, and, catching no enemy fire, dropped two colored smoke canisters to mark the landing spot for the first drop-off. But something didn't look right, so at the last minute came an order from the lead ship to wave off and head for an alternate landing zone about a mile away.

Seventeen Yankee Papas dropping down now, banking right. Which is just when the tree line to the right blinks on like a pinball machine.

IN A FAR DIFFERENT SCAPE, a different kind of urge to go had been blinking on for several months. It's necessary to back up for a minute, say, to January 27, 1965, a decent starting spot.

A government servant sat at his desk in a building on the far side of the Potomac and scribbled comments on a piece of paper. His closest aide on Vietnam, Assistant Secretary of Defense John T. McNaughton, had come to work at 7:45 a.m. with a hastily written memo. The two talked for twenty-five minutes. In Saigon, there had been yet another political coup. ("I've had enough of this coup shit," is one of LBJ's more widely quoted lines having to do with Saigon coups.) The insurgents were winning in the countryside, no question. Something had to be done, no question. But what—start the program of systematic bombing in the north, as the generals were urging? Cut losses and get out altogether? Keep plugging along present ineffectual lines? In *The Pentagon Papers*, McNaughton's memo is registered as Document No. 249, and what's chiefly interesting about it are the penciled comments of his boss, the secretary of defense. Everything is in the go mode.

His comment as to whether the U.S. should keep on the present course? That's "Drifting."

A little farther down, on the question of risk: "This is better than drifting."

Air strikes against the north? (McNaughton had questioned in the paper whether bombing would do anything to improve the political situation in the south.) "RSM comment: Dissent. Help the actual situation."

And as for bombing itself: Isolated reprisal for specific enemy atrocities was "too narrow." The secretary was now feeling they should move toward a program of graduated military pressure. In the inner White House councils, around those conference tables you could drop a UH-34D onto, this program was known as "Phase II." Or, in the lexicon of the moment: "sustained reprisal." The previous November, a Working Group had provided for such a ratcheting upward of their responses: Phase I, in which you slap them back hard after they've come at you. Phase II, in which you begin programmatic bombing, albeit in a scrupulous and moral and controlled and exact-target kind of way.

That same morning, January 27, the secretary of defense talked over Vietnam with McGeorge Bundy, the president's special assistant for national security affairs. It has to be said here emphatically that if Robert McNamara led the American interventionist parade in the first half of 1965, his White House colleague, Mac Bundy, was at the front of the march, too. His fingerprints are on so many crucial documents. These two civilian policymakers, bearing so much burden for the doomed war, share many personality traits. Both of them are a study in the meritocracy unleashed. But there were and are key differences. If the secretary of defense was a Calvinist from pleasure-seeking California by way of the industrial Midwest, then the White House special assistant was the aristocrat, a Brahmin, the eastern egghead insider whose father had graduated from Yale and was first man at Harvard law. Mac Bundy had come to *his* arrogances by birthright. In 1962, when Kennedy was king, a hagiographer wrote of the keeper of the realm: "Bundy is a sandy-haired, bespectacled man with green eyes and brown hair, who stands five feet ten inches in height and weighs around 160 pounds. 'Aggressive' and 'brilliant' are adjectives that journalists have overworked in describing him. Business-like and self-assured, he works at breakneck pace, then relaxes with a game of tennis. Bundy used to travel to his destinations in Cambridge on a bicycle. He is fluent in French and Spanish, reads German, and commands an elementary knowledge of Russian."

The special assistant liked keeping notes with pencils or pens that held the thinnest possible leads and points; he would draw little squares and rectangles on his notepad. These squares and rectangles would be made up of dozens of incredibly tiny lines. They looked like the fine mesh of screen-door patches.

He possessed a pithy way with words in memorandums: If the South Vietnamese politicians "will only pull up their socks." Any attempt at a negotiated American withdrawal from Vietnam "would mean surrender on the installment plan."

Like McNamara, he had arrived at the beginning, having given up his Harvard deanship as McNamara had given up his monthlong auto presidency. After November 22, 1963, both had stayed on to serve the new president, and by 1965 Bundy's position with the coarse Texan had seemed to solidify. It had taken Bundy far longer to make it with LBJ in the dreams and schemes of the Great Society. Possibly the president didn't like him very much even now, Bundy embodying so much of LBJ's paranoia about easterners, but it's clear from the documents that he was listening to what his pinched and brilliant and French-speaking in-house egghead said.

George Ball, the dove of Vietnam, the man wise almost all along on the war, got at some of the difference between the two men in his memoirs, *The Past Has Another Pattern:* ". . . in any group where Robert McNamara was present, he soon emerged as a dominant voice. I was impressed by his extraordinary self-confidence. . . . Once he had made up his mind to go forward, he would push aside the most formidable impediment that might threaten to slow down or deflect him from his determined course." What Ball was saying is that there seemed no particular need for Mac Bundy to crush somebody in a meeting. Bundy's style was subtler.

Ball told me in an interview that after the Gulf of Tonkin charade (his word) there had been a key meeting in which he had bested McNamara in front of the president. In Ball's memory, McNamara glared at him as they were leaving. McNamara refused to speak. Ball had taken issue in the meeting with what the secretary had proposed, and the president had seemed confused. He had turned to McNamara: "We won't go ahead with it, Bob. Let's put it on the shelf." Ball, recounting this: "It was clearly a competition for the president's heart and mind." He had won, that day. He should have won far more often. But one of Ball's problems, as he was the first to admit, was that he could never talk as fast as Robert McNamara, or Mac Bundy, either. Most times he just thought better, which is to say wiser. Most times, he thought better than the whole hot-eyed herd of them—which isn't to make him the unalloyed saint of Vietnam. Ball had his own compromises, too, his own buyings-in, as the documents reveal.

On January 27, the day McNamara met McNaughton at the Pentagon before eight o'clock, and on the same day that McNamara and

Bundy agreed that something must be done immediately on Vietnam, Bundy wrote a memo to the president under his and the defense secretary's name. Among scholars of the war, this piece of paper is known as the "Fork in the Y Memo," and it contained sentences like these:

> What we want to say to you is that both of us are now pretty well convinced that our current policy can lead only to disastrous defeat. . . . Bob and I believe that the worst course of action is to continue in this essentially passive role, which can only lead to eventual defeat. . . . *We see two alternatives.* The *first* is to use our military power in the Far East and to force a change of Communist policy. The *second* is to deploy all our resources along a track of negotiation, aimed at salvaging what little can be preserved. . . . Both of us understand the very grave questions presented by any decision of this sort. We both recognize that the ultimate responsibility is not ours. . . . But we are both convinced that . . . the time has come for harder choices.

Harder choices. LBJ met the two at noon that day. "Stable government or no stable government, we'll do what we have to do—we will move strongly. I'm prepared to do that," Johnson said. He also decided in this meeting to send Bundy to South Vietnam for a firsthand report. Bundy wrote a thank-you to Johnson, sounding like the grateful son at being trusted with so important a national mission. He left Andrews on February 2. McNamara lent him a plane. McNaughton of the Defense Department was in the traveling party and was to help compose the reports.

On February 7, in the middle of the night, while Bundy and party were in Saigon, the Communists attacked the U.S. installation at Pleiku. They had served up a fat opportunity for the urge that was already blinking on in men. "Pleikus are like streetcars," Bundy said some while after to a reporter, meaning that you jump onto one when you need it. Pleiku was the third assault on a U.S. target in three months, and this time there would be swift American retaliation.

Over the next several days there was a flurry of National Security Council meetings. McNamara was ill with a fever, and there was even a report he had gone to a hospital, but he made the meetings. In the second of these meetings, following the somewhat ineffectual Pleiku retaliation, the secretary of defense urged restraint when some others around the table weren't urging it. This should be paid note, because a

lot of McNamara's generals would have put in for a carpet-bombing of
the north.

Shrilled an MGM *News of the Day* newsreel: "A failure to respond
would be taken as a sign of weakness or defeatism. . . . There is no
intention to spread the war. At the same time there are limits to the
patience with which this country will take provocation without
responding to it."

Bundy arrived back from Vietnam with his report, and *go* was all
over it: "The prospect in Vietnam is grim. . . . The stakes in Vietnam are
extremely high. The American investment is very large, and American
responsibility is a fact of life which is palpable. . . . At its very best the
struggle in Vietnam will be long. It seems to us important that this fundamental fact be made clear and our understanding of it be made clear
to our people and to the people of Vietnam." Johnson would disregard
that last part. And the president's men would go along.

Three days following Pleiku, the Vietcong hit a U.S. Army barracks
at Qui Nhon, killing twenty-three Americans and wounding twenty-
one. Once again the president called an emergency NSC session in the
Cabinet Room. The meeting was at 2:10 on the afternoon of February
10. This time McNamara, speaking for the Joint Chiefs and the Defense
Department, recommended immediate reprisal. No notes of restraint.
He also sought a sustained-bombing program. According to the declassified notes, "Secretary McNamara said . . . we will soon be facing the
difficulty of taking Phase II actions even though there are no incidents
created by the Viet Cong. However, the Qui Nhon attack provides us an
opportunity today to retaliate immediately." As Vietnam scholar
William Conrad Gibbons has written: "In other words, McNamara was
advising the president that the Qui Nhon incident should be used as
the occasion for beginning Phase II. . . ." In other words: opportunity
looking for pretext.

From the minutes of NSC Meeting No. 548: "Mr. McGeorge Bundy
said that at an appropriate time we could publicly announce that we
had turned a corner and changed our policy but that no mention should
be made now of such a decision."

"Look, get this straight," Bundy afterward warned his older brother,
William Bundy, another key player in these decisions (he was assistant
secretary of state for the Far East), "the president does not want this
depicted as a change of policy."

It was in one of those NSC meetings, over these four days, following the streetcars of Pleiku and Qui Nhon, that the secretary of defense

ran over George Ball. The man of action had made up his mind; Ball represented an impediment to what must be done. Soviet Premier Aleksei Kosygin was temporarily in Hanoi, and Ball (along with Vice President Humphrey and Senator Mike Mansfield) had voiced concern in one of the meetings about the efficacy of launching air attacks during the Russian's visit. Wrote Ball in his memoirs: "Bob McNamara brushed these caveats aside. I was, he protested, trying to block our retaliatory raid, not merely postpone it (which, in fact, was true). There would never be a perfect moment to begin bombing: someone could always find an objection and time was of the essence. We had to show immediately that we were reacting to the Viet Cong attack. It was the quintessential McNamara approach." David Halberstam, in *The Best and the Brightest,* wrote: "McNamara, the ripper now, his own doubts having disappeared, could not afford to lose an argument, or even express partial doubt. . . ."

But had his doubts disappeared? Or did it only appear so?

On February 12, James Reston, having gotten wind of developments, said in his column in the New York *Times:* "The first casualty in every shooting war is commonsense and the second is free and open discussion. . . . The big black limousines arrive and depart from the White House. Brief statements are issued by press officers on the latest military operations and casualties. . . . The least the president can do is to go before the country and explain his objectives."

On February 15, 1965, Bundy recorded McNamara as saying: "We should have a military action soon. to get off tit-for-tat kick." Next to the words Bundy drew a one-inch-by-one-inch screen-door patch made up of several hundred exquisitely thin lines. The next afternoon, in a meeting with the president and several others, Bundy turned and said to McNamara, "How much more do you need to carry out our decision [to begin sustained bombing of the north]?" McNamara: "Nothing." Both McNamara and Bundy advised the president to release a public statement. Nothing doing.

Friday, February 26: a meeting to discuss a sixty-seven-page, single-spaced "dissent" memo by George Ball. The paper had been written the previous October and had already been argued down by McNamara and others. Years later, in an oral history, Ball remembered that when the paper was passed around, "McNamara, in particular, was absolutely horrified. He treated it like a poisonous snake." And in his memoirs Ball wrote: "Bob McNamara in particular seemed shocked that anyone would challenge the verities in such an abrupt and unvarnished manner and implied that I had been imprudent in putting such doubts on paper."

The president himself had never read this lengthy get-out-of-Vietnam memo, not until now. But now it was late winter, and everything was in the go-mode for sustained bombing. Why hadn't the president seen the memo earlier? The answers aren't clear, although Ball has told historians and biographers—and has also suggested it in his own writings—that the timing never seemed right. And then, too, the memo had been so loudly shouted down by his colleagues several months before. In any case LBJ held a special session on February 26 to discuss the four-month-old paper, which sought to mount arguments against every major assumption held on Vietnam. Again, from Ball's memoirs, which like most memoirs are self-serving: "That he had studied it was clear; he challenged specific points I had made and even remembered the page numbers where those arguments occurred. I outlined my position, and Secretary McNamara responded with a pyrotechnic display of facts and statistics to prove that I had overstated the difficulties we were now encountering, suggesting at least by nuance, that I was not only prejudiced but ill-informed."

Is it possible a defense secretary so pyrotechnically sure on the outside was feeling something different at his interior? Could the man with so large a need to prevail at the big tables have been leaking to his colleagues with the least secret fear? Every now and then, in the documents, you get that sense. On February 16, in a memo to the president, Bundy wrote: "When you were out of the room yesterday, Bob McNamara repeatedly stated that he simply has to know what the policy is so that he can make his military plans and give his military orders." Bundy spoke of a "deep-seated need for assurance." Was he speaking generally—or of McNamara? Is it possible that Bundy in his own way was using McNamara as a wedge to get sustained bombing started as soon as possible? Yes, it's possible. Anything's possible. The truth is so hard to know from pieces of paper. Documents are evanescent, they're only words on a page, cryptic notes in a tiny hand, they'll never deliver the emotion behind the emotion.

But here is a sheen of memory. A decade ago, in Princeton, New Jersey, I spent an afternoon probing an elderly and soft-talking and quite gracious George Ball on McNamara's pyrotechnics. I was to go back to Ball's home several times after that, but on this day Ball told me a story I'd heard parts of before, had even read of in books, but never with such vividness as now.

"One of the very oddest things I can recall from that whole period is the—what would I call it?—almost schizophrenia of his views after one of my dissent memos. I'd write one, and Bob and Mac Bundy and the president and of course Dean [Rusk] would be the only ones to see them. Well, almost invariably I'd get a call the next day, sometimes even the same day, from the Pentagon, and Bob himself is on the line and he's saying, 'I'd like to come right over and see you.' Now I was the junior man theoretically, I should have been coming to see him. But no, he'd insist on coming to my office. He often brought along McNaughton. And the two of them would be wringing their hands. 'Gee, George, you're right, everything you say here is exactly the case. The war is going nowhere but down a rat hole, we've got to find a way to get out.' Et cetera, et cetera. And you know what? The next day, in a meeting with the president at the White House, there'd be not a trace of what had gone on the day before. The first time that happened I wondered if I were dreaming. 'Did I make up that scene yesterday?' I mean, here was Bob, twenty-four hours before, telling me, 'George, you're right, and John here has been writing some of these same things. Of course he's not going as far as you are in his conclusions. But fundamentally we're in principal agreement with you, George.' And the next day, before the president, nothing. It was as if the day before had been canceled."

On February 26, 1965, with systematic bombing of the north scheduled to begin at the earliest moment, the secretary of defense blew past the undersecretary of state. The White House diary indicates McNamara and Ball left the meeting at 8:35 p.m. It doesn't say whether they left together or if they spoke on the way out. (Ball couldn't recall.) According to the diary, the president himself was far from retiring. At 8:50 he told the White House operator to call the garage and get his car to "pick up Mr. and Mrs. Edward Clark and Mr. and Mrs. Denius at the Carlton Hotel and bring them in the South entrance and tell them to go to the sitting room in the mansion." At 9:10 his daughter Lynda Bird joined him. At 11:25 he ordered dinner. At 1:30 a.m. the president went to bed, or so recorded his calendar-keepers.

A helo squadron, green in several ways, had been in Vietnam nine days. A war photographer for *Life,* who had big balls, who had shot bullfighting in Spain with Hemingway and had toured England with Billy Graham, was rolling over in his mind then the idea of doing a long photo essay on an American military unit. He wasn't sure which unit. But he knew he believed in the American commitment. Then he did.

* * *

MIDDLESBORO is in southern Kentucky, just over the Tennessee line. Jim Farley was born there in the early fall of 1943. The family legend is that his mother's people came into nearby Harlan County in covered wagons. It was the ones on Farley's mother's side who were the hillbillies noted for their cussedness (his grandmother is said to have buried four husbands and kept on walking), while the other half, which produced the military men, were a more intellectual and equivocal Yankee bunch.

The latter-day Farleys don't seem to know much about their paternal side. What they know is that James C. Farley, Sr., grew up in a Pennsylvania orphanage, served with Patton in World War II, fell in love with a no-nonsense woman. "He was very mild-mannered at home," reports the eldest son. "I remember him trying to kill a chicken country style, you know, wringing their neck. Three twists and a jerk. . . . Dad couldn't do it. That was a big family joke for a while."

After the soldier-father died, his namesake began to experience sinus and respiratory problems. Drainage from his sinuses would drive him awake at night. James couldn't seem to keep food down. He would be so nauseous in the morning he couldn't eat. "Take him to a dry climate," the doctor said. June Farley had a brother named Walter Roberts in Arizona.

In Arizona, the no-nonsense Kentucky widow with three young children met a widower with two young children. Soon the two families got together. But it wasn't a contract made in heaven. June Farley and Al Grenier found property on the east side of Tucson, in the Rincon Hills. They named their patch the Lucky 7 Ranch. It had mesquite and cactus and greasewood. There were a couple of burros and a horse for riding. The widow and the widower had come together out of convenience and need and loneliness, and pretty soon there was a lot of fighting at the Lucky 7. The sensitive-cum-angry eldest son with the respiratory problems studied violin, served Mass, rode his bike and the horse, got into fistfights, lassoed snakes in the arroyos with his half brother, Jerry. Increasingly, he felt lost in a bickering parental shuffle. Increasingly, his mother and stepfather found they couldn't control him. June Farley Grenier decided to send her son to a Christian Brothers academy in Santa Fe, New Mexico.

Farley: "My mom said she'd lost control and by God somebody was going to get control of me." But the next year there wasn't enough money to send him back to the Christian Brothers, and besides James had broken lunch trays over the heads of some fellow students, and so the religious brothers of Santa Fe weren't so keen to have him back anyway. Farley: "High school, when I think back, was basically a fight. If I wasn't physically fighting, I was angry with the teachers."

By his junior year he had dropped out of school in Tucson. By then his mother and stepfather had separated several times. The eldest son was running with a wild bunch, and soon some of the bunch got picked up for burgling a gun store. Farley told me he didn't take part in the burglary but became an accessory after the fact: He was teaching his buddies how to fire the stolen guns when the cops came. His mom and the judge put their heads together and decided that the accessory after the fact should enlist in the Marines, if the Marines would have him. They would. His enlistment was in September 1960, when he turned seventeen, earliest moment he could go. Within four years, he'd be a helicopter crew chief and a lance corporal getting ready for Nam: fast rise. The corps would have done its job and straightened him out.

In Michigan the rocket-risen, forty-four-year-old executive vice president of cars and trucks at Ford Motor Company, who never needed any straightening out, was worrying right then about the rise of a helmet-humped little West German import called a Volkswagen. He was in the midst of preparing a twenty-three-page, single-spaced speech with graphs and charts and schematic evaluations for the company's upcoming Greenbrier Management Conference. The final draft would contain sentences such as: "In our forward programs all of us must give added emphasis to controlling and reducing the tooling and facility investments, engineering costs, and other fixed costs. . . . These costs and their control. . . ." It was all control. Within three months he'd be out of Dearborn and into Camelot.

I once asked Jim Farley about the physical symptoms he seemed unable to control after his father's death. I was trying to get at questions of an eight-year-old's psychosomatic responses to grief. I was trying to get at the idea of tough facades and soft innards, and how someone who may never have been really right for the Marines in the first place got into the corps by chance and circumstance and did with it what he could, until one day when his humanity overwhelmed him. On the day I brought up this question we had gone to lunch at a fish-and-burger joint. I noticed that while I was tearing into my sandwich, having slathered it with ketchup, the rough and brutal ex-Marine was digging little dollops of mustard out of the lid of a mustard jar. He had taken the top off the jar the way you might take the back off a watch. He worked his table knife delicately, retrieving the bit of mustard that was trapped on the inside of the lid. He applied it to his sandwich, cut the sandwich in half, began to eat. I was finished by then.

As to what I had asked about psychosomatic responses to grief, Jim Farley said a little later, stubbing his cigarette: "I don't like to look at the past like that. I don't like to try to figure out some of the reasons connected with my dad's death, or what it did to us. He died. He's dead. That's where I leave it."

AN INSERTION, about some physical things *I* couldn't control.

In the just-spring of 1965, I was twenty-one years old and hermetically sealed away with my doubts and beads and self-absorptions and stomach pains in a Catholic seminary in the Deep South. The place was called Holy Trinity, Alabama. I weighed 135 pounds and had a Marine haircut and also bowels that felt as if they had razor blades in them. My name was Brother Garret. I had been in religious life for seven years, having cast off the world at the age of fourteen. I had another six years of study remaining before my ordination, but what I had come to know by that spring was that I wanted out of the missionary life—and didn't know how to do it. I didn't know how to admit it, least of all to myself, because leaving the seminary, when all of your energies and all of your peers were focused toward the goal of ordination, seemed such a terrible admission of failure.

I won't say I had never heard of Vietnam. But I couldn't have told you where it was located or what America's commitment was there, except perhaps to help a friend in need. Nor do I know how I found that issue of *Life,* since we weren't normally allowed to have any secular literature. But it got into my hands. Maybe the town shopper had brought it home and inadvertently left it in the dining hall for the priests. In any case, I stuck it inside my religious habit and spirited it over to the jakes, which was our name for the cans. I remember looking at an ad for a Daiquiri Collins. I remember looking at the feature on Don Schollander, the eighteen-year-old Olympic phenom who had won four gold medals in swimming in Tokyo and was now enrolled at Yale (as the headline said) as "a bulldog for Old Eli." There was a picture of the muscled swimmer touring campus with his all-America steady, Patience Sherman of Upper Montclair, New Jersey. He had his Yalie blazer on and he had his hands stuck in his pockets and he was throwing back his head in such an easy laugh and the impossibly beautiful Patience of Upper Montclair thought he was swell as hell.

Mostly, though, I looked at the cover story. I looked at it over and over, especially the last shot of a Marine hiding his face against a box. He and I were the same age. He was there, I was here, safe and cloistered and doubt-filled.

Within three months I was gone from Alabama and religious life, though I wouldn't want to suggest that a photograph brought me out, not exactly. I didn't join up; I did the opposite. I finished college, obtained a deferment for grad studies, got summoned for an Army physical, was saved by some old bowel and asthmatic histories, implored a liberal doctor to sign some papers, passed out leaflets for Gene McCarthy, thought of myself as an intelligent and humane liberal. By then it was the darker half of the sixties. I was in my mid-twenties and figured I had the Vietnam thing beat. If you lived in a college town, it was something to be proud of. Then it was.

3 1 6 5 . I N Y P - 8 , Lieutenant Wendell T. Eliason (they call him Eli) turns sideways with a sick smile and falls forward on the cyclic stick. One bullet, two seconds: He's gone.

Third lift. In YP-16, Captain Buck Crowdis, an Okie ex–fighter pilot, takes a round in his leg. The bullet travels through his NATOPS manual (Naval Aviation Training, Operations, Procedures and Systems), which is in a zippered pocket of his pants leg, and keeps on going.

In YP-13, the cockpit glass and the instrument panel have been blown out, and the aircraft's commander, Peter Vogel, has been nicked in the neck. Vogel, realizing a sister ship is in trouble, sets down close. Over the mangled intercom, he tells his crew chief to see what he can do to get the pilot out. The copilot of YP-3, Jim Magel, along with a gunner, Billie Owens, have escaped Yankee Papa 3 and have been helped inside YP-13.

So the crew chief does what he's ordered to do. He might have done it anyway. He runs low. Standing in a foothold and leaning into the cockpit, with his back to fire, he is certain he's staring in at a dead man. Lieutenant Eddy has been shot through the right cheek (he had been looking over his right shoulder when the hit came), and the bullet has exited at his spine, just below his neck, causing an instant shock paralysis. Not that the crew chief has this figured out. He just sees the blood, the hole in the neck. Eddy's shoulder strap is unbuckled and he's limp and across both seats. The officer, who can neither speak nor move, sees the crew chief reach in and turn off the magneto switches, which operate the rotors. He can see the crew chief trying to pull him up and get him through the small window. He can see the crew chief's face, which is as white as paper. Dale Eddy can't communicate, but he can think, and after the crew chief disappears from the cockpit window, he thinks: *I'm going to burn up in this little bitty piece of magnesium. Or get shot again. Or get captured. Okay, so I'll say good-bye.*

But Lieutenant Eddy will shortly be rescued by Major Bennie Mann and the crew of Yankee Papa 2. Years hence the saved man will take his two teenage boys out to California to meet the ex-major who rescued him. And more years hence Dale Eddy of Fort Worth, Texas, will say over the phone to an author who never wore a military uniform or went to a war: "You know, I once went to the picture archives at Time-Life in New York. I wanted to look at the glossy photographs. I saw some of the pictures that weren't published. I can tell you this. As Farley is climbing up the side of the ship, there are no holes in the outer skin of the plane, not that I can see. And when he's up there trying to save me, there are all kinds of holes. In that minute or two, with his back to the fire, he risked everything."

Back in his own ship, with Magel and Owens bleeding on the floor, a crew chief turns sideways from his M-60 and screams, "Get me the first-aid kit!" This caught instant is going to become the cover shot of *Life* magazine, although the editors in New York will screw up the caption. They'll write: "Under fire in Vietnam, two wounded U.S. Marines—one of whom is dying—lie on the floor of the helicopter Yankee Papa 13, while the crew chief shouts, 'My gun is jammed! Cover your side—I'll help with these guys!' "

Quick cut, to the California kitchen and the tense of modern times. "My gun got jammed, that's true. But that's not what I'm screaming. I know what I'm screaming. I'm screaming to Wayne Hoilien to get me the first-aid kit."

At the Vietnam wall, the names James E. Magel and Wendell T. Eliason are etched side by side on panel 1E, line 98. As John Hax has written in the moving unpublished war memoir *Life of Pops,* which he was determined to get down on paper for his wife and grown daughters: "Try as I might, I had to concentrate very hard to keep their loss from being almost abstract. . . . It is still that way when I touch their names on the wall. All that pain, and something has kept me from feeling it. I don't know if it is something I should be guilty about, or whether it is one more thing I have learned about being human." And then, as if speaking for all his squadron mates, Hax ended his account of 3165 with this: "I would not have missed it for anything. That's the guilty truth plainly stated. The year 1965 I can remember almost day by day and some days, like March 31, can almost be remembered hour by hour. The years since I left the Marines have been very happy ones with Lizzy and the four girls, but there are some from which I can now remember nothing at all."

Wayne L. Hoilien's name isn't on the wall, though Vietnam aided in killing him. Early in April 1965, after an ordeal, but before a magazine came out, Farley's gunnery mate—who had been heroic at his gun position that day—wrote home to Viroqua, Wisconsin: "Dear Mom. I want you to buy 10 issues of *Life* next week and keep for me because I cant buy any hear. Theirs going to be a 14 page story on me and another guy. . . . Im pretty excited to think a small town boy like me in a big magazine. Now be sure and get 10 issues. At the end of month plan on going on two days 'R and R' rest and relaxation to Bankock, Thiland, get hotel and just rest. maybe find a girl and just have a good time."

The writer of the letter lived another fifteen Aprils. When he was done with war he went home to Wisconsin and the family farm. On April 7, 1980, a funeral card was handed out to mourners at the Westby Coon Prairie Lutheran Church: "Wayne Lewis Hoilien died suddenly, Friday April 4th at Lutheran Hospital in LaCrosse of a heart attack. He was 35 years, 6 months, and 7 days. . . . He was employed at American Motors in Kenosha for several years. In recent years he farmed and made his home near Bloomingdale, located in Clinton Township, Vernon County." Hoilien's older sister, Jean Peterson, a lifelong rural Wisconsin woman, told me: "I believe the trauma from Vietnam killed him. He drank. He had a heart attack. The combination of hard work and Vietnam, I don't know . . ." She didn't finish the sentence. I tried to say something about hard lives on the land, hard lives in a war. "He liked to be alone," she said.

IN A WAY, it's all there, the unseen webbing, without names, with few particulars, on the front page of the April 2, 1965, edition of the New York *Times*. In Vietnam, the crew chief of YP-13 was recovering, as were his squadron mates. HMM-163 was taking what's known as a maintenance stand-down day. The day before, on the first, some big American bombers and attack aircraft had flown into the flat green valley between the two bloody rice paddies and leveled it with cluster bombs.

At the top of the April 2 *Times,* this two-deck headline: "PRESIDENT ASSERTS STRATEGY ON VIETNAM IS UNCHANGED." Two news stories lower, this smaller headline: "BATTLE IS PRESSED IN DANANG REGION." You could draw a straight downward line between the two pieces. The first, filed by the White House correspondent, reported that the U.S. was planning no far-reaching change in its strategy in Vietnam; and that the president had yesterday insisted (in a surprise five o'clock news conference) that there were no new crucial policy developments in the offing, as had been rumored abroad and around unofficial Washington. The president didn't care what had been rumored. "I know of no division in the American government," he said. "I know of no far-reaching strategy that is being suggested or promulgated." But it was a lie wide as the Mississippi.

The second story, filed by a *Times* foreign correspondent out of Saigon, gave a sketchy description of the ambush during the troop-ferrying mission up north two days before: "Two of the three armed American helicopters downed by ground fire . . . have been recovered. One Marine helicopter remained in the rice paddy where it had fallen. The losses were the heaviest taken by United States helicopter crews in one engagement, with two Marine officers killed and seventeen Army and Marine officers and enlisted men wounded." There were no names listed. No mention of a lance corporal named Farley, no photographs of his box. (Larry Burrows's film hadn't even been shipped to Hong Kong yet, first stop on the way to Time Inc. in New York. Early issues of the magazine wouldn't be out for about another ten days. If *Life* had never come out, this would have been just one more war story.)

The front page of the *Times* on April 2 also had a story on Helena Rubinstein, dead at ninety-four. Also a story about LBJ borrowing money to pay his income-tax bill. Also a photograph of a Negro's fire-bombed home in Birmingham. The beatings of Selma and the March to Montgomery had lately happened. The struggle for civil rights was that other erupting war in America threatening LBJ's plans and dreams for a Great Society.

Readers of the *Times* had been unwittingly duped. The policymakers had just officially turned Vietnam from a defensive conflict into an offensive one. The mission of American ground forces had just been changed from protection of U.S. air bases to active combat. America was now embarked on a land war in Asia, although it wouldn't be until midsummer that this land war would be acknowledged in any official way. As Vietnam scholar Brian VanDeMark has summarized the significance of this moment in his carefully researched 1991 book, *Into the Quagmire:* "U.S. ground forces would now directly enter the war. . . . The course of American involvement had shifted dramatically. . . . With these decisions, LBJ had carried the United States, unmistakably, across the line from advisory support to war in Vietnam."

The document that allowed these things to happen is known in the scholarship as NSAM-328 (National Security Action Memorandum No. 328). If you went looking for it in the river of 1965 declassified paper, you would be disappointed: It's bland as can be. As VanDeMark has written, the decisions of NSAM-328 got "framed in the evasive and misleading language of a president fearful of their domestic political consequences." But the meaning behind the evasive words wasn't evasive at all. And the lies that flowed out of the document, as policymakers strove to protect its secrecy, could fill up rooms.

It was three pages long and what it did was codify the president's latest deceptions. At the moment of the two April 2 *Times* headlines—the one at the top about strategies unchanged; the one a little farther down about an unnamed and ambushed helo squadron—the decisions of the document hadn't yet been committed to paper. But that was only a bureaucratic delay. The decisions themselves had been made and approved. They were made and approved in two meetings—on April 1 and April 2—and the more important and supposedly off-the-record meeting began literally minutes after the president had stood before cameras in the White House theater late on the first and told a roomful of reporters: "I know of no far-reaching strategy that is being suggested or promulgated." The president said that and then walked to the Cabinet Room where McNamara, Rusk, Bundy, and six other decision-makers waited for him. There they took up the decisions that would become NSAM-328.

What was approved in the meetings of April 1 and 2, in addition to a relatively mild upping of troop numbers, was the overarching decision to sanction offensive war. In the document it would be described as "a change of mission." A change of mission "for all Marine battalions deployed to Vietnam to permit their more active use under conditions to be established and approved by the secretary of defense in consultation with the secretary of state." Several days later the document would be put on fancy stationery embossed at the top with "The White House / Washington." Thirteen years later, in 1978, the historians would get the piece of paper declassified.

As the makers of the 1983 thirteen-episode public-television series *Vietnam: A Television History* have said: "A U.S. president for the first time had authorized ground troops for offensive operations in Vietnam."

In the language of LBJ's National Security Council: ". . . to change the mission of our ground forces in South Vietnam from one of advice and static defense to one of active combat operations against the Viet Cong. . . ."

In for a dime, in for a dollar.

Almost from the dropping of the first bombs on the north, in the February days of their secret Phase II meetings, there had been the escalating pressure to commit ground forces. Thirty-five hundred Marines had landed on the beach on March 8, and, yes, their orders were strictly limited: to protect the airfield at Danang. The mission was defensive. But it was a mud slide. Nine days after this landing, General Westmoreland cabled the policymakers asking for another BLT (Marine Battalion Landing Team), this time to guard the helo base at Phubai. Two days after that, Admiral Ulysses S. Grant Sharp, who was commander of American forces in the Pacific, and Westmoreland's superior, supported Westmoreland's request and moreover asked for another battalion for Danang. The following day the Joint Chiefs recommended to McNamara that two divisions from America and one from South Korea go to Vietnam.

Like that, the thing had acquired a life of its own.

In the secret papers of March, as opposed to the documents of February, the words "combat deployments" are everywhere.

"Where are we going?" the president said to McNamara, Rusk, and Bundy during his weekly Tuesday luncheon in the second-floor dining room on March 23. Bundy, taking notes in the vernacular, had the screen-door patches all over the page. "Do they know we're willin to talk," LBJ said. At the bottom of Bundy's notes, this from the president: "I was a hell of a long time gettin into this. But I like it."

Eight days later, on April 1, the decision to begin an offensive war was officially made and approved. "If we can first get our feet on their neck," LBJ told his faithful in that meeting. "We have set our hand to the wheel," he said. A moment later: "payin enough money—payin enough information. we got to find em & kill em." Once again, Bundy had taken the notes, and apparently they are the only notes that exist, or at least that have ever come to light.

Under Point 11 of the written document No. 328: "The president desires . . . premature publicity be avoided by all possible precautions. The actions themselves should be taken as rapidly as practicable, but in ways that should minimize any appearance of sudden changes in policy, and official statements on these troop movements will be made only with the direct approval of the Secretary of Defense, in consultation with the Secretary of State."

Even before the decisions could be put down on paper, on April 6, the president directed McNamara to go ahead with a two-division combat deployment. Scheduling battalions of troops for Vietnam was one thing, but making plans to deploy two *divisions* of fighting forces was big potatoes. On April 5, the secretary of defense told the chairman of the Joint Chiefs to proceed on "earliest practicable introduction of 2-3 Div into SVN."

It's one level of mendacity to deceive the press and the American people about what you're doing; it's another to deceive the chairman of the Senate Foreign Relations Committee in a closed executive session. On April 7, McNamara and George Ball went up to Capitol Hill and did that. The chairman of the committee was J. William Fulbright, Democrat from Arkansas, whom Lyndon Johnson would take to calling "Senator Halfbright," after he had broken bitterly with the administration over its war policies. Almost no one noticed this hearing at the time; it got four lines in the New York *Times* the next day.

The front-page news was the president himself, who choppered up to Johns Hopkins University in Baltimore on the evening of the seventh and delivered a major televised speech on Vietnam. (It was seen or heard by an estimated 60 million people.) Holding out the carrot, LBJ proposed a vast new United Nations development program in Southeast Asia: a kind of TVA on the Mekong River. On the way back, he got an aide by the pant knee, leaned in, and said, "Old Ho can't turn that down. Old Ho can't turn that down." But old Ho could, old Ho did.

Formally, the Fulbright hearing on Capitol Hill on April 7, with McNamara and Ball as the witnesses, concerned appropriations. The first part was a public hearing and dealt with the proposed fiscal year 1966 foreign-aid-authorization bill. But afterward, Fulbright and his

fellow senators went into an executive session with McNamara and
Ball, and it was then that the subject of Vietnam and rumored troop
increases and new policy decisions arose. At one point the testimony
went off the record, so that even the official stenographers from Ward &
Paul, 917 G Street Northwest, were made to leave the room—or so it
seems from the internal evidence. From the exchange that takes place
when things are back on the record, it's clear that certain numbers were
given to the senators by the secretary of defense, though not *the*
planned-for numbers of April 5 (which is to say the two to three divisions of combat troops). And apparently nothing at all about the change
of mission from passive security of bases to the active combat now
sanctioned by NSAM-328. Nothing about the tremendous war corner
that had just been turned. And more than this, to judge from the transcript itself, a deliberate and skillful mislead, to slide the talk toward an
approved 18,000- to 20,000-man increase in logistical/support forces
that were also shipping to Vietnam as provided for in the decisions of
April 1 and 2.

NSAM-328 had been typed the day before. McNamara's memo to
the chairman of the Joint Chiefs to go ahead with plans for two to three
combat divisions had been put on paper two days before.

But let the record chart the lie:

> THE CHAIRMAN. BACK ON THE RECORD: . . . It looks now
> as if the administration is assuming that no longer—no fur-
> ther consultation or approval from the congress is necessary
> in view of the resolution of last summer. Is this true, is this
> the attitude?
> SECRETARY BALL: No, Mr. Chairman. I would say that the
> president has every intention of keeping in the closest con-
> sultation with the congress on all moves of this kind.

Farther down:

> THE CHAIRMAN: I don't know what the responsibility of this
> committee is, whether or not we should be kept advised and
> whether or not we should approve. It seems to me we
> should. . . .
> SECRETARY MCNAMARA: Mr. Chairman, may I say that I
> think there is a difference between adding logistical person-

nel, engineer corps personnel of the kind I have outlined, on the one hand, which I do not believe will lead to enlarging the war and, on the other hand, introducing major combat elements such as a division of personnel. I am certain that it will be the president's desire and purpose to consult with the congress, the leadership of the congress, members of this committee, before undertaking any combat moves of personnel that would potentially enlarge the war.

Farther down, Fulbright to Ball:

> THE CHAIRMAN: Would you have anything to enlighten the committee in this respect, Mr. Secretary?
> SECRETARY BALL: Well, I would certainly subscribe to what Secretary McNamara has said, that there would be every intention to consult with the congress on a move which appeared to engage us in a land war in Asia or appear to enlarge the American activity to the point where it could very likely lead to an expansion of the war.

A little farther down:

> SECRETARY MCNAMARA: I think it is important to differentiate between new moves that will influence the course of the war, raise the risk as the chairman mentioned a moment ago. These are not those kinds of moves.

In the spring of 1995, in his critically savaged memoir *In Retrospect,* Robert McNamara wrote that he and the other faithfuls of the Kennedy and Johnson administrations "acted according to what we thought were the principles and traditions of this nation." In his preface he talked about people's "honest mistakes." A couple paragraphs down: "I truly believe that we made an error not of values and intentions but of judgment and capabilities." In the second chapter: ". . . Dean [meaning Rusk] and I, and our associates, gave frequent reports to congress and the press. Were they accurate? They were meant to be." Two chapters from that: "I tried to avoid misleading the public about our progress." On page 180 of this "confession," the author actually—and fleetingly—referred to that particular hearing of April 7, 1965 (he didn't identify the committee or name Fulbright or source it in his endnotes), but, oddly, he decided to quote a line from George Ball's testimony, not his own. He sort of lumped himself in with the mendacity, but put the light on Ball.

In the summer of 1986, twenty-one years after those hearings (which are minor in the scheme of things), I went to see William Fulbright with a set of partially declassified transcripts in my hand. This, of course, was long before McNamara's book came out or, so far as I know, had even been dreamed of. A record of that April 7, 1965, session had been "sanitized" and printed with the public part of the hearings At the time I talked to Fulbright, I was in the process of using the Freedom of Information Act to get committee members to declassify the entire hearing, public and private, including all the portions that had been previously deleted. I was successful, though it took several months. In the meantime, I knew enough about April 7, 1965, to go to Fulbright and ask how he felt these years later about having been flatly lied to. Because even the sanitized versions of the executive session, which had long been available to researchers, gave the game away.

Fulbright was eighty-one then: strong mentally, round in the middle, tanned, funny, aphoristic, smaller than I would have guessed, a Southern boy up so many years ago on the morning train from the mountains. He was in a tiny office in a big law firm on Connecticut Avenue. I was in my high righteous dudgeon, because I had transcripts. And what's more, I knew that the unadulterated lies from that hearing would eventually be coming to me courtesy of the Freedom of Information Act.

He sat framed by a water cooler and piles of books. He looked out from behind them with a glassy lizard smile. He croaked like a smart old frog. He wasn't mad at anybody.

"But look at how they deceived you," I said.

He said, shrugging, "You find lots of people in public office who suddenly feel they have this special responsibility to this abstraction we call the state, even if they were quite ordinary people before."

A moment later he said, "Well, Lyndon was a big powerful Texan. You know how Texans are. Power is what they're about. Muscular power if you herded cattle, mental power if you were playing politics. It was primitive and American, not special to Texas, by the way."

A moment later he said: "Well, you get what you deserve finally, don't you?"

A moment later he said, "Well, we're brought up here in this big country thousands of miles from these older countries. . . . We're a parochial people. . . . In a sense you feel sorry for them, given these huge responsibilities they're not prepared for. . . . I'm always torn about it. . . . I think sometimes this system is unworkable. . . . Well, he didn't know a thing, did he—he'd had a great success making cars, the Mustang or whatever, and then he is running the whole military. . . . Then Lyndon comes in, I mean, my God, nobody was ever more parochial than Lyndon, my God, he'd hardly ever been out of the country."

A moment later he said, "My God, I'm just an old fuddy-duddy." (I'd said I was enjoying hell out of my visit.)

A moment later, after I had told him how naïve I had been about the Vietnam War and its policymakers, he said: "Don't feel bad. I was not only naïve, I was ignorant. You see, there was a time in my career, very late, when I felt governments told you the truth, too."

On April 7, 1965, in the republic of Vietnam, Helicopter Marine Medium 163 hauled 48,360 pounds of cargo from Quang Tin province headquarters to Tien Phuoc. A crew chief was back in the air, presumably whole. In a Manhattan skyscraper, editors were madly assembling a knockout story.

WHEN IT HIT STANDS in Tucson, a mom was working on a Holy Thursday outfit for her youngest child. The phone rang. It was a neighbor from church. "June," the neighbor said, "I think you better get over to the grocery quick and buy *Life,* because James is on the cover." When a reporter for the *Citizen* tracked her down that evening, Jim Farley's mother said, "A fella doesn't tell his mother much about the fighting or the girls when he writes home from a place like Vietnam."

The week it came out, a nun in a New Orleans convent—her name was Sister Maura—took a look at the final photo and said, before she could think about it, "No, that's not my brother, my brother doesn't cry like that, that must be somebody else." It was as if even in the instant of saying it, she knew how much she would regret it. (Twenty-nine years later, with many life changes behind her, Marilyn Farley sat in the warming winter sun of a Tucson backyard and told me quietly, "I remember being embarrassed later that I would have been so narrow-minded, that I demeaned my brother, really, demeaned his emotion. . . .")

A student nurse was in her dorm at Winslow Hall on Maple Avenue at the White Plains Hospital School of Nursing in New York. Meg Byrne later sat down and wrote: "Dear Sir, I don't know whether to call you James, Jim, Jimmy, Jas or hunk. I think that I'll settle for Jim. You should never have let *Life* do that spread on you. We girls on the fourth floor have obtained your address from the Dept. of the Navy. You'll probably be receiving quite a few letters like this in the near future."

Yeah, bags. "Answer some of them, Farley," the guys in the squadron said. But he never did. He'd hand them out unopened.

"Dear Jim," wrote somebody who signed her name "Gratefully, Susan": ". . . I want to thank you personally for being in Vietnam. Although I am a girl, I feel as though I can understand in a small way how you must feel. . . . To see a man there only two years older than myself is quite a shock and after seeing the picture I cried because death is so near you all over there but please remember that there is a God who cares."

Wrote Senator John Tower to *Life:* "Larry Burrows' photos are by far the most revealing and powerful that have come from Vietnam. He and *Life* have performed for American citizens a service fully as significant as the service of the men he photographed."

Wrote James B. Gibson of Montreal to *Life:* "I feel that your photographic coverage went beyond those limits laid down by the requirement to inform the public and transgressed laws of common decency. I am left with great pity for the dead copilot's parents who must now witness such blatant advertisement of their dead son."

On the Easter weekend that fourteen pages of photographs in the April 16 edition of *Life* magazine were being studied with dropped jaws, the secretary of defense and his wife were the houseguests of the president and Lady Bird at the LBJ ranch in Texas. On Good Friday—the sixteenth—the president toured them around in his big white Caddy convertible. The wives sat in the backseat with a dog. The quartet inspected the tanks, the family graveyard, the schoolhouse. On Holy Saturday LBJ told forty reporters in the front yard that the "outrage of this country and the world must be visited" on lawless Communist aggressors. Lady Bird forgot to put out the cookies. In Washington, Joan Baez and Judy Collins were appearing with some 15,000 others at a Vietnam "peace protest."

Did the president and his houseguest have *Life* put in front of them by an aide? I've not been able to determine that from any record. But one certainly imagines they saw the essay, that they were appalled, though perhaps for different reasons.

I know this: On Easter Monday, April 19, the defense secretary left Washington for a hastily called high-level conference in Honolulu. The ground-force numbers were about to be upped some more—doubled, in fact. Additionally, there was some internal warring among high players that needed to be patched up. There was a sudden sense of things deteriorating. General Westmoreland flew in from Vietnam, as did Maxwell Taylor, now U.S. ambassador in Saigon, who had gone soft on the idea of escalation. One reason he had gone soft was because he had been flooded with Washington cables since the beginning of April to rush in combat troops, now that NSAM-328 was officially on the books. As Admiral U. S. Sharp later wrote in a bitter book called *Strategy for Defeat:* "In a series of messages, the Secretary of Defense expressed his desire to move ahead quickly with the introduction of U.S. and third-country ground forces and their employment in a combat role." And as McNamara's own commissioned *Pentagon Papers* would later put it: "From April 8 onward, Taylor had been bombarded with messages and instructions from Washington testifying to an eagerness to speed up the introduction to Vietnam of U.S. and Third Country ground forces and to employ them in a combat role, all far beyond anything that had been authorized in the April 2 NSC decisions."

Planeside at Andrews, evening of the nineteenth, the secretary was asked if his quick trip to Hawaii constituted an emergency meeting.

"No, certainly not."

Four times in two minutes, McNamara deflected, dissembled, evaded, misled. To read a two-page transcript of this impromptu conference, to study film clips and audiotapes of it, is to feel in touch with every bright shining deceit about Vietnam. It's not an effortless or cynical kind of lying—no. There's the stammer, the shift of eyes. He keeps telling his auditors of the "logistical support and training and advisory personnel" bound for the war.

> QUESTION: More Americans?
> MR. MCNAMARA: No, principally logistical support—arms, munitions, training, assistance.
> QUESTION: As many as 5,000, sir? We've heard this report.
> MR. MCNAMARA (the sudden look away, the mixed-up sentence): No. Uh. I'm not discussing primarily additional personnel, but primarily this logistical support needed to support the increase in South Vietnamese military strength. . . .

The following day, leaving Hawaii, having nailed down a consensus on the new numbers and having brought Ambassador Max Taylor into line, he does it again, the skillful mislead and deflection. "The number of additional American advisors . . . will not be large. The quantities of equipment, of course, will be very substantial indeed." Inside, toiling in shirtsleeves, the secretary and his men had just raised the recommended numbers of U.S. ground troops from 33,500 to 81,700, an increase of 48,200. As historian VanDeMark has put it, "The number of American troops fighting in Vietnam would jump 150 percent." It had been a strenuous McNamarian workday: After the long overnight flight from the mainland on the evening of the nineteenth, he had shown up at the Pacific Command War Room at 8:30 a.m., carrying his brown travel case stuffed with papers. At 12:20 p.m. the group went to Keehi Lagoon for hamburgers and pineapple salads. He put on a bathing suit and took a four-minute dip.

The memo to the president, written on the nine-hour plane trip home, broke the Honolulu numbers into categories and summarized the conference's other recommendations. The door was left open for "possible later deployments." And yet, this should be emphasized: McNamara's memo closed by urging that Congress be informed of what was going on. LBJ wouldn't buy. A defense secretary would go along.

The sec/def had been to Hawaii and back in less than thirty-six hours.

In *In Retrospect,* McNamara devoted a couple of chunky paragraphs to that Honolulu meeting, but made no mention that he had misled the press. In the fall of 1994, eight months before the book came out, I wrote him a letter, specifically asking about the conference and the deceptions I had studied on archived film and in Pentagon transcripts. I asked how he would reconcile what he had said publicly with what he had done secretly. This letter was one of several more or less frosty exchanges between us in the previous few months. I had written to him proposing that we try to find a way to begin some kind of direct communication again, in that our relationship had long ago lapsed into silence. I was hoping for a face-to-face sit-down interview or interviews, but I was willing to settle for less—written questions, written answers, for instance. Even this didn't materialize. We couldn't agree on how it would be done. He wished to see all the questions ahead of time, with no commitment to answering them. We argued back and forth about it in the mails.

In the end, I submitted three "sample" questions to him, and the 1965 conference at Honolulu was one. I wrote: "I have the documents and public statements in hand, and as a journalist I am able to report the apparent bald discrepancy. But as a journalist, I'd also like to hear your explanation and points of view. It's only fair." It took four months, but I got this reply: "I don't have the documents in front of me and, therefore, I cannot address the issue of specific differences between my reports to the press and the president following the meeting. In general, I can say my reports to the congress and public were meant to be accurate. With hindsight, it is clear the reports on the military situation were often too optimistic. The reports on the political situation—which I always stressed as a precondition for military success—were both more accurate and pessimistic." He closed: "As for further exchanges, I doubt they would be productive. The opening sentences of your letter indicate your approach is basically adversarial." He signed it "Bob" below a close of, "With best wishes for the New Year."

But back to 1965, and its mixed messages: Admiral Sharp, for one, didn't like the summary of views the secretary presented to the president following the conference. Many years later he wrote in his own book of the main points, in which he felt McNamara had summarized not according to veracity but according to McNamara: "The foregoing is, in fact, a distortion of the view I took at that conference. However, as with most conferences that Secretary McNamara attended, the published results somehow tended to reflect his own views. . . ."

Not every reporter beyond the closed Honolulu door was fooled. Some journalists were able to ferret from their sources what had really happened inside: that combat numbers had been seriously raised; that the ground war in the south would now be increased; that the whole nature of the conflict had changed. And, certainly, correspondents in the war zone could see these changes. And yet many newspapers continued to buy and publish the ongoing administration untruth: It was still the ARVN war. As William Conrad Gibbons has summarized it: "On April 22, President Johnson secretly approved the Honolulu recommendations. There was no NSAM, and no public announcement of the decision. For the press and the public, Johnson and his advisers continued to portray the situation as normal, involving no dramatic decisions or changes."

One week before the secretary flew out of Hickam Field in Hawaii, back to the five sides of his power, two wounded Marines from a helo squadron flew into Hickam Field and got decorated with Purple Hearts. Their names were Dale Eddy and Billie Owens. They were on their way to the States and their families. For them, the war was finished. Their C-135 wasn't scheduled to refuel in the islands, but the top officer of the Marines in the Pacific, General Victor Krulak, decided that the plane should be rerouted so he could preside at a small decorating ceremony. When the general pinned the heart on Dale Eddy in the VIP lounge at Hickam, he said, "I hope you'll be proud of your medal. I'm proud of both of mine." In the sense of being physically in the same space, seven days apart, you could say this was as close as any Marine of HMM-163 ever got to Robert S. McNamara in the lie-laden and long-ago just-spring of 1965.

SO THE CREW CHIEF came home. Home to some deceits and old lies and new infamies and big liars in public places. But also home to his own screwups and confusions and weekend drinking binges and misdirected rages, as he now understands.

He got out in 1966. He had been sixteen months in Vietnam, six years in the corps. He won nine air medals and the Silver Star, the latter being the third-highest military decoration that exists for a Marine, behind the Navy Cross and the Congressional Medal of Honor. Of his homecoming Jim Farley once said, "I got a hamburger. My sister paid for it." His story, "One Ride with Yankee Papa 13," had made it into the pages of *Paris Match, Pravda,* a German picture magazine called *Quick.*

At home, a wife he barely knew was divorcing him. He had met her a month or two before leaving for Vietnam. The divorce papers had been mailed to him while he was still in-country. Among the uncontested charges, he says, was the charge of nonsupport. Farley: "No, actually, she comes to mind now and then. Can't picture her too well sometimes. No idea where she is."

He tried some vet groups—and hated it. "They were sitting around feeling sorry for themselves. So I said, 'The hell with this crap.' " He helped put on mock gunfights for the tourists at Jeremiah Greene's Territorial Gunsmith Shop in Old Tucson. He gave awkward talks on his exploits at VA hospitals and Tucson-area schools. Much of this was instigated by his uncle Walter, who loved his nephew and wanted to watch out for him on choppy civilian seas but was also getting some reflected glory out of it. It was Uncle Walter who pushed his nephew toward an ill-fated singing performance at a VA hospital. James froze, forgot everything.

Farley: "Oh, it's not all bad. Somebody forces you into some things you might not ordinarily try. It's not all bad. Sometimes you surprise yourself. . . . I am a good teacher. I am a good singer. The thing there, I got scared off of it."

Coeds flung themselves at him. Were they in love with a black-and-white abstraction?

He taught remedial bilingual reading to sixth- and seventh-graders. "I love working with young children," he told a reporter, "but it can be a rat race." In the summer of 1969, working toward his bachelor's in elementary ed, he was a counselor at a camp for Chicano kids. One day he took the kids out to Old Tucson, and the local reporter tagged along. There was a nice-sized feature. But somehow his el-ed adviser at the university got the idea the vet was trying to engineer publicity for himself at the expense of the Chicano kids. The vet blew up. He threatened the adviser, standing over him with his bulk and his voice. He swore and walked out, not just of the guy's office, of the school. College was done. They could have it. But the more complicated truth may be that Farley had discovered by now he didn't want to be a teacher anyway. Relatives and others had pushed him toward it, and he had gone along, done what he could.

He got married again, this time to Jane Bonner, who had a daughter of her own named Carmen from another marriage. The university dropout, needing dough, opened a repair garage. He could do cars, he knew that. His mother helped stake him to the purchase of the place. Presently, Jane Bonner and Jim Farley had a child of their own. They named her Lorie. Presently, the couple was fighting a lot in front of their children. "I think it was because of Vietnam," Jane said much later to a reporter. "It was not in his personality to be violent." The repair garage at Swan and Speedway went into the ground.

They moved to Idaho, thinking they would try again. (Some of his wife's people were from up there.) But things went lousy. The vet found work as a warehouseman, operating forklifts. It was a job. On weekends there were opaque hours in front of the TV set. "He would startle easily," Jane was to tell *People* magazine. He blackened her eye in his sleep. Once, when the fighting and the night sweats grew particularly bad, he started walking down the middle of a freeway, hoping to be struck by a tractor trailer.

Shamed, angry, broke, the hero of YP-13, so good with kids, medals in a bottom drawer, lit out for California. There was another uncle on his mother's side, Wilburn Roberts, who lived in the Bay Area and was said to own a hydraulics firm. The vet made it to the Bay with $25 in his pocket. Uncle Wilburn took him in, and although the mechanically inclined nephew proved to be adroit at hydraulics, the two had trouble getting along. They kept trying. After his uncle died, Farley took over the firm. But the problem was, he didn't know how to manage a company; he knew how to design hydraulics.

Now and then magazines and papers and TV crews hunted him up, and he seemed willing to have his picture taken, his story told. In 1979, *Life* did a catch-up feature. In most of these where-are-they-now pieces, there was a not so subtle undercurrent: Hey, Jim, give us all of your posttraumatic stress, huh? He seemed both humble and hyperbolic. In one piece, he told the reporter, "My mother and grandmother always taught me to do the best with what you have. Some people have more crosses than others and you have to do the best you can while living with them. I'm not fulfilled, but I hope to get there."

In the *Life* piece (his segment was brief, but it opened the story), the man who looked on the outside like an aging hippie, or maybe somebody in a California motorcycle gang, posed with his daughters, Lorie and Carmen. He held them tenderly; a warm smile fought to get through. The piece was subtitled "The Unforgettable Faces of Vietnam—Then and Now." That same year, 1979, a bad movie sequel called *More American Graffiti* came out. One of the characters, headed for the Nam, tells friends he's going to "kick ass, take names, eat Cong for breakfast." Pretty soon he's down on the floor of a transport helicopter, bent over a comrade who's bleeding to death. The scene in the movie was such a cheap rip-off of what had been published fourteen years earlier in *Life,* and the Farley-like character bore no similarity to the real Jim Farley.

One day the real Jim Farley had a kind of epiphany, though that wouldn't be his word. Farley: "I can't remember when it was, but I can see it. Cool day and the sun is shining and I went out to get warm and said, 'Hey, you better knock this shit off.' "

He became president of a second company, Applied Hydrostatics of Oakland. It too eventually failed, but the man himself had begun to fail less. And somewhere in here—so many of the dates remain a blur—he met dark-haired Mary Mallon of Ireland. She was twenty-three and from County Monaghan and her father was a victualler, which is to say he had a meat shop. The hydraulics man was trying to live on accounts receivable, but on the other hand he was tooling around in a 914 mid-engine Porsche. There was something dangerous and gentle about him. "I think it was the Porsche and the green card," Mary Mallon said later, trying to figure her instant attraction. In a way there wasn't anything to explain. She was the no-nonsense Irish woman with a yen for excitement, much his junior, abhorrent of violence, who didn't mind taking hold of the reins, in the same way that there had once been a no-nonsense and big-hearted Kentucky hillbilly woman named June Roberts who had fallen headlong for a small-boned gentle soldier named James C. Farley.

Anyway, the vet chased her to Ireland in his wild hair and cowboy boots. Mary Mallon's father liked him fine and got him drunk on the local moonshine, known as poteen, made out of potatoes. He must have passed the test. He married Mary in 1985, and although money was still a struggle, and although his back had begun to give out on him, his life seemed to travel upward nearly from that moment. In 1990, just before the vet's forty-seventh birthday, the two had a son. It was as if no father on the planet had ever had a son before.

WE'RE ON OUR WAY to Orange County to visit Colonel Norm Ewers. It just came up. I had located the colonel the day before, found out he was retired and living in a garden condominium close to the old Marine air station where 163 had first mustered its men for Vietnam in the fall of 1963. Farley hasn't seen his CO in twenty-nine years. He's nervous as a cat on a slick rock. How do you address an old skipper, anyway?

The day before, in Farley's kitchen, the phone rang and it was the colonel. (I had set it up as a surprise early that morning from my hotel room.) "Oh Jesus, not you. Wow. How are you? I'll be damned," Farley said, nearly blurting it. He had a cigarette, he was pacing.

He said, "Oh, not bad, not bad. I'm trying to get off disability at the moment. Doesn't look too good. What's that? Oh, I took a fall on board a ship. Oil skimmer. Going down into the engine room and ended up breaking the vertebrae. So now I don't move from the rib cage to the hips. . . . What the hell, I'll find something else to do."

A moment later: "You're seventy? You're too young to be retired."

Before the call came, Farley and I had spoken again of his back problems. "They're talking two more operations. To fuse the L5S1, and then an operation to take the steel pins out. The L5S1 is the lowest flex-ible vertebra. The doctor said he should have fused it along with the others. That's it. They ain't cutting my stomach open again. Screw that. Of course I may reconsider. If the pain gets bad enough."

He said it and then ratcheted himself down with a paper towel to wipe coffee stains off the floor. "If I don't get these brown stains off, Mary will have a piece of me tonight," he said.

Mary Mallon Farley had told me at the outset of my visits to Castro Valley that she didn't wish to be directly involved: It's Jim's life, she said. I felt nervous around her at first, afraid she might try to talk her husband out of participating in this book. Mary is a warm and yet direct person who wants what anybody would want: to protect her family. On my first visit, Mary and Jim and Matthew and I had gone out to a restaurant. Jim got up from the table and took his son for a walk. He said he needed to stretch his back. While they were gone, I tried to say something to Mary about her husband's decency. I was trying to win her over.

"Well, that's right," she said. "Because I know what's underneath. There's all this tough stuff, and this talk, but underneath. . . ." She shrugged, as if to say: It's all there in that photograph you seem to admire so much.

On the plane to southern California, Farley said: "She was the kind of wife I was looking for all along. Someone who knew what they wanted, and could go after it." In the air, Mary's husband kept swallowing and corking open his mouth.

I asked what kind of officer Ewers was. "He was with his men. Pride in the corps. Pride in what you do."

At John Wayne Airport, we got the rental car and drove into the parking lot of the condominium. The colonel lived only ten minutes from the field. Now it was as if neither of us wanted to go through with it. Farley said, "Let's walk up and down here a little bit, Paul." He was sucking in a cig.

The colonel's front-door knocker featured a golf motif. A trim, balding, smallish man in wire rims answered. He peered at us. He was tanned. "Let's see, let's see now, which one of you is Farley?" he said. Twenty-nine years earlier, on March 29, 1965, two days before Black Wednesday, Farley had crew-chiefed the colonel's ship. They had flown together a good deal after that, too.

We took seats on a sofa in the den. Everything was tidy and stowed away. "I got elected to the Marine Corps," Farley said. "I don't think you were alone," Ewers laughed. He was in golf slacks, seated in a black swivel chair.

I asked where that day bumps up in his Marine memory.

"The max thing. I'll never forget it. Every March 31st comes around, I think about it. I think about these guys who died."

His grip tightened on the armrests of his chair. "I've had drinks with men in the squadron who were wounded. I've corresponded with the families. I've never forgotten it. . . . These were two young officers. . . . I wrote a condolence letter to Magel's family. I tried to say what they died for."

He was choking, and yet the recovery was swift. He turned to Farley. "I wanted you guys to see me—do as I do, act as I act. Then everything'll be all right."

He asked me what another word for "humane" is.

"Compassionate?" I said.

"Yes. In that same context, I was not as compassionate as I later wished I was."

I said, "But, sir, you were just breaking up a second ago—"

He cut in, "Yeah, but you've got to communicate that. In retrospect, I did some things that were kind of chickenshit."

"Were you hiding things you felt for them?" I asked.

"Not consciously."

I listened to them bat names around: Ken Tiger, Bones Wright, Shadow Wilson. After an hour, we drove out to the air station for lunch at the officers' club. I sat in the back of the colonel's car, which looked like it had just come from the showroom. Farley was pointing out scenery. "Yeah, our barracks were over there. And there's the theater. And, Norm, they used to have the dispensary over there. Hell, I used to ride my motorcycle through these orange groves." The *Norm* had fallen out.

I tried to reprise a subject I had brought up in the colonel's den: their feelings about McNamara. At his home Ewers had said, "I feel sorry for him. I think he made mistakes and knows it. . . . A brilliant mind." I had hoped for little cluster bombs of anger. The truth is, I'd never really seen that much anger toward McNamara from Farley, either, though once, early in our interviews, he'd said, "He was ass over teakettle backwards. That whole political premise is not the way to fight a war. You either fight or you don't friggin fight." And another time he'd said, "The body count was a farce. . . . Screw that bullshit. You're out there to kill people and destroy supplies and by God do it or get out." But I remember him saying right after this that he didn't hold personal grudges against McNamara, and if I was looking for that, I was probably climbing the wrong trees. I felt a kind of reproof.

Now, from the backseat, I said to the colonel: "Do you mean that you feel sorry for McNamara because he knows he gave the president bad advice and it torments him?"

"Yes."

In the officers' club, which had a kind of forlorn feel, the colonel snapped open a yellow paper menu. He scanned the contents. "Mmm, chicken salad," he said, "I think that would be good." We agreed.

"This base is on the closure list. Sad," the colonel said.

I asked if he goes to movies about Vietnam. No, he said. "Well, not for me, really, more for my wife."

"Too violent?"

"I guess so."

Norm Ewers went into World War II as a college freshman. He flew B-25s for the Marines in the Solomon Islands. He saw duty in Korea. He logged hundreds of chopper hours in Vietnam. These days he does much volunteer work for his church.

Turning to me: "See, 163 would re-form itself out here on the coast. Kids like him straight out of tech school, some experienced NCOs, a few experienced officers and junior ones. You'd train for a year, really get it up to snuff, and then deploy to Vietnam. At the end, the flag would come back here and re-form all over again."

A moment later: "Paternal. I felt like a father toward them. I didn't drink with them. Some COs did."

A moment later: "We worked every day. There'd be a break for church on Sunday."

I asked if he felt he was in the middle of a war that day. "Hell yes," he said. "What else was it?"

I told him how the wider Americanized ground war came to be sanctioned right at the time of their Black Wednesday. There was little reaction to this. It was as if both were telling me: Those coincidences are for writers.

After lunch we walked across the grass over to an old UH-34D. The ship was sitting near a fence on Red Hill Road. Above us, commercial airliners were whining in and out of the afternoon sun for set-downs at John Wayne. The dry-docked Yankee Papa from an Asian war had now been painted a wild and kind of phosphorescent green. It had Major Bennie Mann's name stenciled beneath the cockpit glass. Mann, the executive officer of Squadron 163, was the pilot who went in with his crew to save Dale Eddy after Yankee Papa 13 had left the death zone.

Farley was walking eight or ten feet behind us, as if he knew there were things I wanted to ask out of his earshot. I brought up the last picture in Larry Burrows's essay. Did the idea of one of his Marines breaking down like that in the outsize pages of *Life* bother him? The colonel didn't seem to hear my question. "It's hard to remember after so many years," he finally said. "I think I was mostly concerned about the effect of Magel's death, and the gruesomeness of that, and how that was pictured."

In his driveway Ewers shook our hands hard. The seams of contained emotion looked ready to split open again. He kept waving as we drove off. Farley didn't say much on the way to the airport. But in the marble corridors of John Wayne Airport, as we talked of Ewers and the feelings for his men he'd shown, Farley said: "Maybe that's why I stay away. Maybe I'm protecting myself unconsciously. So I don't have to bring all that stuff up again."

He got on an airplane and headed north to the Bay Area. I got on an airplane and headed east to Washington. Before he disappeared down the ramp, a found Marine, with a wrecked back, a good Irish wife, and a young son he's mad about, told me: "I feel I'm very fortunate, really. A lot didn't work out, but I feel pretty lucky to be where I am right now. I have a sense of where I am."

In Vietnam, in the second half of 1965, as a lost ground war got waged, men stepped on Bouncing Bettys, which were only the size of a fruit-juice can, but which blew away buttocks and tore off arms and sent heads flying out ahead of their bodies. You stepped on a Bouncing Betty and in a billionth of a second the world was different. You never got a sense of where you were.

LYRICS FOR A BUNKER

Yet at the cruel edge
of your five-faced cathedral of violence,
the church of the spirit is ever being rebuilt.
                    —*Alexander Laing, in* The Dartmouth,
                                        November 12, 1965

The ensuing months of 1965 were cheerless ones.
Even in the face of the increasing buildup of
American forces in South Vietnam and the intensified
bombing of the north, the enemy still seemed unim-
pressed and unaffected. . . . By the autumn the war
began to intrude seriously on the normal life of Ameri-
cans. Draft calls had increased substantially, American
casualties were now beginning to be felt across the
country, military funeral corteges moving across Memo-
rial Bridge and among the trees at Arlington Cemetery
were a common sight. . . . Some McNamara-watchers
claim the secretary underwent a discernible change in
mood in late 1965. It was not so much a transition from
"hawk" to "dove" (these observers would say that that
metamorphosis took place much later); it was rather a
change from overflowing confidence to grave doubts.
                    —*Chester L. Cooper,* The Lost Crusade

THERE ARE, COUNT THEM, somebody has, 7,748 windows. And 685 drinking fountains. And 280 rest rooms. And 4,200 clocks, most of them identical. These clocks are in cafeterias, locker rooms, halls, corridors, bathrooms, bays. There's one in "the tank," which is where the Joint Chiefs convene. There's one on the fourth floor of D Ring, corridor 7, bay 61. But the most crucial clock in the entire building, who would argue, hangs head-high on a southwesterly wall in suite 3E880. Muckety-mucks with scrambled egg on their visors come into this office and plant their behinds in a gold-studded leather chair. They're going to make a presentation to the sec/def. From where they're sitting, it's impossible to see the clock without turning around. But he can see it, it's straight ahead of him. He has his inner eye on it and sometimes his outer eye. It's just a harmless government-issue clock, making sixty-second quiet revolutions, its face flat as a dinner plate, with a brown rim and black numerals. But somehow it feels the size of Idaho. Always there is the presence and pressure of McNamara's clock. Time is more than money in this room; time is so sensate you can hear it ticking.

The building is famously five-sided, hence the name, but really it should be called the Pentacube: five sides, five floors, five rings. There's three times the floor space of the Empire State Building. It's twice as big as the Merchandise Mart in Chicago. You could fit the U.S. Capitol into any one of its five wedges. They constructed it in sixteen round-the-clock months in the early part of World War II—something like 13,000 construction workers on the site at one point. "This thing would not come to pieces very early, would it?" a congressman on an oversight committee asked. "It certainly should not. It shouldn't ever come to pieces," testified a brigadier general.

It rests on 41,192 concrete piles, driven into what used to be a swamp called Hell's Bottom. The basement floats on hydraulic fill dredged from the river. Get below ground in the Pentagon and you may never come out: subbasements, mezzanines, double-floor sections, alleys, connecting gangways. Real spacey down there.

Some smart-ass writer named Scheer for some hippy-dippy West Coast rag, *Ramparts,* toured the place recently and did a piece that began: "The Pentagon Building, whether by choice or design, seems always to be at war. The lights in its endless corridors are dim and flickering, as if powered by some temporary generator. The offices are in 'bays' connected by 'rings,' and the dull pigment of the walls renders the effect of a bomb shelter." The article went south from there.

Fact is, it's a design and engineering marvel. The five concentric rings on the five main floors are connected by ten spokelike corridors (going from the inner, or A Ring, to the outer, or E Ring), so it's a checkable fact that no two offices are more than 1,800 feet apart: about a seven-minute walk, tops. To a first-timer, these interior spaces and hot walking canyons are a bit terrifying, dizzying, yes, and in this sense the building nicely fits the man: beyond calculation. And yet once you get the hang of the locating system (floor, ring, corridor, room), the inner vastness turns quickly navigable. As the OSD historian (that's Office of the Secretary of Defense) will one day write in a book-length tribute to the bunker: "Born of necessity, built in great haste, and occupied section by section, it turned out to be a much better building than anyone expected or had a right to expect. In appearance and soundness of structure it exceeded expectations." As the edifice, so the man.

Instead of elevators, there are wide terrazzoed concrete ramps between floors—you could pilot a low-slung tractor trailer down any one of them. The ceilings throughout are low, and this adds to the general queasiness. But you can always go down to the concourse for a relieving stroll. On the Pentagon concourse there's a bookstore, bank, post office, barbershop, dry cleaner, florist, pharmacy, candy store, Western Union, optometrist, photo supply, jewelry shop, shoe repair, dental office. The concourse is like Grand Central depot before air travel came in.

There's a special barbershop for the OSD guys, run by a merry little clipper known as "Tos," as in Toscanini. One time Tos kept the sec/def waiting for four or five minutes while he finished up another head.

In the center of the building is an open-air courtyard, and in the center of that is a hot-dog stand. The Russians are reputed to have intercontinental ballistic missiles aimed here: middle of the middle of the middle. The courtyard itself, summer-lush with magnolias and crape myrtle and dogwood, is an official no-headgear zone. It's five acres of "no salute," which is to say that a sergeant on a park bench reading his newspaper doesn't have to leap up when he sees a bird colonel coming down the walk. For some reason the courtyard gets a lot of starlings. The pesky iridescent things come in at night.

The building has its own phone book, about the size of Toledo's. They put a new one on your desk every three months. In the current edition he's on page 101, line seventeen: "McNamara Robt S Hon The Secy of Defense 3E880 Pnt-55261." His entry takes up an extra line, but that's the only difference, no bold or enlarged type. He's wedged between "McNamara Lawrence Capt JAG-A 2E439 Pnt" and "McNamara Walter W OCSS 2738 T-A."

People who work for McNamara will look back many years from now and testify that security in his part of the E Ring seemed curiously lax. There's no sergeant at arms, at least not anywhere nearby, although one secretary has some kind of buzzer under her desk. The two civilian secretaries are Margaret S. Stroud and Frances W. Shareck, Peg and Franny, and beyond them are two female military receptionists (marines). Two male military assistants are also in here. The door to his office is almost always unlocked, so it's theoretically possible that a distraught mother or worried priest or nutcake with a derringer could gain access to the building itself and then make his or her way to the correct ring and corridor and room and then move swiftly past the head-down typists and receptionists and turn the handle on the narrow wooden unmarked door—and boom, that mother or priest or derringer-bearing nutcake would now be standing face-to-face with the embodiment of the Vietnam War. If the embodiment's in.

A secret: There's a door to the Sanctum Sanctorum right off the hall in the E Ring. It's unlocked and unmarked. People who are very close to him are permitted to stick their head in and say, Bob, got a minute?

Likely as not he'll be in shirtsleeves behind the massive flat-topped piece of polished wood originally built for General of the Armies "Black Jack" Pershing. He'll be framed, like a painting, by two desk lamps; five wood in-and-out boxes; an oil portrait of the first defense secretary, James V. Forrestal, who, shortly after leaving office, leaped to his end from the window of a sixteenth-floor room at Bethesda Naval Hospital on May 22, 1949.

Not this guy. Maybe he'll have just taken thirty minutes of squash or will soon allow twenty-two minutes for lunch in the adjoining conference room. In the latter instance, the stewards will set up a small table, with napkins and silverware and starched linen. He likes to saw away on a good government steak, though he's also keen for raw carrots and celery sticks.

He has a private elevator to the National Military Command Center (NMCC). As Jack Raymond of the New York *Times* has described it in a recent book (*Power at the Pentagon*), this Strangelovian center "is the nucleus of a labryinth of soundproof rooms built with walls of acoustic tile, connected by a narrow, dead-end corridor, including rooms within rooms." Whew. Who would guess such a place, such a building, would inspire poems? And yet right now, in the late autumn of 1965, poems are happening. Well, it isn't so much the Pentagon itself that's inspiring the poetry but an act that has taken place out front of the building, "at the cruel edge of your five-faced cathedral of violence." The act occurred only days ago and the poets are trying to sort it out. One of the first works to land itself on a printed page, at Dartmouth College, has called out directly to the man inside this concrete bunker:

> *Mr. Secretary, you were looking another way*
> *When grief stalked to your window to forgive you*

But what was that grief, and who did the stalking?

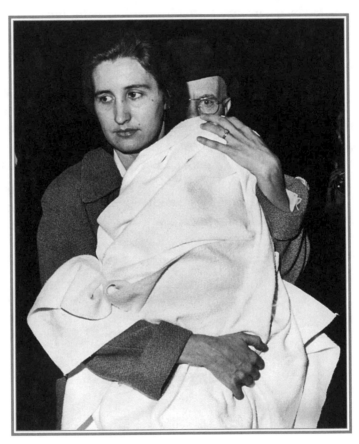

FORT MYER DISPENSARY, WASHINGTON, D.C.,
NOVEMBER 2, 1965. ANNE MORRISON,
CLAIMING HER CHILD, ON THE NIGHT
OF HER HUSBAND'S IMMOLATION.

THE BURNING OF
NORMAN R. MORRISON

*M**ines in the same Ground meet by tunneling.*

—*Emily Dickinson*

I SAY THE NAME. This funny pause. It's as if I've struck a lacuna, a cavity of air, in the marrows of his refusals.

"He wasn't forty feet away from my window," says Robert McNamara, shooting his arm outward. "He was a Quaker, you know. It was a personal tragedy for me."

Are his eyes glistening? Can't tell. But his voice is squishy—even looking toward the window can't hide it.

"And the guy was insane enough to have a baby in his arms—" I hedge, anything to keep it going.

"No, not insane. I don't like that word. That's a value judgment. In some ways he may have been correct. If by such actions he could bring to bear the attention he sought."

"By the way, ever been down to the Vietnam Memorial?"

"Yes."

"What was it like?"

"I don't want to talk about it. That's Vietnam."

His fingers have come up in front of his face, as if to interpose them between himself and the world. The chilliness in his voice is almost scary. And why not: It was a transparent question, the kind that has quagmires and guerrillas waiting at the back of it. Who could win that kind of war, who could win on that kind of question?

THE QUAKER DID IT one rush-hour evening, in gathering dark. No Buddhist monks were present to feed peppermint oil on the flames and keep down the smell of burning flesh. The fire shot ten to twelve feet into the air—so said a Pentagon guard who tore to an alarm box to call the fire department. (They got there quickly but it was pointless.) The flames, people said, made an envelope of color around his asphyxiating body. The sound of it, one witness said, was like the whoosh of small-rocket fire.

What made it so horrifying, awesome, and impenetrable all at once was that Norman R. Morrison had a child, his own infant daughter, in his presence. Her name is Emily, and she was nine days from her first birthday. Had he held her in his left arm while he'd soaked himself with his right? Some thought so. Did he set her down ahead of time and then move off ten or fifteen paces before removing the cap from the glass gallon container that contained the yellowish liquid? This too was reported. Did he release her just as the flames were licking up from his shoe tops, which is where he had apparently struck the match, and, if so, did he do it of his own volition or out of a panicked response to the screams of onlookers?

Another way of framing the last question might be: If he did put her down at the critical second, which is my hedging belief, was it out of a confusion and fear, or out of his love and mercy?

It will never be known. We don't have a videotape. Eyewitness accounts conflict. That night's news flashes and the next day's newspaper stories were maddeningly contradictory, imprecise, hedgy— often within the same story. Some of the second- and third-day reports turned hedgier still. I know: I've spent a fair amount of time these many years later poring over them, trying to cross-analyze, make them jibe. They won't be jibed.

Some accounts had the burning man handing his child off to a woman never identified. I don't believe it. And yet what is true? The deeper I've sought to go, the more unreachable the answers seem, and not just the answers to those blurred final seconds. Maybe I should have understood this much from the beginning.

All right. No earthly intelligence will ever be able to sort out or say precisely what a pacifist Quaker from Baltimore did or had in his terrified mind vis-à-vis his baby daughter late on the immolating afternoon of November 2, 1965. But what I've also come to think is that maybe it isn't necessary to know. Indeed maybe trying to pin the Emily part of it down goes in a mistaken direction. Because no matter what happened at the last, or what the intent was, a child was saved, was led away from death in an eye's blink, in the way Isaac was led away when an angel on a mountain stayed a knife in Abraham's raised hand. The Old Testament story of Abraham and Isaac, grieving father and unwitting son, going up to make a burnt offering to a demanding God is a terribly difficult parable to comprehend. But I think the parable has to do with this: Obedience to a perceived divine call is a high value. And yet love is an even greater value. Writers and philosophers from Kierkegaard to Robert Graves have struggled with the seeming madness of Abraham's readiness to slay his son, until he was told not to.

Could angels have been out front of Robert McNamara's stone fortress that evening? A mushy and unscientific thought. Poets might call it the hope of things not seen.

This was seen: Emily was unharmed. In ways not revealed, she fell, dropped, or floated to her safety. She found spongy prewinter earth, or was placed on it, while her father disappeared to another place. She was wearing light-blue coveralls, and they weren't so much as singed.

"The only thing you could smell was burning flesh," said a doctor at the scene.

"HUMAN TORCH AT PENTAGON—BABY IN ARMS," said the New York *Herald Tribune* the next morning, that headline just beneath the even larger headline about John Lindsay's winning the New York mayoral race. For several days running, the man wreathed by light on an off-year election day was front-page news in America. And then it was as if somebody had doused it. The ballad of Norman R. Morrison, Quaker of Baltimore, fell to the minds of poets, one of whom, James Bond of Florida, wrote: "He lit a flame / And round the campfires of the world / He dances in our eyes."

It happened at about 5:20 p.m. Pentagon workers on their way home to Suitland and Hyattsville gazed out from their cars as if experiencing visions. Employees, coming out the doors of the river entrance, took off running toward the ribbons of fire. "Drop the baby!" some were crying, or at least those three words appeared in uncounted metropolitan dailies the next day. *Newsweek* made it the headline on its treatment, as if to encode madness.

Two men in uniform, one an officer, one a sergeant in the Air Force, tried beating out the flames with their hands and thrown-off coats. But it was too late. The Quaker, his life extinguishing like a candle, had pitched forward into a narrow trench, a narrow grave, shooting streaks of orange from his close-cropped head. He was trying to get out last words nobody could understand. That morning he had worked on a lecture for an adult class. He wrote: "Quakers seek to begin with life, not with theory or report. The life is mightier than the book that reports it. The most important thing in the world is that our faith becomes living experience and deed of life."

Some news bulletins had him standing on a three-foot retaining wall and shouting to passersby as he combusted into fire—but I don't think so. The reason I don't think so is because I've spoken to the three principal eyewitnesses, none of whom had been reached by a journalist in three decades. Each man held his own memory, though all were pretty sure Morrison was behind the wall, not atop it, in a raised rectangular garden cut by brick walks and bordered by trenches. A small, not very important detail, yes. But I have gone to that garden, behind that low wall, trying to conjure the precise spot, hoping it would all turn clear. It didn't. I've gazed up at the curtained window behind which the concealed man used to work. (The garden is farther away than forty feet, the distance McNamara cited with conviction in 1984; he put the same figure into his 1995 memoir.) The trench on the forward side is filled in now, and the place isn't tended so well, and a line of high shrubs has been planted. I would almost want to use the word peaceful.

The enlisted man who vaulted over the wall and tried to beat out the fire with his uniform coat suffered a neck burn that puffed up like an adder. His name is Robert C. Bundt. When I talked with him he was at the family hardware store in Michigan. He told me the flames didn't cause the burn on his neck—the heat did. "I couldn't see his face," Bundt said. "It was too black." He said he could see arms and hands sticking through the fire. Bundt remembered that detail and then he was choking on the other end of the phone wire. He said he still has a scar from the heat burn, and sometimes, in the rag of summer, when there's a certain excitability in him, it'll welt up again.

A twenty-seven-year-old doctor from Brooklyn, on duty in the Pentagon dispensary, got a two-word call: "Somebody burning." That evening Robert Ruderman, M.D., told the New York *Herald Tribune:*

"The crowd let us through. . . . He was unconscious, but still alive; his body was smoldering and smoking, and he was giving his last gasps. His face was unidentifiable. We couldn't work in the small area. We got a stretcher and lifted him on it. I was unable to get pulse, and he was having terminal-type respiration. He died a few minutes after we got him into the ambulance. . . . We got there the same time as the firemen. They got out oxygen equipment. . . . I didn't know anything about a baby until after we got into the ambulance and the firemen came by with a baby wrapped in blankets."

At 5:20 p.m. on November 2, 1965, a time-calibrating man was in a meeting. Wan streaks of daylight were coming through. An aide interrupted to say something was happening outside. Robert McNamara went over to the long windows and saw two ambulances. Paramedics were bundling a form. "It's what?" he said, his face whitening. He was informed of a child. "What?" he said.

And what of that child? Well, her mother claimed her that night at the nearby Fort Myer dispensary. They presented Emily to her wrapped up in a flannel Army blanket from which her chubby arms protruded and from which the smell of kerosene was unmistakable.

More than a decade ago, having come on this story for the first time, I went in search of a child named Emily—and also in search of the rest of her family. I found Emily in a fourth-floor walk-up on a block of the East Village in Manhattan where I saw somebody urinate on a car and little kids were out at night shouting obscenities at nervous strangers. I was really searching for her father, not knowing exactly why it seemed so important. This was in the late autumn of 1985. I hadn't even made the connection in my mind that it was the twenty-year anniversary of Morrison's act. All I knew was I wanted to find somebody who had his blood.

Emily Morrison Welsh was finishing a degree in drama at New York University. That day she had received in the mail a sweater from her mom for her twenty-first birthday. She was taking final classes and holding down several part-time jobs. She had huge expressive green eyes and dark hair falling everywhere. She was five feet ten and stalky as August corn and I remember something silvery and approximately the size of a bass lure dangling from her left earlobe. She was—there is no other word for it—beautiful. She told me about the time, a few years earlier, when she went to see a psychic. "Do you have any memory of the first time you experienced pain and fear on a terrifying level?"

asked the psychic, who Emily swore knew nothing of her history. Emily, who thought she was prepared, started crying.

I stayed three or four hours. At one point Norman Morrison's daughter told me, and it seemed all right then, "What's crucial, I think, is not whether my father had actually decided to take me with him but whether he loved me enough, his last child, to want me there in the final moment of his life." The window in her apartment was open and a neon narcotic night poured through. A few minutes later she said: "Maybe he wanted it debated." Then she said, "Was he a brutal enough man to take his daughter with him? That's what they want to know, right? That's what you want to know, right?"

Going on: "For years people who loved me said, 'Emily doesn't remember, don't worry, there's no way possible Emily could remember, everybody knows memory doesn't start that early.' I mean, even my mother, who loves me so much, who came to get me that night, kept saying that as I grew up. 'Emily doesn't remember.' I can recall when I was about three or four crying one night to my mother: 'He didn't love us, Daddy didn't want to be with us, that's why he did it.' And she came over and said, in this real soft voice, 'No, no, Emily, he loved us too much.' But, you see, she never thought I knew it in a memory way. Well, I simply believed on some deep level of my being that I experienced it."

So her cells knew, if her memory didn't? "It was just in me," she said.

Would the "it" be the crying and the yelling and the explosion of color and people running and the handing off, or the releasing, or the gentle placing down? Could "it" also be the oddly sweet smell of the fuel? "It's like our dreams," Emily said. "We say we don't remember them. What we mean is we don't let ourselves remember."

Emily and I talked some more and then we went down to the street and found an outdoor cafe, and I can still see a blurred man's child fingering the foam in her café au lait and then reaching across the table with her slender arm to help herself to some of my butter and bread. I was pretty charmed. There was something knowing and fetching and unselfconscious and wise-beyond-the-years about her; also something disarmingly vain and a little theatrical. Emily said she was going to a party later that night on Bleecker. There would be dancing. She said she had been to a lot of auditions of late and was waiting for calls from agents. I might not have thought right off to call her Quakerly, but that is what Emily turned out to be, beneath the semiglitter and the mild

Manhattan vanities. She told me that night that she would never let go of her Quaker values and heritage, but at the same time she needed to move on. She wanted to make it in the world as an actress or some other kind of artistic performer, this is how she saw herself, sharing her gift for self-expression. I can report that Emily still works at this dream, and has known success, although perhaps not the big technicolor kind. She has even lived in Hollywood, though I suspect she's too true for Hollywood. A few years ago she came back to Carolina. She's in her early thirties, daughter of her father's fire, child of his history.

In the space of ten days in that 1985 autumn, on the twenty-year anniversary of Norman Morrison's act, I visited two other surviving members of a remarkable family. It began to occur to me that this family, like the rest of a country, was just then in a process of beginning to sort out all that had happened two decades before, during a war they were too young to know. In the North Carolina mountains, I found Anne Morrison Welsh, Norman's widow, who had married twice in the years that had gone by since fate had handed her the strangest kind of news. Emily's mother was and is an extremely decent, plain, caring, and compassionate country woman whose life has known an uncommon hardness. She bore three children by Norman Morrison, two daughters and a son, but only the daughters made it to adulthood. The son, Ben, her eldest, died of bone cancer at sixteen, a decade after his father gave his life away in the vain hope of stopping a war. Some of his final words were, "I don't want to die." Anne Morrison Welsh cried just once on the day I met her, and that was when she said Norman never got to see how fine his children turned out. Anne and I have corresponded much in these last several years as I have tried to make sense of the riddle of her first husband's life. She has given me large benefit of the doubt. I've written rambling letters to her, full of unanswerable questions, and she has always responded—maybe not immediately, but with honesty and often enough an eloquence. I've almost never encountered her anger, much less her rage, and I've puzzled some about that, because had it happened to me, I would still be raging at God.

In one letter several years ago she wrote: "To this day, I do not know for sure if Norman sat Emily down or if so, when he sat her down or if he dropped her or if he gave her to someone else. The accounts conflict. . . . All I know is Norman did not (and, I believe, ultimately could not) take Emily to his own fate. Of course, for which I am forever and ever grateful, amen." In that same letter, she said: "My thinking on it all is deeper now, more aware of complexities, more objective, and I'm more in touch with my feelings. . . ." She also said in that letter, in response to a question I'd asked: "I strongly doubt that Norman knew enough about the Pentagon layout to know he was under McNamara's window. Unless I had evidence to the contrary, I would call it synchronicity or coincidence. Yet, had he known that was McNamara's window, I think he would have selected that spot, even though he was protesting the War itself (and secondarily, the war machine and the Pentagon in general). I don't think he had especially hard feelings toward McNamara himself; I don't remember him speaking that way. It was the impersonal, mechanistic thinking and the acceptance of violence toward the innocent in Vietnam that he was witnessing against, and the Pentagon was its representative."

On that day more than a decade ago when we sat down together with sandwiches, Anne Morrison Welsh said: "But there is above all an element of mystery. . . . You just have to remember the mystery and the desperation." I'm not so sure I listened so well. I believe she meant desperation in terms of all that her husband felt about the Vietnam War, and the path it was on in the darkening year of 1965, but I've since come to believe she was allowing for more personal meanings as well. Anne also told me, and again I didn't listen so well, "I think poets can understand this act better than other people."

In that same period, the fall of '85, I had a long walk and conversation with Tina, the other daughter in the family. Christina Morrison is Emily's older sister. When Norman Morrison ignited himself in the presence of his youngest child on the far bank of the Potomac, Tina, the second child, was a five-year-old in Baltimore. Twenty years later, when I spent a fall Sunday with her, meandering around a placid Carolina college town, stopping to sit on benches and to pick up brightly colored leaves, Tina Morrison was almost twenty-six, and, like her sister Emily, a physically beautiful person, all angles and edges, rail-thin, a sort of New Age woman with her father's unmistakable square Scotch jaw and a smile that slipped up on me unawares. I remember the tiny braided bracelet on her right wrist. Tina said she hadn't found her true vocation yet. "Healer," she said. As part of this, she was studying massage: the gift of putting hands on people in soothing ways. She also told me as we passed under old Chapel Hill trees: "I didn't get angry at Norman until just lately. There was never any context for being angry. You don't get angry at a dead person—what's the point of that? I couldn't talk to my mother about it. I think I was afraid of her feelings. I think we were all afraid of each other's feelings. . . . We've been waiting for twenty years for someone to come around and ask us these questions."

Quakers believe that in the silence of waiting, answers will come, the spirit will speak.

Questions? Those talks with the Morrison family were in another decade, and it's as if in the time since, my impatience and questions have only doubled over on themselves. I've kept on searching—for what? After I met the three Morrisons in 1985, I wrote a long story for the Washington *Post*. I see now far too much was centered on the spared child; it was the predictably newspapery thing to do. While I wouldn't disavow the article now, I see all I missed. One thing I didn't understand nearly enough was the inherent unknowability of the act itself; what was so mad and useless on the surface may have had its own inner logic and moral trajectory—from childhood onward. A decade ago I knew little about Norman Morrison's childhood, but I know now it was a largely gray and pained childhood, even as it was spiritually imbued and high-minded.

The second thing I didn't appreciate enough was the linkage—or what I can only think of as linkage—between somebody standing at a retaining wall in twilight with a child and a jug of kerosene; and somebody else, behind a wall, inside a building, crunching his numbers and just beginning to crack with his hidden doubt. An external destruction, Norman Morrison's, an internal dying, Robert McNamara's.

Because it is clear now from scholarship on the war, and not least from McNamara's own testimony in a New York libel trial, and also from what's tucked between the lines of his 1995 memoir, that the season in which a secretary of defense began to make a turn against all he had made and masterminded was the same season in which a husband and father who resided at 5304 St. George's Avenue in a north Baltimore neighborhood known as Govans got into an old car with his youngest in the back and drove approximately forty miles and found a space in a restricted lot at the mall entrance of a mammoth building and took a plaid picnic bag from the trunk and went around front and paced back and forth for about forty-five minutes before picking his spot and opening the package and bringing an end to his life. Having either dropped his child or set her down before the fire could hurt her.

I have thought a lot about those forty-five minutes of pacing, and the pyres of will it must have taken to go ahead and raise the jug and pour it on himself. Was he hoping the angels would stop him? Did he know he was being called to something more powerful than clear?

I used the word linkage. In December 1984, nineteen years and a month from the act, Robert McNamara, long gone from the Pentagon, war minister no more, American soldier on the run, stopped barely long enough from his intercontinental runnings and refusals to testify at the Westmoreland/CBS trial. He showed up hugely against his will, but he showed up; an act that required a great deal of guts. (Most of the other Vietnam icons managed to stiff-arm the trial.) I attended large portions of the tedious and disappointing drama, and I happened to be in the courtroom on the day this exchange took place between McNamara and the cross-examining attorney for CBS:

Q. You said, Secretary McNamara, that you had reached the conclusion that the war could not be won militarily no later than mid-1966. Is that correct?
A. I said I believed I had reached the conclusion the war could not be won militarily no later than sixty-six.
Q. And am I correct that it was your recollection, at least at the time of your deposition, that you might have reached the conclusion as early as 1965?
A. I believe I may have reached it as early as the latter part of 1965.

When he said that, McNamara took a paper towel and very carefully wiped the spot on the ledge of the witness box where his Styrofoam cup of water was sitting.

The public burning of Norman R. Morrison took place in the gathering dark of a mistaken Asian war that Lyndon Johnson and his brainiest advisers were making more mistaken and incendiary almost by the week. One hundred and seventy-five thousand men were in the process of going in. American bombers had been raining destruction on the north since the previous February. And a thirty-one-year-old, deeply faithed Baltimore Quaker whom almost nobody in the wider secular world had ever heard of—certainly not Robert McNamara—sat on a wooden stool in his kitchen one fall day and wiped his hands through his chestnut hair and said to his wife, "What will it take to stop this war?" Was he insane, was he messianic, was he inspired beyond what is earthly?

In South Vietnam, monks had been immolating themselves as an expression of witness and faith for two years, but this burning seemed vastly different. For one thing, it occurred in our own civilization, right at the cruel edge of the five-sided bunker. (A week later, in New York, a twenty-two-year-old Catholic named Roger LaPorte would set himself on fire at sunrise in front of the United Nations.) Anne Morrison Welsh knew more than I imagined when she told me it was poets who understood this thing her husband had made with his life. In a poem titled "Emily, My Child," written by a North Vietnamese poet named To Huu, the third stanza begins:

> *McNamara,*
> *Where are you hiding? In the crypts*
> *Of your vast five-cornered house—*
> *A corner for each continent?*
> *You hide away from the fires you ignite*
> *As an ostrich hides his head in the sand.*

Another poem, published in *Poetry* a year after the act, played on these themes:

> *And Norman Morrison, Quaker, of Baltimore Maryland,*
> *burned what he said was himself.*
> *He said it with simple materials such as would be found in*
> *your kitchen.*
> *In your office you were informed.*
> *Reporters got cracking frantically on the mental disturbance*
> *angle.*
> *So far nothing turns up*

Later still, another poet, Hugh Ogden, who had known the immolated man in boyhood, wrote:

> *As you drove by the refineries*
> *flaring gas near Baltimore you suddenly*
> *needed*
> *to go to the Pentagon*
> *with her in the car seat beside you.*
> *You forgot how*
> *a baby gazes up at an adult.*
> *Oblivious and wild for peace you breathed*
> *close to murder*
> *and then put her aside*
> *to change our history.*

I have no doubt the burning shocked McNamara. In *In Retrospect* he wrote: "I reacted to the horror of his action by bottling up my emotions and avoided talking about them with anyone—even my family." Nor can there be doubt of this—it's in the secret documents: Within a month, the secretary of defense, back from another of his ritualistic blur trips to Vietnam, was urging the president in memos and in White House meetings and private conversations to consider a bombing pause. Yes, he had pressed for bombing pauses earlier; in fact, on the day following the suicide, there had been an early draft of a fifteen-page memo recommending a cessation as a way of trying to induce the enemy to the bargaining table. (The paper, a collaborative effort, had been started before the burning.) But by late November 1965, and into December, in memos, meetings and private talks, McNamara would be pushing harder for bombing pauses and other kinds of options and cessations than he'd ever pushed. Those November–December McNamara papers and transcripts, now fully declassified, along with notes of key meetings, also declassified, are in such contrast to the spring-and-summer documents. Taken as a whole, they unmistakably reveal the beginning of the shattering.

And the public never knew, not for a long time. Even on the inside, many didn't know, not for a long time. Only astute McNamara-watchers on the inside could begin to detect a different man, who, for swirls of complicated reasons, was going to continue managing the doomed war for the next two years, a war he believed could not be won on the battlefield, while the casualty rates of the dead, dying, wounded, and missing spiked past the 100,000 mark and the country tore apart and his own deep slow incineration went on. An external destruction, Norman's, an internal burning, McNamara's.

One fire is over in a few seconds. It shoots up, an overarching sort of thing. The other, inside a building, cordoned off, under fluorescent lighting, has fire walls built around it. It's a tortured and oozeful kind of incineration that stitches itself low along the ground. Do I sound too fanciful? And am I suggesting that a ten-foot-high flaring in near-darkness "caused" the apostasy behind the wall? No, I'm not saying that; it's not so dramatic or linear. Nothing is ever that straightforward with McNamara; too many other things swirl in the mix. And yet what I fervently believe, and cannot prove, is that Norman Morrison's act became the emotional catalyst for the secret turn. What I believe, and cannot prove, is that the fire in the garden became the deep sensitizing agent for a revelation that began seeping into the secretary of defense about a fortnight later. It was a revelation having to do with numbers, what else, and it arose from the ashes of a supposed military triumph in a ghostly place called the Ia Drang Valley. But hold that story, until I can go into it a little more.

Because I have a question. Is it mad to think that a pacifist Quaker who had little power in the world save the power of his own life could somehow have known in his bones and in his cells on the afternoon of November 2, as he gathered his child and assembled his simple materials and drove by the refineries of Baltimore, that he was bearing strange gifts to a receptive authority? But what did this receptive authority do with the gifts laid at his window? What he did with them, as a record of documents shows, is full of paradox and zigzag. But there's no riddle or zigzag in this: Not one high figure in government resigned after Norman Morrison's suicide, the Vietnam War went on, the bombing pauses never worked, the balloon of death kept going up and up. This isn't their story, though, not right now. In a way it's not even Norman Morrison's.

IN THE TWO-TONED old Cadillac he piloted down from Baltimore, police found two bottles of milk, half a dozen diapers, a couple of pacifiers. The Cadillac wasn't his; fellow Quakers who had gone out of town had left it in his safekeeping. When he exited the machine, he left the keys in the ignition.

The ambulance drivers were the first to see that the uninjured, still-unidentified little girl had kerosene on her clothes. (The dead man was being driven away in another ambulance.) What exactly did this mean? What Anne has always believed is this: As Norman locked her to his heart in the final embrace, and then bent down to catch reflections from evening red, Emily Morrison's clothes, like the rest of her life, soaked clean through to his.

"Well, the facts are these," I can remember a steady-voiced, middle-aged woman deep in the mountains of Carolina telling me with a steady gaze one noonday in 1985; I had been in her presence about twenty minutes. Anne Morrison Welsh, who had on a corduroy jacket and wore her graying hair tied in a bun, strained forward in a chair. She reminded me a little of Joan Baez, and her voice had something of that same sonorous quality. ("Maybe Joan Baez's mother," she said later, laughing the comparison away.)

"When I received her that night, when they gave Emily to me, there was not a thing wrong with her—not a cut or a mark or a bruise of any kind. If something had happened to Emily, I think it would have been . . . well, very difficult for me to accept what Norman was doing. But I'm telling you, her hair was not singed, there was no smell about her of burning. Yes, it's true, there was the odor of kerosene. But there were no lacerations of any kind. The next day I took her to a pediatrician, and he confirmed her condition for me."

Back then, Anne Morrison was working at a group home for people with Down's syndrome and other disabilities. We talked in the kitchen while she tended to tasks. Her charges were out at their day jobs. She has since moved around in her work, but the work has always held to its Quakerly values—and underpayment. Her psychology degree is from Duke University. I've long wondered where her degree of acceptance is from—maybe rural Georgia, which is her native ground.

I remember the corn shocks that stood outside the window. I remember the sticker on the fridge that said: "Let Nicaragua Live." I remember the jar of homemade relish she brought out for our impromptu lunch. I remember how she got distracted in the middle of some of her sentences and looked down at her hands and laughed at herself. I remember how she wore no makeup or any other kind of frill, and yet how attractive she seemed in her large-boned and countrified way—an interior attractiveness, shining out from around and behind November 2, 1965.

And I remember when she said, "I hate that story, frankly!" I had brought up the Bible story of Abraham and Isaac. It was something like anger, but then it died.

The phone rang, and she said to the voice on the other end, "Oh, are you, honey? Of course I'll come and get you. You just wait. I'll be right there." She left in a van to go get one of the people she was looking after.

When she came back, she said: "It was suffocation. The flames choked off his air. He was entering eternity. He had a call. If you believe in angels, as I do, then I think they were there. I mean, I saw his coat—it wasn't even burned that much. . . . I kept his pocketbook for a long time afterward, you know. It was hardly touched."

She told me of her former husband's impatience. "If you have deep ideals and passions about how the world ought to be, then you're terribly impatient. I know. I'm impatient, too."

She spoke of his rather amazing intuition, perhaps the more amazing for a man who was never easy with people.

"I think we should have talked about it more," she said. "I mean myself and the children. In the beginning, there was all that media.

Then we were trying to get on with our lives. For so many years after his death, I was his widow. Even after I remarried, I was his widow. I think what I did was postpone the grief. Oh, we didn't know as much about grieving then as we do now."

A few minutes later: "This is my retrospective feeling about it. . . . I think he got the clear calling that he should decide to go to Washington. I mean, why did he take all of this *equipment* if he was going to be gone in an hour, and her with him? My own sense is he held her for the moment—and then the angel of God intervened."

I have come to believe that the supply of extra diapers and milk and pacifiers argue much for a merciful state of mind. But I've also thought about how that mind could have changed itself many times on the drive to death. And how it could have changed itself many times again in the forty-five minutes at the wall.

Anne, going on: "He set her down of his own volition. Well, I don't think the volition was rational."

Anne: "You think about it—no one would have noticed him until he lit the match. You're out there walking around with a child. Who's going to notice? It's a little strange, maybe, that you have a child."

Anne: "On a practical level, she was consigned to his care that day." (Yes, come to think: What was he going to do, leave her in the parking lot?)

When the first call came, Anne thought: He's walked into the Potomac, that's it, Norman has walked into the Potomac with Emily. Nobody said anything about burning, about suicide. The first man on the phone just said "some kind of protest." He was a reporter from *Newsweek*. He choked on the words when he realized she didn't yet know. "He said my husband had been involved in some sort of protest or witness and that I should call Fort Myer." Even the people at the Army hospital stopped short on the phone. "They didn't tell me he was dead. I think they wanted me to make a positive identification. Finally someone told me three-quarters of his body was burned."

Several days later came this letter to Emily Morrison from a woman in Troy, New York: "By holding you he made his point; by dropping you he spared a life to continue, carrying his name, to work for peace. Honor his acts, and love his memory. No medals for Norman Morrison could reward his death as you can, living."

Several days later came this letter to the Pentagon, addressed to McNamara and the Joint Chiefs, from a doctor named Marian E. Manly:

"Gentlemen: It is easy to dismiss Norman Morrison's dreadful act as the meaningless self-destruction of a deranged fanatic. It was desperate; it was futile; but it was not meaningless. What he was trying to say was: 'See what it is like for a man to die by fire. See it for yourselves. You, who make impersonal war, devising strategies and tactics in your air-conditioned offices, look and see!' "

Anne, going on: "Norman had a sacrificial, utilitarian sense about his life. He felt there was a role some people are called to play. . . . What I felt was that if he really wanted to do this with his life, then I'm glad he succeeded. That may sound horrible, but what I mean is I wouldn't have wanted him to go through life with those kinds of burns or the terrible feeling he had failed at what he felt was called for at that moment in history."

With a sudden little slap at her palm: "Oh, he had been thinking of shooting a hole through his hand, or maybe a couple fingers off. He had talked of it, yes, with certain friends. Oh, I don't know, we're entering a realm of faith here, aren't we? He was so terribly impatient. If he looked on any of this rationally, I think he felt something needed to happen that would speak to people's hearts. He told me once—oh, maybe a year before he died—that in terms of the movement of history, sacrifice for the common good, even martyrdom, was sometimes necessary. 'The world doesn't need many martyrs,' I remember him saying. 'But it needs a few.' "

He had another expression. "Anne," he used to say, "the world has a lot of good nurserymen. But not enough peacemakers." Norman Morrison had a gift for making things come up out of the ground.

What kind of man was he? He was tone-deaf—and loved polkas. (Couldn't sing for beans, but he could wriggle his oversize ears beautifully to the beat.) He suffered hay fever and allergies. He could wear a beret at a mildly rakish angle. He loved baseball and knew the intimacies of it and as a kid was crazy for Connie Mack's Philadelphia A's. (He could barely play toss and catch.) He rode a secondhand bicycle and found the stock market fascinating. (Never owned any stocks.) He drove a Volvo and an old VW. He was a Scotch puritan, but he was good for a beer and even a cigar on occasion. When he got excited, he was apt to stammer. He thrilled in his ability to be cheap. (He would get his suits for $2 and $3 at Friends rummage sales; they looked damn fine on him.) He could fix you with a flat, disconcerting stare. He had a way of keeping his spouse and others off balance with the seemingly stray but probably calculated remark. He was kind to pets and the dispossessed. There was a quotient in his life to be silly. There was a quotient in his life to be violent. He was cryptic, syllogistic, inward, a man of deeds, especially of physical tasks. He was someone for whom the spoken word got in the way. And yet he wrote beautiful letters.

From a letter: "It is nearly impossible for most Quakers or anyone else to sit in silence for an hour with other working minds without feeling their individual and collective futility and dependence upon the will and power of Christ."

"Anne," he used to say, "most people live at the level of the Old Testament." He meant: eye for an eye. He meant it in terms of owning a less complex view of the world, though he also must have meant it in terms of retribution. In high school once, he put a classmate in the hospital. (The sorry kid had been swatting him on the back during study hall.) In college once, he opened up a couple of stitches over somebody's eye. (They were in the showers, and the guy had provoked him; Norm reared back and hurled the cake of soap at point-blank range.)

I have wondered if the deep commitment to pacifism and nonviolence didn't have its origins in the need to combat his inner self, which he understood as essentially sinful. Norman R. Morrison, the violent pacifist.

James C. Farley, the peace-seeking street fighter.

Robert S. McNamara—the what?

I have wondered if he did "it" out of his very inarticulateness. Because he couldn't get out all he felt.

He had a philosophy of what he called "the guided drift." He used to joke that there was sometimes more drift than guide.

From an essay bearing his name: "Without the inspired act, no generation resumes the search for love."

On the day we met, I asked Anne if she had been deep in love with him. She nodded, not so vigorously. "We had a relationship that was sort of . . . we were like two workhorses hitched to the same wagon, and the wagon was destiny. I don't think we ever had a romantic relationship. We just had a sense of loyalty to the marriage. It was workmanlike." (A decade later, rereading some of her husband's early letters, Anne would be surprised and pleased to see more romance in those letters than she would have guessed.)

Today, when the name Norman R. Morrison remains semihidden in the country of his birth, Vietnam still venerates him as a high hero. He is known up and down Vietnam, not just in the north. In museums there are Morrison memorials. The name Emily has a special reverence and resonance there, too.

In the aftermath of November 2, 1965, the North Vietnamese, eager, you might callously say, to cash in, issued a stamp. It bore his picture and cost twelve dong and had lettering down the side and across the bottom that said: *Norman Morrison Hy Sinh Cao ca'vi chinh nghia.* It means, "Norman Morrison, the ultimate sacrifice as duty and purpose demand." Ho Chi Minh himself cabled Anne and invited her to Vietnam. Ho's troops, making their way southward, down the trail, were said to have sewn on their backpacks and pasted to the fenders of their bicycles and onto the dashboards of their lampless trucks small likenesses of a man who had grown up washed in the blood of Presbyterianism and under the roof of an acidic Erie, Pennsylvania, dentist.

BUT THEN IMPROBABILITY is what this is about.

On December 29, 1933, in a cold corner of Pennsylvania, Buehler Brothers Meat Market is selling pot roast for eight cents a pound. There's an ad on page seventeen of the local paper: "Readings Daily, Phone 56-1098, 1219 Holland Street, rear." The Green Mill restaurant on Glenwood Park Avenue is accepting New Year's Eve reservations: seventy-five cents a head. And Hazel and Stanley F. Morrison, loyal members of the Church of the Covenant, are grateful to God for the safe delivery of their first child. They will christen him Norman Robert and bring him home under the gray-grim skies of Erie.

Out in California, a frosh at Berkeley has been commuting to school in a Ford roadster with green wire wheels, and that frosh's father, a seller of shoes, is passing Oakland evenings in the small downstairs room off the kitchen, saying little.

History. They brought him home to an old, dark, brick house on the east side, close to the lake, near the paper mills. Doc Morrison had been a dentist four years then, a graduate of Pitt. His practice was in a storefront at 1140 East Lake, eight buildings down from the family's flat, and seems to have chiefly served the immigrant laborers of the factories. In Erie the prevailing winds are from west to east, which is why the east side is where immigrant families have historically been forced to cluster: close to the work, where the stink is bad.

Dreary Erie. The Mistake on the Lake. Never mind that this smoke-stacked and much-maligned city can sometimes know beautiful summer light. Never mind that Erie has fine beaches for swimming and fertile farm country at its perimeters. "Erie is truly a city of home and happiness," a travel brochure claimed the year after Norman was born. Then as now, Erie was one of the least sunny spots in North America.

His mother, by every account that survives, was sweet and prayerful and light-filled, very much a lady. His father, by every account that survives, was an intense, demanding, driven person: a perfectionist personality. And yet Doc Morrison must have had a redemptive love for literature, especially Emerson. He purchased the complete works, and they were well-worn at his death. There were tags of poetry in him. He was a thirty-second-degree Mason and belonged to the Zem Zem Temple Shrine. He owned a pale-green metal operating chair with a spittoon attached and a leather headpiece and also a foot pedal that the tooth extractor would pump like an organ when raising or lowering a victim.

Doc Morrison, the story goes, dug his grave with his teeth. Which is to say he wouldn't stop eating incredibly rich and fatty food, even as it tore holes in his stomach. He was gone from this world in his forties, when his older son, Norman, was a month past thirteen and his younger son, Ralph, was a few months past ten. A bleeding ulcer was given as the cause of death. He had smoked like a chimney. He had left some savings. "DR. S. MORRISON, DENTIST, IS DEAD," the obituary in the Erie *Daily Times* said, and there was a picture. Twenty-eight years onward would be another picture, same paper, under these headlines: "FORMER ERIEITE IN TORCH DEATH / MORRISON QUIET BOY, NEIGHBORS RECALL."

The gray grimness of dentistry, a profession known for its suicide rates. The gray grimness of Erie, an outpost on a lake in a snowbelt. The gray grimness of the firstborn apprenticing himself to the church at a far too ripe age. But there must have been comforts in that apprenticeship, too. Early on, Norman knew he was going to serve his Lord, in ways not yet revealed.

But more than any of the above: the gray grimness of your father dying so stupidly at the beginning of your teens. This fact alone has made me wonder how Norman Morrison could have done what he did on November 2, 1965, knowing the effect it would have on his own children for the rest of their lives. But families have a way of reliving their own histories in spite of everything. Several weeks after Norman Morrison ended his life, his widow, with amazing grace, and perhaps with some denial, posed for a picture with her three children and told a Quaker reporter for the Baltimore *Sun:* "[Norman] was dismayed by the view of so many people that their chief obligation is to their own family. He felt that we're all one human family. He just didn't make the usual distinction between the obligation to his own family and the rest of mankind."

Between 1933 and 1939, when Norman turned six, the family moved at least four times. They always stayed close to the practice, around the corner or on the same street. Somewhere in the forties, the Morrisons moved to a brown-shingled and substantial house at 2963 Peach Street, a mostly German section of town. The dental rooms were in the front, the family lived at the rear. Doc Morrison died there on January 29, 1947. And in the bitterness and grief and impecuniousness that followed, something good resulted: Norman, now the figurative head of the family, convinced his mother and his younger brother that they should sell the Erie house and regroup at their small summer home at the Chautauqua Institution over the border in New York State.

Chautauqua. It sits frozen in time, a symphony in old wood on a narrow blue lake. Teddy Roosevelt once called these 750 acres the most American spot in America. A Methodist bishop founded the institution in 1874 as a summer retreat for Sunday-school teachers, and ever since it has been devoted to the total man, where summer colonists from Pittsburgh and other eastern points convene to write poetry, weave rugs, hear chamber-music concerts, study ballet, practice the flute, swim, play tennis, sail, listen to orators, partake of the literary and scientific circle, and of course worship God. Whole families praying and playing in the fields of the Lord.

You walk through the main gate, down miniature streets named Palestine and Ramble Avenue: You're backward in time and collective memory. The Morrisons lived at 19 Peck Avenue. The house is still there, one of the more modest on the grounds. The lake and the docks are maybe 150 yards down the lane, past the Athenaeum Hotel, with its old canvas awnings and wicker furniture. An elderly Chautauquan named Alfreda Irwin told me of looking out the library windows night after summer night in the late forties and fifties and there was a young man in a white shirt and skinny tie, waiting for the program to begin in the "amph." It was Norman. "I think he was one of those who cared too much," said Irwin, who also remembered how he used to sit and talk kindly to the ladies of Chautauqua.

In "Chautauqua," poet Hugh Ogden, who knew and looked up to Norman in the fatherless and reborning years in western New York, wrote:

I see you sitting on the grass outside an amphitheater
listening to Bach's B Minor Mass,
your eyes oblivious to the brown bats
that flit from the roof.
I see you getting out of an old Cadillac
in the Pentagon parking lot.
You wrap your daughter in a plaid blanket,
then carry her under one arm,
a gallon jug hung from the other.

He had a wooden rowboat and a single-cylinder outboard engine. He had a little garden plot at the south end of the grounds, and he'd fertilize it with fish guts. He joined the Scouts and got the God and Country award. He belonged to Hurlbut Memorial Church where the wooden altar had these words cut into it: "In Remembrance of Me." The minister from Norman's time is dead, but his wife told me: "Always sort of felt that a guy like Norm could be compared to Jesus. How many come along that we crucify before they have a chance?"

In the winter the place was ghostly, the old hotels shuttered against the cold. The institution was waiting for those nine weeks of summer light and swelled population.

Norman and his brother, Ralph, three years younger but two grades below, would walk out of the main gate and across the road to Chautauqua Central School. It wasn't that Norman was unpopular at school, it was that he was so uneasy. And the uneasiness was complicated by the fact that his only sibling was exactly opposite: athletic, natural with girls, gifted at friendship. You can sense the difference in photographs. Ralph is the one with the sunny smile and relaxed body language; Norman is the one in the buttoned-up suit, maybe holding a book.

"People idolized his brother," a Minnesota kidney specialist named Milton Bullock told me. Bullock was a year behind Norman and became a good friend of both Morrison brothers. He was attracted to Norman's "intense interest in politics and world affairs . . . in a rural school where there wasn't much interest, where a lot of it was interest in agriculture." What Milt Bullock saw in Norman, besides the fertile mind, was an "incredibly honest person who struggled with the social graces. . . . I recognized quite clearly it was an uphill battle for him, especially in terms of his brother, Ralph." Bullock, like everybody else, could recall the doggedness, decency, high-mindedness, the wish to do something important in life. Bullock was studying medicine at Yale when he heard the news reports. He had been out of touch a good while.

In November 1965, Norman Morrison's little brother was a Peace Corps volunteer in Gondar, Ethiopia, when a Voice of America report over a transistor radio reported the Baltimore Quaker's killing himself at the Pentagon with a baby in his arms.

Ralph Morrison has been dead a good while. He died suddenly in his forties, coming home from a family outing. You can save your life by not doing something like your older brother did—and still perish young. People close to the family have told me that Ralph never really found peace with Norman's act, although this wasn't true of Hazel Morrison. Norman's mother had long accepted it, and was able to drop his name and memory into luncheon talk with the ladies of the club. For many years before she died, Hazel Morrison worked at the Chautauqua library, a wonderful old place.

While his brother went around as if he were skating on air, "Norm couldn't walk ten feet without stumbling over something," remembered Lowell Rein, who was probably his closest friend in high school, but who, like Bullock, drifted from him in the years after. Part of the reason for the drift, for Rein as well as Bullock, was that it became increasingly difficult to talk to Norman about much other than the causes he was preoccupied with. He didn't want to let a lot of light in for something else; the intensity levels got uncomfortable. "I never remember him even once saying anything loving about his father," Rein told me. He has since reflected on how angry Norman must have been at his father for the way he allowed himself to die. Rein, unlike Bullock, was able to recall instances of the temper. "I saw him violent several times. . . . He had tremendous strength anyway, and so when it's held in check but then comes out in that adrenaline rush, it's almost super-human," said Rein. Their friendship basically ended in an argument, and for years Rein felt regret about it. They were adults by then and their lives were in pursuit of separate goals.

For a time during high school, Norman drove a laundry truck. He would come by the Rein house on his run to grub a meal. He would sit and talk to Lowell's dad about baseball. Rein now understands how his best friend was trying to reach out to an older male figure. Rein: "He was an achiever, and I was an achiever. But he couldn't do anything *with* his achievement." That sounds a little harsh. Norman wrote columns for the school paper, attended the national Boy Scout jamboree at Valley Forge, made senior patrol leader, managed the basketball team, won oratory contests, was in the honor society his freshman year. "The Best. To My Best Pal," Norm Morrison wrote to Lowell Rein in the 1952 Chautauqua yearbook, the *Indian,* at their graduation: twelve boys in a rural class of twenty-eight. Norman stroked the words in his awkward hand. In his class picture he has a warm smile and a checked tie. "Norman Morrison," it says opposite the picture. "Moses."

In the fall of 1951, a seventeen-year-old high-school senior uneasy in his skin filled out an application to the College of Wooster in Ohio. He wrote an essay called "A Brief Story of My Life." It's notable for its honesty and plainspokenness. He said of his junior year: "I seemed to go through a general period of doubt and uncertainty and turned to reading Ralph Waldo Emerson; and also studying thoroughly the pacifism movement in this country. . . . My grades suffered during this year and my social life declined." Farther down: "My main hobby has been a small farm of five acres located in the city of Corry, Penna. I was able to make the purchase myself because it was land that was already in the family. I am, on a small scale, an apple grower, bee raiser, and flower bulb encourager." He closed his life story: "I am prepared to do all in my power to become a Christian minister. . . ."

Personal rating forms were sent in from teachers and clerics. He earned high marks for industry, integrity, and intelligence. The evaluators wrote comments such as: "Norman does not win support of fellow students. Needs to learn to be tactful." And, "Norman needs coaching in human relations." And: "At the present time he has become much interested in pacifism, and has earnestly studied the subject. He has determination and eagerness in presenting this matter to others."

The College of Wooster, like Chautauqua, is an ivied cocoon; it sits an hour southwest of Cleveland. In their evangelistic urge to establish a Christian community across America, Protestant clergymen of the nineteenth century created small denominational colleges as a stay against the devil and darkness. Wooster was founded by Presbyterian synods. The college president of Norman's time once told *Time* magazine, "You simply do not have a liberal education when you divorce learning from man's deepest inquiry." It isn't an accident that the Wooster of the fifties sent 10 to 15 percent of its graduates into the ministry. And yet the image of a little pious Republican coed institution with its greenswards and collegiate Gothic architecture is both correct and incorrect. The liberal traditions of Wooster would see to it that the college contributed a disproportionate number of volunteers to JFK's Peace Corps in the next decade. And at the Vietnam Moratorium in Washington in the fall of 1969, the second-biggest collegiate delegation in America was from the College of Wooster in Ohio.

"PACIFIST SUICIDE LOCAL GRAD," headlined the Wooster *Daily Record* on November 3, 1965, noting that "McNamara—the principal target of the drastic protest—was in his office at the time Morrison met his fiery death." I have wondered if the public burning of an alumnus, class of '56, didn't uniquely prepare a college for the more fiery second half of the sixties. A Wooster professor of Russian studies named Dan Calhoun, who arrived the year Norman graduated, and never met him, told me one day several years ago over coffee in the student union: "He made it a moral question; you couldn't intellectualize it after that. I know I felt a little angry at him at the time. It forced me to face it. I wonder if it didn't make McNamara face it, too. 'How dare you not let us keep this any longer at the level we wanted to keep it at.' " Professor Calhoun also said this, regarding the lighting of the match: "At that moment, you don't have choice. At that moment, it's inevitability. At that moment you have no freedom, whether it's divine providence or whatever else you want to call it that's driving you."

His best friend that first year was Don Reiman, also from Erie, whose folks had been friends with Norman's parents at the Church of the Covenant. As teenagers Norman and Don Reiman had both been taken under the care of the presbytery, which means they were in preparation for a life in the ministry. (Although the Morrisons lived at Chautauqua after 1947, they retained their Erie church membership and would come into the city regularly.) Reiman is now a widely recognized scholar of the life and work of Percy Bysshe Shelley. In June 1993 I spent the better part of a day talking to him about his old friend and about the culture of Wooster. Reiman said that when Ike won election in the fall of their freshman year, students broke into chapel and rang the bells. Norm Morrison, espouser of nonviolence, flower-bulb encourager, hitchhiked to Washington for the inauguration.

Reiman and Morrison were mostly outsiders, odd fits, and again, you can sense it in photographs. Wooster didn't have real fraternities; it had "sections" in the dorms. It was good to be able to play ball and to sit around afterward in the section in your penny loafers and college sweater, shooting the shit. Norman would have been awful at that. But he played intramural football for his section and he ran cross-country for the school itself. The runners lost to Slippery Rock and Oberlin in the '52–'53 season, and in the yearbook was this: "Letters were awarded to Captain Dick May and to Jim Landes. Stu Hills, Chuck Schneider, and Norm Morrison, all key men who had been counted on by the squad, suffered injuries that kept the Scots from reaching their full potentialities."

Early that year the Sophomore Court picked out Reiman and Norman, among others, put blindfolds on them, drove them up near Akron, and dumped them by the side of the road. That night the two had to knock on the door of a farmhouse to find shelter. Back at school the next day, having survived the test, Don Reiman sat on the shoulders of a blocky Norm Morrison, and the two "dishorsed" a gaggle of soph riders. Dishorsed them damn well.

"He was always trying to talk me into pacifism that first year—and I was not amenable to that," said Reiman, who, in the early years of the war, was an apologist for Vietnam—that is, until an unreal act on a darkening eve in 1965. And then it was as if Don Reiman awoke, saw. He started calling newspapers and TV stations, trying to tell whoever was on the line that the dead man wasn't the strange delusionist of their inflated accounts. On a pink sheet of paper he scribbled to himself: "His child Emily symbolic of Vietnamese children. The Americans who felt revulsion at the idea she was endangered would look & feel differently at news accounts of children napalmed in Vietnam."

In the fall of '53, soph year, Norman began attending Friends meetings. There were only a dozen or so Quakers on campus, including faculty. Their Sunday-morning meeting in the east room of the library basement was like a religious cell in the Presbyterian midst.

Between semesters or on a holiday weekend, Reiman and Norman would hitch home. Once, Norman started telling Reiman about his five acres of land in Corry, Pennsylvania. Reiman: "It was a surprise to me. It was a facet of his life I didn't know anything about. I was impressed by it. . . . He was a sort of a Thoreauvian character. . . . He believed in independence, in symbolic action more than words. . . . Let's put it this way: Thoreau is trying to express the kind of person Norman was. . . . He didn't have any display in him. He was not trying to catch the public attention in any way. So far as I know, he never got up and gave a speech."

From a letter to Reiman: "When I opened up the typewriter to do your letter I knocked a plate off the wall and broke it, but what I really felt like doing was breaking it over the segregationist's head. I guess I am still the mixed-up pacifist that you knew back in your college days."

Following the act, Reiman, a rising university professor, wrote a long letter to another Wooster classmate: "Norman Morrison, I am fully convinced, made a rational decision to do what he believed some individual had to do to witness against a course of national policy that he believed was rushing the world toward destruction. . . . I have known many who were brighter and quicker, many who were easier with people and more articulate, but Norm was one of the few people whom one could trust to hold to his beliefs and act on them. . . ." The classmate, a clergyman in Illinois, replied: "Yet it does seem to me that idealistic movements such as Christian pacifism may themselves become instruments of cruelty, sacrificing others piecemeal to preserve a 'peace' which is really 'no peace.' "

In 1981, sixteen years after the burning, Don Reiman went back to Wooster to receive an honorary degree. People thought he would discourse on Shelley and the romantic poets. He called his talk "Witnesses." It was about Norman, and it was moving and brilliant. He quoted Kierkegaard's *Fear and Trembling* in regard to the biblical Abraham and his higher duty: "The tragic hero has need of tears and claims them," but "One cannot weep over Abraham. One approaches him with a *horror religiosus. . . .*"

I asked Reiman if what his friend did was selfish. We had been talking for hours and he was now almost twitching about his basement (we had gone downstairs to fish out the Wooster yearbooks): emptying trays of rubberbands and screws, dusting the top of a painting, reshelving tomes, plowing a hand through his long white hair. It was as if he had gotten the word about Norman only the day before and was trying desperately to decode it. "I don't think so. . . . You see . . . no, I don't think it's a selfish act. . . ." In an earlier conversation, on the phone, Reiman said: "You see, he did the thing that was true to his nature, and he did not do the thing that would have been untrue to his nature." He meant: He did not kill his child.

In the late summer of 1955, at Chautauqua, about to return to college for his senior year, a twenty-one-year-old history and religious-studies major, so hard to fathom, uneasy in his skin, possessed of his religious instincts and Thoreauvian impulses, met an earnest and intellectually bent southern woman named Anne Corpening. She was up from Duke on a summer job. She spoke at a Sunday vespers-campfire service in the Ravine. The topic was ethics. He pursued her single-mindedly for two weeks.

Anne Morrison Welsh: "He gave me his fraternity pin right before I left to go back to school. I said, 'Look, I'm not going to take that ring.' Finally I told him I'd hold it for him, I certainly wasn't going to wear it. He would have left it there on that park bench."

In the late summer of 1955, Ford Motor Company was getting ready to bring out the new fall models, including the Crown Victoria, featuring chrome side moldings running from the headlamps to the back fender, with a cheeky dip at the A-post. The Crown Vicky came in two tones of shocking pink and tangerine and other colors; inside, you could get candy-pink leather seats that looked like something at Hedy Lamarr's dressing table. These were odious facts of life to the head of Ford Division, who knew one had to sell the wares in America, make display.

ONE WANTS DESPERATELY to find clues to the inexplicable. Four days before Norman Morrison killed himself, he attended a meeting in Philadelphia of the American Friends Service Committee. (Four days after the act, on November 6, 1965, John Corry of the New York *Times* reconstructed a kind of prose calendar of the last hours and days, and I am indebted to it here.) The theme of the Philly conference was "Inward Renewal and Outward Works." Norman drove to Pennsylvania with several associates from Stony Run Friends in Baltimore, which was and is the name of the Quaker meetinghouse on North Charles Street where he used to sit in Sunday silence with his spouse and wait for what is called the Inward Light.

One of the conference speakers was a Friend just back from South Vietnam, who asserted that for every member of the Vietcong who dies, three civilians must also die. Norman and the others from Baltimore stayed overnight. On the way home, Norman, who served as the executive secretary of Stony Run Friends, and who was paid $6,400 a year for this more or less full-time and quasi-ministerial position, took out a worn blue notebook and talked from the backseat about some of the things he had just heard. He focused hard on the innocent civilian deaths.

This was Saturday. The next day, Norman told his fellow Stony Run Quakers that he was impressed by a scientist who had stated in a paper that new discoveries in science served only to increase his sense of wonder. After the meeting the members went into the library for coffee, and Norman gave $2 to the wife of the man who had used his own car to take the group to Pennsylvania. It was for the gas, and please, he said, you must take it. He looked rather spiffy. That evening, the executive secretary of Stony Run stayed home to take care of his three children while his spouse went back to the meetinghouse to view some slides of a Friend back from Japan.

On Monday Norman worked over a statement whose heading was "Dear Editor." It was about Vietnam and he was hoping it would be used on a local television program. In Washington the Pentagon announced that American planes in South Vietnam had accidentally killed forty-eight civilians.

The next day, Tuesday, his last on the earth, Norman read a letter to the editor, asking those who thought the Vietnam War "a mistake from the beginning" to write to their congressmen, so that Washington would not convince itself that no one "except draft-dodgers and addlepates" were against the war. His reaction to this published letter in the *Sun* was visceral: Good God, man, I've already done all those things.

At 9:30 a.m. he called his secretary at the meetinghouse, just a short distance away, to tell her he had a cold and wouldn't be coming in. Later in the morning, Norman received in the mail his regular subscription copy of *I. F. Stone's Weekly.* In the paper was a full-page account, reprinted from *Paris Match,* of American bombers destroying a French priest's village near a place called Duc Co, after the Vietcong had already been through. A French correspondent had found the cleric stretched out on a bed in the St. Paul Clinic in Saigon. "I have seen my faithful burned up in napalm," the nearly out-of-his-mind priest told the *Paris Match* journalist. "I have seen the bodies of women and children blown to bits. I have seen all my villages razed. By God, it's not possible! . . . They must settle their accounts with God."

The next morning, readers of the *Sun* awoke to a triple-deck headline: "BALTIMORE QUAKER WITH BABY SETS SELF AFIRE . . . Pacifist Releases Girl as Flames Engulf Him in Front of Building."

The following day, Anne Morrison found in the mailbox outside her shingled house on St. George's Avenue a letter from her husband. The envelope carried a Washington postmark of November 2, which meant he had made sure to stop off on his way to death to drop it in a box. This tiny fact alone, suggesting a seeming presence of mind, might argue for a person far less irrational than the one pictured in news accounts. When Anne took the letter out of the box on November 4, she had this strange feeling he was still alive, even though she knew he had been cremated the day before at the Lee Funeral Home on Capitol Hill. (It was the only private mortuary in Washington with a crematorium.) The letter, which has never fully been published, began: "Dearest Anne: For weeks, even months, I have been praying only that I be shown what I must do. This morning, with no warning, I was shown as clearly as I was shown that Friday night in August, 1955, that you would be my wife. . . . Know that I love thee but must act for the children of the priest's village."

The letter also said this, with a chilling simplicity, referring to the story of Abraham and Isaac: "I shall not plan to go without my child as Abraham did."

A WITNESS. Major Richard V. Lundquist is coming out of the eighth-corridor entrance on the Potomac side. He's on his way to an economics class in another building. Someone behind a retaining wall is yelling. This person has a child.

Lundquist, remembering three decades later: "I looked up and expected to see a long-haired, unkempt, young person, but instead I saw a well-dressed man with a child in his arms."

Lundquist: "You hear a jet go overhead and you look up and see a Piper cub. You do a double take."

In Pentagon dusk, the major sees flames shooting up the left side of the man behind the wall. He starts running. People behind him are running. The officer climbs over the wall and discovers the child on the ground. She's on a path, in blue coveralls. He's the first to reach her. He picks up Emily and carries her some distance away, to the back of the garden, where he hands her either to a woman who has a blanket or to Pentagon guards.

Lundquist, remembering: "I'm not a doctor. The whole thing is happening in seconds. But when flames go up past your nose and mouth, it doesn't take very long for them to cut off your oxygen, and you lose your ability pretty fast to stand or hold on to something."

A second witness: Lieutenant Colonel Charles S. Johnson, then of North Venice Street in Arlington. In November 1965, he's working in mid-range planning in the office of research and development. He's come upon the vision from a different angle.

Johnson, remembering three decades later: "The child was knocked out of his hands."

Interviewer (startled): "Who did the knocking?"

Johnson: "I did."

But then, several minutes into this memory, the certainty is slipping away: "Going back to square one. I looked up and saw this man flaming with a child." A minute later: "On second memory, maybe the child was on the wall when I got there."

Down in the trench, Colonel Johnson risks his life trying to pull a man's head down out of the flame. When it is over, he goes to the Pentagon dispensary. There are burns on his hands and face. He calls his wife and says he'll be home a little late. She has already heard the radio flash.

A third voice: Sergeant Robert Bundt is standing outside the building, waiting to be picked up by Russell Banks and his wife, Sue. Bundt always rides home with the Bankses. They're getting their car at a lower entrance and will pull around up front. Sergeant Bundt got back from Greenland two years ago, and they posted him here to the Pentagon. He works in war-game theory for the Air Force. He and his wife, who's pregnant, have a place off Columbia Pike near Bailey's Crossroads.

He's on the sidewalk when a man with a baby brushes past him. The man is carrying a package of some kind in his other arm. He's in street clothes. Bundt doesn't think anything of this. Thousands of people in the Pentagon wear civvies. The man is probably taking his child to work, the sergeant thinks. He's done that himself. It's true the guy looks pretty distracted.

Russ and Sue Banks still haven't come. Must be a jam getting out of the lot. Bundt's back is turned to the raised garden. There's a loud noise. He turns, sees smoke, hears shouting. People are running from several directions. By the time Bundt has jumped over the wall and gotten into the trench, the baby has been taken away. In fact, Bundt never sees the child.

On the way home with the Bankses, the sergeant's hands begin to blister, so he stops off at the service station where he has an evening job to tell them he won't be in. The next day the sergeant doesn't have a dress uniform to wear to work; it's black and smells foul. Bundt's name doesn't appear in any of the newspaper accounts: He has gotten away before reporters can find him. Several months hence he'll receive a commendation medal from the Air Force. He'll also receive a note of quiet gratitude from the wife of the immolated man.

THE IMMOLATED MAN, a decade earlier, would have left a Wooster ring or pin on a Chautauqua park bench, had not Anne Corpening sighed and said okay, she'd hold it. He was Presbyterian, she was Methodist, but they were both finding paths to Friends, and that's how and where Anne and Norman got married in the fall of 1957: in a plain Quaker service in a plain brick meetinghouse in Durham, North Carolina. By then he had finished at Wooster and completed his first year of seminary studies at Western Theological in Pittsburgh. Anne had finished at Duke. After the wedding they left for Scotland, where Norman planned to do his second year of seminary at New College in Edinburgh. Anne would stretch the tuna and grilled cheese and take some psychology courses.

Before departing they posed for a picture. Norman is in a coat and tie and looks almost relaxed; Anne is holding a small camera and is in a two-piece suit. They're the same height; her smile is far easier. His feet are planted at forty-five-degree angles and the arm of his jacket is too long. A notebook or maybe a case for glasses sticks up from his vest pocket.

At Christmas he wrote to Don Reiman in the States. He used a soft blue parchmentlike air letter, the kind you fold open and write your message on and then fold back into fours and send off at reduced postage. He typed the letter single space, cramming it to the margins: "We both get thrilled from time to time just considering our present state of marital bliss and how we actually got this way. I hope we are not in for any jolts when we hit the routine of American life next year." They were living on $50 a month, not counting rent, and eating very well. He intended to apply to Yale for his last year of seminary but probably he would wind up back in Pittsburgh.

They did end up back in Pittsburgh for the '58–'59 school year, his last before ordination, though apparently ordination was no longer fig- uring in his plans. From a Christmas 1958 note to Reiman: "I have man- aged to preach every Sunday since the middle of September and am enjoying it a great deal, but I am not seriously considering ordination until I have really tried something else." Six months later, on May 27, 1959, he wrote again to Reiman and his wife, Mary:

> Pittsburgh has been the scene of much activity this spring. In our own lives the big rival events both happened on the same day. Benjamin Howard Morrison was born on the 12th of May, the same day that daddy graduated from seminary. I got my PA about 10 hours before my B.D. . . . . Pittsburgh itself is celebrating its 200th ann. and the Sprague, the largest paddlewheeler ever to labor on the Mississippi is tied up at the bottom of our hill. Last weekend the United World Federalists held their con-

vention in Pittsburgh for the first time, and Harvey Haddix of
the Pirates just completed 12 innings of perfect baseball in one
game to break all previous records only to lose in the 13th
inning to Lou Burdette of the Braves, who allowed 12 hits but
no runs.

The other news was that he and Anne were moving south to organize a Friends meeting in Charlotte, where six Quakers had already
been assembling informally for two years. "My three years in Presbyterian seminaries have made me a better Quaker," he wrote. Accepting
ordination to the ministry would imply he was better than the people
in the pews he was trying to serve. He was joining a faith where there
was no distinction between laity and the clergy, between men and
women. A sect that held nonviolence as a way of life, not as liberal
ethic. Several of his Pittsburgh seminary professors and classmates
tried to talk him out of it, but that was like talking to stone.

Before leaving for Carolina, Norman had a fight with Lowell Rein.
The family Volvo had conked on the Pennsylvania Turnpike and Norman had called his best friend from Chautauqua days, who was now in
the Pittsburgh area. Rein's memory is that the plea for aid came at night.
He got dressed and drove out to the turnpike. Norman was waiting by
the side of the road. There was a service plaza across the barrier divide.
Norman wanted Rein to push him at right angles against traffic through
a small break in the barrier. Rein refused. It would be crazy to do a thing
like that, he said. Rein: "He got violently angry. The bumpers wouldn't
even line up." This came close to finishing their friendship.

From a letter to Reiman, shortly after reaching Charlotte: "Honestly,
Don, I learned and digested a lot in the last 7 years and it has left me
with no clear and sincere choice but to refuse ordination and become a
Friend in order to remain true to what I have learned from the very people who are being paid to keep the church doors open by training ministers." He closed: "Among a host of other things I am most thankful for
the union of two lives that Anne and I have achieved. . . . Anne has
given me confidence and abundant patience and understanding as I
have gradually learned to communicate with her, and I trust more of the
world from now on."

A reporter from the Charlotte *Observer* came to observe the Quaker
cell in the city's midst. Fourteen Friends sat in a living room in their
Sunday silence. Wrote the journalist-guest, watching the waiters:

"After intermission, Morrison called on Carroll Mullis to read John Greenleaf Whittier's 'First Day Thoughts.' Then there was complete silence. Some bowed their heads and closed their eyes. Others looked straight ahead. . . . You could hear airplanes overhead, cars going by. Wind rustled the leaves of the huge oak trees. A dog barked. A boy fired his cap pistol. Inside, quiet Quakers listened for the voice of God." After twenty-two minutes, somebody spoke.

Time went on in Carolina. More dogs barked. Additional folding chairs were set up in spare living rooms. John Kennedy got elected president of the country. Some inroads were made against bigotry and social injustice. Norman picked up a copy of *The Mind of the South* by W. J. Cash and couldn't decide whom it was meant for. ("Most southerners would hardly believe it and any Yankee is encouraged to despair of the southern mind," he wrote to Reiman.) More time passed. He and Anne negotiated to buy a small ledge of land at Ginger Cake Mountain Park, where they hoped to build a small primitive cabin someday. They helped draft a statement supporting nonviolent protest against segregated lunch counters: "If we dismiss these protests as mere isolated events and of no importance, history shall overtake us before we know the cause of our own undoing." Another child, Anna Christina, blessed their lives.

But what you begin to sense between the lines of this correspondence is disenchantment, for the South, maybe also for the job. You also hear the wear of parenthood and family life, even as he seems to have loved it. In any case Baltimore would be the next place for the Morrison clan, although not before a summer-camp stop-off in South China, Maine. Norman had lived in Charlotte three years, and good things had come about as a result of his presence and spirit. Just before leaving, in May 1962, he wrote to Reiman about the prospect of seeing Maine: "It is a thousand miles away, and I have never been above Boston, but that is where my thoughts are straying much of the time now; especially in this hot dry weather we have been having."

From the Friends camp, Anne wrote to the Reimans: "We are enjoying the cool ruggedness of Maine, with its clear blue lakes everywhere and its alpine climate. . . . We are learning a lot about camp directing and teen-agers. . . . Norm has accepted a very generous offer from the Baltimore Friends Meeting to become their Exec. Secretary. It would be a 2 year contract, at least. Although there were 2 interesting possibilities here in New England, the Baltimore position was just too inviting to refuse. Theirs is an old, well established Meeting, quite large in comparison to Charlotte. They meet for worship on the basis of silence and are liberal in their social philosophies. So it would be a different situation from Charlotte, although Norm's work would not be *that* different."

On April 13, 1963, a small piece appears in the Baltimore *Sun;* Morrison has been a resident of the city for seven months:

> For the second year in a row Norman R. Morrison has withheld $5 from his income tax and sent it to the United Nations for refugee work. Mr. Morrison, executive secretary of the Stony Run Friends Monthly Meeting, said he called the attention of the Internal Revenue Service to the $5 shortage both times. . . . "Even though we are Christian pacifists we agree that our Government has an obligation to provide for the common defense but under the present circumstances we feel that our military budget is only preparing us for mutual suicide."

He gets involved with the city's pacifist community. He plays ice hockey on the Gunpowder River with homemade pucks and sticks. He helps build a cabinet in the kitchen of a farmhouse for a fellow Friend. He demonstrates for civil rights, gets arrested in a nonviolent protest at Gwynn Oak Park. But in truth, the cause of social justice is giving way now to a new intensity.

George Webb, longtime Stony Run member: "In the early years I kept wondering why in the world he was worried about Vietnam. I mean, Kennedy was in, there was excitement in the country, Vietnam didn't seem like a problem."

Christmas 1964: "Merry Christmas from the Morrisons!" says the mimeographed letter that goes out with the cards. The Morrisons have been in Baltimore two years. "Now that there are five of us, Christmas 1964 in our home gives evidence of being more wonderful than ever. Emily Fuller Morrison was born November 11, a healthy nine-pounder with brown hair and blue eyes. Already she has claimed a significant place in our family life and is the bearer of much joy. Ben (5½ years old) and Tina (4 years) are enjoying kindergarten and nursery school at Friends School this year."

He and Anne make a down payment on a two-story house with a nice porch. It's a few blocks over, on an integrated working-class street. There's a fir and a maple out front, a yard in back for the kids. He tells friends he can make a stake here; Anne was the one who had pushed to get it.

On August 3, 1965, the *Sun* publishes a letter signed "Norman R. Morrison." The letter has been prompted by a nationally televised press conference of a few days before, on July 28, in which Lyndon Johnson has announced that 50,000 new troops will be sent immediately to Vietnam and that draft calls will be doubled and more Americans will be sent as needed. In reality, the president and his men have already planned for an additional 150,000 troops for Vietnam, what's known as the full "forty-four battalion request." It has been in debate for some two months in the councils of power. The president stands under a silver-colored light-reflecting umbrella in the East Room (the secretary of defense is in the front row, to his left) as he plaintively asks the nation, "Why must young Americans, born into a land exultant with hope and with golden promise, toil and suffer and sometimes die in such a remote and distant place?" Twenty-eight million Americans are reported to be watching this historic news conference, which has been deliberately staged at midday during the week when TV audiences are down.

One of those watching is a Quaker in north Baltimore. Who sits down afterward and writes a letter to the *Sun*. McNamara's name is in it, but the writer seems to be focusing his rage on the president: "How long can a president who had to begin his most recent address by again defining the enemy, after Americans have been dying at their hand for well over a year, hope to continue to demand that more of us give our lives in the struggle?"

In three months, less a day, he'll be on fire.

NORMAN AND ANNE MORRISON took a small lunch together on November 2, 1965. It would not be precisely accurate to say a spouse had no hint. But not in her wildest imaginings would she have thought this. They talked about the filthy war and the burning of the French curate's children and finally Anne changed the subject and said she wanted a suit for Christmas. It didn't have to be a new suit.

A few weeks later she was to tell a Quaker reporter for the *Sun* regarding that last lunch: "Somewhere in the conversation he said he had never felt better or more right. I can see him sitting there on the stool in the kitchen, but I can't remember the exact words or how they connected with the rest of the conversation. But nothing about it seemed abnormal. I'm sure he wanted me to know that he was sane in what he was about to do."

They had their meal and then at three o'clock Anne left in the family's VW bus. "I'm going over to school to pick up Ben and Tina," she said. "Back in a jiff. Will you take care of the baby?" Norman nodded. While she was gone, he gathered his tools and collected Emily and slipped on the sport coat that he had bought in Scotland in 1957, maybe the one piece of clothing he had ever spent a little money on.

That night, two Friends from Stony Run drove Anne down to Washington to get Emily. The car bearing the shocked people from Baltimore pulled onto the post at Fort Myer, crossed Custer Road and Lee Avenue, found the dispensary. Norman's body was in an ambulance parked in a narrow drive on the side of the building. Anne never saw the blackened corpse. George Webb, accompanying her, and whose slides of Japan she had gone to see a couple nights' previous at the meetinghouse while Norman stayed home with the kids, read a statement in front of reporters. Anne wrote it with the aid of others in an anteroom of the dispensary, but she didn't want to read it or meet with the press herself. The statement said, "Norman Morrison has given his life to express his concern over the great loss of life and human suffering caused by the war in Vietnam. He was protesting our government's deep military involvement in this war. He felt that all citizens must speak their true convictions about their government's action."

At 9 p.m. the Arlington County medical examiner arrived at the dispensary to make his report. Under *Body Heat,* the doctor wrote "cool." In the box marked *Probable Cause of Death,* he wrote, "2nd + 3rd degree burns 70 percent body surface." The examiner didn't date and sign the document until four days after, and he seems to have relied on press accounts in compiling the summary of what had happened: "He apparently drenched his clothing and that of his daughter. Then he stood on a wall where he could shout to the workers as they left at 5 p.m. His clothing was then seen to catch on fire—the onlookers screamed for him to drop the baby which he did. The child landed unharmed in a bush—he was completely engulfed by the flames and died." (Three decades after that report, in the summer of 1994, Anne Morrison Welsh, at my request, okayed its release from Virginia state archives. She carried a copy around in her purse for a week and then she forwarded it with a letter that said with characteristic simplicity: "I had a good cry, reading the report; I thought of Moses saved in the bull rushes.")

Early on the morning of November 3, 1965, two children were informed, though not all of it. Tina Morrison was just beginning to sort out how the moon and the stars and the air and all our lives are webbed. When her mother told her, she said, "Oh, I understand, Daddy has gone and now his love can spread." Ben, six, older by a year, didn't say anything. The next day he hid in the garage. They called and called but couldn't find him.

SOMETHING I'VE WONDERED: How long had it turned in his mind?

Anne Morrison Welsh has told me and said to others that her husband never once discussed self-immolation with her, and I have no reason to doubt that. But it's clear now he had talked with people outside his family about it. Was his talk in a hypothetical context? Sort of. And did he stop talking about it at the end? It seems so.

In the first news accounts, a Baltimorean named John Paisley, a conscientious objector in World War II, was quoted as saying: "We had to talk him out in the same manner last year. He wanted to do it when the monks in Saigon were killing themselves that way." Afterward Paisley wrote to Anne and said he'd been misquoted. Paisley wasn't a member of Stony Run Friends; he and Norman had met informally at peace meetings around town. On the day in 1994 when I knocked at Paisley's door, he was very old and very ill and couldn't focus on my questions.

John Roemer could. He had been a close friend, and within minutes of our sitting down in the early summer of 1994, he put the events of November 2, 1965, in this context: " 'I have a moral call.' The trajectory leads right down there. . . . The moral trajectory, right to its logical conclusion." Roemer and I were seated in the library of the north Baltimore school where he teaches. His arm shot out. He was pointing southward, about forty miles.

Roemer said, "We debated this in the halls, in the classroom. We talked of it a lot. There's no question." He is a thin, intense intellectual who runs marathons and teaches courses in ethics and history at a private elementary and secondary school called the Park School. He became a Quaker at Princeton in 1957. In 1965 he and Norman Morrison were the young radicals of Stony Run Friends, always pushing the older and more established members of the meeting. But Roemer emphasized that Stony Run never rejected Norman in death. I've spoken to some of those older members and I'm convinced it's true. For more than a year, Stony Run helped provide for Anne out of its comfortable pockets.

Roemer told me that Norman came to his classes at the Stony Run school and discussed doing it. Perhaps this was as much as a full year before he did do it. It was hypothetical talk, sort of. "We talked about the monks in Vietnam. We talked about all kinds of things. Maybe we ought to do what the monks do. Moral witness demands it. He said, 'Nah, that wouldn't work.' " They talked of nailing Roemer to a cross and carrying him into a church. "Nah, sends the wrong message." People would think they were nuts. Roemer: "And it's not only a practical decision, it's a moral one: You're leaving behind a family."

Then what turned in his mind? "I don't know. I don't know. He fought the war more and more deeply. I mean, when are you one of the Germans? . . . You have to be mentally different to fly in the face of received wisdom on this in this country. He played it out in his mind, I think, in terms of being a moral witness."

Roemer and I sat there in the quiet of a school library so many years later and spoke of the *mechanism* of doing it. I watched Norman's friend shudder. "When you're going to your execution, you may be lucid till those last couple hours. Then, who knows? . . . I'm sure he wasn't quite right. . . . He wasn't insane, but he also wasn't quite right. . . . Look, you're going to your execution."

I asked Roemer if he was shocked upon hearing. "I was shocked he did it—and I knew right where it came from." I asked if he felt any guilt afterward. "I never thought this was animating his behavior." A moment later, holding his arms tight against his chest: ". . . he was a grown-up white boy. If, on the other hand, I'd been dealing with some unbalanced nineteen-year-old. . . . I never took heat. I never hid it."

At a memorial service in Washington three weeks after the burning, John Roemer of Baltimore stood and said: "In a society where it is normal for human beings to drop bombs on human targets, where it is normal to spend 50 percent of the individual's tax dollar on war, where it is normal . . . to have twelve times overkill capacity, Norman Morrison was not normal. He said, 'Let it stop.' "

AND WHAT OF THE "receptive" man behind the wall? He was waltzing with the Tiger Woman, the president of the United States was calling him night and day on the secured phones, he had just jumped in and gotten Alcoa and the copper industry to rescind their unfair price increases, the columnists were enthusing as to how Lyndon might soon anoint him an "assistant president."

Call this part the trajectory of the turn. It's the dying not visible to the ordinary eye. For one thing, you would need documents, and some knowledge of a faraway battle.

On Sunday, November 14, 1965, the first of 457 soldiers of the First Battalion, Seventh Cavalry Regiment, U.S. Army, came by helicopter into a remote valley of the central highlands of South Vietnam. Almost immediately these high-tech Americans of the superbly equipped and trained First Air Cav Division were surrounded by two regiments of regulars of the People's Army of Vietnam—more than 2,000 troops. As Neil Sheehan wrote in his landmark *A Bright Shining Lie*—in a sentence Hemingway would have admired—"The men of the two armies met among the trees where the rain forest began."

The Ia Drang Valley ("Ia" stood for river in the language of a local Montagnard tribe) had long been known as a Communist sanctuary and infiltration route. It was scrub brush, ravines, stunted trees, elephant grass, tigers, and termite hills sitting below a mountain outcropping known as the Chu Pong Massif. The Chu Pong was a 2,401-foot mountain with forests that stretched five miles into Cambodia.

The Ia Drang was the first major face-to-face engagement of the war between large-scale U.S. cavalry units and NVA regular-army forces, as opposed to pajama-clad guerrilla units. Like Norman Morrison, the Ia Drang was a big story in America, but only briefly. It flared and went out. The Americans fought against the far greater numbers, and won. But 234 U.S. lives were taken in four days and nights of savage fighting—against ten times as many losses on the enemy side. The North Vietnamese regulars and the supporting cadres and main forces of Vietcong died profusely, as Sheehan later wrote, partly because they had made themselves the attackers. It was a U.S. victory in more or less conventional stand-and-fight warfare. Except that the Communists read the Ia Drang as a confirmation that *they* would prevail in the long run—while almost all of the high-ranking U.S. military and decision-makers in Washington and in Vietnam saw it as exactly otherwise. Which is why some students of the war think of the Ia Drang as "the fatal victory."

And it was in the days and weeks after this trumpeted American military triumph in the shadow of the Chu Pong that I believe a numerically brilliant defense secretary came to grasp what so few others at the time in either Saigon or Washington were able to comprehend: That America couldn't win the war, not on the battlefield. That the strategy of attrition was doomed, militarily speaking. That the Westmoreland concept of search-and-destroy was bankrupt before it had really begun. That there had been a terrible, terrible miscalculation. It was in the numbers.

In essence, what McNamara and a handful of others at the high echelons of strategy and analysis began to see was this: No matter how many men our side was willing to put in, the enemy would be willing to put in more. They would match us, and up it. They would give a million dead over to their cause. And keep going.

The human story of what went on in the Ia Drang has been told in a moving 1992 book called *We Were Soldiers Once . . . And Young.* It was written by the commander of the First Battalion of the Seventh, Harold Moore, and by a reporter named Joseph Galloway, who was in the killing zone with a camera, notebooks, and a rifle. Back then Galloway was a twenty-four-year-old reporter for UPI. Their collaboration is an almost minute-by-minute re-creation of a four-day war in two clearings—first at LZ X-Ray, then at LZ Albany—whose lessons, meanings, and bloodbaths were largely ignored or covered up by a civilian elite at home and by a military hierarchy in its Saigon villas.

The low-echelons who went into the Ia Drang had names like Willie Godbolt and Ernie Savage and Galen Bungum—who was off a dairy farm in Hayfield, Minnesota. They were men like Clinton Poley of Ackley, Iowa, who would say in a letter many years later to the authors: "Every night I rub a towel over all my scars and see them in the mirror. . . . In a way, I never feel as bad as when I'm feeling good."

Men stood up in that place and urinated on their eighty-one-millimeter mortars, lest the shells inside the mortars "cook off." Men stood up and said, "I'll be forty-three years old tomorrow, but I don't believe I'll live to see it"—and were then shot instantly in the head. Men stacked other men into Chinook helicopters and then raised the tail ramps and watched the blood squish through the hinges, like orange rinds in the back of a garbage truck.

In Washington (it was day five in the Ia Drang and the guns had turned quiet), Maxine Cheshire of the Washington *Post* was reporting to her readers on a very gay White House party held the evening before, November 17—the premier social event of the season. Henry Ford II and his wife were guests, as was the secretary of defense and his wife, who had driven up to the gate in their own car, a five-year-old Ford

Galaxie. Wrote the society reporter: "The ravishing Christina Ford, who has been described as a 'tiger kitten of a woman,' was the sensation of the evening as she danced and danced and danced and danced with Defense Secretary Robert McNamara. . . . Mrs. Ford, suntanned and with tawny hair that hung down her back, displayed a magnificent figure in a strapless white crepe dress which required her to stop periodically and tug it back into place. At one point, she didn't quite react fast enough."

Sixteen days earlier, a Quaker had been carted away from a raised garden.

Hobart Rowen of the *Post* wrote an economics column. It appeared a couple of days after the strapless story. The piece was headlined "McNAMARA EMERGES AS ECONOMIC CZAR." Wrote Rowen: "With the copper problem and its solution having followed so closely on the heels of the aluminum flap, McNamara seems to be running not just the war economy, but all of it. The performance has left Washington quite breathless. . . . The talk now in Washington is that Mr. Johnson would like to make an assistant president of McNamara. Whether or not he gets the title, he seems already to have the role." To read the newspapers is to suspect nothing.

On the day before the First Air Cav had entered the Ia Drang, on November 13, 1965, the *Post* had published a small one-column bar chart bearing this legend: "U.S. War Dead in Vietnam." It was beneath the headline "35,000 MORE GIS SLATED FOR VIETNAM." For the year 1961, the black bar was almost invisible to the eye. For 1965 the bar of death went the width of the column—a sliver of what was to come.

Ten days from that death chart, after many bodies had been stacked at the Ia Drang, General Westmoreland, believing he was now in a conventional war he could win, cabled Washington for 41,500 more troops. The reason provided was the unexpectedly high rate of NVA infiltration. Five days after this cable—now it was the end of the month—the secretary of defense, with no hint of what was swelling at his interior, flew from Paris to Saigon on a virtually windowless Boeing military jet with cramped double bunks and limited office space. It was his seventh visit of the war and this one would last just two days. He wore heavy mountain climber's boots, sweat socks, and suntan work clothes. Said the New York *Times* on arrival: "An official spokesman agreed tonight that his shortest visit on record here was a 'nuts and bolts' affair, and not the kind of trip that would lead to major new recommendations to the White House."

Back home, 25,000 people calling themselves SANE had formed a ring of war protest around the White House.

The secretary winged to a base camp where he was briefed on the Ia Drang by Lieutenant Colonel Harold Moore and other officers. Years later, in *We Were Soldiers Once,* Moore would recall: "During my twenty minutes I did my best to convey to McNamara and his party a vivid picture of the North Vietnamese soldiers who had fought against us at X-Ray. . . . McNamara's silence as I concluded was significant. He now knew that the Vietnam War had just exploded into an open-ended and massive commitment. . . ."

At press conferences arriving and departing Vietnam, McNamara used the expression "maul and dismember." Odd macho language. He employed it in reference to the Vietcong's effort to divide the country in half, but in one press conference he turned the phrase around and spoke of our "dismemberment" of their battalions. The usage sounds jolting on the tapes. In his departing Saigon press conference of November 29, having been in Vietnam thirty hours (at one point he took nine briefings, back-to-back), McNamara said: "First, let me say my most vivid impression is that we have stopped losing the war." His voice sounds sure.

A reporter asks him to comment on the significance of the fighting in the Ia Drang. On the two tapes that exist of this news conference, there is a sudden pause. There is this thin high quality in his voice, at least at first. It's just two old audiotapes in a drawer in the National Archives, you can't see a face, you have to imagine that face. But a shaken quality—it's there. He tries to seal it off.

SECRETARY McNAMARA: Uh, I don't think I'm in the best position to do so. I think General Westmoreland, Ambassador Lodge, and others here can speak more authoritatively on that than I. I'll simply say that the decision by the Viet Cong to stand and fight, recognizing the level of force we can bring to bear against them, expresses the determination to carry on the conflict that can lead to only one conclusion. It will be a long war.

He flew back to Washington. Chester Cooper, McGeorge Bundy's assistant in the White House, told me some years ago that McNamara seemed different in the corridors of the White House after that trip. "It's based on viscera," said Cooper. "Somebody is a believer. And then the words 'devil's advocate' begin to slip into his conversation—not that I ever heard McNamara use those exact words. And then some people move to being real devil's advocates. The devil's advocate role is a bridge, if you will, between believing and disbelieving. It was clear to me that from his questions, some of this was happening in McNamara."

He handed in a three-page memo. Daniel Ellsberg told me once that the problem with trying to decipher bureaucratic memo writing is that the documents are always a hodgepodge, an admixture—a John McNaughton or Paul Warnke line here, a McNamara revision there. I don't doubt that, but at the same time I think of something I once read in a book by the great California storyteller and essayist M.F.K. Fisher: "There is an urgency, an insistent beauty, about words written while they are hot in the mind, soon after something has happened to make them burn there."

The relatively short McNamara message dated "30 November 1965" and signed in his angular hand is a striking document with its own kind of insistent beauty. Something was hot in the mind. The memo said: "We have but two options, it seems to me. One is to go now for a compromise solution . . . and hold further deployments to a minimum," and the other was to "stick with our stated objectives and with the war, and provide what it takes in men and materiel." If the latter course was chosen, then 400,000 troops would be needed in Vietnam by the end of 1966 and 600,000 by 1967. And yet, faced even with that kind of scary buildup in the next two years, "We should be aware that deployments of the kind I have recommended will not guarantee success. U.S. killed-in-action can be expected to reach 1,000 a month, and the odds are even that we will be faced in early 1967 with a 'no-decision' at an even higher level."

Before enlarging the war, the secretary urged "a three- or four-week pause" in the bombing. Why? ". . . we must lay a foundation in the mind of the American public and in world opinion for such an enlarged phase of the war and, second, we should give North Vietnam a face-saving chance to stop the aggression."

Five months earlier, a wholly different Robert McNamara had been proposing to the president that America call up the reserves, extend tours of duty in all services, mine the enemy's harbors, obliterate their airfields, wipe out bridges and railways—an all-out offensive to "destroy the war-making supplies and facilities of North Vietnam wherever they may be located." This was on June 26, 1965, and on paper at least he was taking no prisoners. It's true that a month later, near the end of July, he had tempered his hubris. He had come back from his sixth trip to the war zone and had closed his report: "The overall evaluation is that the course of action recommended in this memorandum—if the military and political moves are properly integrated and executed with continuing vigor and visible determination—stands a good chance of achieving an acceptable outcome within a reasonable time in Vietnam." As *The Pentagon Papers* would later put it, with a little stab, "Never again while he was Secretary of Defense would McNamara make so optimistic a statement about Vietnam—except in public."

This point should be stressed in McNamara's favor: Back during the summer, in a *Memorandum for the Record* dated July 22, the secretary was recorded as saying in a high-level meeting the day before that he "felt that we should make it clear to the public that American troops were already in combat." The contradiction wrapped once more in the riddle.

That was then. Now in the gathering dark of winter, this bleak three-page secret assessment with its two grim options, neither of which he seems to have any heart for, and both of which he seems to be saying between the lines won't work. Vietnam historian William Conrad Gibbons once told me that, for him, the real import of McNamara's November 30, 1965, memo to the president is that here was the principal architect of the war policy psychologically bailing out on what he had created in the space of about four months—even as he was electing to go onward.

On December 6, McNamara sent Johnson an even grimmer version of his November 30 message. "The United States must send a substantial number of additional forces to Vietnam if we are to avoid being defeated there." The next day there was a final version of the paper. In the conclusion: "It follows, therefore, that the odds are about even that, even with the recommended deployments, we will be faced in early 1967 with a military standoff at a much higher level. . . ."

There's no question he was serving up the bad news.

Chester Cooper told me in an interview, "Here's a guy who saw the edifice falling all around him."

McNamara's pushing on the inside for bombing pauses and for new ways of thinking about the war in this period is something that must be paid attention to. The pushings were an act of conscience, I believe. They demonstrate moral courage from a shaken man. But McNamara's subsequent reversals and continued deceptions about the war over the next two years must equally be paid attention to. He would grow more darkly pessimistic, and he would stay. He would serve up the hard truth on the inside, sometimes, and he would nonetheless go on, agreeing to and designing further escalations, sending more platoons of the low-echelon into the high elephant grass. For extremely complicated reasons, and not just cynical needs to stay in power, a secretary of defense would continue running the military half of a doomed war while soldiers in their teens and twenties rode home in body bags and shiny aluminum government-issue caskets. But even on the inside, Robert McNamara was fully capable of reversing himself, circling back, contradicting, confounding. As LBJ's White House counsel, Harry McPherson, has said: "McNamara was still providing the president with an enormous amount of detailed, optimistic information . . . that this thing was working." As late as the summer of 1967, the secretary of defense would tell Johnson that this thing was working, it's *not* a military stalemate out there, sir.

George Ball told me, "He couldn't face the implications of his own logic." Norman Morrison, you might say, did face the implications of his own logic.

In mid-December, six weeks from the burning, the president convened two days of debate in the Cabinet Room on the McNamarian bombing pause. The second day's session started at 12:35 and lasted four and a half hours. From the declassified notes and transcript:

> THE PRESIDENT: The military say a month's pause would undo all we've done.
> McNAMARA: That's baloney—and I can prove it.
> THE PRESIDENT: I don't think so. I disagree. I think it contains serious military risks.

Farther down:

> McNAMARA: Military solution to problem is not certain—one out of three, or one in two. Ultimately we must find solution, we must finally find a diplomatic solution.
> THE PRESIDENT: Then, no matter what we do in military field there is no sure victory?
> McNAMARA: That's right. We have been too optimistic. One in three or two in three is my estimate.

According to several accounts, Johnson sighed, stood up, looked around the room, and then said to McNamara, "We'll take the pause." He left the room.

The bombing pause began at Christmas and lasted for the next thirty-seven days. It was a flop.

On January 6, 1966, the secretary of defense had dinner at the Georgetown home of Arthur Schlesinger, Jr. He had asked the historian of Camelot to arrange a private meeting with some old Kennedyites, among them John Kenneth Galbraith, Carl Kaysen, and Richard Goodwin. From Schlesinger's account: "McNamara told us that he did not regard a military solution as possible. His objective, he said, was 'withdrawal with honor.' I noted, 'He seemed deeply oppressed and concerned at the prospect of indefinite escalation.' " The stressed balloon was leaking air.

Not long after, McNamara met Victor Krulak privately in his office. The Commanding General Fleet Marine Force Pacific, who had a very good relationship with McNamara, flew in from Hawaii, where he had written a seventeen-page memo on a mountain overlooking Pearl Harbor. The paper laid out how and why attrition would fail. Attrition was the enemy's game: The enemy could turn the fighting up or down at his will. The document then presented the arithmetic. Krulak calculated that, between North Vietnamese regular army units and cadres of Vietcong, "there is probably a military manpower pool of two-and-a-half million men" for the enemy to call on. If one took as a given the official kill ratio of 2.5 enemy for one American or South Vietnamese government soldier, it would then "cost something like 175,000 lives to reduce the enemy manpower pool by a modest 20 percent."

Neil Sheehan, in *A Bright Shining Lie,* credits Krulak with being the original high-echelon mind in piercing the darkness of the realization that attrition was bankrupt, the land war was over almost before it had begun. In Sheehan's account, after arriving at his shattering conclusions in Hawaii, the general first showed the memo to his immediate military bosses, and then brought it to the secretary of defense, who looked at the calculations, who read the exponential meanings—and essentially did nothing. Krulak, in his own 1974 memoirs, seems to support this account, without precisely saying so. In *Lie,* Sheehan wrote: "The secretary was struck by Krulak's mathematics of futility— 175,000 lives for 20 percent of Hanoi's manpower reserves. 'I think you ought to talk to the president about this,' he said." In the meantime, at

McNamara's suggestion, Krulak went to see Averell Harriman of the State Department. Nothing happened there. Again, Sheehan, in *Lie:* "McNamara did not follow up his implied promise to arrange a meeting with the president. Krulak did not realize at the time that although he could catch McNamara's attention momentarily, he could not hold it." In his own memoir, *First to Fight,* Krulak writes, in regard to the figures of futility he had carried personally to the Pentagon: "McNamara made only brief comment. He rationalized his own alternative of a slowly intensifying air campaign, 'the tightening screw,' he called it, designed to persuade the North Vietnamese that they could not win."

When I spoke to Krulak on the phone in September 1995, he said of that face-to-face with McNamara: "The numbers got his attention. . . . I just know he listened to me. . . . I can't say what was in his mind. I can only report the facts. There's an expression—*idée fixe.* As the French say. Fixed idea. I think Mr. McNamara had this fixed idea."

McNamara saw Krulak in mid-January. Norman Morrison had been dead two months. Early in February, at a quickly convened Honolulu conference, the defense secretary invited a few reporters to his room, one of whom was Stanley Karnow, who years later would publish a best-selling account of the war: *Vietnam: A History.* On page 498 of that book: "I first discerned the change in February 1966. . . . His face seemed to be grayer and his patent leather hair thinner, and his voice lacked the authority it had once projected when he would point briskly to graphs and flip-charts to prove his rosy appraisals. . . . A rural society could not be blasted into submission, he said with unusual emotion: 'No amount of bombing can end the war.' " The turn had been made, with zigzag and riddle.

In the memo of November 30, McNamara had been saying to the president in an unvarnished way that even if America were to triple the number of soldiers it sent to Vietnam, the U.S. would still have no better than a fifty-fifty chance of winning the war. William Bundy, assistant secretary of state for East Asia, has since said to Vietnam scholars that option number one of the November 30 McNamara memo—that is, cutting losses and freezing buildups and negotiating to get out of Vietnam as soon as possible—was never seriously considered around the White House table. And that option number two of the McNamara memo—deciding to go on with the war and increasing the deployments to 600,000 men or beyond by 1967—was bought by all around the table, including McNamara.

In *In Retrospect,* in Chapter 8, McNamara discussed those late-fall and early-winter reversals. He wrote of Norman Morrison and of the Ia Drang and of how he had pushed for a sustained pause. He also disclosed something not widely known in the scholarship: that he had made a special pilgrimage from Aspen down to the presidential ranch in Texas over the holidays to plead personally the case for a longer bombing pause. But nowhere in Chapter 8 did the terribly sorry author of *In Retrospect* explain to his readers how it was possible to go on running a war he had lost faith in militarily; go on for another two years.

I should add something else. In that chapter, but even more so in subsequent ones, McNamara wished to suggest he had been "increasingly skeptical" about progress on the military front. That is the way he would like the picture painted for history: a continuum of agonizing doubt culminating in his 1968 departure. But neither the weight of the evidence nor his own sworn testimony in a libel trial will so easily support that sanitized expression of the picture. On the stand in the Westmoreland/CBS trial, the witness stated under oath that no later than 1966 he had come to believe the war *could not be won militarily,* and that indeed he may have arrived at that conclusion by the latter part of 1965. He was under cross-examination, and he didn't mince. He didn't use words like "increasingly skeptical" (page 234 of *In Retrospect*) or "growing doubt about the wisdom of our course" (page 257); no, he said to the court and to history: "I had reached the conclusion the war could not be won militarily."

But stayed in until February 29, 1968.

Is it mad to think that if the nation's secretary of defense had resigned after his November 30, 1965, memo, there would now be something known as the McNamara Prize, and that this prize would be coveted by men and women of conscience around the globe? But there is no such prize, and today this ex-servant of the people is skulking in the shadows of his own history.

I N 1 9 8 1 , Anne Morrison Welsh wrote a letter to Don Reiman. He was getting ready to go to Wooster to get his honorary doctorate. While drafting his speech, Reiman had posed some questions to Norman's widow. Now Anne wrote: "In some perhaps simple and naive way, Norman may have thought his act would really stop the war; I don't know. At its deepest and most significant level, the decision, I feel, was one of holy and compelling obedience to an inner directive, rather than a calculation. I do know, as fact, that it deepened the consciences of many individuals, and made them take a more serious approach to their own levels of commitment . . . to peace; to ending the war in Vietnam; to life itself."

She couldn't let it rest there. Four days later she wrote again to Reiman with an eloquence born of so many years of trying to explain to herself the unexplainable:

> What I want to say is that Norman wanted to *give his life away;* perhaps for a variety of reasons, not all of them totally healthy. Norman felt compelled (I think from childhood or at least early adolescence) to do/be something significant with his life. He wanted to serve some useful purpose, beyond the tending, carding and spinning, or husbanding a family. He wanted to add to the moral dimension of the universe. At first, he thought the way to do this was by being a preacher. And in the pursuit of that goal he became frustrated and disillusioned. Then he wanted to be a Quaker leader and peacemaker. He tried this, with some success but also with some failures. . . . He was in the process of thinking of *other* ways to serve within the Society of Friends, professionally. But, even though he was at a kind of frustrating crossroads in his work career, he was not apparently depressed about it, to any significant degree.
>
> As you may have known, Norman had a theory of "guided drift"; he felt that some greater Hand had hold of his life, beyond his knowing. Maybe because things hadn't all worked out for him professionally, it was easier somehow (a little bit) to give away his life. I don't know, Don . . . but I would not, no, *would not* call it suicide. (He wasn't unhappy enough, desperate enough, depressed enough for anything like that.) This attitude of the guided drift went back far, in his life, maybe to boyhood. Somehow it manifested itself very clearly that day of his death (perhaps glimpses came weeks earlier? I don't know). Maybe the unsettledness and lack of clarity about his next professional moves somehow coincided with his great concern about the war in Vietnam, and its significance to the people there, and here. Maybe his sense of easiness (& uneasiness!) about his own life, his lack of possessiveness about it, made him able to be more sensitive to an inner calling, or the inspiration of the Holy. I do know that he felt absolutely clear about how one should respond when those inner signals come. He had told me before, more than once, that his very life depended on *a fidelity to guidance.* When inward guidance came, he *dared* not ignore it. (If he did, what would be left of him, he asked.)

Enough of this rumination. All I want to do is to add to the complexity of his act, maybe acknowledge its mystery, for myself. None of what I've said, I hope, detracts from his dedication to peace, to ending the war, to being faithful to inner and Holy guidance, to looking at life on much deeper levels. Those all stand true and clear when it comes to Norm.

Four years after that letter, in the autumn of 1985, I met the surviving Morrisons. I didn't know about the letter, I didn't know about a lot of things, but it didn't stop me from writing a long story in the Washington *Post*. I talked to Anne and then went to New York to see Emily and then flew back down to Carolina to spend a day with Tina. I remember Tina telling me she thought a lot of what her father did was motivated by fear and frustration and his own need for approval. "This is what I know about him as a person," she said. "I really see these two strains in him: this unconditional love of humanity, the desire to serve, to give; and this very frustrated, approval-seeking, frightened, angry man who had never really dealt with his own pain. . . . My mother told me he used to make Ben recite math tables at the dinner table. That was a terrible thing to do. . . . But his own father had done it to him." None of it was said without softness or compassion, nor was this: "I think the main thing I got out of his death back then is, 'The world is unsafe, the world is mean, the world is not okay.' That things can happen to you at any time; that you can come home from school and be told that your father is dead, and not only dead, but that he killed himself, and for this weird reason. What I have done since then is a whole lot of emptying, not refilling, not yet."

Tina told me of a memory of lying on a couch with a thermometer in her mouth. She bit into it and broke it. Her father got so angry.

Growing up, there were times when Tina couldn't tell playmates about her father. It was too intense. She made things up, said he died in an accident.

And yet time has its powers. In early 1996, I received letters from Emily and Tina. Emily wrote: "No matter what could have happened to me, I believe I was purposefully with my father ultimately to symbolize the tragedy and brutality of war. Because I lived, perhaps I symbolized hope as well. Although I wish I could have known my father, his writings as well as the words and open arms of all those who understood and honored him have let me look into his eyes and feel the fullness of his heart."

Wrote Tina: "I've released a lot of anger and tears in the past ten years, and it's been a big relief to finally let go of my resentment toward my father. I still grieve his absence from my life and would love to have received some word or token of love and farewell from him. Yet I now realize that he left me what he could, and he left me a lot. He gave me a strong, rhythmical body; a sweet, compassionate, exuberant spirit; an inherent sense of justice and morality; and an ability to exalt in the simple joy of living. He also gave me, by his example, a great role model of courage and faith."

In the late fall of 1985, on the twenty-year anniversary, just as I was meeting the three Morrisons for the first time, I attended a memorial service for Norman at Stony Run Meeting House in Baltimore. It was a damp Sunday evening. Emily came down from New York, Tina came up from Carolina. Anne was unable to attend, but she sent a message and it was read aloud. The two sisters sat side by side in a fine old wood-and-fieldstone building on North Charles Street that traces its Quaker roots to 1792. The meetinghouse is set back from the street amid oaks and maples. On the door it says: "In this place, Quakers—members of the Religious Society of Friends—gather for worship. Our worship is based on silent, expectant Waiting for the experience of God in our hearts. From this silent worship may arise spoken messages."

I watched from the other side of the room as Emily and Tina held their hands and tears. Other Quakers all around them were crying. A woman rose and said, "It's hard to remember what the world was like in 1965." George Webb, an elderly man in bright-red socks recovering from a heart operation, rose and said: "Every time I use kerosene, or smell kerosene, I remember holding Emily wrapped up in an Army towel, in the back of a car."

A story was told about a silent vigil at Norman's wall on the first anniversary of his death, in 1966. Some Quakers had come down from New Jersey, and others from Stony Run had joined them. Every once in a while, on November 2, 1966, a man in a white shirt on the third floor of the Pentagon would come to the window to gaze out. He was silhouetted. He came back to the window two or three times in an hour. It was thought to be the secretary of defense, though no one on the ground standing in the rain could tell for certain.

Emily and Tina were the last to speak at the twentieth-anniversary service. "I could think of a thousand reasons not to get on that train and come down here . . . ," Emily said. She put her head on her sister's shoulder and cried a little. Tina said, "Norman's gift grows in love and strength, thank you, Lord."

N O T S O L O N G A G O , I called up Anne. We hadn't spoken for several years but now we spoke for a good long while. She was very warm. Finally she said she wished, at least for the present, to keep her relationship with me at a correspondence level. She said she would help me in my new research in whatever ways she found herself able to— suggesting boyhood friends, clarifying chronologies, granting release of certain documents—but that she had been interviewed enough by people who wrote things down for a living. It was just too painful. Soon after, I got a letter. With her usual directness, Anne said: "After almost three decades, I am beginning to be more able to look at our tragic and challenging family history than at anytime before. In re-experiencing the past (and it is very painful) I find that I am also reassessing it. Christina, Emily, and I are all going through this, each in our own way."

Several months later Anne shared something with me that I had long had hints of: Emily, the last child, had special meaning for Norman and herself because she was born a normal infant despite a German measles scare during Anne's pregnancy. Anne had been the one contemplating abortion; Norman had helped talk her out of it. And his faith had been rewarded. When I brought this up in a letter, Anne responded: "I will say (and you may use if you wish) that I think Emily's health at birth, after the German measles scare, represented to us both an answer to prayer, and a validation of faith and of Norman's intuition. Although I took a more rational, exploratory approach to the issue of aborting the pregnancy, Norman never expressed a doubt that she wouldn't be OK at birth. So, her pregnancy and birth were of special significance to us."

Why wouldn't a man have carried his special child to the last wall that night?

Anne and I continued to write out our thoughts, and on rare occasions we spoke on the phone. I always found her willing to trust in what I was doing without directly being a part of it, at least in terms of face-to-face interviews. In one phone talk, I mentioned how her first husband has a funny way of popping up when I least expect—a footnote here, a poetry anthology there. (Someone once showed me a street map of Hanoi with the words "Rue Morrison.") It's a hidden kind of impact, a sly kind of impact. Anne grew animated. "Really? Oh, my. If what you say is true, then he would have really enjoyed that. That's exactly what he would have wanted, Paul. That sort of impact. What? Oh, I don't know. Whimsical. And unexpected. That's *exactly* what he would have wished for. I know the man."

In that same conversation she said of McNamara: "I myself feel he's looking for light, I really get that sense. I think he's trying to pull it out, put it all together, find his place in history, square himself with history. The problem is, he's got so much baggage, as we all do." I felt envy for the way she could say that so forgivingly. I asked if some of her suffering might psychologically be linked to McNamara's suffering. "Yes. Maybe."

In August 1992, three months before the presidential elections, *Newsweek* published an essay bearing the byline "Robert S. McNamara." It was titled, "On Avoiding the Draft." An editor's note said the author ". . . was moved to write the following by the controversy over Gov. Bill Clinton's 1969 letter about the draft. His article was not solicited by the Clinton camp."

The author, referencing his past, said: "But I write also to say that I knew then, and I know now, the anguish of those who honestly and sincerely—and perhaps correctly—opposed the war. I tried to keep in touch with them while our decisions were being made: Sen. William Fulbright, chairman of the Foreign Relations Committee; the Rev. William Sloane Coffin, chaplain at Yale; the young Quaker who subsequently burned himself to death below my window in the Pentagon; Sam Brown, a friend of my children, who, after leading marches of protest against the president and me, would dine at my home."

Anne saw that piece and sent a note of thanks to the author in care of the magazine. She didn't hear back. I should add that no one in the family of Norman R. Morrison in the long-ago year of 1965, at least insofar as Anne Morrison Welsh knows, ever heard from Robert McNamara "while our decisions were being made," as modern-day readers of *Newsweek* were made to think from a slender deception in 1992. Mark Twain once said that a lie can circle the globe while truth is getting its boots on.

Three years later, in the spring of 1995, Robert McNamara came out with his own book about the war, and the response in America after six days—to quote the front page of the New York *Times*—was "broadly and almost relentlessly negative." But what the nation's editorialists or book reviewers thought of *In Retrospect* didn't stop a forgiving woman deep in North Carolina from releasing this statement: "Thirty years ago, on November 2, 1965, Norman Morrison gave his life in agony over our war in Vietnam and in a desperate hope of somehow ending it. . . . To heal the wounds of that war, we must forgive ourselves and each other, and help the people of Vietnam to rebuild their country. I am grateful to Robert McNamara for his courageous and honest reappraisal of the Vietnam war and his involvement in it. I hope his book will contribute to the healing process." McNamara called Anne after that. She told me in a letter that it was very warm between them, and that he expressed his deep gratitude, and that he also said as how he might like to use the statement. Anne said that would be okay. Soon there were her words and name at the top of a full-page ad for his book in the New York *Times*. In Washington McNamara was handing out Anne's letter to reporters.

Part Four:

SHADOWS, AND THE FACE OF MERCY, 1966 IN AMERICA

Coming from a religiously committed position, Professor Davis has drawn a conclusion that I (an unbeliever) strongly endorse from clinical experience with Vietnam combat veterans who experience severe psychological injuries: The healing of the combat veteran is inextricably connected to our capacity as a community to hear what the veteran has to tell us and to be changed by it. It is no overstatement to say that their healing and our own are bound up with one another. In biblical terms, Davis sees the Vietnam veteran as called to (or stuck with) a prophetic role. . . .

> *—from an article published by the Harvard Divinity School*

Oh Christ, where shall I begin? There once was a man who saw 250 bloody brothers in a single afternoon. Two were the first I ever saw (he ever saw), one hysterical and bleeding from his nose and ears and the other one with most of his hand blown away. And that was the way the day started and the day went on unending and has never ended. Time ended. Time broke apart. Living broke apart. . . . Simple sight of some things stains a man.

> *—from a letter by an ex–Marine medic to his psychiatrist*

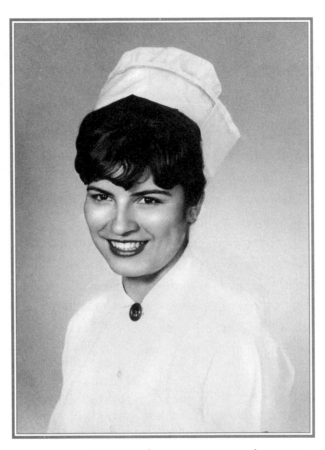

MARLENE VROOMAN (NOT YET KRAMEL) IN HER
GRADUATION PORTRAIT, REGINA SCHOOL OF
NURSING, JULY 1965; TWO MONTHS BEFORE
INDUCTION INTO THE ARMY NURSE CORPS, AND
EIGHT MONTHS BEFORE LANDING IN VIETNAM.

THE WAY IT COMES TO US
IN DREAMS

SO MUCH REMEMBRANCE, forgetting too, bandaged in one small word: push. That's what they called it, that's how they used it in a sentence: *A push is coming, get ready for the push.* In the parlance of war nurses, it meant time was ending, about to break apart. There wasn't day or night, just the red river you couldn't stanch. In a push the corpsmen ran them in on litters from the big Chinooks blowing up dust right outside the door. They would keep running them in, litter after litter. In a push the docs in the OR never had time to suture wounds—they just got to the trauma point and did what they could and sent the cases over "dirty" to Recovery. In a push you could end up on your feet fifteen, eighteen, twenty hours at a crack, gobbing in the amphetamines, stuffing back down your fright and fatigue. In a push you could end up holding some boy's head in the bowl of your fingers while his brains leaked through. But an image like that isn't where the story begins. It begins with a milder image of a war minister in North America who is making a speech—no, two.

TUCKED SOMEWHERE INSIDE every animus is a corresponding anima, and sometimes, for some reason or other, our opposite face wishes to come out into the light. On May 18, 1966, a split man endeavoring to cope with the disarray of his inner world flew to Montreal and delivered an astounding address before the American Society of Newspaper Editors convened at the Queen Elizabeth Hotel. No one in the audience was ready for what he said. He spoke about the inadequacy of guns and bombs. He spoke about international security as a matter of economic and social development, not of warfare. "Security is *not* military hardware—though it may include it," he said. "Security is *not* military force—though it may involve it. Security is *not* traditional military activity—though it may encompass it." Toward the close, he grew eloquent and philosophical even as he seemed to be losing his Pentagon marbles. "Who is man?" he asked. "All the evidence of history suggests that man is indeed a rational animal—but with a near-infinite capacity for folly. His history seems largely a halting, but persistent, effort to raise his reason above his animality. He draws blueprints for Utopia. But never quite gets it built. In the end, he plugs away obstinately with the only building material really ever at hand: his own part-comic, part-tragic, part-cussed, but part-glorious nature."

References to a conflict in Southeast Asia were almost nonexistent. But running through the text like an underground stream was the clear cold implication that Vietnam was an unwise commitment—a mistake, to be frank.

The president of the United States (with whom it wasn't cleared) is known to have been furious at the Montreal address. Washington commentators are known to have turned themselves inside out over the Montreal address. ("McNAMARA DROPS A BOMB ON WASHINGTON—WARMTH" was one headline.) The speaker himself was to say a few months later (he was at a dinner with academics in Cambridge, Massachusetts, and that afternoon some unruly students had sought to harm his person and his car until campus police led him away through steam tunnels) that while he had come to regard his remarks in Canada as foolish in terms of his role as the nation's chief military person, he could not have *not* said what he said and survived in his job. Some in the capital thought he was running for president, though others gauged that this was a moment when interior conflicts were showing public light. And four days after Montreal, on May 22, 1966, this time in Pittsburgh, the animus-turned-anima did it again, gave the light, flashed a kind of night-shadow, this time as the commencement speaker at small, privileged, and all-female Chatham College. The speaker employed Latin, quoted two Greeks, two saints, two poets, one dramatist, and Abigail Adams. At times he was genuinely witty. He said such un-McNamarian things as ". . . the ambivalence of technology grows with its own complexity. . . . The real question, clearly, is not whether we should have tools. But only whether we are becoming tools." At the close, as in Montreal,

he seemed almost plaintive. He talked of the dangers of depersonaliza-
tion. He spoke of the special insights of women. He said it was the gift
of womanhood to love, and the world had such a terrible need of it. He
said:

> If there *is* a danger of depersonalization in our society, then it is
> *you* who are best endowed to save us from that threat. For the
> gift of womanhood is precisely the gift of being able to *person-
> alize:* to relate to the *individual,* rather than to the mass; to the
> *specific* rather than to the generic; to the *existential,* rather than
> to the abstract.

SITTING IN THAT GILT HALL on those stiff chairs that Sunday
were 114 well-bred American daughters, one of whom was Robert
McNamara's own middle child, Kathy. A graduate named Pam Armstrong didn't know that one day she would hook up with a man who
had been instrumental in helping Vietnam Veterans Against the War
organize its first big Washington march. A Chatham woman named
Susie Cohn didn't know that in a year she would take a job (it was waiting across the country in San Francisco) as an educational counselor to
amputees home from the war. A recalcitrant senior named Cordis
Heard, whose father worked in the Pentagon, didn't know that two
summers hence she would have her face shoved up against a wall of the
Conrad Hilton Hotel in Chicago by some of Mayor Daley's finest at the
Democratic National Convention. (The disrupter's two-year marriage
would be kaput by then, but she would have found herself as a stage
actress, the actress with the deep political bone, the ex-deb from Chevy
Chase with perfect teeth who had gone radical.)

There was a woman present named Jeff. (Her real name was Jennifer but everybody in the class called her Jeff.) She had signed up for
the Peace Corps and was heading to Thailand. Jeff Potter didn't know
that soon, as a regular loathed occurrence, she would be able to walk
outside, in Maha Sarakham, and see big B-52s and boss Air Force jets
making their destruction runs to the north. (Did I say going to the Peace
Corps was an accommodation in part to what she felt about Vietnam,
and that it was further complicated by the fact that her dad, whom she
adored, was career Air Force in the McNamara Pentagon?)

There was a woman on that stage named Lynnette. She had a
brother named Skipper who had been drafted six months earlier. One

night about a week before he went in, Skipper and his friend Bob, also bound for the war, had spent an evening marching around Skipper's parents' house, in and out of doors and even windows, waving broomsticks and wearing pots on their heads. They were calling out imaginary and ridiculous orders to each other. As Lynnette Burley Fuller would describe it years later, writing down the memory, it was such a goofy-serious and bizarre evening, watching her brother burlesque his terror like that. (He would survive the war, though in another sense lose the peace.)

And one more: Jean Wiest. Her immediate connection to what was pulsing under the floorboards was that her dad was a professor at a local Presbyterian seminary; he had given the baccalaureate address earlier in the day. After the baccalaureate, at the coffee hour in the Andrew W. Mellon Garden, in the middle of campus, Jean and her folks had a chance to meet the commencement speaker, who hadn't given his address yet, and which was going to be presented, for security reasons, off campus, a couple miles distant, in a big, stiff mausoleum of a building called the Carnegie Music Hall, first time ever (or at least in memory) a Chatham graduation couldn't be held outdoors, in the May sun, on beautiful Mellon Lawn. Anyway, Jean Wiest's father had been pretty impressed at that morning coffee hour by the guest from Washington, by his seeming softness and shyness and interest in others, even if it's true that Professor Walter Wiest was opposed to the war the speaker was prosecuting. Long afterward, the giver of the baccalaureate would recall one thing about his encounter with Robert McNamara: Far from being upset by the outside agitators who were planning to picket the afternoon graduation, the guest seemed actually to be welcoming them. "Let them come! It'll be fine! I'm in favor of it!" is what the seminary professor would recall the defense secretary had privately said. It didn't come up in the chat that Professor Wiest had once been mentor and friend to a taciturn Pittsburgh seminarian named Norman R. Morrison, who had immolated himself, though not his daughter, in a Pentagon garden six months back.

And probably you get it by now. A ceremony, a moment, a speech: awash with all kinds of cross-tensions and undercurrents and seethings not yet known—perhaps a funny little connecting node or cross-tension for every graduate or relative or robed teacher in the room. Probably any of these Chatham College connecting points of May 22, 1966, could be probed more fully now for hindsights on roiled times. But what if I told you that far from that commencement weekend, under some flapping tents, inside some dim Quonset huts, in a place called Qui Nhon, in a hospital known as the Eighty-fifth Evac, there was another young American woman, not of any privilege, not emblematic of roiled times, but who in effect was the *manifestation* of what the man at the dais was saying, and maybe even saying in some half-understood way about himself? Fact is, at the moment of the Pittsburgh saying, this American daughter may have been more or less stuck with (or called to) her prophetic role. Fact is, she may have been in the middle of the very first push. . . .

SHE'S TELLING HOW they used to scrape it off with their fingernails. She means mud. A woman sitting on a blue wooden swing in a Louisiana backyard forms her hand into a claw. Her nails are brushed with clear lacquer. She's got little pearl balls in her ears. Her blue-striped blouse has CHIC written over the breast pocket.

"They thought they were dead," Marlene Kramel says. "When they woke up, they thought they'd died. They'd say, 'Did I die? A round eye? Where am I? Am I in heaven? Are you my mother?' See, they'd be starting to smell my perfume. It was either White Shoulders or Shalimar. I can't remember anybody wearing anything else but White Shoulders. But especially Shalimar. That's what I wore. We could get it inexpensive. We'd put it on our neck, behind our ears, on our wrists—"

(She's dabbing on pulse points, emptying a bottle.)

"—and they'd sort of blink awake, and smell our perfume, and ask us about being in heaven. And we'd say, 'No, no, you didn't die, you're not dead, we're Army nurses. . . . We're here, it's okay.' "

I ask, "Do you see their faces?"

She turns her head sideways, as if having just caught something on a table at a junk sale. "Their feet," she says. "What I keep envisioning. It's mixed in with all the mud. The feet. I keep seeing their feet."

"Do they have their boots on?"

She studies that. Are their boots off? It's so gauzy. Maybe their boots were already off, yes, maybe it was their knotted and sticky rags she was yanking on and trying to cut away with her surgical scissors. So she could get down to the mud. Which was all over them, like dried lava, thick and crusted, brownish-yellow, as if red had been stirred into it.

She remembers one night when she got so tired she kept downing diet pills. She wasn't on duty, she says, and wants to stress that. (Earlier she had said that if somebody had asked about it after she got home, she would never have thought to say, "I took drugs in Vietnam." That would have been an unreal and unfair sentence, somehow. A circumstance out of context.)

A moment later: "I never saw the choppers. I could hear them. I was inside."

A moment later: "I think we totally blocked out what was happening. It just seems we did what we had to do. I remember so many times feeling I didn't know enough. I remember feeling, Oh God, I won't get through this."

A perch or crappie or maybe it's a smallmouth bass pops on the surface of the pond that's out in front of us. It startles the stillness, it startles me.

"I remember one of the comments somebody made. It may have been one of the other nurses. It may have been after a push. I don't remember. I remember the comment: 'Whatever they've been through, we have it all over us now.' "

"When was that first push, Marlene?"

She extends her right leg and pushes her foot into the pine needles beneath the swing, creating drag. This was the leg that was due to be sliced off up to the pelvis—no, I don't quite have it right. Not up to, but into her pelvis, a sort of hindquartering. "Hemipelvictomy" is the term Marlene Kramel saw on her medical chart one night at Walter Reed Army Medical Center—and started screaming. Which was uncharacteristic, really. She'd been home from war five years then.

That leg didn't get taken off. That leg, which has muscle and tendon and hamstring missing, is creating drag. The swing we're sitting on, swaying on imperceptibly in the gauzy Louisiana breeze, comes to rest. The Yorkie that has been asnooze in her lap is stirring.

She says, "I don't have the date. Maybe two months after I got there. Yes, I think so. Because the plane taking us to Vietnam left on March 5th from Travis. I'm pretty sure of that date. So let's see, two months, maybe around the middle of May. I'd say maybe the middle of May 'sixty-six. Why?"

I don't really answer, just let it hang in the soft afternoon air. Where unconscious forms in blood-sticky rags have the wrong uniforms on— that's what I keep thinking. Somehow I keep thinking they're the Confederate, not the Vietnam, dead.

THIS IS ABOUT a virginal, Catholic, twenty-one-year-old nurse who went to Southeast Asia nearly straight from her virginal Catholic nursing program, and got stuff all over her, and came home afterward to years of unexplained medical illness. A woman who grew goiter-sized knots and a football-sized tumor. Who was informed she might lose all rectal control. Who developed a draining sinus on her right buttock that lasted three years and smelled foul and had to have its dressing changed nightly by her good husband, who would pour the peroxide and try not to wince at the flesh on his wife's behind that had blistered and reddened from all the taping and retaping. A woman who suffered sieges of nausea and what clinicians call FUOs—fevers of unknown origin. Who got up one night in a blurred fog at a stateside military hospital and made her way to the bathroom only to find all this hot and thick and lavalike reddish-orange stuff coming out of her. It happened so fast that the patient, who knew a lot about crisis medical situations, wasn't even clear where it was coming from. Was she hemorrhaging to death right on the damn toilet seat?

"Good God, doctor, come quick, Mrs. Kramel's ruptured a kidney," the night nurse at Fort Polk cried when she looked into the room and saw the flowage making wider and wider circles on the floor. It wasn't a kidney rupture. It was a massive abscess.

But here's the swerve to the story. This is the part that will fool you. Marlene Kramel is the American daughter who went to war in her patriotic urges and Florence Nightingale dreams; and got stuff all over her; and came back to much suffering; and has caves of Vietnam sadness inside her now; but who somehow never got trapped in a rage or bitterness—then or now. If anything, the opposite would be true, which, given her history, given what happened after, seems not quite plausible, seems a little loony. I know I didn't want to believe it. I know I kept thinking when I first met her: *Something is off, she's plowed it under.* I know I wished to see it all as some far subtler form of Vietnam victimization. Fact is, there's a part of me yet that I don't like so much that still wishes to see it like this, even against a weight of accumulated evidence.

Although I've changed my mind from where I started out, or mostly so, I'd like to leave open the question of whether she blocked out what was happening to her—leave it in suspension, because she's willing to do so. The word "block" as a possibility comes up fairly often when you sit talking with a religious and gracious woman on a blue wooden swing facing a family pond that's fat with fish in Libuse, Louisiana.

You look out at that pond, and everything is still. The turnoff to Happy Acres Road is past a sign for the Serenity Chair Company. And yet . . . the person who lives in these clean-smelling piney woods suffers migraines; will tell you she didn't experience her first flashback—or something that seemed like a flashback—until she had been home from war twenty-six years and had gone to Washington for the dedication of the Vietnam Women's Memorial. Things here may be simultaneously less and more than they seem. Some things may never break the surface.

Marlene's husband, a retired Army lieutenant colonel who is regular as tap water, a good ol' Libuse boy (beer out of the can; hush puppies out of the sack; the Mamou Playboys on the Cajun boom box), might be pitching hay behind the swing as you talk. He'll sort of be eavesdropping on parts of the talk—and why not? His name is Glenn. He did two tours in the green dream of Vietnam. He was an infantry officer. All he wanted to do, after more than two decades in the military, was get back to Libuse, which you pronounce like "caboose." And he did, with Marlene right beside him.

From everything I can tell, Glenn and Marlene, who met in Vietnam and have two grown sons and have been together for a quarter of a century, have a fine marriage. They are wonderful hosts. They spend a lot of time together on weekends. But this stuns me: They have seldom talked about Vietnam. Doesn't seem to come up. Doesn't seem to need to come up.

The urge is to call them Vietnam innocents—but how could that be?

Marlene, still a nurse but no longer a bedside RN, works as a coordinator for women veterans' health programs at a VA medical center in Alexandria, Louisiana. She has proven administrative talents, and her job has gained her statewide recognition and respect. Additionally she's become a spokesperson in her region for women who went to Vietnam. She's had a lot of experience in the mental-health field and knows much about PTSD: posttraumatic stress disorder. There was a time not so long ago, in the higher Washington strata of veterans' affairs, when that term, that disorder, was considered nonapplicable to women: Nurses and other females who were in the war never saw combat, so how could they have PTSD? Marlene has sat as a counselor in groups in which she has said to damaged figures in robes around her, "What makes you so sure *I'm* all right?"

A VA social worker once said to Marlene, after Marlene was able to go on medical-surgical hospital floors without feeling the building swim, without thinking she was seeing something through a thick pane of warping glass, "Well, Marlene, you finally got rid of your PTSD." "I don't *have* PTSD," she answered.

Marlene has showed me snapshots of herself at the wall in Washington. Her arm is outstretched and her fingers are touching the polished black granite; a sad woman is gazing back toward the camera. The woman, sometimes surrounded by other female veterans, looks as if she's trying to balance herself more than touch chiseled names. She looks as if she's trying to cry through the photographic paper. "I'm trying to remember. I'm trying to see faces," she said the first time we looked.

I've talked to some other nurses about the way faces will hide. Marlene's best friend from Vietnam, a woman named Becky Goller, who lives in Florida now, told me: "It was almost like Scarlett. 'I'll think about it tomorrow.' He died. Maybe he was nineteen. Okay. I'll not let myself think about it." Becky and Marlene were roommates in the war. They went through nursing school together, signed up together for the Army student-nurse program, passed their state boards together, entered basic together at Fort Sam Houston in Texas, trained together at Letterman Army General in San Francisco, left America on the same plane from Travis Air Force Base. (They had been out of school not quite eight months.) After they got back, Becky was the maid of honor at Marlene's wedding. But Becky, who must have gotten bad stuff on her, didn't come home to grow desmoid tumors in her leg. She has raised a family and still works as a hospital RN, and loves Marlene much, and I have seen photographs of them at the Vietnam wall, holding on to each other. Like Marlene, Becky Tapia Goller is a religious woman who wishes to remember Vietnam as a positive and life-affirming experience. And mostly does. Only now and then does something else seem to be seeping out, like moons of dark ink.

"There are two or three faces I still see," Marlene says.

"Did you ever want to run out of there?" I ask.

"No. No. The adrenaline was so high. I never felt like running out of there."

A little later I ask, "Did you cry much?"

"I never ever remember crying."

"How were you able to do that?"

"I don't know. I don't know. I know I got tired. I got to the point of fatigue. I may have cried without remembering. I don't remember anybody ever crying. I don't remember Becky crying, either. I must have blocked that out, too."

Tomorrow, after church, Marlene will relate a dream she occasionally has: "I'm at work at the VA, in the mental-hygiene department. There's a TV in there. It's as if the whole room is a TV. Everybody's leaving. Then I'm in there, on the screen, in this big panoramic view. I'm in a helicopter. And the helicopter's lifting up. And I'm reaching down. All these bodies are reaching up and crying and screaming. They're bleeding and crying. And holding out their arms. 'Please, please, don't leave me.' I'm screaming to the pilot of the chopper, 'Stop, stop. We've got to go back.' All I see down there is the filth and the blood." As she tells the dream, while we're parked at a Mobil station on the way home from Sunday Mass, Glenn Kramel will be standing outside the van, pumping fuel, gazing in at his wife and me through a thick side pane. There will be the saddest hound-dog look on this good man's face.

By tomorrow Glenn's wife and I will have talked for maybe twenty hours. It will be the end of my second visit to the big fine house Glenn built for Marlene on the family pond off Happy Acres Road. And what won't have come up, not yet, is that Marlene once met America's secretary of defense. On an October day in 1966, Robert McNamara walked into her recovery room at the 67th Evac, a rather startling coincidence and statistical improbability when you consider that something like 11,000 women served in the military during Vietnam, and maybe 7,500 were nurses, and so what might be the odds that the one I had picked to write about in the year 1966—as much for her goodness as for what puzzles me about her—was there, on the unit, at her station, maybe getting ready to hang blood or check vitals or insert an intravenous, when the khaki-clad and open-collared apparition broke from the press of generals and MACV public-affairs flacks around him and came right up, stuck out his hand, and said something like: *It's my pleasure to meet you, ma'am. Thank you for this very important work you're doing*—what would be the odds of it?

I'll have come back three times and swayed on the blue swing before this sliver of memory falls out. We'll be looking at some old faded color war snaps of Becky Goller's, and the soft-talking middle-aged woman with the face of mercy and the frosted hair and the scent of Shalimar that makes me think of my own mother will say, laughing at herself, "I must have blocked that too."

THINK FOR A MINUTE not of the synchronistic or serendipitous but of the *prophetic,* which is commonly used in religious contexts.

Think too about faces. Robert McNamara made the cover of *Time* three times in the sixties, and by themselves those magazine covers seem to tell a story, chart a line, of what was gaining on him from the inside. The first face is in 1961 and it is all jaw-jut and split of New Frontier grin. By 1963 the face is no longer looking the world cold in the eye. There is something monkish here, as if it were the face of a medieval melancholic. And by the summer of 1966, when pillars of greasy smoke began to billow up from within even McNamara's own family, the face from the artist's brush at *Time* is something deeper than melancholy. The tight-lipped mouth has returned, the set jaw, but the look in the subject's eye is a barely suppressed scream.

Statistics and data won't tell the story, but here's a set: Army nurses in Vietnam averaged 23.6 years of age; only a third arrived at the war with more than two years of professional experience. The typical nurse was pretty much fresh from nursing school, and for some reason so many of those programs seem to have been Catholic. Army RNs worked six days a week, twelve-hour shifts. The wounds that doctors, nurses, and corpsmen treated, as opposed to what were treated in some other wars, were extremely "dirty." Rocket-propelled grenades and rapid-fire weaponry don't make fine holes. Shrapnel and debris got hurled into jagged openings. And a point about evacuation: In World War I, the average time between a wounding and surgical care was between ten and eighteen hours. In World War II, the time between a trauma and treatment in a field hospital was reduced to six to twelve hours. In Korea, the time went further down. And in Vietnam, our high-tech war, the average elapsed span between a battlefield injury and hospital attention was cut to 2.8 hours. Sometimes the dust-off choppers delivered them there in minutes, tracheostomies in, IVs going. This rapid evacuation was wondrous, but there's another way to think of such a statistic: Nurses, medics, and surgeons were constantly receiving people in litters who were only technically alive. Bodies had been lifted out of the muck and were still in this world but so many of them weren't going to make it. Hence the practice of triage, which means sorting: Let the dying die. We've only got so many resources. We'll tag that one as an "expectant" and set him in a corridor to make room for someone else who's got a chance. In Vietnam there were many things, not least the dedication of the healers, that combined to keep the massively wounded from dying. But if you were a nurse, a doctor, or a corpsman in a forward hospital, there would have to be two edges to the swift sword. In 1986 the first in-depth study of women and war stress found that 50 percent of female veterans had symptoms suggestive of PTSD. A little earlier, a medical researcher for Louis Harris and Associates concluded that, based on their "exposure to death and dying on a regular basis, it's entirely possible the women may have higher levels of stress and disorder than males."

Finally, a third kind of quantitative data. On June 17, 1966, which would have been roughly a month after a split man gave two speeches in the space of four days, a systems-analysis office in the Pentagon produced a document. It was a study of press response following Montreal and Chatham, and it had headings such as: "Summary Data / Quantitative by Content." There were useful subheadings: "A. Secretary McNamara's 'New' Image / 1. Humanist, Intellectual. 2. Portent of New Policy—Or Just Words?" There were paragraphs such as this one:

> The broadest consensus of editorial and feature opinion savored (27 out of 37 items) what *WashSunStar* and Marder (*WashPost*) called McNamara's "unusual" speech. *WashPost* topped it with a reference to his "highly unusual" speech. Childs (*WashPost*) and Wolfson (*ProvJnl*) pulled all stops to call it "extraordinary," Fritchey (*WashStar*) thought it "exhilarating," Reston (*NYTimes*) termed it "remarkable," and *ChriSciMon* called it "a bombshell."

To go back now and read those stories is to be struck by two thoughts: how a man was seeking, consciously or otherwise, to save himself, was acknowledging and taking his pain out into daylight, if only for a moment, because there was no place else to take it; and how the nation's premier journalists had decoded perfectly the mysteries of a divided self—without seeming to recognize the implications of it.

On the day after Chatham, Mary McGrory wrote in the Washington *Star:* "The real Robert McNamara stood up again yesterday. . . . Washington, which was still in a state of shock over his delivery of a humanist manifesto in Montreal Wednesday, reeled again. . . . What has happened is that the secretary of defense has suddenly started talking in public the way he has increasingly talked in private . . . the total emergence of the other McNamara in two speeches—the first lofty, far-flying, and liberal beyond any dogmas, and the second, fatherly, witty and poetry-spangled—was entirely too much for the simple politicians of the city. . . . [the] more seasoned students of the ways of Washington think that the secretary's declaration was spontaneous, and that it was the long pent-up outburst of a man mistaken for a hawk."

In the New York *Times,* on the day McNamara was speaking in Pittsburgh, James Reston wrote of the Montreal bombshell: "This startled Washington, which is a funny town, and thinks of McNamara as the mechanical man who always defines Administration policy with geometrical accuracy, which is both true and wildly inaccurate. He is a philosophical computer, and the philosopher in him is stronger than the computer."

Columnist James J. Kilpatrick would soon write: "The two speeches, taken together, seem to say that McNamara wants to escape from his equations and flip-charts, from cost accounting and computer input. He is taking on a new dimension. . . ."

On the front page of the *Christian Science Monitor,* Richard L. Strout would soon write: "Nothing on a personal basis in the past couple of months has stunned and charmed Washington so much as the discovery that Defense Secretary McNamara, known as an icy human computer, is a warm, witty, and philosophical person underneath."

Wants to escape from . . . total emergence of the other McNamara . . . long pent-up outburst of a man mistaken . . . person underneath. It was as if McGrory, Reston, Kilpatrick, and Strout were giving the chronicle of a death foretold. In almost a prophetic way their pieces were putting bare the struggle between technology and the soul, and the pathologies of Washington power, and the manner whereby public men stand behind masks, and what happens when the head doesn't listen to the heart—but that wasn't their tone. Their tone was full of glow. It was as if these esteemed journalists couldn't see what they had written because they were in thrall to the other self showing full-length suddenly in the daylight mirror.

I confess to another thought after reading the Montreal and Chatham pieces. The word I kept forming was "surrogate." I thought of a helicopter lifting up. And a woman reaching down. The man on the ground was bleeding. He was holding out his arms. He was crying for someone to help him. The woman in the helicopter was screaming to the pilot: *Stop, stop, we've got to go back.* She was willing to go back down to the muck, take on somebody's pain, get strange stuff on her, offer it up.

It was only a gauzy thought, my confused dream.

FROM A PAIR of old letters—documents, you could call them.

The first was written to Sister Alma from a place deep inside the war. Sister Alma was the director of Regina School of Nursing back in

Albuquerque. Sister Alma, who belonged to a religious order called the Sisters of Charity, had presided at Marlene's capping. That was the day, early in her three-year diploma program, when she had approached the communion rail with her other classmates, knelt, bowed her head, took the Nightingale Pledge, and received the official headgear of a nurse-in-progress. So white, so starched, such a simple and beautiful and ridiculous cottony thing to have placed on your head like the crown jewels of England. At Regina, your capping was a little like a betrothing.

But the letter written from Qui Nhon, mid-tour 1966; it said this: ". . . last Saturday and Sunday 115 casualties came in. The doctors were up around the clock, trying desperately to save life and limb. You should have seen us in the Recovery Room. We have only nine beds, so we were really pushing those patients out. And there was no time (let alone enough sheets!) to change linen between patients. . . . When things are slow in Recovery, I work in Intensive Care. I love the work and am gaining a tremendous amount of experience. The patients are number one—the USA can really be proud of its fighting men. You see young men with amputated arms and legs not bitter, just concerned about how their buddies are. They are a great bunch."

The second document. It, too, is in the form of a letter, though essentially a letter to oneself. It has a different tone, but not so great you wouldn't recognize it. It was written a decade later on cheap penny paper with a blue ballpoint in Palmer-perfect penmanship. It was four pages long and had been composed on a sunless winter afternoon in Minnesota as part of a course in spiritual renewal, though "composed" is probably the wrong word, because the letter seemed to dictate itself, without pausing for grammar or spelling checks. Marlene Kramel sat curled on her living-room sofa. Glenn was at work, the boys were at school. The rock-solid Minneapolis earth was getting another coat of white. It was 1978 now, and she had been home from war not quite eleven years. She was a mother and a military wife who had survived eight tumor operations; survived so many middle-of-the-night airlifts to military hospitals that, like all the places she had lived in as a child, they almost defied chronology.

That day in Minnesota, as part of a course in spiritual healing called Genesis-2, Marlene wrote: "During my lifetime there have been many experiences which have caused me to lose my childhood qualities briefly, but usually there is some out force—a friend, a coworker, my husband—which have helped me regain them . . . perhaps one of the most significant events of my life, and the time I often refer to as when my balloon became deflated, was my assignment as an army nurse in Vietnam . . . our eyes and hearts will never forget the young GIs waking up without arms and legs—the pain, the heartache. Soldiers bodies mixed with blood and dirt. And it goes on and on—12 hr. shifts for nurses which run into 15–16 sometimes 18. Doctors up round the clock fighting desperately to save life and limb. You wonder why! What's it all about! An occasional POW comes through and it's all that you can do to touch him. Bitterness, hate, intolerance crepe into your world. Your balloon is all but deflated! And you keep asking why. . . . We laughed a lot. We made the heaviest situation as light as we could. We all grew up. We lived day by day and hoped for a tomorrow. My balloon is almost full again—I'm learning to look at things as a child but face them as an adult."

A fifty-year-old woman wearing perfume, with a husband pitchforking mulch on the pine trees behind us, shows me those old letters now. She says, "There were eight of us in that Genesis class. I read it aloud to the others and cried. I think I was the only one who took the assignment seriously. This was really the first thing I'd ever written about Vietnam. It's the first time I ever cried about Vietnam. When I look at it now, it sounds so childish. And yet I can see the incredible difference between it and what I wrote to Sister Alma. It was as if I'd been blocking it all out. Was I blocking it out? I mean, that's what we were supposed to do, in a sense. How else were we going to do what we had to do?"

THAT WAS EARLIER. Now her arms are out. Her slim torso is making a kind of half twirl. Marlene's in a New Mexico roller palace. "You just floated, you could just lose yourself, I do that a lot," she says.

"It was turns and swirls to the organ music," she says. (I hear the music—I think it's "Lady of Spain/I Adore You.")

"You've got this little thing on, and your skates, and you just glide around," she says. (Yes, she's got on a black skirt, frilly blouse, white lace-up leather skates with turquoise wheels. They're Chicagos, a nifty brand. Her folks gave them to her for her birthday. All around her, other postpubescent bodies are ovaling in ultraglide.)

"Tangoes. Waltzes. The fourteen-step. We'd walk up there after school or sometimes take a bus. I met a kid named Bobby. Just get out there and skate and skate," she says.

"I remember dreaming about Dreamland," she says.

The roller palace that became a second home in the last year of high school and for the several years after was on San Mateo Boulevard in Albuquerque, off Central Avenue, up by the fairgrounds. Its name was Dreamland. Except it wasn't.

Dreamland was where Marlene met Bernie Rocasso. He was from Greenfield, Massachusetts, and was in the Air Force, and worked at a little military installation outside of town. Marlene was a freshman at Regina, eighteen, and Bernie was a couple years older. It lasted about three months. He two-timed her.

After she found out, she wrote Bernie a letter and wrapped it inside the U-Mass sweatshirt he had given her. She called up a disc jockey and asked him to dedicate "I'm Losing You" to a fellow in the Air Force. Then Marlene told a friend of Bernie's to let Bernie know a special tune was coming on the radio for him that night. Then the student nurse (Bernie had come to her capping) went out to Bob's Drive-In on Central and cruised the circle in another car with another boy, and pretended not to care when the two-timer drove his own rod in.

It sounds a little like the movie *American Graffiti:* heartbreak and teen innocence, so long as you keep gliding on the surface of the story. For instance, there was that time she met Elvis when he was on Waikiki filming *Blue Hawaii.* Marlene Vrooman (her name was Vrooman before she married Glenn Kramel; it's Dutch) was a junior in high school. Her family had just uprooted her to Hawaii, following a three-year stay in Texas. "Oh good, I'll get to graduate with all the leis and those beautiful landscapes" is the way a Navy kid says she reacted when her folks told her they were leaving Kingsville and transferring to Honolulu— which also may have been a way to cope with the fact of having to make friends again.

The dream of Hawaii turned out to last a year. But she met Elvis. She and a newly made friend were hanging outside the set when a man came out and said, "It's over right now, Elvis is going to lunch." He took her hand. He was so shy, soft-spoken.

Dreamland. "He was nineteen on the *Hornet,*" she says. "He fell in love with Rosie the Riveter in Oakland." She's talking of her father and mother, and how they met, and how her skinny and good-looking and flat-topped teenage dad went to World War II in his patriotic urges. He was a flight mechanic on the aircraft carrier from which General Jimmy Doolittle's B-25s got launched. Somebody made it into a movie: *Thirty Seconds Over Tokyo.*

Dreamland. She has a book describing the Civil War glory of her great-grandmother's father. He was a Yankee and his name was Rudolphus Robbins. He was killed on May 15, 1864, in the Battle of Resaca, Georgia. *Trials and Triumphs: The Record of the 55th Ohio Volunteer Infantry* tells how Major Robbins died charging down a hill at the head of his men, with "the Johnnies returning the fire at a lively rate." He was thirty. "His name is enrolled among those of the immortals," it says in the book. "See, I had all this behind me," she says.

She had barely touched Elvis on Waikiki when her parents came to her and her kid brother with the inevitable: We're going again. "And I was devastated." There would be no graduation with leis around her neck. Marlene's father had become a Navy chief, but rather than setting sail for Midway Island with his unit he had opted for retirement. The family would take up a new civilian life in New Mexico, where Marlene's mother had kin. But jobs were scarce in the desert, and the ex-Navy chief went to work as a night janitor. The four Vroomans located in a trailer park in the southeast quarter of the city, not far from a hulky old skating palace. They had lived in many trailer parks in their lives, near bases, so an American daughter didn't think this was anything to be self-conscious about.

She made a close friend, Nancy Dlouhy. One day Nancy said, "Let's do the candy-striper thing." Oh drudge, Marlene thought, but went anyway. At Presbyterian Hospital she filled up jugs of water and sat next to old women, hearing their stories, holding their hands. She brought patients their dinner trays and helped feed them. Her work was in a nursing-home component to the hospital, and to her great surprise the seventeen-year-old who loved to whirl at Dreamland found she liked it. "I think it made me feel good," she says. "That's when it hit. 'This is it. I could do this.'" Mrs. Vrooman couldn't understand. She felt nursing would be a life of bedpans. But it was as though Mrs. Vrooman's daughter had seen something through a pane.

But how would she pay for it? A four-year undergraduate program at the University of New Mexico was out of the question. "Well, I really don't have the clothes to go up there," she told herself, perhaps as a way of pushing college from her mind. (She was near the top of her high-school class.) Marlene's folks decided to leave Albuquerque and go to San Diego, where they had once lived. Jobs might be better there. This time Marlene refused to go. Her parents managed to secure a loan for the first year at Regina. The school and the dorms were next door to St. Joseph's Hospital, very Catholic, very virginal. The big rink off San

Mateo assumed greater importance—an escape from the pressure of classroom theory mixed in with work on the wards.

"Did you see dying?"

"I think I can remember three. Two of them were older, and I think it was kind of expected. One of them was a mother, and I sort of identified with her because of my own mom. She was a leukemia patient, probably thirty-nine or forty. They knew it was a matter of time."

"What could you do for her?"

"At that point, nothing. Cool cloths. Pillows. Turning her. I can still look up at her: the old hospital bed. I can see the light. She was up in a corner. She knew she was going to die. She had a wonderful attitude."

I ask, "Did you see blood?"

She says, "No. I never saw blood. I never remember blood as a student nurse."

Circling back: "Oh, wait a minute. OB-GYN. A young unmarried mom. This was a young girl and she's hemorrhaging all over the sheets and full of blood and, and, I'm just there sort of in shock. The head nurse was walking by. 'I'll be right there,' she said."

Item from the Albuquerque *Tribune,* June 19, 1963: "The freshman class of Regina School of Nursing, their escorts and guests, attended a Hawaiian luau on the lawn at Regina Hall recently. The luau followed a swim party at Four Hills Country Club. . . . Miss Marlene Vrooman, a freshman, performed hula dances and gave hula instruction."

She and Becky were like sisters by now. Becky was from a Hispanic family in Santa Fe—not poor, though not of means, same as Marlene. "REGINA HONOR LIST NAMES EIGHTEEN NURSING STUDENTS," the local paper said one day. Marlene cut the story out and pasted it in her memory book and wrote below: "I actually made it!" And yet every once in a while, in between the exclamatory captions and snaps of parties on the lawn, there's a glimpse of a different student nurse: the one in a black cape with "RSN" written on her high-buttoned collar whose face looks startlingly sad, old, grim. It's just above a luau shot.

She graduated on July 24, 1965, a Saturday evening. (A crew chief named Farley was four months past his box in a Danang shed; a Quaker named Morrison was three months shy of his Pentagon match; a president was four days from announcing to the noontime nation that he was sending in 50,000.) Marlene's final year of schooling had been paid for by the Army Nurse Corps in return for a two-year commitment to active duty. Becky had also signed up for the Army as a way of finish-

ing school and maybe finding a little adventure after. The new RNs took
their boards, got their orders, flew to San Antonio. Marlene had never
been on a plane before. At Fort Sam—everybody called it that—the offi-
cers-to-be learned protocol. Marlene took pictures of the Alamo and
affixed them in her album with those little black paper corner-holders
that you buy at Woolworth's. Next to a picture of herself and Becky, she
wrote: "Pals—Side by Side in army green!" They had found another pal
now, Mary Beth Shoene. She was from Louisville and a tennis player
and a lanky extrovert. They were three musketeers.

There were 350 nurses in that fall Officer Basic Class at Fort Sam. It
was said to be the largest number of incoming nurses since World War
II. Nobody had to ask the reason why.

They got commissioned as second lieutenants and were assigned to
Letterman Hospital at the Presidio in San Francisco. Marlene worked
on the pediatric wards: "peeds," in the lingo of RNs. The musketeers
found an apartment off the post, and toured Fisherman's Wharf, and
hung from the side of cable cars, and ordered cocktails at the Top of the
Mark, and went to the Venetian Room at the Fairmont Hotel to hear the
McGuire Sisters. (Marlene brought home the table card and a little sack
of sugar.) They leased a secondhand Corvair with no defroster and
brakes that always seemed ready to give out as they were sailing down
the city's hills. The RNs went to a folkie joint, and Marlene came back
and pasted the evening in: "The Drinking Gourd. Folk Music. 1898
Union Street. Cheese and Crackers, .85. Imported Beer, .70."

Yes, rumors of war, but they were in San Francisco, having an
adventure, across the bay from where a defense minister grew up, not
that they knew or that it would have mattered.

Weekends, an Air Force captain whom Marlene had met in Texas
would sign out for a plane and jet-jockey it to the coast to see her.
Thomas Edward Brand would take his RN dancing, hold her sweetly at
the waist. He would fly home in his T-39 and wire flowers.

One day Marlene and Mary Beth went to a personnel officer at Letterman and asked to be sent to Vietnam at the earliest opportunity. "I
don't know how you can say you were bored with San Francisco, but
somehow, I don't know, it was just as if we'd done everything, and it
wasn't enough." The chief nurse at Letterman asked them if they were
sure they wanted their names on the list. Becky got angry when she
heard. She wasn't interested in going to Vietnam, not so soon. She felt
a little betrayed. She and Marlene were on the Army-buddy system,

and so if Marlene was going, it meant almost certainly Becky was going. In her hurt and confusion, Becky moved out of the apartment and back to post, but in the end the two patched it up.

"Becky was the one always playing Bob Dylan and what's her name, oh, you know, that woman singer with the guitar?"

"Joan Baez?"

"Yes. Becky liked those songs. You know, antiwar stuff."

"So you really didn't know what was coming?"

She thinks about it. "I remember after the war listening to Walter Cronkite interviewing some nurses who said they'd gone over totally unprepared. In a sense, this makes me mad. We just didn't look at the world like that. . . . I don't think we looked at the news that much. I thought I could do something great. I thought maybe that's what nursing's all about—going where they need you most. Even though I didn't know what I was going to, I still thought: 'This is what it'll be all about. I'm supposed to do this. It's right.' "

Let this chip of the dream end with this: There's no Dreamland in Albuquerque, New Mexico. The skating palace where an American daughter made beautiful ovals was called the Rainbow Gardens Roller Drome. It's still there, at 204 San Mateo: I dialed and got a recorded message, something about one of the world's greatest rinks and one of the world's finest maple floors. "Make a date to roller-skate," urged a dreamy voice.

"Dreamland? Where did I get that? How did I come up with that?" says the woman who went to war and skated on the dark half of the moon but didn't let it take her down.

IN HIS EARLY and valuable McNamara biography, Henry Trewhitt wrote of the year 1966: "He was under tremendous strain and showing it more frequently." In her much later and more comprehensive McNamara biography, Deborah Shapley wrote of the year 1966: "The war manager who seemed so certain before the television cameras was inwardly lost." And *Time* magazine, in a sentence written not specifically about 1966, but which describes it well, once said: "As the war widened he consistently underestimated its cost—in life, in spirit, even in money." That assessment was made in 1971, when McNamara had been running the World Bank for three years, just as *The Pentagon Papers* were flushing out in America, documenting deception, miscalculation.

Even in money. David Halberstam, in *The Best and the Brightest,* tells in detail how Lyndon Johnson, with the secretary of defense as the point man, set about hiding the true economic cost of Vietnam, not just from Congress and the people but even from some of the administration's own key financial planners. Wrote Halberstam: "The result was that his economic planning was a living lie, and his administration took us into economic chaos . . . the failure to finance the war honestly would inspire a virulent inflationary spiral. . . . Thus was the fatal decision made not to go for a tax increase, a decision made in early 1966, which resulted in the subsequent runaway inflation. . . . It was not the war which destroyed the economy, but the essentially dishonest way in which it was handled."

That's the received wisdom about the '66 money lie: that if McNamara and LBJ and several others at the inner circle had put the country on an honest war footing; if taxes had been raised and not just subterfuged; if an open accounting had been made; then the American economy wouldn't have gotten trapped in the inflationary chaos from which it has never really recovered. But an open accounting couldn't be made in late 1965 and early 1966, because Lyndon Johnson wanted guns and butter both. He intended to have his Great Society. He couldn't afford to give the impression the U.S. was involved in a major war. Thus the money deceptions. (I should say here that Shapley and others have since questioned whether the initial inflationary spiral of Vietnam was unavoidable. It's one of the ongoing historical debates, and books will continue to debate it.)

There are a lot of twists to the late-1965 and early-1966 budget deceptions, but at the center of the lie, insofar as McNamara is concerned, is an old, sad fact, clear from documents: The secretary *wanted* to increase taxes and to call up reserves, wanted this as far back as the previous summer, 1965, when the president committed large-scale forces. But when these recommendations were denied, when the advice was rejected, the secretary went along. No, he didn't just go along: He argued brilliantly for positions he didn't privately hold. I'm not suggesting McNamara was alone in this kind of loyal hypocrisy; he just did it better than most, and besides, he is the one whose riddles I am struggling to pierce.

In the budget message that was sent to Congress in January, Johnson said: "We are a rich nation and can afford to make progress at home while meeting obligations abroad. . . . I have not halted progress in the new and vital Great Society programs in order to finance the costs of our efforts in Southeast Asia." The defense budget of early '66 for the next fiscal year (that is, July 1, 1966–June 30, 1967) was a record $58 billion, of which $10 billion would go directly toward financing the war. But the true projections of Vietnam's cost—as McNamara and several others in an inner circle had reckoned—were not $10 billion but in the range of $16–$18 billion. Thus was the $6 or $7 or $8 billion lie made. To make it work, a budget was constructed on the arbitrary assumption that the war would be over by June 30, 1967. A two-step approach was taken. As William Conrad Gibbons has written: "In order to use this two-step approach while remaining within the requirements of the Budget and Accounting Act, however, a way had to be found to limit the estimated cost of the war. The answer was found in an act of budgetary legerdemain by which it was assumed that the war would end and defense expenditures would return to their pre-Vietnam level. . . ." A mighty assumption, since America's secretary of defense was calculating in circles other than economic that there could well be 600,000 U.S. troops in Vietnam by 1967. To use Gibbons's words, the president and his men had "devised the logic to justify avoiding either a tax increase or the full amount of appropriations needed." Which is to say they had baked the books. And as history shows, the *actual* cost of Vietnam spiked in the next fiscal year: from $10 billion to $20 billion. And the deficit climbed to an *actual* $9.8 billion.

A decade ago, in an interview in Princeton, William Bundy told me—almost offhandedly—of a small dinner McNamara once attended at his home. Bundy first thought the dinner was in late 1967, but then said, no, it had to be spring '68, maybe fall. (In that case, McNamara was out of the Pentagon and at the World Bank.) Several from the Johnson administration were there. According to Bundy, McNamara talked that night about how he had bought into the big 1966 economic lie. Bundy told me he could see McNamara's conscience hurting him.

Under tremendous strain and showing it more frequently: On March 3, 1966, a secretary's picture appeared at the top of the fold in the New York *Times.* (Two days hence, a planeload of nurses headed for war will lift off from Travis Air Force Base.) The face in the paper wasn't a face of mercy. The body was hunched, the finger was jabbing. The day before, McNamara had held a press conference on four hours' notice, during which an investigative reporter for the Des Moines *Register,* Clark Mollenhoff, lobbed Mollenhoff cocktails. Mollenhoff, a six-foot-four, 245-pounder, had stuck in the McNamara craw before. He was a famous Pentagon agitator.

"Look, if you are not going to maintain order, will you please leave?" McNamara said.

"No," said Mollenhoff.

"There are others who want to ask questions," McNamara said.

"I want to ask you a question," Mollenhoff said.

"You have asked three," the secretary said.

"You dodged it three times," the reporter said.

"I will take other questions."

"You seem to dodge everything, Mr. Secretary."

The *Times* said McNamara was "edgy and angry," and the story was paired with another front-page story, about casualties. This was the lead on the second piece, which was placed on the page just below McNamara's jabbing finger: "In the first two months of 1966, the United States suffered more than 4,300 casualties in the Vietnamese war. American casualties for all of last year were under 7,000."

Ten days later an animus under Pentagon strain went on a skiing trip in Switzerland with his wife and fifteen-year-old son. There were reports he had left town under orders from the president. A diploma RN from a New Mexico nursing program was now in Vietnam. And it wasn't long after he had gotten back from the spring snows of Zermatt, knowing nothing of a Lieutenant Marlene Vrooman in her Qui Nhon recovery room, that the animus under strain held a meeting with a new Pentagon speechwriter. This speechwriter, a career government wordsmith, had come over from the United States Information Agency. His name was Jack Maddux, and it was his first introduction to the secretary of defense, who talked crisply but kindly to him in his office that day, saying, Look, Jack, can I call you Jack, I have to give a speech in May, no two speeches, one's up in Canada and the other's in Pittsburgh a couple days after, I don't really want to give that one, but I let my daughter talk me into it in a weak moment, but anyway I have certain things I want to say in both, and my secretary Peg here's going to give you some memos, and I want you to immerse yourself and then come back to me with questions, because this is a priority, okay?

I'll get right to work, sir, said the new McNamara wordsmith, Jack Maddux, who had a certain flabby and deceptive softness about him—a likable Washington type who would strike you as a definite anima. Yes.

*   *   *

"*LAWRENCE OF ARABIA* was showing the night we got in," she says. (I'm thinking camels in the jungle—how can it be?)

"Eight of us to share one shower, and it was just this little trickle," she says. (Her fingers are miming a dribble.)

"We wanted to feminize it," she says. "We mixed lavenders and pinks. We went out and got all this fabric in the markets. We named it the Purple Pad." (Yes: draped footlockers, floral sheets on iron bunks, a sign over the door made from construction paper. It says, what else, The Purple Pad.) Marlene had the top bunk, Becky was in the middle, Mary Beth took the bottom.

The Pad had once been a squalid room in a military compound, but now it was the lavender Shangri-la of MACV where three RNs sought refuge and sleep after all-night shifts. Mary Beth Shoene's mom sent a portable sewing machine through the mails from Louisville to aid in the makeover. Mary Beth was a whiz at sewing. Her mom also mailed tennis rackets for off-hour pursuits. From the villa's rooftop balcony, you could look out across the asphalt road and see a lovely beach: palms and white sand. The view was straight out of a tourist brochure. Except the water was so polluted the RNs couldn't go in. The beach stank from human feces. But the MACV compound was fragrant with flora.

At Christmas Marlene's mom sent a silvered tree with ornaments, the kind you screw the arms into.

It sounds a little like Gidget goes Vietnam, so long as you don't dwell on, say, somebody's brown belly swelling up and eviscerating—no, popping like a tire going out—before you can get the hot towels on.

Once Marlene popped in so many amphetamines her heart began to pound wildly. She thought it was going to tear through her chest. The next morning it was still pounding. A doc at the hospital made her lie down. "I could have stroked out," she says. Sometimes the Seconals she took would act in reverse. "You felt so hopped up," she says. There were nights on the unit when she would start manically cleaning a counter, scrubbing a floor.

Memory: "There were many times it was quiet. It's another misconception. It annoys me. You read these books about Vietnam, nurses who went to Vietnam, and you think it was just crisis and push all the time, and when it wasn't that it was drinking. It wasn't *China Beach.* . . . And it was a lot of fun, too."

Fun, yes, they got to see Bob Hope and Joey Heatherton and Danny Kaye and Vikki Carr. Roy Rogers came through—the king of the cowboys brought his own photographer and had his doo-dadded pants stuffed inside his hand-tooled boots. He and Marlene posed side by side in a pre-op ward in a Quonset while Roy's man made a Polaroid snap. Roy was such a gentleman, like Elvis, on the other side of another dream.

Once, the occupants of the Pad and some other RNs were trucked up to the big base camp at An Khe to see an Ann-Margret show. Mid-performance, the round-eyes in their fatigues and Shalimar found themselves being hauled up onstage. "Here's one of ours!" boomed the guy at the mike. "This is Marlene from the Sixty-seventh! This is Mary Beth! And here's Becky from Santa Fe!" Seas of GIs screaming and whistling in the dark.

When was that time she woke up delirious and talking about her mother? She hadn't been there long. It's so gauzy. What she remembers is that there wasn't any room for her at the hospital, so she went to bed in the Pad. The delirium and fever were judged to be an Asian virus. "I think it was from bathing in contaminated water," she explains.

Another time she and Becky caught a ride on a chopper to a special-forces camp in a Montagnard village. It was sort of illegal. On other days off, she and Becky had volunteered their time at a Qui Nhon orphanage; not today. At the camp the adventurers put on green berets and posed for a picture. They lined up with some village kids. It's a wonderful sepia moment, two Yankee faces in field uniforms and nursing caps standing behind maybe twenty children, some of the kids naked, others yawning, others grinning in incomprehension at the strange photographic box. You feel the watery fields against the flat sky, mountains beyond. Behind the nurses, a temple or shrine.

And yet . . . while they were in that Montagnard village, four captured VC were brought in. The RNs took pictures. A week or so later, Becky wrote on the back of a print: "These are four suspected Viet Cong in a big hole held for questioning—supposedly but I think they killed them that night cause they don't usually keep prisoners."

It's as if a different Vietnam is captioned on the back of every Vietnam image Marlene Kramel owns; just flip the slide over. And yet I have encountered much the same flip-flop in others—Becky and Mary Beth, for instance. I once spent a lovely afternoon in Florida with Marlene Kramel's old Vietnam roomies. We met at the regional hospital above Fort Lauderdale, where Mary Beth Shoene Cooper is a nursing supervisor in charge of several departments. Becky Tapia Goller had left her hospital job early and driven down from Palm Beach Gardens to join us. She's a small dark-haired woman who tends to be taciturn until she's drawn out. Then she'll go like sixty. Until several years ago, Becky and Mary Beth had no idea they lived within an hour of each other.

"Weren't we going over [to work] in deuce-and-a-halfs?" Mary Beth said.

"Remember how during alerts we'd jump out of bed in our pajamas and combat helmets and lie on the floor till they told us it was all clear?" said Becky.

They talked about the time a drunk GI got into the Pad. It was Becky who awoke to find the horny paw polishing her backside. They had gone to sleep with their tops off, it was so hot.

"Remember that night we were eating [in town] and it was a pigeon head?" said Mary Beth. More laughter. But then soon after, Becky was saying in a flat voice: "The head cases were always the expectants." Mary Beth told me about a boy with no arms trying to get out of his bed to salute General Westmoreland.

Once, Becky opened a fresh dressing. There were ants crawling around in an unsutured wound. The patient was a VC. "They were just as scared as our boys," Becky said. "They'd look at you with these scared eyes."

Quick cut: to the Libuse blue swing—the third roomie just looked over with scared eyes: She's remembering a patient who begged her not to turn him over. He was in a special bed for his circulation. He needed to be turned. "I told him, 'I have to turn you. You'll be okay.' But he begged me. I promised him. I utterly promised him I'd be back. He kept saying, 'Please don't turn me. I'll die.' 'No, no,' I said, 'you'll be okay.' "

Then: "I can't tell you why I didn't get back. I just can't remember. I don't know what I was doing. But I didn't. I didn't get back. His eyes. I can see his eyes. I went back over. I couldn't get a pulse. There was no blood pressure, and he was dead, and I didn't get back there." She means: She didn't get back in time.

I say, "Were you able to tell anybody about this?"

"No."

And then: "Only time I did anything with it was in the class in Minnesota, and I wrote it down, and other people wrote things down, and we put them in a pile and burned them."

Best she recalls, Lieutenant Marlene Vrooman of Albuquerque met Captain Glenn Kramel of Libuse about six or eight weeks before she caught the freedom bird home. She had made first lieutenant now. Maybe she had seen the captain earlier, but nothing clicked. And besides, she thought he was engaged. (He sort of was, he says—to a woman he had met in Germany before being shipped to Vietnam.) One night, at a movie in the compound, Glenn asked Marlene to sit down beside him. She said no. A while later she ran into him at the officers' club. This time she sat down. They talked until three in the morning—and she had to get up at five-fifteen. In his infectious drawl, the infantry officer asked if he might walk her to quarters. At the stairwell the nurse kissed him lightly on the cheek. He had asked her for a kiss.

"He went like this." (Her finger is tapping against her rouged and puckered cheek.)

Three nights after they met, the captain asked the lieutenant to marry him. "You're crazy," she told him. "It's the war." Until that moment Marlene thought she was still in love with the jet-jockey she had met in San Antonio. "Look, whatever made it happen, it happened," Glenn said.

For the next several weeks, two innocents necked pretty passionately in an area called "the porch," but that was as far as it went. "Not that he didn't want more," says a woman who has a chasteness about her even now, in her long-married middle age.

CARL JUNG, the Swiss founder of analytical psychology, once wrote: "The persona, the ideal picture of a man as he should be, is inwardly compensated by feminine weakness, and as the individual outwardly displays the strong man, so he becomes inwardly a woman, i.e., the anima, for it is the anima that reacts to the persona." Which may only be saying how we seek our hidden self, if we just knew.

I am walking down a Washington street with the man who ghosted Montreal and Chatham. It's the tense of modern times; a decade ago. A rambling, shambling, and altogether inquisitive mind is remembering the first encounter, his first double-smithing job, for a figure he still reveres, even if the figure is in hot disrepute. All the way down K Street, Jack Maddux, who would be pretty hard to dislike, has been talking high-pitched and squeaky. He's been rambling and shambling in his black oxfords and black buttoned-up trench coat—pointing out this, digressing on that. He reminds me of some ribald and aging bishop.

On the day after Chatham, in her story about the "total emergence of the other McNamara," Mary McGrory of the Washington *Star* wrote: "It is known that in addition to a new lease on life, the secretary has a new speechwriter, a U.S. Information Agency recruit named Jack Maddox [sic]." Two weeks later, with the Montreal and Chatham speeches still confounding the capital's collective mind, columnist James J. Kilpatrick wrote, "Now, skeptical souls will contend that all this reflects not so much a new secretary as a new ghostwriter. In part, this is true. But the first task of a good ghost is faithfully to pull together what his mortal principal wants to say."

A story from the ghost about the mortal principal: For nearly all the years he wrote speeches for McNamara at the Pentagon and World Bank, Maddux suffered a serious weight problem. He would balloon, go on crash diets. Sooner than later he would be a fatty again. It never came up with McNamara, not even in passing. It was as if the secretary never noticed the periodic loss or gain of fifty or seventy-five pounds in his wordsmith. Talk like that would have been personal. Maddux had a role, and, as the policymakers liked to say about Vietnam in the early days, it was limited and defined. Which isn't to say McNamara wasn't cordial. He was always very cordial.

Maddux, remembering: "He had very definite ideas about that speech. [He meant Montreal.] He was very serious about the gravity of it. He said, 'I want to show that security is not just military hardware. True security is in the character of the differing relations between countries.' I remember he was throwing numbers at me like crazy, hundred thousand this, and if you take the square root of that." (Some of that got into the speech, despite the ghost's best efforts to keep it out.)

McNamara was emphatic about making a proposal "that every young person in the United States give two years of service to his country—whether in or out of the Army. It could be the Peace Corps or some other developmental work. He said, 'Jack, I want to make this point at the end. The draft is inequitable. Smart people can get out of it. It isn't right.' The first time I wrote the speech, I left his two-year thing out. There was so much else crammed into the speech, I thought: 'Who needs it?' I almost can't believe I was that arrogant."

He decided to write the Chatham talk first, even though it was much less important. The wordsmith felt tight for both tasks and didn't complete the Montreal speech until 3 a.m. on the morning it was due in McNamara's office. He took it to the message center near the secretary's office where the cables come in. Then Maddux went home and climbed into bed. He was living in somebody's Capitol Hill basement and didn't have a phone. About eight, the people from upstairs were rousing him: "The secretary of defense is on the line."

"Look, Jack, I've just read it, I've read both, you did very fine, I like them a lot, you got most of my ideas in, but look here, you've left out my two-year proposal for national service."

"Yes, sir," Maddux said. "I'll have it in there by noon."

The Pentagon printed both speeches, and the next day McNamara called for Maddux. The secretary was taking lunch in his conference room, and for a palpitating moment the ghost thought he was going to be asked to sit down. "I want to make a change, several changes," McNamara said.

"But, sir, you approved it yesterday and I think they've already printed them."

"Oh, that's no problem, just get the text back," McNamara said, sawing on his meat.

I asked Maddux if he had any sense that his first penned McNamara words were going to cause a sensation. "I guess I didn't think of it that way," he said. But I thought I saw a sly nod. "There wasn't even that much talking it out between us, really. I just got to work." I asked if it was possible that each saw in the other an uncompleted part of himself. The ghost laughed. "What I'm surprised about is the guy could put up with me all those years."

We shambled some more and I said, "You read his mind, Jack." To which a droll, verbose man in spongy shoes and a white drip-dry shirt replied, "Oh, no, I never flatter myself that way."

WE HAVE TO GO BACK for a moment to that commencement stage in Pennsylvania and what was pulsing under the floorboards. Because it's a thread in the dream, a stitch in the moral.

Think of it this way: On a May Sunday in 1966, while a Recovery Room nurse in Vietnam was relating to the existential, a man riding and hiding his pain dipped down into the land of the anima, Chatham College, and let something out. But the place where he let it out wasn't necessarily what it seemed, either.

What was Robert McNamara letting out on May 22, 1966? If you went by text, he was letting out some soft-sided and even squishy things about himself that he had carried since his childhood in Oakland, things he didn't wish to deny or conceal so much as keep down, keep boxed and compartmentalized for their acceptable nighttime use. But if you were trying to go below delivered words, to subtext, then McNamara was letting out to the women of Chatham, one of whom was his own child, that Vietnam had destroyed his universe, or at least his image of himself.

"It is not really the computer that is in question; it is whether or not Dr. Strangelove is sitting at the computer's console," said the guest that day, who happened to regard the cinematic character of Dr. Strangelove as a personal attack on his middle name.

In Washington, between and beneath the lines of documents, reaching as far back as six months, a turn had been made—albeit with zigzag and riddle. And now, at a tiny women's school in western Pennsylvania, this different acknowledgment, publicly.

What was Chatham College from its outside on May 22, 1966? It was a little preserve of brick Georgian privilege sitting on a hill in a neighborhood called Shadyside. It was a ninety-seven-year-old institution with classic liberal-arts values and certain standards of excellence. (No one would have suggested it was Wellesley or Sarah Lawrence.) But under that truth lay other truths. Under that Chatham fact lay other facts. Think of it this way: Beneath the gowns of 114 daughters, waiting for a piece of parchment, were 114 stories, seethings, ironies.

Someone was gay, and had lately come to it. Someone heard Dylan go electric at the Newport Folk Festival. Someone had had a secret abortion. Someone wasn't wearing anything under her robe. Someone had done the almost shocking thing of going out with Negroes. Someone had ridden a bus to Selma the previous spring after sitting in her room at Bennedum Hall and watching people on television getting hit with billy clubs. Someone drove her moldy VW bug up to Harvard for teach-ins on the war. And someone else, years from that moment, was going to stop off in Springfield, Illinois, on the way home from Granny's with her husband and children to see Lincoln's tomb and then sit down and write the lines: "Today we teach our children about imperialism and racism so they will remember: remember wars fought for conditions they have not experienced and for causes no one understood. Remember to care for the wounds buried under the scars of another generation." That Chatham woman's name was Patty Williamson (now it's Patty Baker), and she and I have spent some pleasant hours together talking about concentric circles and what was more illusory and far less sheltered than you would ever have guessed.

At Chatham College in the sixties you couldn't wear slacks to dinner. (The way to get around it was to go over in your slacks but keep a skirt in the cloakroom outside the dining hall.) At Chatham you worked on undergraduate theses with big-think titles: "The Czechoslovak-American Intellectual: A Study of the Political Behavior of a Select Group." At Chatham you were obliged to come to teas and convocations in a white dress with your class ribbon fluttering from your shoulder. At Chatham you lived in dorms that were the onetime mansions of nineteenth-century steel barons. The mansion Robert McNamara's daughter slept in her senior year was Berry Hall, and she and her roomies could have gone out the back door and left campus and walked across the street and, like that, been standing on the doorstep of the private Shadyside residence where Norman Morrison and fellow Quakers used to sit in Sunday silence. McNamara's daughter, her classmates have told me, used to nip around Shadyside and Squirrel Hill on a hot little green Vespa motorbike.

Chatham College, such a tony finishing dream on a Pittsburgh hill. And under the dream, so many twists.

I found no terrible connections vis-à-vis McNamara and his speech of May 22, 1966—say, a brother who got killed the following year at Quang Tri or a fiancé who ended up a POW in Hanoi. Instead I found uncounted Chatham connections and ironies—none calamitous, all real—which revealed the deeper, if plainer, truth: I doubt it was possible to be breathing in the mid-1960s, even or especially at a tiny women's college in Pennsylvania, and *not* have felt some personal intersection with the man who embodied an age.

Out on the sidewalk that day were a hundred pickets. "Bohemian youths in sandals . . . to graying, middle-aged men and women," the Pittsburgh *Press* reported. The demonstration was pretty restrained, sort of like Chatham.

Five days before, the president of the United States, speaking at a Democratic fund-raising dinner in Chicago, urging unity on his countrymen, said, ". . . there will be some Nervous Nellies and some who will . . . break ranks under the strain." That has a certain ironic ring. Ten days before Chatham (which would have been six days before Montreal), a U.S. spokesman in Saigon reported that 82 American servicemen had been killed and 615 wounded in the previous week, the second time in five weeks that U.S. battle losses had been higher than those of the South Vietnamese army. And even as the speech was being delivered in Pennsylvania, a Buddhist bloodbath was going on in Vietnam. Saigon police and troops were using bayonets and tear gas to break up anti-American demonstrations. Vietnamese students were burning U.S. vehicles.

Riding and hiding your pain.

So how was his wisdom about womanhood received? Would his speech even be recalled now?

Most didn't remember; what they could recall immediately was the feeling of disruption, this and the fact they had had no say-so in who had been invited to address them in the first place. What was in almost every memory cell was that the class couldn't have its graduation on beautiful Mellon Lawn in the middle of campus but instead had to have it down the hill, at the Carnegie Music Hall, closer to the grit and stink of the city. There had been a famous meeting about this with the college president in the chapel basement. "I know a concern like that may sound a little obscene in the context of 58,000 names on a wall—but it seemed real enough at the time," someone told me. It didn't sound obscene; it sounded in context.

I sent the speech to Helen Read Steele. She was class president. She teaches school and has a sheep farm in the New Hampshire mountains. On the phone Steele said, "I remember the general feeling of hostility. And yet I can remember meeting him at a luncheon. . . . I almost felt at that luncheon a shift. I can remember thinking, Oh, what do we know. We're just a bunch of women college graduates."

I sent it to Sharon Smith, who lives in Washington and works for the National Geographic Society. On the phone she had said, "What I remember so vividly is he was saying to us you as women have a unique gift you can give to the world and your point of view is important because it's nonconfrontational, it's softer, and you have to recognize your contribution and do something with it." Smith said she sometimes sees him now coming up out of the subway—head down, body bent forward, so old. No, she's never tried going up.

I sent it to Cordis Heard. She's the Chatham woman who was shoved up against the wall of the Conrad Hilton at the Democratic National Convention two summers after graduation. She got married in a dress she found in a Chatham prop box. Cordis, ever the rebel looking for the cause, ended up an accomplished actress, with stops for political causes, which she wouldn't think of as causes so much as decent human justices. She lives in New York and has acted on Broadway. Her brother, John Heard, went out to Hollywood and became a pretty well known movie actor—but Cordis's career has stayed at the fringe of fame. She thinks that's okay. "I've never even had the opportunity to sell out," she told me. "The closest I got to it was when I did a series of voice-overs for Con Edison. The text wasn't that offensive. It wasn't saying nuclear power was safe, it wasn't going that far." We were sitting in her tiny but elegant West Side apartment drinking herbal tea; in a minute she was due to go around the corner and fetch her nine-year-old from school. She had just topped fifty, and there seemed something fetching, angular, sexy, sexless, and still so wonderfully outsiderish about this Chatham woman who had grown up in a big house in Maryland, and who had gone to a convent high school in Georgetown while her dad toiled in McNamara's Pentagon as a civilian engineer. He had been an outsider, too. We talked about the apparent coziness of a place, while behind it things may be falling and crashing. The actress said: "I wanted to be able to stand up that day to that liar and say, 'You're a liar.' I was so torn. I wanted to be out there with the protesters. I'm thinking, Why am I sitting here listening to this man trying to placate us with this bunkum? What do they understand, anyway? They're feeble people." I asked the old disrupter why she didn't walk out. She said, catching a dilemma of the sixties, "You don't say fuck you to your father. That's not who I am."

I sent the speech to Lynnette Burley Fuller. She's the grad with the brother named Skipper who, on the eve of induction, went broomsticking around the house with a pot on his head—a skit that might have been hilarious if it hadn't been so anxiety-filled. Lynnette Burley Fuller became an Episcopal priest with advanced degrees; she's also a practicing therapist. She read the text of the speech and mailed back a literary deconstruction that sort of took my breath away: "You are being cued as to what you are to do or be. There is no 'I believe' you are. 'I hope' you are. 'I wish for you.' No connection between the speaker and the hearer that gives the hearer an option to exercise their own thoughts or feeling. . . . Jung students could use this as a text for the pain that is caused when you separate Spirit and Soul, taking one and assigning the other. . . . This is a tiresome man, who shows little insight into himself or others. He is a passive-aggressive, aggressive-aggressive. He is deceptive in his agenda. I can see why I forgot this address. I probably disassociated, murmuring to myself: 'Life is real. Life is earnest. And the grave is not its goal.' "

I sent the text to one more grad. I didn't try to phone her beforehand, just enclosed a note, asking if she would be willing to recall her feelings about the moment. I didn't hear back from Kathy McNamara, who became an economist at the World Bank.

IN THE SURREAL PROSE of a Consultation Report, this one typed on Standard Government Form No. 513 and signed by doctors at Walter Reed Hospital on January 20, 1975:

> This thirty-year-old woman has a four-year history of recurrent desmoid tumors involving the right leg and buttock area. She first presented with a mass in the posterio-lateral thigh on the right and this was excised in February 1970. In November of that year, she had a popliteal recurrence which was excised along with the origin of the gastrocenemius. She remained free of the disease until October 1971 when a right gluteal recurrence was noted and excised followed by a second recurrence in the same area in July 1972 and a third recurrence in July 1973. At that last time, a recurrent mass in the popliteal fossa was noted and biopsied. It was felt to be unresectable because of entrapment of neurovascular structures. In December 1974, the right popliteal mass was still present and there was also a good size mass in the right gluteal area. This was reexcised recently and proved to be a large mass of recurrent desmoid tumor as reported on pathology report S-75-226. At the time of the surgery, it was felt that the tumor could not be completely excised because of penetration into the pelvis in the region of the sciatic nerve sciatic notch. At the present time, she is recovering from her latest surgery and has a drain still in place from the buttock incision. . . .

Marlene Kramel and I are looking at a framed color portrait of herself and husband and baby son. It was taken in 1970, five years before that report. She and Glenn and little Glenn Allen (Rick, their second son, hadn't been born yet) were living at Fort Benning, Georgia. Marlene had been home from Vietnam three years. The tumor dream was under way. "This picture is maybe three surgeries later," she says. "No, I think two."

The woman in the 1970 portrait has her hair in a bouffant. It isn't that she's so shockingly thin, it's that the structure of her face seems to have been altered. It can't be the person who posed with Becky in the green beret in the Montagnard village; it can't be the virginal RN in the graduation picture at Regina—which wasn't even five years in her past.

"It's almost as if you've changed bodies," I say.

"I know, I know," she says.

This part of the story is about the kind of shadows that show up on medical film.

Chronology of an illness. A woman, no longer so naïve, returned from war in March 1967. She was twenty-two. What she was carrying on her, what she had gotten inside her, isn't possible to know. On leaving she had been presented with a certificate proclaiming that ". . . she successfully achieved all her objectives in working for the counter-insurgency program against communism in the Republic of Vietnam." She had six months of active duty left, so she was assigned to an ortho unit at Fort Monmouth, New Jersey. She hated it—there seemed nothing in it after what she had experienced. But more than this, she missed Glenn terribly. So mainly she focused on her upcoming wedding. At her discharge, Marlene left behind in Jersey a whole trunk of her military things. She wanted that part behind her.

Glenn followed her home and they were married on an Army post in Louisiana in October 1967. (But nothing is as smooth as it sounds: At the last, before Glenn left Vietnam, a distance had grown between them and the marriage seemed momentarily threatened.) Within weeks of getting married, Marlene got pregnant. Within weeks there were rumors that Glenn and his unit would be going back. Had her leg already begun to hurt? "Like a hamstring, back up in my right thigh," she says.

Adding: "I remember going to buy some hush-puppy shoes. I remember saying something to his mother. And she said, 'Maybe it's your shoes.' Oh wait a minute, that was later."

(Her hand has moved up under her buttock, lifting it off the seat of the swing. Funny, I've noticed only now how slack this leg is. I've also just noticed what is written on her silver bracelet: "Give O Negative only. Roman Catholic.")

With their two sticks of furniture, the newlyweds moved from Fort Polk, Louisiana, to Fort Carson, Colorado. Marlene put up paper curtains and tried to feminize. The hidden thing growing inside her wasn't making her limp, not yet, so she said nothing. "I do that with pain, I toss it aside," she explains.

Glenn Allen was born in the summer of 1968 and afterward the father left for Vietnam. Doing her postpartum exercises on the floor, the baby's mother found she couldn't straighten her leg. Marlene mentioned this to her mother-in-law, and they decided it was probably her shoes. "It's just me, I'd tell myself. I'd just kind of toss it away. I'd think about it and I'd say, 'Oh, it's just something to do with me. Something quirky.' "

A year passed. Glenn got home safely. They were at Fort Benning, 150-C Kessler Drive, Custer Terrace. Christmas came. The pain worsened. Almost nightly Marlene rubbed Ben-Gay on her leg. Putting it on one evening in the new year she said, "Glenn, do you have a knot like this in your leg?"

"No, I don't. Maybe it's a pulled muscle," he said.

"Yes, that's probably it," she said.

But a few days later, standing at the sink at Custer Terrace, there was a pain that came close to making her fall down, and this time she went to a phone and made an appointment to see a doctor. In the office the next day, a female physician rubbed the ache and looked concerned. Still, it was probably nothing, something itty-bitty, which is how Marlene described it to the wife of a colonel who was planning to host a cocktail party in a day or so: "This little benign tumor removed—that's all they're going to do." Except at the post hospital they asked her to sign a consent form for amputation.

"I remember what one of the surgeons said. The words were 'Or it may mean the whole leg.' I can remember they were wheeling me down the hall to surgery and I'm wanting desperately to say to them, 'No, no, you can't have the leg.' But I was so drugged."

The initial benign tumor turned out not to be itty-bitty, nor even the size of a golf ball. It was monstrous, extending from under the bend of her knee up to her buttock.

There were three surgeries that year, 1970, and somewhere in the middle a scared woman and her worried husband and baby son went to a photography studio in Columbus, Georgia, and posed for a color portrait: It's the one where Marlene seems to have changed bodies, altered faces.

The next year, Glenn got orders for Korea. Marlene was catching the knots fast, so they weren't talking amputation. "I was getting down onto the floor into every position imaginable to feel for them," she says. She became pregnant with her second child (her doctors had advised against it), and once more Glenn was forced to leave. But halfway through his tour he managed to get back on a short visit and saw his wife suffering.

By the summer of 1972, just before Glenn finished in Korea, there were sharp shooting pains in Marlene's buttocks. She was mom to a four-year-old and a five-month-old. A little earlier, some stupid doctor at an Air Force base in Louisiana had told her that it was all in her mind—she was an hysterical wife with nothing but phantom scar tissue and a husband overseas.

The woman in the tumor dream was moved from a hospital at Fort Benning to Walter Reed in Washington. At Walter Reed, late at night, she saw an opened envelope with her name on it. Someone had left the document lying around. Marlene read the first words: "Purpose of transfer. Transfer to Walter Reed for hemipelvictomy."

"I was crying and sobbing," she says. "We'd just gotten there. Glenn and I went up to the ward and it's dark and they'd been painting in there or something and I see this lady in a bed in the hallway and she's got the sheets pulled back and there's this stump of a leg."

By daylight, the doctors told the patient that the tumor was well into the artery and the nerve. They said, "If we don't do this, it's going to get into the pelvic cavity, and your liver, and you're going to die." Glenn, who had been at Marlene's side for every surgery, said the same: "Princess, they want the leg." But once more the leg seemed to have a will and a life of its own.

Over the next several years: more surgeries, more air evacuations on a military DC-9 with a big red cross painted on its side. Sometimes Marlene would spend a whole day or night on a transport, lying in a litter, bouncing along with other military dependents who were being dropped off or picked up at Scott Air Force Base in Illinois or at Fort Benning or Walter Reed. She was like a piece of government cargo being shipped through the skies. Often she lay in the litter dog-sick. "I'd spike temps, they were running malaria smears on me," she says.

In January 1975 she was at Walter Reed again, and again that talk of slicing it off. Glenn, who had become expert at pacing the grounds of hospitals waiting for word, bent down over Marlene's bed and said it: "Princess, they want to take your whole leg, otherwise it's your life, and maybe in a year." But two months earlier, something strange had happened. Marlene experienced what she is still convinced was a religious vision. It was as real to her as if she had been kneeling at the glowing bush at Fatima. "There was a knot behind my knee," she says. "It felt like a goiter. I had this vision it was melting away."

Not only did the patient's leg not get sliced off in January 1975, but the tumors began to dry up, following an experimental course of radiation. Marlene: "I think it was 6,300 rads to each area." It's true that she still had ahead of her some massive bleedings and other unexpected troubles. But by that January it was as if an American innocent had beaten the odds of the learned men writing surreal prose on Standard Government Form 513.

THE GREAT DANISH WRITER Isak Dinesen said, "All sorrows can be borne if you put them into a story or tell a story about them." So let me tell this: I once spent several hours talking to a Vietnam nurse named Dusty. I'll call her Dusty and not give her last name because this is her wish and besides "Dusty" is how she signs much of her published poetry—which has deceptively simple lines such as this: "I went to Vietnam to heal / and discovered I am not God." Those Dusty poems are widely quoted by Vietnam veterans, especially women, especially nurses. There are some other pieces of Vietnam nursing literature that have had a wide readership: an oral history called *A Piece of My Heart;* Lynda Van Devanter's *Home Before Morning,* and Winnie Smith's *American Daughter Gone to War.* These last two are autobiographies. But the Dusty poems have seemed to speak for and cut to the deepest part of the Vietnam nursing bone. Marlene has read some of the poems aloud at Louisiana veterans' functions, especially one called "Hello, David," which begins: "Hello, David—my name is Dusty / I'm your night nurse," and which ends: "Goodbye, David—my name is Dusty / I am the last person / you will see / I am the last person / you will touch / I am the last person who will love you."

Dusty was an Army nurse in Vietnam when Marlene was, but they didn't know each other. When I talked with her, Dusty was a typist in what she referred to as a big, disgusting Republican midwest law firm. When I asked her why she left nursing, she said, "Because I just didn't want to be responsible any more for trying to keep somebody alive." When I told her that her talents were being underused, I thought I could hear someone spitting on the sentence through the phone wire. Then she said, with a breathing that sounded as if she were climbing stairs, "Well, that's flattering. But on the other hand I'm no different from about half the other women in the world." Then Dusty said, "This war is just such a running sore that it's going to run till the last Vietnam veteran dies."

Of Marlene Kramel, about whom she knew nothing save what I had described, Dusty said, without any judgment in it: "Sadness is such an acceptable emotion for a woman; rage is not. It's her coping mechanism. You can get over a death, but not the reason. If it was all a waste and a lie, how do you face that?"

Another female friend of mine, whom I've talked to about Marlene, said, also without judgment: "Marlene could be a present-particular tense if she were a grammar form. It would be a very loving tense. But those desmoid demons must have horror, disgust, terror, fury in them somewhere."

I remember the night Glenn and Marlene and I were sitting by the edge of the swimming pool. Blue light was rising. Marlene and I had talked for hours, much of it down at the pond. That morning we had gone to Mass in a little crossroads church out in the countryside, past sweet-potato fields owned by Glenn's people. In the liturgy book in my pew, I read: "Jewish theology at the time of Jesus held that God sent certain afflictions to people because of his mercy; he did this to raise them to a higher state of virtue." Marlene was one of the eucharistic ministers at the service, and when it came time to help with communion I watched her climb out of our pew and gimp toward the altar. Her hands were folded like a child's. She had on a buttery silken suit and she was trailing perfume and disguising the gimp. If she doesn't use it much, the leg and the ankle won't swell. She'll still get the numbing sensations, as if something isn't there.

Glenn Kramel seemed to be praying hard at church that day. He's a convert. Marlene's faith brought him over.

It was evening now and we were sitting poolside in the cooling dark. Even when swimming season is over, Glenn keeps the pool filled, because his wife loves to look at the purling blue water. I asked Glenn if he felt the war caused Marlene's tumors. The ex-soldier was using a pocketknife to trim pieces of rubber off his sneakers. He folded the blade. He put his hands together and blew into them. "I don't know if it did or not," he said.

Marlene: "We've never been able to prove it was service-related. I go back to the way we showered—in all that bad water. And Agent Orange. Who knows what they came in with?"

Glenn: "Maybe there was a predisposition and something triggered it."

Me: "You must have thought you were going to have to care for an invalid the rest of your life."

Glenn: "Yep. And trying to be an officer at the same time."

Me: "There's an incredible history behind that gimp." The three of us laughed.

Glenn got up and went into the house to turn on lights and watch a football game with his younger son, Rick. I turned to Marlene. "I guess I just don't understand why you're not angry."

"Why get myself into something I can't do anything about now? What good would it do? My life is too full of things to let anger consume me. I've been angry about things in my life, but you've got to let it go. I come home and I want to be with my husband, my family. It takes a lot of energy to keep refueling your anger."

"But what about all the lies?"

"Well, I know there was a lot of profiteering going on over there on the part of some Vietnamese generals and things like that." I said I wasn't thinking about profiteering, I was thinking about the lies of policymakers on the Potomac.

"I know. But it's over. If I want to be angry I can be angry about the drunk drivers. Or the crime. The people who are killing people in the streets. Not that. That's gone. That's over with. I've seen what anger does to people, and maybe that's part of it." Her voice rose. "If I'm going to say what I don't understand, okay, it's why they didn't allow us to get in there and finish the thing. But it's over. There's nothing I can do about it. I just don't want to go into that place. What can I do with that anger? I've had to overcome too much. I just have too much life around me. And I have a very deep faith. It's not a faith I live on Sunday. It's an everyday faith."

I said, "Maybe you would have gotten the tumors if you'd never gone."

"Who knows? If I'd never gone to war I'd have never met Glenn. I wouldn't be sitting here, which I call my little heaven on earth."

We talked about people who have come to take things for their research purposes—like me. She answered evenly. "They're disappointed, I think, when I say I don't have PTSD. They seem angry. They keep pushing and pushing." She paused. "I've said to the PTSDs I've worked with, 'Look what anger's doing to you.' "

"What did they answer?"

"I don't think they heard me."

THE ANIMUS, taking things from people, flexed back, as if he had not heard his own voice at Montreal and Chatham. He refitted the mask, as if no stricken self were inside. A technician stood before his pull-down maps at press conferences. And in the fall of that year Robert S. McNamara went again to his war.

In October he made the eighth trip in fifty-four months, and this one lasted four days. Vietnam is twelve time zones away from America, and it takes better than twenty-four hours to get there in a 707 tanker rigged with compartments for sleeping and other compartments for working at bolted-down tables and chairs. "BRIEFINGS AT THE FRONT" headlined the newsreels and papers as he departed. The last time he had gone out to Vietnam for an inspection was after the battle of the Ia Drang, in November 1965, and in the succeeding eleven months the number of American troops had risen from 170,000 to 328,000. At the start of the trip, the New York *Times* published an editorial about the "dreary sense of futility." A weekly casualty list, given out a little while before this, showed that 967 Americans had been killed or wounded in a seven-day span: highest yet.

Just before the plane touched down at Tan Son Nhut, the South Vietnamese police aborted a Vietcong plan for Robert McNamara's assassination.

He inspected a new field hospital. It was called the Sixty-seventh Evac and was located in Qui Nhon, a coastal city 270 miles north of Saigon. He strode into Recovery there, flanked by brass, and shook the hands of several startled nurses, told them what important work they were doing. It was just a flash; he was on the unit, he was gone. "He's coming, he's coming," a corpsman had shouted to a perky RN from Albuquerque, who had recently transferred over from the Eighty-fifth Evac. The photographers from AP missed the moment, although they got him bending over a bed talking to a soldier, who may or may not have been one of Marlene's patients.

Back in Saigon, another news conference. His opening words: "The military operations have progressed very satisfactorily during the past year. The rate of progress has exceeded our expectations. The pressure on the Vietcong, measured in terms of the casualties they have suffered, the destruction of their units, the measurable effect on their morale, have all been greater than we anticipated." In a private press backgrounder, immediately following, he was somewhat more truthful.

Morley Safer of CBS filmed a report from Saigon: "When Mr. McNamara's giant Air Force jet swept away, he left this city at once puzzled, relieved, depressed, disappointed, dismayed, angry, and excited. The dope sheets of CBS cameramen who ran after him for the past four days testify to time and energy that this visit characterized. They read: 'Mr. McNamara into helicopter, Mr. McNamara out of helicopter, shakes hands, into building, out of building, into plane, plane leaves, plane lands. McNamara shakes hands, into helicopter, waves, leaves, flies, lands, into building, shakes hands, leaves.' Well, it wasn't really that bad, but little was announced."

The party left at night and flew toward the West and the secret report to the president was prepared en route. Arrival at Andrews at 7:30 a.m., October 14, balmy fall Friday in the capital. Again, the public shine for public consumption at the foot of the transport (nothing like the real facts): "Today I can tell you that military progress in the past twelve months has exceeded our expectations." And the secret document? Gloomy wouldn't catch its tone. "McNamara's report to the president on his October 1966 trip to Vietnam was a watershed," wrote Neil Sheehan in *A Bright Shining Lie.* William Conrad Gibbons has said that the recommendations from that trip were "sobering if not startling. . . ." The memo went eight pages, with a two-page appendix. The secretary said he saw "no reasonable way to bring the war to an end soon." He wrote of "the spectre of apparently endless escalation of U.S. deployments." He said he saw a strategy on the other side of "attriting our national will." He said, "In essence, we find ourselves . . . no better, and if anything, worse off." Among his recommendations: Put a cap on troop increases; put a cap on the bombing of the north; install an electronic barrier at the seventeenth parallel to stop infiltration; press toward a settlement, one provision of which might be a coalition government with the Vietcong in the south. In *In Retrospect,* McNamara quoted from this memo at length but didn't mention how he had sought to deceive the press.

Stanley Karnow, in *Vietnam: A History,* pointed out his deception—quoting what he had professed on the outside, and what he had told the president on the inside—and then said of the memo: "This was not a prescription for surrender but a scenario for restraint. Hold the line, buy time, minimize the costs and hazards of the war, McNamara was saying, and the American public will support a protracted struggle that promises neither defeat nor victory yet might, eventually, finish satisfactorily." Two pages later in that book Karnow told of a 1966 CIA summary that had to do with air strikes against North Vietnam: "Hundreds of bridges had been wrecked, but virtually all of them had been rebuilt or bypassed. Thousands of freight cars, trucks and other vehicles had been destroyed, but North Vietnamese traffic was moving smoothly. Roughly three quarters of the country's oil storage facilities had been eliminated, but there were no fuel shortages." Futility.

It translated into an even greater hubris in Robert McNamara, or so it would seem. It was as if old macho ways were revisiting now, redoubling. The following month, November 1966, he was at Harvard University when a bad scene erupted. Students for a Democratic Society rocked his car and shouted obscenities at the figure on the other side of the pane. I once got to ask him about this semifamous encounter. McNamara replied: "Well, I did get in trouble once. Not at the Pentagon. At Harvard. You probably know all about it. That one was pretty rough. The demonstration against me occurred when I went up there to speak to Henry Kissinger's classes."

As he tried to leave Quincy House about 3:30 p.m. on November 7, a large crowd composed of both students and nonstudents closed in and stopped the car. Only a fraction were SDS, which was still a not-well-known radical protest group in America. One account had him climbing onto the car, with the roof making a buckling sound, but I believe he was on the hood. By almost every account but his own—which can be found in his memoirs—he taunted the crowd. *They* began the disturbance, *he* enraged them, then they were out for his blood. That's what I think happened.

From United Press International: "When I was at the University of California at Berkeley, I was both more tough and courteous than you are."

From a transcript of CBS News footage: "I must say there was one difference between you and me. I think I was both tougher and more courteous. [APPLAUSE AND BOOS] I was tougher then and I'm tougher today, and I was more courteous then—"

"Are you courteous to the Vietnamese people?" a woman shouted above the din.

In *In Retrospect,* the author explained that he was hoping to "avert further violence by making clear that their threat would not intimidate me." Thus his words about "tougher than you." However, a Harvard poet-to-be and conscientious-objector-to-be named John Balaban, standing on the fringe, startled, experiencing shame for everybody present, saw and felt it differently. He later said of the moment in his own beautifully captured Vietnam memoir, *Remembering Heaven's Face:* "It was as if he had clobbered an enormous cow." Balaban meant the *I'm-tougher-than-you* taunt, which seemed to be flung right in their faces. Louder now the crowd yelled at him: "Fuck you!" and "Murderer."

Again, from a transcript of CBS footage: "McNAMARA: Now I want you to recognize two things (SHOUTS)—one, that we're in a mob, people can be hurt in a mob, and I don't want to be hurt and you don't want to be hurt, so behave yourselves. (SHOUTS) Why don't you come up here and answer the questions? You've got all the answers."

And yet . . . things here may not be what they seem to a camera's eye, to a reporter's notes, or to any witness's recollection (I've talked to four). What may have happened atop the buckling car, if it did buckle, is that extreme fear somehow functioned as a taunt. What came out might have been the opposite of what was intended. I can squint and feel my own fear for a hated man on a hood pinned in by the howling intelligentsia. A decade ago Michael Ansara, one of the leaders and SDS organizers, who was right up close, told me that what has always stuck for him was McNamara's trembling. He remembers how the pants legs shook. "He was simply exposed as a human being," Ansara said. Ansara said he was pretty scared, too.

The authorities, one of whom was Barney Frank of the sponsoring Kennedy Institute (in *In Retrospect,* McNamara described Frank as an undergraduate but it wasn't so), helped him get away through the campus steam tunnels. Frank would one day become a liberal congressman from Massachusetts, though then he was just a chagrined and very junior university official who would get much blame for this. A while later McNamara was seen browsing in a Harvard Square bookstore. That night he was the guest of honor at a private campus dinner. SDS wasn't there. A man who knew him well, who had worked for him at the Pentagon, said: "Secretary McNamara, why did you give that moving speech last May, the one in Montreal?" And he replied, "Oh, that. It was childish. I never should have done it. Here I'm the secretary of defense and I'm supposed to be the inspiration for our troops in the field. But I was so frustrated." According to McNamara's memoir, the idea for *The Pentagon Papers* emerged from this dinner.

The next day Harvard publicly apologized. McNamara replied no apology was necessary, that he understood.

Another sixteen months in office remained to a split man. A daughter who owned a snappy green Vespa motorbike had lately been graduated from a school in Pittsburgh. Another daughter had lately been wed in a big, fine Washington ceremony, and the president himself had stopped by the reception at the McNamara home on Tracy Place. And yet this also is true: By late 1966, Robert McNamara's wife and son, his only son, both had raging ulcers, and the son, a sensitive soul, like his mom, was having trouble reading and found he couldn't concentrate and so was having to repeat his tenth grade at St. Paul's School in New Hampshire. His name was Craig McNamara, and in a way he was just a surrogate for suffering. Which might be an epitaph for 1966.

IN THE SPRING OF 1995, twenty-nine years after she had gone to Vietnam, and twenty years after the fall of Saigon, Marlene Kramel spent a week in the Texas hill country with thirteen fellow nurses whom she had known in Qui Nhon. Becky and Mary Beth came from Florida; others made it to the reunion from as far away as Seattle and Los Angeles. Two were widows, two had gone through divorces, one had suffered the death of a grown child, at least one had been in counseling for depression. And yet overall they seemed a remarkably positive bunch. It was as if each was an extension of the person I had spent hours with on a Louisiana swing. These fourteen women, older, bulkier, took rolls of pictures. They sang "If I Had a Hammer." They sat up listening to old Barry Sadler tunes about green berets and nurses who had carried the load. And they cried.

They permitted me to stop by on their last day. I arrived into a chaos of curlers, half-packed suitcases, and coded jokes. Four evenings earlier, Robert McNamara had arrived in Texas—as part of a big cross-country signing-and-selling tour for his Vietnam apologia. He spoke to a select audience at the LBJ library in Austin (most were patrons of the library), and they had brought him in the back way so as to avoid the pickets out front. I hadn't gotten to Texas in time for the event, but on my way down to the nurses' reunion in the hill country I collected the write-ups in the Austin papers. One began, "Since the release of his book, *In Retrospect,* former Defense Secretary Robert McNamara has been verbally pilloried by Vietnam veterans (some likening him to Hitler). . . ." Another story quoted a Laverne Ransbottom, of Oklahoma City, who had lost a son in the war and had come to protest: "I would have to call him a coward of the worst kind. . . . To even imagine that he could let all those people die, the wounded and the maimed and those abandoned over there, without speaking up, there couldn't be a worse crime."

So now I was in a time-share condo on a lake with some Vietnam vets, only these vets didn't seem angry. What they seemed was dismissive. It was the emotion of mild contempt.

Said one: "It matters not." Said a second: "Let him write what he has to write." Said a third, grinning wickedly: "Little mercenary in his timing, don'tcha think?"

I said, glancing toward Marlene, who was on the sofa with her bad leg tucked beneath her: "The book can't dishonor what you did?" Marlene wasn't the one who answered.

"How could it dishonor?" said the one who did. "We made a difference in somebody's life. We did it honorably. Nothing takes that away."

Part Five:

WOUND LIKE A WHEEL, 1967–1968 IN AMERICA

If any question why we died
Tell them, because our fathers lied

           —*Rudyard Kipling*

Time has its revenges, but revenges seem so often
sour. Wouldn't we all do better not trying to under-
stand, accepting the fact that no human being will ever
understand another, not a wife a husband, a lover a
mistress, nor a parent a child? Perhaps that's why men
have invented God—a being capable of understanding.

        —*Graham Greene,* The Quiet American

ROBERT McNAMARA, IN A PENTAGON BRIEFING, ABOUT A
YEAR AND A HALF BEFORE HIS REMOVAL.

IN THE SHATTERING

H E   H A D   S U P P R E S S E D and contained the emotion of living
with lies for a long time—licking his lips, gripping the rostrum
tighter, covering his mouth, jumping across an opening word or phrase
like a record needle seeking the groove—but finally he couldn't contain
or suppress it at all and the grief and rage and humiliation began spilling
out with hydroelectric force.

Sometimes the lying had been monstrous, and sometimes it had
been trivial, but was it ever without conscience? No, you'd say. It was
always storing something up, was always being purchased at the larger
psychic price. The fact that he owned a significant conscience, which
he struggled against and was continually willing to compromise, only
deepened the lessons of the destruction.

Today marks the end—well, really tomorrow, since this is a leap
year February, and there's yet another good-bye ceremony scheduled for
noon at the Pentagon, with bands and Air Force flyovers and another
medal bestowed. But today Robert McNamara is getting the Medal of
Freedom from the president, with his wife and children and one hundred or so Washington potentates and power-lovers looking on. This
afternoon, February 28, 1968, in the East Room, is the spiritual end.

Yesterday, the twenty-seventh, in a working luncheon in a private
dining room at State, before some peers and mid-echelons and his successor (Clark Clifford), the emotion had spilled over the side again, the
rawness of it in that small perfect place shocking and upsetting everyone. The unleashed rage was so great you could have believed he was
going to rise and sweep the glasses and plates off the table, yank the
starched cloth off the table. On the way back to the White House two

hours later, it was all Harry McPherson and Joe Califano—they are key men in the president's sweatshop—could talk about: *Geezus, Joe, do you believe what you just saw? How long did it last?* But that display was in a closed setting, it wasn't filmed by network cameras. Today's fissure—not rage, but something so pure in its misery it will almost seem childlike—is going into film archives. You could label the can How Not to Live Your Life.

There's Rusk, taking his seat. Here comes Sarge Shriver, glad-handing. There's the chief justice. There's Max Taylor. There's Bobby and Teddy with their wives. There's Dean Acheson, Washington wise man. And isn't that Alice Roosevelt Longworth? These figures, these faces, are arranging themselves like daguerreotypes in a photo album. The room is clearing its throat, adjusting its brocade chair, murmuring low. The guest of honor and his family are up at the front, behind and to the left of the podium, framed by flags. Marg has a red dress on. Bob, arms clasped behind him like a soldier, has a four-in-hand knot in his striped tie. Already his temples wear a baker's glaze of perspiration. He looks as wan as someone getting over malaria.

Craig, his youngest, is down from school in New Hampshire. Studying this sensitive teenager with the helmet of hair, you would somehow know he's the kind of kid who can't get his father's attention. Once, at school, Craig had gone into a phone booth and dialed his father and nearly blurted, "Dad, can you provide me with some information? Some written documentation of what we, as the United States, are doing in Vietnam?" Dad had sent some literature and fliers. Craig—who's seeing a psychiatrist in Boston—has pretty much come to know the war is heinous, although he hasn't turned radical yet. The problem is, the boy so deeply loves his father.

Earlier today some White House apparatchik suggested on engraved stationery as how the president might want to read the citation of the Medal of Freedom rather than just present the award. More personal that way. A flunky had typed the script for the one o'clock ceremony: ". . . President enters and proceeds directly to podium. . . . President speaks. . . . Possible response by Secretary McNamara. . . . Receiving Line." Everybody knows these working scripts are made to be departed from. That may happen, given the sense of neurasthenia up front.

There has been a lot of talk around town in recent weeks, some of it published, as to how Lyndon Johnson has deftly slid his once most-trusted man Bob out of the Pentagon and into the presidency of the

World Bank as a way not only of removing him from the war but of silencing him on it. Almost certainly there are particles of truth in this, but dare any man or woman in the room who knows the relationship between these two say it's that easy? No, the seeming out-of-the-blue appointment of McNamara to the bank ninety days ago, like nearly all Johnsonian enterprises, has to be a textured thing of chicanery and manipulation and genuine caring and solicitude. Almost a father-son solicitude. Solicitude for someone who, in the president's view, has gone not just dovish on him but seems close to going mad on him. A bunch of times this past autumn, to different White House aides, the president has fretted aloud as to how his man Bob is liable to crack and kill himself if he doesn't get out from under the goddamn war. Could some of these frettings-aloud to underlings be understood as part of the chicanery and manipulation? You bet. At the same time the dismissal or removal or whatever you wish to call it has to be more complicated than the ruthless boss axing the unstable deputy. For one thing, the buying-silence angle tends to ignore how much Bob McNamara himself wants the bank job, has long been interested in development work in third-world countries. It's something like a perfect fit. You can say the all-but-broken secretary is going over to the bank to do penance for Vietnam, and that dog'll hunt. But there are a couple more dogs in the story.

Several years from now, himself in exile at the ranch, LBJ, in one of his King Lear soliloquies, will put the tentacled and layered McNamara leaving this way to his biographer Doris Kearns: "McNamara's problem was that he began to feel a division in his loyalties. He had always loved and admired the Kennedys; he was more their cup of tea, but he also admired and respected the presidency. Then, when he came to work for me, I believed he developed a deep affection for me as well, not so deep as the one he held for the Kennedys but deep enough. . . . Then the Kennedys began pushing him harder and harder. Every day Bobby would call up McNamara, telling him that the war was terrible and immoral and that he had to leave. Two months before he left he felt he was a murderer and didn't know how to extricate himself. I never felt like a murderer, that's the difference. Someone had to call Hitler and someone had to call Ho. We can't let the Kennedys be peacemakers and us warmakers simply because they came from the Charles River. After a while, the pressure got so great that Bob couldn't sleep at night. I was afraid he might have a nervous breakdown. I loved him and I didn't want to let him go, but he was just short of cracking and I felt it'd be a damn unfair thing to force him to stay. When he told me in November that the only job he really wanted then was the World Bank, I told him any job he wanted in the administration he could have."

Enough. The thing is starting. Fanfare, and not for the common man. The president is making warm remarks. "Mr. Secretary," he says, and it comes out, "Mr. Sekkaterry." He speaks of "your seven long years of unshakable loyalty to the republic, to the president." He talks of "the larger work you now undertake." He reads the citation. He turns to the honoree. "If I may be very personal, I am giving the world the very best that we have to win the most important war of all." The honoree's nostrils are flared, he's blinking. The room is on its feet.

A second ago his hands were clasped at mid-button of his suit jacket, but now he's raking them up and down in a wild way. The two men say something to each other the film camera can't catch. The president steps away. He's there at the podium alone.

"Mr. President—"

Coughing, turning around to look at LBJ, coughing, facing the audience again, hunching forward, starting over.

"I cannot find—"

Coughing, the voice with a crack in it, a fault on the spine of time. McNamara can't speak.

"—words to express what—"

More coughing, struggling to hold.

"—lies in my heart today—"

His jaw is quivering. He's crying. It started on the word "lies." And yet by "today," he's caught himself.

"—and I think I'd better respond on another occasion."

It's done. Almost before they can react, he is standing over by the president, his mouth sawing funny, as if grinding soundless words. From the evidence of what's on film, the president doesn't put his arm around the abject son, although years from now at least one person in the room will remember it this way. LBJ's body language seems to be saying: Buck up, boy.

If you came in right here, and knew nothing else, you would be astounded at what happens next—or maybe not. What happens is that the abject son starts grinning and shaking hands. He goes over to his wife, who somehow looks peeved, and turns her around, as though to head her to the receiving line. (Their eyes don't meet.) But he veers off.

He's reaching over to grab hands in the first row. He gets Earl Warren's hand. Has he just been made pope or vice president? He's like a pumped campaigner reaching down from the back of the train.

In the receiving line moments later, this same strange split, the high old time, laughing, hand-grabbing, no clue as to what just happened back there at the microphone.

At the microphone he had spoken a total of twenty-three words, and the four words in the middle had started him to bawl, though only for an instant. *Lies in my heart:* such a perfect unintended double play. You have to think God designed it. Call it song for the life, coda for the close.

IF THE YEAR 1965 is when the Vietnam War transformed itself into the huge Americanized conflict (with the architect of the policy becoming a secret apostate within months of the major escalations); if the interim year 1966 is when things widened in the crimson gyre; then 1967 and the first two months of 1968 are the point at which it all came apart and sat exposed—if not quite for America herself, not yet, certainly, for Robert McNamara. For America it didn't all unravel and seem to go mad until a little later in '68—on a motel balcony in Memphis and in a hotel pantry in Los Angeles and in a lakeside park in Chicago named for a Civil War general.

More than a decade ago, the makers of *Vietnam: A Television History* wrote with wonderful simplicity: "First a handful of advisers. Then the Marines. Finally an army of half a million. That was the Vietnam war. It was an undeclared war, a war without front lines or clear objectives." In a sense those five sentences are all that's required to understand how as a country we got from the just-spring of 1965, when an awesome man was pushing and jamming to go, to the late winter of 1968, when the same man, no longer awesome, was taking a small eternity to get out twenty-three words under the chandeliers. It was an eye-blink of time in America, barely three years, during which so much happened, so much went wrong. It was when we found our own second Civil War.

Essentially what happened in that time line of history, insofar as the principal architect is concerned, is that he lost faith in all he had made, lost it early, came to feel it wasn't possible to win militarily, and yet stayed on to prosecute the war. He tried to hold the lie inside him and found he couldn't and in that sense the story is biblical. The fact that he didn't resign and stalk off into his honor and maybe anonymity is the box Robert McNamara would never be able to get out of for the rest of his life. David Halberstam has spoken of "the crime of silence," and for Halberstam and others, myself included, there would be two prongs: First, that the man in charge of America's military forces didn't quit when he no longer held out honest military belief; and second, that he didn't speak out afterward, while the war was still being waged, though not by him, but when his voice and decision to tell the truth might have changed history and saved thousands from their graves or wounds.

But the "loyalist" didn't stalk off. The alleged "loyalist" didn't speak out after, while he was lodged at the World Bank and the war went on and the ghosts of 58,000 were finding their way to the eventual wailing wall on the national ellipse. *Qui tacet consentire* is one of the turning-point lines in Robert Bolt's play about Sir Thomas More, *A Man for All Seasons.* It's a drama about loyalties to the sovereign set against the obligations of conscience, when your own death sentence is possibly in the bargain. *Qui tacet consentire:* He who is silent gives consent.

A bookending set of numbers: At the point when the secretary of defense appears most likely to have lost military belief, in the late fall of '65, after the battle of the Ia Drang Valley (and about three and a half weeks after the burning at his doorstep of a Quaker from Baltimore), the official U.S. casualty figures stood at 1,335 dead and 6,131 wounded. That's a total of 7,466: awful, but pretty low. Almost two years later, in early October 1967, which was the approximate point when LBJ began setting out to remove McNamara from his job, the casualty figures had hit 100,278. Which is to say nearly 93,000 Americans were wounded or were reported missing or met their death or suffered another kind of misfortune of war in the period of veiled disbelief. I say veiled, not secret, because by the fall of '67 the apostasy of Robert McNamara was an open Washington secret—and not just at Hickory Hill in McLean (Bobby's place) or in the liberal dining salons of Georgetown, where once again a split man sought to accommodate, play to the night field. In those salons he was known to raise a glass and say, "Bless the doves— we need more of them."

And yet this also needs quickly and strongly to be said: You study the internal documents of 1967, once again that endless river of declassified paper, and what you find, no question, is that McNamara was doing a lot of hard pushing from the inside to cap the war and alter his fatal mistakes. In that sense he wasn't being silent at all. In that context he wasn't giving consent to the sovereign at all. In fact, what the year really reveals is how much McNamara did speak up—even as he would accommodate and circle back. Neil Sheehan, in *A Bright Shining Lie,* has termed some of this hard pushing from the inside—especially in regard to a now-famous McNamara/McNaughton memo of May 1967— as "an act of abundant moral courage." I agree. But the trouble is, what the record also shows is the inconsistency and paradox, the riddle and zigzag. The old McNamara story. The maddening one.

The deeper truth of 1967 may be this: He wasn't capable of getting himself out. So he saw to it that he was gotten out.

When everything is scraped away, there is the twin fact: He didn't leave when he no longer believed it could be won militarily. And he didn't speak out after, not for almost thirty years, when it was too late. Those facts form the box he can't get out of, the double prong in the biblical lesson that is his life. The lesson sits there, shining, intractable.

Was it his need to stay connected to power? Was it simple moral failure of nerve? Was it the tragic flaw of character interwoven with the terrible ambition? It seems hard now to say otherwise, no matter how he would explain, no matter how the word "simple" seems nonapplicable.

A year after McNamara was gone from the Pentagon, Nixon's war now, James Reston of the New York *Times* wrote: ". . . the art of resigning on principle from positions close to the top of the American government has almost disappeared. Nobody quits now, as Anthony Eden and Duff Cooper left Neville Chamberlain's cabinet, with a clear and detailed explanation of why they couldn't be identified with the policy any longer. . . . Most [of those who stayed on] at the critical period of escalation, gave to the president the loyalty they owed to the country."

"Do you know what I'd do?" Gloria Emerson, author of a great and savage Vietnam book called *Winners and Losers,* once said. "I'd chain all of [the politicians] to that haunting Vietnam memorial and have them read—slowly—every name aloud. Then the war would end for me. Take all of them, all of them who gave us the war—all of them who, like McNamara, began to doubt that the war could be won and still kept it going. Chain them to the memorial for several days, if need be, and have them read each name aloud. Wouldn't that be something? Justice at last."

More than a decade ago, a Washington player named Morton Halperin, who was in the Pentagon during the McNamara era, told me:

"The following statement is true: Not a single person who was working full-time on Vietnam held a press conference and said, 'I was working on Vietnam until yesterday, and I'm resigning in protest.' You have to judge McNamara in some sense by this standard."

Although it's a major plank in the edifice of rationalization, I think McNamara has always believed that, had he quit in 1967 or earlier, far worse things would have happened, larger fools than he would have taken over. And besides, didn't he make this mess? And yet . . . scrape it away: Whom was he serving, his conscience or his president? That would be his grief now, that would be his flight, although I believe the flight and grief are bound up with so much else too, not least the hard death by cancer of his beloved wife. Marg McNamara lived until 1981. But after 1967 her health was never really the same.

Something a study of the year 1967 will reveal, although it won't necessarily be revealed through the river of declassified paper, and it won't wish to be heard by the vengeful: the degree to which he suffered. He's so caught and trapped inside the lie. In midsummer he's just back from Vietnam and showing up unshaven and looking like the face of death at Marg's bedside at Johns Hopkins hospital in Baltimore. (She's gone in under another name for surgery on her bleeding stomach.) In early fall someone tries to torch his not-even-finished new house in Snowmass. (It gets six lines on a Saturday, page twenty of the *Times,* above an ad for Dr. Ervin Seale and the Church of the Truth.) By December SDS is gathered outside his home on Tracy Place with hats and horns. (Party time in America: He's leaving.)

The overriding image I have of Robert McNamara in his last year and two months in office is of a man with whirling disease—and probably no moment conveys it better than the moment in August 1967 when the sec/def, prepared to his eyeballs, went up to the Hill and brilliantly, wickedly, devastated himself on the air war and the bombing issue. That day becomes a paradigm for all the McNamara paradoxes. He wasn't trying to condemn the entire bombing program—his aim was opposite. But his withering sarcasm to those hawkish senators, not to say the arsenal of his numbers, made it almost impossible to think he wasn't ridiculing and abusing everything about the bombing—and by extension the war itself—and thereby creating unbridgeable gulfs between himself and the president. Even as he denied the fact. Even as he implied—and stated—he believed it could be won militarily. The left hand relentlessly chopped off the right that day. After that day it was just a matter of time.

But this was far from the best-known moment of 1967. The best-known was when a primeval sea snake came writhing and roiling toward him across Memorial Bridge. There were cameras and helicopters and TV cars and protesters by the thousands. Some of their names he knew: Norman Mailer, Jerry Rubin, David Dellinger, Benjamin Spock, and the poet Robert Lowell. But there were names he would never know—the young black man who had a placard that said "No Vietnamese ever called me a nigger." They had come to protest what Mailer called Uncle Sam's Whorehouse War. It was the March on the Pentagon. It was October 21, 1967, and from his command post on the roof, the secretary saw it all.

He described it to me once, in 1984. We were seated in his office. He hadn't yet cut me off, hadn't yet decided I was an enemy out to expose him. The "retired" man was just back from a place I didn't catch and his raincoat was turned inside out on the sofa, sitting alongside his single piece of soft luggage. Tomorrow he was going somewhere else—Chicago, I think. In the outer office, where I had waited for him to come through the door, were an Einstein Peace Prize plaque; a book about Steuben glass; four deep-red chairs around an immaculate glass coffee table; three pieces of art on the wall, one a tad crooked; two philodendrons and two standing plants; a book about Paul Klee, the Swiss abstract painter; and a secretary, Evelyn, with a faintly British accent and a bag of Lay's potato chips on her desk.

Now I was inside and he was remembering armies of Mailer's night. The primeval sea snake, writhing and roiling.

"It was terrifying," he said. And then, "You know, there wasn't one shot fired. I'm very proud of that to this day. Our troops didn't even have ammunition in their guns."

His voice was oddly soft. "How many of them were there?"

"About fifty thousand?" I said.

"Okay, fifty thousand. I thought it was forty thousand. But can you imagine? Christ, yes, I was scared. You had to be scared. A mob is an uncontrollable force. It's terrifying. Once it becomes a mob, all the leaders are useless. It was a mess. But there was no question I would be up there. You don't delegate something like that."

It was almost as if there were not a connection in his mind between the march and the war. "There's no natural means of defending the Pentagon, you know. There's an asphalt drive around the perimeter. We put troops shoulder to shoulder on the drive"—he was up out of the chair now, at attention, trying to mimic soldiers standing shoulder to shoulder with unloaded guns—"and at the very top of the stairs the TV crews had all their cameras. So the troops are right there and the girls in the mob are trying to make them flinch. They're rubbing their naked breasts in the soldiers' faces, they're spitting on them, they're taunting them. God, it was a mess. My impression is that the mob lost public support. All we had was that one thin line around the edge of the building. The Pentagon is hollow inside, as you recall. We'd brought in some troops by helicopter."

I said, "What if it had gotten out of control?"

"We had plans. I guess we would have used tear gas. We had plans."

There was still something far back and strange in his voice, like a phone going fuzzy. He came forward and slapped his fist. "They did it all wrong. I mean, the marchers. The way to have done it would to have been Gandhi-like. Had they retained their discipline, they could have achieved their ends. My God, if fifty thousand people had been disciplined and I had been the leader I absolutely guarantee you I could have shut down the whole goddamn place. You see, they didn't set up proper procedures for maximizing the force of the day."

He repeated it. "Gandhi-like."

I would like to tell in more chronological fashion what I know about Robert McNamara's last whirling year and two months. And I've decided that maybe the best way to illustrate a parable of How Not to Live Your Life is by pairing it with the converse. It's about a family he never knew. Their name is Tran. They were ripped and plundered and dispossessed in the aftermath of the second Indochina war, which is another way of saying the American war, the McNamara war. Theirs is the wound like a wheel. But somehow they retained their discipline, stayed Gandhi-like.

The Tran family are Vietnamese, only they are not in Vietnam anymore. They are spread to the winds.

THREE PICTURES, a triptych. The first:

A long time ago, in a war-divided city in a war-divided country, there were nine people who lived in a lovely and slightly decaying old walled villa close to the presidential palace. The address was No. 198 Hong Thap Tu, and the phone number and district were listed like this in English directories: "Saigon 3. Phone 25.866." The villa was across from Tao Dan Park, where despite the war little kids played with boats and lovers strolled head-to-head at twilight. The house, which sometimes felt almost more like a ship than a house, had big airy bedrooms with ceiling fans and louvered doors and a wonderful view of the park through the trees across the boulevard. There was a Chinese cook here who did French cuisine. There was a nanny here for each younger child. There were drivers here to take you off to school in the family Fiats and Peugeots and then collect you in the afternoon. There was a garden here with a fountain and sculpted mountains and thirty or forty varieties of roses imported from Europe: the yellow Grace Kelly Rose, the Brigitte Bardot Rose, the purple Cardinal Richelieu Rose, this last opening in blooming time bigger than your balled fist.

Important people had paid visits to this homestead in French Saigon—Mr. Graham Greene. Mr. Ngo Dinh Diem. Mr. Edward Lansdale of the Central Intelligence Agency.

The mother in the family was as elegant as a French cinema star. In English her name meant "happiness." Evenings, Tran Thi Phuc came down to dinner in a long flowered tunic and white silk trousers—the traditional Vietnamese *ao dai*. She was only in her forties but already had a heart condition, and there seemed an ineffable sadness about her. She had grown up an orphan and had never known anything about her own parents.

The father in the family was a lawyer and public servant and lifelong nationalist who, instead of being driven in the car, sometimes pedaled off on his bicycle to an appointment. He went to bed every night at 10:30 and got up at 5 to practice tai chi and kung fu. Afterward he would collect the papers (the city had innumerable rags) and sit down to coffee blacker than road tar with a crony who had come by to talk politics while the Saigon morning was still sweet and moist as something in a Somerset Maugham novel. This father, who was more like a patriarch, spoke half a dozen languages, including Mandarin. His licentiate in law was from Hanoi University. He had already held important positions in his country, though higher ones were yet to come. There were all sorts of interesting biographical facts about him. For instance, though he was essentially a public man, Tran Van Tuyen had written a novel as far back as 1944. (In English the title meant "Loneliness.") His memoir of the 1954 Geneva Conference was titled *Hoi Ky Hoi Nghi Geneve*. He served on innumerable boards—the encyclopedist group of Vietnam, the Free Workers Confederation, the national Boy Scouts. (In his youth, in the thirties, he had been a founder of the Boy Scout movement in Vietnam, which always had a kind of nationalistic fervor to it.) His roots, as were his spouse's, were in the north, but history and destiny had driven him and his family here to the lusher southland. For almost as long as he could remember, Tran Van Tuyen, anti-Communist, advocate of human rights, democratic socialist, had worked on one dream: to make Vietnam independent and unified and free of colonialist and other tyrannies. Despite how weighted he was with life, the patriarch managed to get home almost every midday for siesta time so that his children and wife could have him—if not for long, at least for something. In the culture of Vietnam, especially among the bourgeoisie, there exists between parents and offspring "the thin curtain." But in this family the children had grown up playing under Daddy's desk in his study. They always called him that—*Daddy*—even if he was a feudal overlord in the way he set tones.

There were five sons in the household, and the older boys went on scouting jamborees in the Dalat Mountains and took their exercise at the Cercle Sportif, where you could do fencing, lawn bowling, boxing, tennis on clay courts. Generally the sons thought of careers in the law, the family profession. There were two daughters in the household, and they played their Frankie Avalon and Paul Anka records, and studied at the best academies in the city and read Daphne du Maurier novels up in their room for pleasure—you know, *Frenchman's Creek* and *Rebecca,* whose opening line is, "Last night I dreamt I went to Manderley again." It's a British romance where the mansion known as Manderley is seen burning to the ground in the last paragraph, a blaze against the night sky.

This is the first mental picture, and does it sound too exotic, too Manderley-like? Because certainly war was everywhere around, had always been everywhere around, it was the history of this country, it was the history of this family. As a family they had already known separation and loss because of war. And yet at this moment they had their bondedness, their wall against what was outside. What was outside were armed sentries posted throughout the city. What was outside were sidewalk cafés with nets strung around them to ward off the grenades and pipe bombs.

I should clarify something. The family didn't own the house at No. 198 Hong Thap Tu. They were well-off, yes, they were galaxies removed from betel-nut-chewing peasants in thatched huts, but they weren't wealthy. For one thing the father's career as a public servant and pro bono lawyer had kept his income down. And for another, the father neither cared nor understood very much about money. The real wealth of the Trans lay in education and in the kind of moral values that seem to penetrate the lives of children almost by osmosis more than anything that is instructed.

The date of the picture must be somewhere around 1955 or 1956 or early 1957—which is to say at the bitter conclusion of the French experience and right at the innocent dawn of the American one. The date can't be 1959, because by then the mother in the family is dead.

But we need to get on to the second picture, and for this one it will be necessary to jump almost twenty years and more—not just to that April of 1975, when a skinny Southeast Asian country fell and the world sat transfixed but beyond that moment, into some of the chaotic and imprisoned years after. The second Indochina war is concluded. The Americans have come and gone. The Communists are the victors and rulers of Saigon, which isn't officially Saigon any longer but Ho Chi Minh City. The tanks flying the flag with the yellow star have crashed and crumpled the presidential gates. The helicopters crammed with the weeping and newly homeless—a fraction of all those begging to be saved—have long since escaped the roof of the U.S. Embassy.

Millions in this defoliated and cratered country—from the bourgeoisie in cities to the peasantry in the villages to the military in all its forms and contradictions—are dead. In the whole country, north and south, the figure may be something like 3 million dead. That garden with the fountain in the middle and Brigitte Bardot and Cardinal Richelieu roses has been paved over into a parking lot. That walled homestead with the big airy open rooms has been cut up and made into a soulless transportation agency. But this is real estate, what of the occupants?

The mother who had been as stylish as a French cinema star is long since dead of malaria and heart ailments. It was the first real incomprehensibility, especially for the younger ones. They came home that March afternoon and were taken to her room where Mommy looked asleep in a rose tunic with the weeping aunts bedside. She was forty-seven. Ten times in her life she had been pregnant. The common feeling is she'd worn herself out.

The father who had set the moral compass and never deviated is dead too. Tran Van Tuyen died in a forced-labor camp in the north eighteen months after the country fell—not that his family members knew of the death at the time it happened. They had to wait almost another year and a half, until 1978, to receive word, and then only through an intermediary in a foreign country. They don't know how he died (there was a report of a cerebral hemorrhage), or where he was buried, or if he was buried at all. In a culture that holds such traditional reverences for forebears and family tombs, the not-knowing only adds to the feeling of desecration. What is so wounding for the family is that he might have gotten out on one of those helicopters fleeing the roof of the American Embassy on April 30, 1975—there almost certainly would have been a place for a person of his stature. But he had declined. "I don't want to die like an old dog in a foreign country," he had said on the phone at the last minute to his oldest daughter, who was safe in America with her own husband and children and had pleaded with him to leave.

On the day Saigon fell, the old lawyer had been home reading a book. He knew they would come for him, and that June they did.

Tran Van Tuyen had remarried after the death of his first wife, and had been in love, and two more daughters had come into his family. But in a way it was as if the cord had been cut and every subsequent loss prefigured with the loss in 1959 of the woman whose name meant Happiness. That death had come even before Kennedy was elected president. That death was six years before the Americans had bullied their way in with the big land war. The patriarch always seemed to know that if the Americans came with a big land war it would only double the disaster.

But to go on. In the aftermath of Communist victory, the eldest son (he had grown up to work with his father at the Saigon bar) was carted out of town and made to dig ditches, work on roads. But Huyen developed internal bleeding. They let him go home, except where was home? How could this son have known then that one day he'd end up with his own nuclear unit in California, having moved from Orange County to Bakersfield to a renovated garage next to a freeway in Oakland? (In driving time, it would take about six minutes to get from that renovated garage to 1036 Annerly Road.)

Another son, Nhue, escaped with his fiancée at the bottom of the twenty-fourth hour—the Communists were rolling through the gates. Nhue would find his way to Massachusetts and computer work for IBM.

Another son—his name was Quoc and he had grown up to become a soldier in the ARVN—was sent to work in the rice paddies, and stepped on a buried spike left over from the war, and got gangrene, and nearly lost his foot, since no one in the new "government of national reconciliation" was willing to treat it.

Another son was imprisoned for the crime of having once played in a concert for the South Vietnamese army. His name was Mien and he was the baby of the family in the original clan of seven kids and two parents. When the country fell he was a law student and amateur musician. They shaved his head, tortured him, and soon he developed a heart condition. Baby Mien would escape to France, where he would find a wife and take up the law and spend his weekends playing piano on pleasure barges going up and down the Seine—a Tran so far from home, improbably saved.

A son-in-law was taken to a reeducation camp for thirty months, and that man's wife—which is to say Tran Van Tuyen's second daughter, Lananh—had to scrounge for food. She wasn't allowed to work because she was a member of a "reactionary" family. Eventually this daughter and her husband and kids would flee as boat people, ending up, though not immediately, in a split-level on Black Latch Lane in Cherry Hill, New Jersey. (On their swamping scow to freedom, they would be forced to throw everything but themselves into the South China Sea.)

And then there's the case of the fifth child and third son. He too had grown up and gone into the military and become a captain in the ARVN—working in both the national police force and in counterintelligence operations. He's the son to whom the patriarch and moral beacon had said, in that smoky Saigon June before being led away, "So many of my dreams have failed." This fifth child and third son was the one fated to bear the longest and most ingenious tortures of all the Trans—close to fifteen years of detentions and involuntary disappearances at the hands of his own countrymen.

His name is Thanh. You pronounce it "Tang." He's the final picture in the triptych. In Vietnamese culture the family name goes first and the given name goes last, so his is like this: Tran Tu Thanh. To hear Thanh's voice we must jump again, to the tense of modern times. We'll need to go to an apartment-cocoon of Vietnamese memory, on the Richmond Highway, in the Washington suburb of Alexandria, ten miles south of the building where a whirling war minister once ran a war, ran it badly.

It's four o'clock on a weekday afternoon. On my way to Thanh's today, as last week, and the week before that, and the week before that, I drove across Memorial Bridge, passed the Pentagon, gazed over at it, thought again about something I can't quite formulate, much less answer. About as far as I get are these four words: the price you pay. The price you pay, on the one hand, for lies and deceits and living out of harmony with yourself. And the price you pay, on the other, for decency and honor and being steadfast with your values. How is it that both ways can so perversely lead to the same end: immense suffering?

I'm in the living room, Thanh is in the kitchen preparing our food. Each time I come he serves something exotic (to me). Today's meal will feature a gelatinous rice-powder ball with burger meat inside. We'll flavor it with odoriferous fish sauce from a bottle. Each visit I ask him not to go to any trouble, and with his apologetic child's pained smile and elaborate courtesies, Thanh ignores my request. "It was our parents," he tells me. "They wish always to make a guest in their home happy."

It wouldn't be possible to narrate all that happened to this man in the jagged space between 1975 and 1990, but this would be some of it: They broke his eyelid, his jaw. They shackled him at the ankle and put him in a box about the size of a large man's coffin. They sat him in a chair in an interrogation room and came up behind and kick-boxed him in the neck. (He thinks there were seven interrogators in the room that time, plus the chief, and they were circling and demanding that he confess his treasons until the kick-boxer jumped high and got him in the neck—this is all he recalls.) One night they pulled his prison pajamas to his knees and attached electrodes to his genitals and then gave a hard crank to the handle of the radio box sitting on the floor. It was an old captured U.S. Army ground radio. Now would the son of Tran Van Tuyen admit to his crimes against the people? "I fell down from my chair, and excuse me, I piss my pants," he says.

He pinches his forefinger and holds it out. "I use my blood to write things on the wall of my cell. I sign it, 'A patriot.' "

On one wall of the living room is a framed picture of a gentle-looking man with a high forehead and rimless glasses: his long-dead father. Framed on the same wall is an artist's rendering of the two-sentence confession the patriarch made to his captors: "I have committed no crime against the Vietnamese fatherland or the Vietnamese people. If I have done anything wrong, it is only that I am anti-Communist, anti-colonialist, anti-dictatorial, and anti-injustice." In 1976 that confession was smuggled out of Vietnam, and got to the West and landed on the op-ed page of the New York *Times,* where a journalist called Tran Van Tuyen the "Solzhenitsyn of Vietnam's *Gulag Archipelago.*" The political prisoner was thought to be alive, though no one knew where. The following year Amnesty International named him one of its worldwide prisoners of conscience. But he was already dead.

The son of that dead patriot is down on all fours in an apartment in America, making hand stretches on parquet squares. He's describing the box. Last week, too, I got him to talk about the box.

"Eighty-five centimeters in width," he says, marking off several of the squares. "From here to here."

He turns the other way, a carpenter measuring. "Length, two meters, five."

"Did you have a pad to sleep on?"

"No, no," he says. The idea nearly breaks him up. "That's cement there."

"What's here?" I say, pointing to the air between us.

"A wall. It's a wall. I'm in a box."

"There was no light?"

"There's a small lamp in the ceiling. Less than ten volts. And a vent. It's like a grate where a little air comes in."

"No windows?"

"Nothing, nothing."

"How long?" (I already know the answer.)

"Four years, six months."

Four years and six months in the nearly lightless tomb.

"Exercise?"

"No, no." But that leads to this: "You know, I piss in a pot. And seven or eight days of waste in the pot before the guard comes. I'm pounding on the door for them to come and take it. The smell, you know."

"What is the door like?" I say.

"Steel door, with a small swinging window. When it is time to eat, they unlock the door, take off my shackle, he comes in, gives me the bowl of rice."

"Did you have toilet paper?"

He tugs his pants leg. "My pant. I use the whole pant."

"Where was this?"

"T-84, Phan Dang Luu prison," he says. "Ward C-1, cell number 25. I was in sixteen camps. They moved me around many times."

All of this is told too quietly, too apologetically, to be untrue or even embellished—that's what I think. And besides Thanh has documents—from the International League for Human Rights, for instance—attesting to things he and his family went through. Long ago Thanh's father founded the South Vietnam affiliate of the International League.

The fifth child and third son is a small man with raven hair lying in flat sheaths on either side of his face. It's an old-looking face able to light up like a child's hovering over a birthday cake. Thanh's French is flawless and his B.A. is from the University of Saigon, faculty of law— but I have seen him attacking food like an animal that's been too long caged. And I have seen him shrink, recoil, when I've stood too close.

The first time, the Communists held him in prison for eight years. Once, Thanh's wife rode a train 1,700 kilometers to the north in hopes of seeing him. She brought Thanh's five-year-old son, Bao-Long. He'd been born in February 1974, fourteen months before the country fell, and Thanh had been taken away in June 1975, two months after the fall, same month as the patriarch. During the three days of the train ride to the north, Bao-Long developed diarrhea. The child was left with friends in Hanoi while Thanh's wife went the remaining 200 kilometers to the prison camp in Vinh Phu province. She walked the last forty kilometers. At the camp she had ten minutes with the detainee, and in those ten minutes he had to be told that the five-year-old he barely knew was ill with diarrhea in Hanoi.

Thanh and his wife aren't married anymore. The war ripped that away too. But he has his son. They're in America together.

When I came to the apartment today, Tran Tu Bao-Long answered the door, just as he did last week. There the young man stood, nodding, as if in silent rebuke to the failed attempts to wipe his family's history from the face of the earth. In English Bao-Long means "Precious Dragon." "I will get my daddy," said the grandson of Tran Van Tuyen, and in a minute Bao-Long's father, with his apologetic child's smile and elaborate courtesies, emerged and went to the kitchen to ready our food.

In 1983 Thanh was let out of the camps for about a year. On the December night a year later when the cadres came for him again (they seized two of his brothers that same evening, at the same hour), Thanh said to the chief of secret police, "I just have one request: Please don't shackle me in front of my son." But Bao-Long, ten then, ran out and so didn't have to see.

Sometimes at night now, Thanh will wake up believing the electrodes are attached to his genitals and that the interrogator is about to give the handle of the old U.S. radio a hard crank. Then he'll recall where he is. Safe. So far from home. "I have a hole in my mind," he said the first day we met. "I always have a strong moral," he tells me today. He means spirit, character.

"Why did all this happen to your family?" I ask.

"Because we were patriots," he says.

"And why did you suffer the most?"

"Ah, but that was the destiny," he says, says it Gandhi-like.

WHIRLING AND TRYING and dissembling: Robert McNamara in 1967. On May 19, the secretary of defense gave the president a twenty-two-page, single-spaced document divided into four chapters and headlined "Future Actions in Vietnam." Essentially the paper said America couldn't win the war and should seek the nearest unsatisfactory peace. There were startling sentences like these: "The picture of the world's greatest superpower killing or seriously injuring 1,000 non-combatants a week, while trying to pound a tiny backward nation into submission on an issue whose merits are hotly disputed, is not a pretty one."

In an asterisk footnote on page 19 there was this: "We should not even rule out, as part of the strategy, changing key subordinates in the U.S. government to meet the charge that 'Washington is tired and Washington is stale.' "

The memo talked of "rot in the fabric" (it was in reference to corrupt government in Vietnam). The memo posed the specter of the doves getting out of hand—"massive refusals to serve, or to fight, or to cooperate, or worse?" Not least, the memo acknowledged that ". . . the enemy has us 'stalemated' and has the capability to tailor his actions to his supplies and manpower . . . the enemy can and almost certainly will maintain the military 'stalemate' by matching our added deployments as necessary."

To read it now is to see crispness, metaphor, doubt, seeming urge to be replaced, will to soldier on. In the fleeing years to follow, Robert McNamara would come to feel that this long and analytical paper in which he said to the president, "Look, it's no go," constitutes his Vietnam exoneration to history. (In *In Retrospect,* the author took five book pages to quote it, then carried the discussion over into the next chapter.) It's a document McNamara has given to many friends, some going back to the Berkeley years. It's a paper—as he once told me—that's "a hell of a reasoned piece of logic that adds up in retrospect to a great McNamara document." It wasn't fully declassified until 1984, during the Westmoreland/CBS libel trial, which is when I had a chance to speak to him about it. What I didn't know at the time was that he didn't write the memo; his closest aide on Vietnam, John McNaughton, drafted it for him. What McNamara did was add his own ideas, endorse it, sign his name three-quarters down on the final page, hand-carry it to the White House. But this somewhat appropriating fact in terms of authorship shouldn't diminish what guts were involved. To use Neil Sheehan's phrase again, the memo was an act of abundant moral courage. To use Tran Tu Thanh's phrase, it required a strong moral. If there are three anchoring points in terms of what removed McNamara from his job in his final year and two months, the May 19 memo is the first.

Two months later to the day, on July 19, 1967, the man who wrote it, McNaughton, died freakishly at age forty-five—and this only added to the McNamara whirlingness.

As Sheehan has noted, McNamara and McNaughton weren't stating "baldly that the war could not be won; that would have been too impolitic in the circumstances of the moment. McNamara and McNaughton let this conclusion become apparent from the actions they proposed and the peace they described." The paper had come about because the ever-voracious general in Vietnam was seeking an additional 200,000 troops. That would increase the total of U.S. forces to 670,000. McNamara and his assistant secretary for international security affairs saw that as calamitous. They told the president he could follow one of two courses: Course "A," giving Westmoreland what he wanted, which would mean calling up reserves and adding $10 billion to the defense budget. Or course "B," their course, granting the general "no more than 30,000," and in the bargain abandoning prior goals of defeating the Communists and establishing an independent South Vietnam. That was kaput. What should be sought was settlement. In the words of *The Pentagon Papers:* ". . . the [internal] Washington papermill must have broken all previous records," as word of the twenty-two-page McNamara/McNaughton DPM (for Draft Presidential Memorandum) got around.

As word was getting around internally, the New York *Times* reported there had been 2,929 casualties in one week, including 313 battle deaths. In one month, 1,177 Americans had died in Vietnam. The war was up to an estimated $24 billion a year.

A month later, the sec/def was in Vietnam again. "NOW THE NINTH COMING," headlined *Newsweek:* It was the last. Seventeen years later, during his testimony at the Westmoreland/CBS trial, McNamara wouldn't remember going. "I have no recollection of the trip, but I undoubtedly did [make it]," he would say.

Leaving Andrews on July 5, 1967 (9:30 p.m., EDT), he's asked by correspondent Bruce Morton of CBS:

QUESTION: Does it seem to you, sir, as some commentators here have said, that the war is turning into a kind of stalemate—that we don't seem to be getting anywhere?

SECRETARY McNAMARA: No, no, I think on the contrary.

A reporter for *Newsweek* asks the same, and this will appear in the magazine: "Emplaning for the front, McNamara was asked if he considered the war stalemated. He replied: 'Heavens, no!' "

Four days into the trip a Reuters correspondent files this lead under a Saigon dateline: "Defense Secretary Robert S. McNamara today claimed that more progress has been made in the Vietnam war in the last nine months than in the previous six years."

There are the usual marathon briefings and on-site inspections. Heading home on July 11, he speaks of "the substantial, and measurable, and evident progress in the large unit military actions." Next morning, back where he started, tarmac at Andrews: ". . . a very clear indication of the success of General Westmoreland's large unit actions." Then to the White House for an oral report to the president, where the secret-meeting notes quote him saying, "No, there is not a military stalemate. . . . For the first time Secretary McNamara said he felt that if we follow the same program we will win the war and end the fighting." (In his own memoirs, *The Vantage Point,* LBJ will write: "I asked McNamara about reports that the military situation was really a 'stalemate,' as some observers claimed. 'There is not a military stalemate,' he answered. He said that 'for the first time' since we committed troops to combat in 1965, he was convinced we could achieve our goals and end the fighting if we followed the course we had set.")

At 4 p.m. on the day he's back, there's a White House press conference, and the star speaker says:

All of the military commanders stated that the reports that they read in the press of military stalemate were—to use their words—the "most ridiculous statements that they had ever heard."

One of the press boys jumps on that.

QUESTION: Mr. Secretary, you said that the military commanders were unanimous in saying there is no stalemate there, but you didn't tell us how *you* felt about that.

SECRETARY McNAMARA: I had read so many reports on this subject I discussed the point with them at some considerable length. I was quite persuaded of their view and the correctness of their appraisal.

Seven days later, in a cabinet meeting on July 19, he repeats, ". . . there is no evidence of a stalemate."

So, has he crossed back? Is he flat-out lying to the president? Many years later, in *In Retrospect,* the author explained: "The optimistic briefings I had received in Saigon had momentarily eased my long-standing doubts. . . ." (But what about what he'd told correspondent Bruce Morton and *Newsweek*'s correspondent on the tarmac at Andrews *before* going?)

Sometimes it takes a while for a transcript of your forgotten words to come back and bite you on the buttock. On the stand in the Westmoreland/CBS libel trial, McNamara kept listing to his left, like a ship taking on water. I was there and watched the listing. The attorney for CBS argued to the judge that his cross-examination about the witness's deceptions were relevant to the basic issue of "how the Vietnam war was managed . . . and the extent to which people in Mr. McNamara's position either were misleading the public themselves or were duped." The judge said it could go on.

At one point McNamara tried telling the court he didn't express his judgment in terms of "stalemate," certainly not publicly. Didn't cast his belief like that. Besides, his real belief was not that the war was at a stalemate by 1967; he just thought it couldn't be won. Someone in the back snickered, and maybe he heard it, because right then he seemed to let up a little on something: "These are rather hairline distinctions and I'm not trying to evade the question. . . ." Shortly, the cross-examiner was handing him another document to make him go dry in the mouth, that ancient *Newsweek* article, Exhibit No. 1432, in which he had said "Heavens, no!" in regard to the loathed word "stalemate." What followed between witness and cross-examiner and even the judge was almost comical.

But this wriggling and denying wasn't until 1984. In July 1967, another kind of truth had caught up fast: Margy McNamara's bleeding stomach. The pain had been dizzying her for months, even as she tried to hide it and go onward with her family obligations and goodwill community work. All one need do to get a sense of this good woman at the start of her vicious decline is to study her 1967 photographs—or look at some of her correspondence. In the Bancroft Library at the University of California, there are a handful of archived Marg McNamara letters to old West Coast friends. Some are written on curlicued inexpensive stationery with the address *2412 Tracy Place NW 20008* at the top. As the Washington years pile up, as 1967 comes on, the handwriting is rushed, punctuation sporadic, the script often going downhill.

Marg entered Johns Hopkins Hospital for stomach surgery just as her husband was leaving on his last trip to the war. It was the same city where twenty-two years earlier she had been immobilized in the children's polio ward. Henry Trewhitt, in his early McNamara biography, describes how McNamara, once he got back, his pallor like chalk under the day's shag of beard, would come racing into Johns Hopkins at strange hours to get a few minutes with the woman who had taken on so many of his turmoils.

It was in that Baltimore hospital room—or so reports Deborah Shapley in her McNamara biography—that the secretary picked up the phone to be told by a military aide that John McNaughton, McNaughton's wife, Sally, and McNaughton's younger son, Theodore, had just been killed on a Piedmont Airlines jet leaving Asheville, North Carolina. A two-engine private plane collided with the airliner shortly before noon on July 19. The smaller plane fused itself into the nose section of the 727, and the fireballs went earthward as one into a trash dump. All seventy-nine on the jet were killed. The McNaughtons had been in North Carolina to pick up their eleven-year-old from Camp Sequoyah. Three, in a family of four, suddenly dead.

I have spent a good deal of time studying the life of John McNaughton. I felt that I could help decode McNamara through someone I had come to think of as "the little McNamara." Nothing has changed my belief that this key policymaker hasn't been brought to light enough. He needs his own biography. Like McNamara, McNaughton was the true believer who grindingly lost his faith. There seem so many correspondencies: the overengineered brain; the quest for precision; the outsider addicted to Eastern power; the gift for hubris. When he arrived in Washington in 1961, McNaughton was a six-foot-four ex–Harvard law professor with the terse, truncated writing style of a newspaperman. His family owned a chain of papers in the Midwest, which is where he'd grown up and once spent a stint as a managing editor on the flagship paper. He had been to Oxford as a Rhodes. He played tennis at the club-championship level. In Cambridge, he and his family had lived on Berkeley Street next

door to the Mac Bundys; close by were the Kingman Brewsters. He loved
Rambler station wagons: practical. He loved a course called Evidence,
especially the Lindbergh case: a purely circumstantial thing. What do
we know? What can be proven? Every Christmas morning, all the
McNaughtons were required to wait at the top of the stairs so Dad could
record the moment with a camera on a tripod. Even as a child, he had a
legal mind mad for documentation. But overall there was something boyish, gangly, and likable.

Once, after he had become a player in the parable of power,
McNaughton took his older son, Alex, to the White House. The Oval
Office was empty. "I want you to sit in the president's rocking chair," he
said. "But, Dad, I don't want to," said the boy. "I WANT YOU TO SIT
IN THE PRESIDENT'S ROCKING CHAIR."

In 1967 Morton Halperin served as a McNaughton lieutenant in
international security affairs. When I asked him to recall McNaughton,
he said, no matter his obvious affection: "Do you know about the lights?
I think that says a lot. The lights were green, orange, red, and white.
Green meant: You can walk in, I'm available. Orange meant: I'm in the
middle of something, but if you must come in, if it's that urgent, do so.
Red: positively cannot come in, unless I have summoned you. White:
He was in his men's room and didn't want you in, even if you were his
deputy, because you might look at his desk."

The McNaughton disillusionment on the war was primarily intellectual, Halperin said, and maybe it came down to this: Westmoreland
was telling the president that the "crossover" point had been reached,
that the American forces were "attritting" more than the enemy was
producing. But if you analyzed it, you understood that *they* controlled
the body count. The American and ARVN forces were chasing *them*
around the jungle. So if the war was going badly, if they were losing too
many, all they had to do was back off, engage in fewer firefights, hide
and run for a while. They could keep up the war forever.

Once, in a moment in which he seemed both scared and cynical,
McNaughton came into Halperin's office, said the crossover thing was
crap, the war a mistake. He left, came back in, mouthed in a big whisper: *Remember, not a word.*

Just before the May 19 memo, McNaughton wrote to McNamara, in
what has come to be a celebrated line among war scholars, that "a feeling is widely and strongly held" around the country that " 'the Establishment' is out of its mind." By 1967 McNaughton was spending

something like 70 percent of his time on Vietnam. He had wanted a change, and had been appointed secretary of the Navy, and was just about to assume the job.

Another McNaughton lieutenant, Townsend Hoopes, author of a perceptive book on Vietnam called *The Limits of Intervention,* told me that on the day McNaughton died, he (Hoopes) had been so distraught he found himself running up to McNamara, who was entering his (McNamara's) office on the E Ring. "Isn't this terrible?" he said. "Yes, it is," McNamara said, and went in and closed the door. And Jack Maddux, McNamara's word ghost, told me he could remember McNamara coming up a Pentagon staircase on the afternoon McNaughton died. It was his regular day to play squash. He was laughing. Split man. Semifatalistic man.

I asked Halperin why McNamara and McNaughton clicked. He said it was because they were blunt men of action. He added, "And both had the ability to do, finally, what you don't believe."

"You know, he changed a lot, I saw that in Dad, he lost, I think, a lot of his humanity in Washington," Alex McNaughton said quietly when I visited him a decade ago in New York. On the day the plane went into the trash dump, the surviving son was eighteen and traveling in Europe and about to enter Cornell.

The funeral was held the following Tuesday. McNamara was a grieving pallbearer. At the last minute LBJ came to the service at the National Cathedral.

Between the death of the closest Vietnam aide on July 19 and the burial in Arlington on the twenty-fifth, America burned: Detroit, East Harlem, the South Bronx. Newark had just convulsed. In Detroit three days of rioting had left thirty-one dead (with twelve more deaths to come), as tank crews blasted away at snipers with .50-caliber machine guns. "The sick society," in the words of Senator William Fulbright. "Each war feeds on the other. . . ." Several months earlier, an American prophet named Martin Luther King, Jr., had stood up and said: "I can hear God saying to America, you are too arrogant. . . . What strange liberators we are." America hadn't even come to its summer of smoke, when twenty-three cities were lit, but the prophet understood the moral bankruptcies of a country wishing to think itself great while slaying faceless enemies in a distant undeclared war.

IN *THE QUIET AMERICAN,* Graham Greene wrote of two Vietnamese couples moving on a Saigon dance floor: "small, neat, aloof, with an air of civilization we couldn't match. . . . If the war seemed medieval, they were like the eighteenth-century future."

So many people are quiet in this world, and seem to live in it tentatively, as if it is not quite theirs, and perhaps this is the central truth about a family who once had their bondedness in a walled Saigon villa, and who afterward, despite ravishment, stayed Gandhi-like. But there was a Tran history before that villa, long before America intervened in Vietnam, and it too reads like Daphne du Maurier fiction: romantic, star-crossed, a plot with uncounted twists. The history of this family is the story of Vietnam.

What I didn't tell up above was that the patriarch, as a young man and young father, had been a schoolmaster at a famous private academy in the north called Thang Long. On that Hanoi faculty were comrades carrying the dream of overthrowing French colonial rule. Professor Tran Van Tuyen taught math. (It was only a high school but the teachers were referred to as "Professor.") He was very poor then and rode his bicycle everywhere and lived in two rooms behind a building that served as the headquarters for the Boy Scouts. He was passionate, yes, but he didn't give the sense of a possessed man. He read political tracts and kept illustrated magazines from the Soviet Union in his room.

His best friend on the faculty, a possessed man without doubt, was a small moon-faced figure who taught French history and whose lectures on Napoleon were legend in Hanoi school circles. His name was Vo Nguyen Giap, and in his library was Marx's *Das Kapital* in French, and one day the world would know him not as Professor but as General Giap.

These two, Tuyen and Giap, brothers against the French, shared their modest meals and worked their long revolutionary nights under weak wattage writing penny underground newspapers and anticolonialist pamphlets. When the papers and pamphlets were printed, the wife whose name in English meant Happiness passed them out secretly in the squares. This was probably 1937 or 1938. (In North America, a native westerner with hair that goes straight back has made his way east to the Boston side of the Charles River, where he is learning a revolution called control accounting.) It was at the point in Vietnamese affairs when a shadowy figure named Ho Chi Minh, founder of the Indochinese Communist Party, was still somewhere abroad, having not yet come home from decades of exile to take charge of his revolution.

In the early forties Giap came nearly every evening to collect his friend Tuyen. The Trans were living then in a small dwelling near two city lakes. Tuyen and Giap would walk the promenade between the peaceful Hanoi waters. The larger and more beautiful lake, Truc Bach, means "White Bamboo" in English. The revolutionaries would stroll while the spouses and children stayed behind. To the Tran children the moon-faced man was *Bac* Giap: Uncle Giap.

In 1943 Tuyen was jailed by the colonial Sûreté (French secret police) for subversive activities. Among other things, the activities included commanding an entire province in armed resistance. In 1945 Tran Van Tuyen became second-ranking member of the foreign ministry in Ho Chi Minh's first Nationalist and Communist coalition government. But revolutionaries have a way of turning on each other. Tuyen was forced to flee Ho's shaky coalition as the Communists started assassinating their non-Communist brothers or giving their names over to the French.

The two brothers on opposite sides of an ideology, Tuyen and Giap, met for the last time in May 1946 at a conference with the French at Dalat, which is a mountainside resort 300 kilometers northeast of Saigon. They went to dinner and Giap worked hard on Tuyen to join the Vietminh. "Return, your place is with the people," he said. But Tuyen declined. They shook hands and Giap said: "Well, we'll remain friends even so."

In 1948 the patriarch joined the cabinet of Bao Dai, the pathetic last emperor of Vietnam. It was a puppet government of the French, presided over by a playboy king who, it's true, wished independence for his people but had neither the character nor the wit to achieve it. The head of the Tran family wasn't long a member of the puppet government. He was too independent, too proud. The French tried to deport him to Madagascar, but he escaped into the mountains of Tay Ninh Province, where he became a colonel in the private army of the Cao Dai Buddhists, fighting Communist forces as well as French. What he and Giap understood instinctively in Dalat had already come true: They were making war on each other.

The nationalist, far more bookish than martial in spirit, practiced law, held other government posts, moved his family south, advanced his income, kept on writing. There are sepia-tinted family photographs in which you see Tuyen and his wife sitting happily at sidewalk cafés in Paris. There are photographs in which you see a thin, handsome, and spectacled man in a cream-colored tropical suit deplaning from a DC-3 at a weedy Vietnamese airfield with other leaders of state. These pictures are at once romantic and sad, and the sad part is in how earnest he looks and how doomed the dream was.

I wish to tell of one more photograph; it's in a gold frame on a shelf in an apartment-cocoon of displaced memory on the Richmond High-way in the Washington suburb of Alexandria. It's one of the few family mementos the Communists didn't get. It's 1952 and the Trans are in the walled villa. A woman is standing in a sun-shadowed yard with three little boys; late afternoon in Saigon. The boys are in anklets and white jackets and short pants. The woman wears a flowered tunic that stops at her shin, and below that are white slacks and a sheer white gauzy material, like a thin curtain. She is beautiful.

The three boys are Nhue, Quoc, Mien. The eldest son, Huyen, isn't in the picture (maybe he's at school), nor is Thanh, because he's being held captive by the Vietminh somewhere in the north. Yes. One more du Maurier twist. The fifth child and third son was stolen from his fam-ily when he was five. It's a convoluted story but the essence of it is that one day, while the family was still in the north, Thanh had gone with his nanny to visit some of her relatives in a village some miles from Hanoi. The Vietminh kidnapped him. It was just a way of harassing the father, who had declined to be a Communist.

And now it's 1952 and Thanh is seven and still missing, and Thanh's mother, standing with three sons in her sun-shadowed yard, bears such a look of ineffable sadness.

I'm holding this picture in my hand, trying to stare past time. A man shortly to turn fifty comes over.

"For two years she had no word of you?" I say. He nods. "Did they mistreat you?" He says, "No, no. I was under house arrest. I had my own tutor. I would go to the fields with one of my guards. I remember he had a huge rifle. A musket."

"Did your mother try to raise ransom money?"

"Oh, there were suitcases. Oh, she removed the whole earth."

When the child got back to his family (probably late 1952), he found he couldn't go to sleep nights unless he lay between his mother and father. For a year he didn't budge from their bed. But for the next few years the Trans had their unity. "And then more of the destiny came," Thanh explains.

HIS   INCENDIARY   BOMBING   TESTIMONY: the   second anchor point. On Friday, August 25, 1967—one month after John

McNaughton's burial, and thirty-six years to the day a knickered Bay Area boy became an Eagle Scout—the secretary of defense went up to Congress and sliced off his effectiveness with Lyndon Johnson at the kneecaps. Not that he intended to. But it was the net result when he was finished testifying before eight Senate hawks of the Stennis committee. The emotional Celt, living the self-lie of coolly rational man, did himself in with suicidal beauty. And it was as if he never saw or knew. But you know what? There was uncommon bravery in it, for all the absurd contradictions and attendant lies.

Part of the reason it happened, I'm convinced, is because a parade of generals and admirals preceded him. It was a stacked deck by the time gone-dovish Robert McNamara got into the witness chair, and he knew it, and so the ever-competitive man, with his overpowering need to win, proceeded to cut off his nose to spite his face. It was as if he went out of his way to heap ridicule and abuse on fifty-seven fixed targets that the Joint Chiefs thought worthy of being blasted to hell and back. By the end of the day his denigration of these fifty-seven targets was about all anybody could remember. It was as if the disputed fifty-seven—which in truth didn't amount to a bootful of piss, to use the LBJ vernacular—had come to stand for a war policy itself, a policy that was futile. Robert McNamara, alleged loyalist.

The loyalist reported to the Stennis committee (formally the Preparedness Investigating Subcommittee of the Senate Armed Services Committee) that the so-called steel factories of the north weren't steel factories at all but rather hapless little operations producing on the order of 5,000 tons of pig iron a month. In his words, "I would have lost that in the back room of what I considered a relatively small pig iron production capacity in River Rouge."

He reported that there were two battery plants on the Chiefs' recommended target list, and how these battery plants put out 600 tons of wet cells per year. "A service station would supply that" was his dismissal, which may or may not have been accurate. Have to be a pretty big station.

A machine shop with 96,000 square feet? ("We wouldn't even call it a machine shop in this country.") A motor pool of 39,000 square feet? ("You probably have on your farms barns bigger than that.") A vehicle repair shop of 48,000 square feet? ("Any garage on any one of the side streets of Alexandria [Virginia] has more than that.") A warehouse of 94,000 square feet? ("It wouldn't fill in the corner of a Sears, Roebuck district warehouse.")

He went on in his numerical vein. To read the transcript is to hear him slapping down aces, one card at a time. Here, boys, have another. Go ahead, try to contradict me on this goddamn math. A rubber factory that puts out thirty tires a day—somebody thinks that's a meaningful target? "I submit to you," he said, "I am secretary of defense and I am responsible for lives and I am not about to recommend the loss of American lives in relation to those targets. . . . I am perfectly prepared to admit that I may be very wrong in my recommendations on these targets, but I am not wrong in submitting to you that the approval of all these targets and the destruction of all of them would not make any material difference in the war, and that is my only point."

But it wasn't. Because in other parts of his six-hour, daylong testimony (the censored version ran to a hundred pages), you find him protesting to the same audience, "I don't believe that there is this gulf between the military leaders and the civilian leaders in the executive branch." You find him saying, "I think it will be a successful war, if we maintain our pressure and our patience." You find him saying, "It is a fantastic air effort and it is a fantastically successful one as any of the ground commanders in South Vietnam will tell you." You find him saying, with no apparent room for equivocation, ". . . I submit it is *not* a no-win program" (emphasis added). I'll come back to this statement in a minute.

After the morning session he came out and said beneath the bright lights, "My policies don't differ from those of the joint chiefs, and I think they would be the first to say it." Senator Stuart Symington of Missouri, who wanted all the bombing and air war he could get, had come out ahead of him to tell the press: "If the position as presented by the secretary this morning is right, I believe the United States should get out of Vietnam at the earliest possible time, and on the best possible basis; because with his premises, there would appear to be no chance for any true 'success' in this long war." *Gee, whatever does the senator mean?* seemed to be the witness's response, like a man with palms turned upward. Then he went back inside and denigrated some more. Even as he kept insisting there was no gulf. It was as if he didn't want his cake both ways, but 132 ways.

To say the occupant of the White House was displeased with this performance is a little like saying Mickey Mantle saw something white and hit it with a stick. LBJ said later it was like a man trying to sell his house, and one of the sons—or maybe sons of bitches—is going to the buyer to say that there are bad leaks in the basement. His man Bob had just strung out the dirty laundry for all to see. The administration wore no clothes. Was it after this Johnson got off the line, "I forgot he had been president of Ford for only a week"? I've heard it a lot but have never been able to pin down exactly when he said it.

The perversity is: In every essential respect McNamara was correct. The perversity is: He hadn't intended to be disloyal or to denigrate the entire bombing program (even though he loathed and despised the bombing), much less the entire war policy. What he had set out to achieve was something much different and far trickier and not lacking in either moral truth or courage. He had brought with him a tightly constructed and carefully balanced eight-page opening statement, worked on for weeks (it was published, in full, the following day in the *Times*), and his central point, repeated many times and bulwarked with all his figures, was this: The bombing was accomplishing its limited objectives and putting a "high price tag on North Vietnam's continued aggression." And yet no amount of bombing could actually *stop* the infiltration of men and matériel to the south—"short, that is, of the virtual annihilation of North Vietnam and its people." It was irrational to think Hanoi could be bombed to the negotiating table. The air war was never intended as a substitute for the land war in the south. It was a supplement.

But it was as if nobody could hear this message. All anybody could hear, could seem to remember after, was the savagery with which he had deconstructed fifty-seven targets on the Chiefs' list. The fifty-seven amounted to a fraction of the total operating list. Something like 1,900 fixed targets had been struck in the north, as well as uncounted targets of opportunity. McNamara told the senators that of the current operating list of 359 fixed targets, 302 had been approved by himself and the president—thus only fifty-seven in dispute. But fifty-seven that, when the day was done, became a synecdoche for the war itself. When the day was said and done, the secretary himself was pretty much said and done. As Townsend Hoopes wrote in *The Limits of Intervention:* "The moderates suddenly possessed not merely a rumored, but a proclaimed, champion within the citadel; the hawks were more certain than ever of their adversary's identity." Vietnam scholar William Conrad Gibbons once told me that August 25 amounts not only to a watershed moment for McNamara but for LBJ, too: He had to know in some sense his presidency was over.

McNamara and the concept of loyalty—such a schizoid thing. Several graduates of Chatham College, class of 1966, have told me that Kathy McNamara used to talk in bull sessions about how her family hated Lyndon Johnson—and one Chatham woman, who knew her very well, remembered Kathy's saying that all the McNamaras thought the White House smelled like "dung" once LBJ took over. (As noted earlier, McNamara's daughter didn't answer two letters I sent, asking to interview her about Chatham and its milieu.)

But ridicule can slice both ways. Gibbons cites an interview in which an unnamed source recalled Johnson's humiliation of McNamara. It was in the summer of 1965 and the secretary, in a moral moment, wanted additional taxes to pay for the secret war. He put the request in a memo, was rebuffed by the president, struck the idea from the final draft of his July 21 report. The secretary had taken the position that unless there was a good-size tax increase, the country would suffer a budgetary deficit, and that would stimulate huge inflation. (Exactly what happened.) This was the president's reply to McNamara, as the source recalled:

> You know so goddamned much about it, you go up there and you get it and you come back down here and give me the names of the people who will vote for it. Obviously, you don't know anything about politics. I'll tell you what's going to happen. We'll put it forward; they are going to turn it down. But in the course of the debate they'll say, "You see, we've been telling you so. You can't have guns and butter, and we're going to have guns."

(In *In Retrospect,* McNamara essentially verified the story. His version has Johnson telling him, "You get your ass up to the Hill and don't come back till you have the vote count.")

Loyalty. On January 7, 1961, when Lyndon Johnson was merely the vice president–designate of the country, a *Times* reporter wrote: "The incoming secretary . . . conveyed the warning that he would not tolerate opposition to decisions. He indicated that he expected his aides to disagree with him, but that once a decision had been rendered he would expect compliance." Three weeks later, at his first Pentagon press conference, McNamara said: "I expect full and open discussion . . . that once a decision has been reached and a policy established representing the decision of the president, or other appropriate authorities, that all members of the department, civilian and military, will be expected to support that decision, publicly and otherwise." Two weeks later, appearing on the *Today* show, he said: "After the president has taken a position, has established a policy . . . I expect that no member of the department, either civilian or military, will discuss that policy other than in a way to support it before the public." Host Martin Agronsky: "Well, if he does, what do you do? Ask him to hand in his suit?" McNamara: "I think that would be appropriate."

From transcripts of a White House meeting on December 18, 1965 (he's fighting hard for the bombing pause): "[Ambassador to Vietnam Henry Cabot] Lodge is a great admirer of the president. He will act like a soldier."

You go back through the record and the word loyalty tolls in him like a bell. It's like that other word, that Harvard business school word, control. In May 1968, three months after he was gone, *Life* published a long piece on McNamara by writer Brock Brower. McNamara himself once sent the article to me, and I was curious why. Brower did his interviews just before McNamara left the Pentagon. He quotes him as saying: "Around Washington, there is this concept of 'the higher loyalty.' I think it's a heretical concept, this idea that there's a duty to serve the nation above the duty to serve the president, and that you're justified in doing so. It will destroy democracy if it's followed. You have to subordinate a part of yourself, a part of your views."

The problem with McNamara and "corporate loyalty"—a term I've heard used by McNamara defenders—is that it won't account for the Montreal speech. And it won't explain 1967 nights at Hickory Hill where he's reputedly telling Bobby and Ethel and other assembled doves that the whole thing's rotten and cruel. And not least will the loyalty argument explain August 25. "Well, it wasn't his only emotion," an early Kennedy insider named Michael Forrestal once said to me.

I remember the time Willard Goodwin—who has known him for six decades and goes back to the Berkeley years—said, as if it gave him not the slightest pause: "Bob's a company man, you see. He did exactly what the boss told him." He meant Henry, as in Ford. And Jack, as in Kennedy; and Lyndon, as in Johnson. Goodwin and I had talked for more than three hours, and loyalty and Vietnam had finally come up. I said, "Yes, but what about the Montreal speech?" And Goodwin said, stumbling, "Well, that's exactly what I mean." Then he brought up the heroic McNamara/McNaughton memo of May 19. What I think he was trying to tell me was that his fellow Eagle was the company man until he just couldn't abide it.

Then why didn't the Eagle resign? But what player did resign, with a bang instead of a whimper, which is Morton Halperin's point? In a 1975 book called *Resignation in Protest,* Edward Weisband and Thomas M. Franck wrote: "It is a disturbing but inevitable conclusion of the statistics and the case studies that, in America, it is both dangerous and costly for those best placed—the insiders—to speak out. One almost has to be a bit mad to resign in protest. Nice, sensible insiders keep quiet. . . . By the 1960s, discretion, not valor, had become both the measure and the rule of those who seek to serve the public weal."

In a sense, there's no place for resignation in the American system. In the British system you can resign in protest and then go to the parliamentary backbench and raise embarrassing questions. In this country you leave with noise, and then you're out, and the next day nobody remembers—or that's what you might tell yourself as you think about the unthinkable.

McNamara told Deborah Shapley that he never spoke directly against Johnson in his now well-known visits to Bobby's house. She quoted him as saying, "I recognized Johnson probably knew about it and wondered whether I was in effect being disloyal to Johnson. I wasn't being disloyal to Johnson, but it was clear to me that Johnson might think so. But that didn't stop me." Defiant son. In his own book McNamara wrote: "I was scrupulously careful not to betray the president's confidences or mention anything Bobby could use politically against the president."

It has never been fully elucidated how much the president knew in advance about what McNamara would say in his August 25 bombing testimony. Most historians have said that McNamara didn't clear his eight-page statement with the White House, except in general terms. On August 18, seven days before the appearance, there was a meeting with the president, McNamara, Rusk, General Wheeler (chairman of the Joint Chiefs), and Walt Rostow, the unapologetic White House hawk whose presidential stock was climbing as McNamara's was diminishing. On page 3 of the meeting notes, McNamara mentions his upcoming testimony—but doesn't suggest what he'll say. On page 4, this: "The president asked what is the answer to the stalemate issue. Wheeler responded there is no stalemate. The president said that's not a good enough answer. He said McNamara gets ridiculed when he says it. The president said he answered it today by saying it was pure communist propaganda." On pages 6 and 7, the Senate date is mentioned again:

"McNamara said the senate committee was trying to prove: 1) we can win it by air and naval power in the north; 2) there is a gap between the chairman of the joint chiefs and the defense secretary or between the chairman of the joint chiefs and the president. McNamara acknowledged that 'sure there are small differences but these are worked out.' "

The meeting ends with a discussion of the 300,000 enemy estimated to be in the south. Of these, 55,000 are North Vietnamese. From the notes: "McNamara commented that these are the ones who have a ticket to death." Odd macho language.

The hearings began at 10:10 a.m. and were over at 5:25 p.m. Early in the going, Senator Strom Thurmond of South Carolina said heatedly: "Mr. Secretary, I am terribly disappointed with your statement. I think it is a statement of placating the communists. It is a statement of appeasing the communists. It is a statement of no-win." The emotional Celt, with his own heat, said, ". . . I submit it is *not* a no-win program" (emphasis added).

Seventeen years later this roosted at the Westmoreland/CBS libel trial. How do you square this? the cross-examiner wanted to know. Doesn't this indicate you believed the war could be won when in fact you did not? Isn't that what you're telling the senator, that it could be won militarily? Everything about the lawyer for CBS's side suddenly seemed to be leaning in and asking: *Aren't you a damn liar, sir?*

Well, he had meant politically, diplomatically.

But you didn't say that, sir.

Well, not that particular day, no.

> Q. If the only thing you have been talking about was the military program, and [Thurmond] was clearly talking about a military program, when you then said in response, "It is *not* a no-win program," wouldn't the normal interpretation that you would expect someone listening to you to have was that you were talking of a military no-win situation?
>
> A. That is possible.

He said the committee knew that he believed it was necessary to have a two-track program, political and military, and that there was right then in the works a secret proposal to Ho Chi Minh to stop the bombing.

(It's instructive to note how McNamara dealt with his damaging "I submit it is not a no-win program" statement in *In Retrospect.* He dealt with it by leaving it out and putting in a later quote. Readers should consult page 290 of the memoir. On that page one finds Thurmond telling the secretary of defense he's placating the Communists, appeasing them, and the uninitiated would then think that McNamara's answer to the senator—buttressed by a colon—is: "There has been no witness before this committee . . . [who] has said the approval of the 57 targets . . . would act to shorten the war in any significant way." The witness said that, all right, in his answer on August 25, 1967. The only trouble is, he said the damaging thing immediately ahead of it. He said: "May I comment, Mr. Chairman, before we go on, on three points. First I submit the evidence from the communists. Ask them whether they think it is placating the communists. Secondly, I submit it is not a no-win program. Ask the field commanders and the joint chiefs." There would be no way for an uninformed reader to know this from page 290 or any other page of the book. Since the reply to Thurmond has become fairly famous among students of the war and students of McNamara, it's surprising that he apparently thought he could get away with it. Possibly he didn't care.)

It's a part of McNamara myth that there was a terrible row with the president at the conclusion of that bitter all-day marathon. You can find pieces of the story in books and in the memory banks of McNamara friends. Roswell Gilpatric, who was deputy secretary of defense from 1961 to early 1964, but who stayed close to McNamara in the Johnson years and after, told me in an interview that he wished to hell he had a tape of the story McNamara told him about the president's tirade that night. Gilpatric said the way he remembered McNamara's telling it was that he had just gotten back into his car and was about to leave the Hill when a message came that LBJ wanted him at the White House. The session went from seven to eleven in the Oval Office, and it was incredible: crying, weeping, the whole range of mythic Johnson emotion—Bob, can't you help me? Bob, you've wrecked my presidency. Recounting this to Gilpatric, McNamara said, according to Gilpatric, "I've been through a lot in my life, Ros, but never so completely drained as after that."

The problem is, the president's daily diary for August 25, 1967, lists two phone calls and no meetings between them. Johnson called McNamara at 8:22 a.m., an hour and a half before the hearings began. McNamara called Johnson at 6:20 p.m., an hour after they were over. The maximum time that call could have lasted—so it appears from the diary—was twenty minutes, because at 6:40 the president had another appointment. At 7 p.m. Johnson left the White House for the Navy Yard, where he boarded the presidential yacht, the *Sequoia*. He was on the boat for the next two days and, according to the archivist at the LBJ library in Texas, there were no contacts between McNamara and the president.

I'd bet the ranch there was plenty of Johnson profanity in that 6:20 p.m. phone call—it's just that a call seems to have been made into a different sort of subtly aggrandized myth. It's a little like telling the Detroit press corps at the dawn of Camelot that you had met with the president-elect regarding the Defense post three times in six days—when really you had met with him twice and talked once on the phone. Puny difference.

THE STORY OF THE TRANS, as their broken history folds into Robert McNamara's, isn't one of coincidence, not implicitly. And yet the circles obtain. I don't have an explanation.

Synchronize it thusly: In a fatal spring, when a man on the Western side of oceans was pushing and jamming to go, a quieter man seemed to know in his bones it would only double the disaster. For this he would get attacked as a weak pacifist by hawkish newspapers in his own country. I'm not saying Tran Van Tuyen was the only—or even most prominent—liberal Saigonese raising his voice against the introduction of U.S. troops. But he was among the raisers, in 1965 and afterward, not that it mattered a damn to the outcome.

We have to back up for a minute, to see it from *their* side. Back up to February 17, 1965. A Marine helo unit, in which there's a bony crew chief named Farley, is getting its first glimpse of a red-dust place named Danang. The head of America's Defense establishment is memoing the Joint Chiefs on the need for more productivity in air strikes against the north. On the front page of the New York *Times,* there's a story on the latest change of government in Saigon. This one is headed by a physician, Dr. Phan Huy Quat. He's an honest man of long political experience—but why should anyone think his regime will last? So many coups and countercoups among all these fractured and weak anti-Communist forces in Saigon ever since the (American-backed) assassination of Diem. No wonder the U.S. must come in and do the job. In for a dime, in for a dollar.

You'd have to read the *Times* story all the way down on the jump page to find the name "Tran Van Tuyen." He's been made a deputy prime minister in the new government. He still enjoys riding a bike. He has those children by a second wife. For three years, 1960–1963, he had been separated from his family as a political prisoner of the Diem dictatorship. His crime? Having helped draft a manifesto for social reforms, a free press, open political parties, civil rights. The *Groupe Caravelliste,* as the signers were known, in that the document had been drawn up at Saigon's Caravelle Hotel. A few months afterward, Diem's men had come for him. But that's past. Tran Van Tuyen is back with his family, Diem is dead, and so is Kennedy, and many governments have come and gone, and the patriarch of Hong Thap Tu has risen to become a deputy premier of his country.

Not that the *Times* story of February 17 goes into this history—no, just the name and a description of Tuyen's new post. On the same jump page of the newspaper there's a photograph of a peasant woman holding a child beside a burning village. The village is identified as a "hamlet near Tam Ky," which is the same spot, six weeks hence, where seventeen Yankee Papas will drop down between the tree lines of a harmless-looking rice paddy to find the world blinking on like a pinball machine.

Odd coincidences. Until I read a book called *In the Jaws of History,* by a man named Bui Diem, I never understood the kind of humiliation Saigon's leaders suffered at the hands of Lyndon Johnson and company during the spring of the bullying-in. William Gibbons told me that while there are hundreds of American works on the shelf rationalizing or condemning or narrating what the U.S. did in Vietnam, *In the Jaws of History* is the only serious study we've had by a Vietnamese who saw the hubris from the inside. In 1965 Bui Diem—who had once been a pupil of Tran Van Tuyen at the Thang Long academy in Hanoi—was serving as chief of staff for the shaky new Quat government. His book was published in the U.S. in 1987.

On March 8, 1965, the first U.S. troops came ashore. Two days earlier a Pentagon press release had declared that the Marines were being dispatched at the "request" of the new government; in fact, Quat and his ministers had not been consulted or even notified in advance. Early on the eighth, Bui Diem was summoned by a panicked Quat and told to draft a joint communiqué announcing the landing. "Be as brief as possible," Quat said. "Just describe the facts and affirm our concurrence."

The Communists had to be overjoyed, for it played straight in. From *Jaws:* "To be openly accused of being puppets was not just personally insulting; it was a wedge that would be driven between the government and the people." And the decisions of April 1–2, 1965, and the document that became NSAM-328? Ditto: a request for Saigon's "concurrence" after the fact. From *Jaws:* "We were completely in the dark about what the Americans intended. . . . We suspected, though, that the Americans were operating from some carefully devised master plan that they had simply chosen not to share with us."

I went to see Bui Diem several years ago. He was an old dapper gent living quietly with his family in Rockville, Maryland. "In my life, I lost many times," he said. But he had also survived politically: After the Quat government fell, he held other posts and eventually was made Vietnam's ambassador to the United States. Bui Diem grew emotional in remembering his friend and high-school math teacher from Thang Long. Bui Diem grew angry in remembering how he and Quat and Tran Van Tuyen and other ministers got treated. "The Americans are very impatient, you see," he said. "They think the Asian way is too slow. The machine was too big. It was like a bulldozer." He put his hand on his maroon sweater, touching his breast. "The Vietnamese felt it in the bottom of the heart to be wrong. But something in the character, in the nature, we couldn't speak up. . . . We were struggling with thousands of problems every day. We didn't even have time to think about it. The only thing we could do was—"

"Sign the paper?" I said.

"Yes," he said.

On March 24, 1965, one week before the decisions of NSAM-328, McNaughton wrote a memo to McNamara in which he said that "Quat is queasy." (One can fairly hear the newspaperman in McNaughton chuckling over the pithy phrase.) Two months later, on May 25, 1965, Ambassador Maxwell Taylor cabled from Saigon to the State Department: ". . . there is no doubt that he [Quat] and his ministers are very sensitive to recurring charge that Americans are in control and that Washington is calling shots." At the bottom of this two-pager: "Note: Passed White House, DOD (Exclusive for McNamara)."

In a 1986 book called *Intervention,* Vietnam scholar George McT. Kahin wrote: "The rapid Americanization of the war was a phenomenon that could not be disguised. One of Quat's deputy prime ministers, Tran Van Tuyen, found him preoccupied by the fear that, if more U.S. forces arrived, his government would appear to be 'a lackey of the Americans.' " In 1970 Professor Kahin traveled to Vietnam to interview Tran Van Tuyen and others.

I remember what I felt in bringing up that word, lackey, to Tran Van Tuyen's son. I'd just been fed exotically. Bao-Long was doing homework and listening to New Age jazz. Thanh said, "My daddy, he told Mr. Quat, 'Never permit American soldiers to come into our country.' He wanted Americans to give assistance, matériel, aid, munitions. But that is all."

"Because otherwise you'd be seen as—" I said.

Before I could repeat it, Thanh said it: "Lackey. Lackey. That's it. That's it. Lackey of the Americans. And you see for a time I did not understand this from my daddy. I was wrong. I was a young soldier. I said to my daddy, 'We need them.' I saw the films about the Americans in Korea, in World War Two. They were always winners."

A little later I said, "But couldn't it be argued that if the Americans hadn't come, what eventually happened to your family would have happened even sooner?"

"No. I don't think so. Because, you see, the Americans came and took over and shoved us aside. We lost our character." I said, "But not your father." He said, "Ah."

The Quat government was out by June. It had lasted barely four months. It was Saigon's last civilian government. A military regime led by Marshal Nguyen Cao Ky and General Nguyen Van Thieu took over. In for a dime, in for a dollar.

That fall, fall of '65, with the waters of intervention crossed, a public man who had survived two decades of political turmoil and was now out of office again, went to a Saigon park and wrote a short story. It was three days before a Baltimore Quaker killed himself. It was eleven days after an Albuquerque RN finished basic at Fort Sam Houston. It was a month before a defense minister turned apostate on all he'd made. It was eleven years, minus two days, from the writer's own degraded death in a forced-labor camp of the north.

The author sat on a bench in Dien-Hong Park and began to write. He titled it "Nguoi khach la." It means "A Strange Visitor." He got into it something of the gothic and visionary. He got into it something of his own terrible weariness, which to my mind makes the story more beautiful. A man dreams on a bench. War is everywhere around, and yet willow branches float softly in the wind and a sampan glides on dark waters before him, "at the rhythm of a mute oar." Suddenly, a sense of someone sitting alongside. This person, neither old nor young, is tall like a Westerner. It can't be known whether he's Caucasian, Asian, or

African. Where has the narrator seen him before—Shanghai, Bangkok, Paris? He talks madness, but with strange logic. When he reveals his identity, it's with a bitter dry laugh: "I am Revolution!" He says: "Where I passed through, I brought along demolition and death. . . . But my objectives are neither havoc nor killing. My objectives are to rebuild. . . . But I am doomed only to destroy, kill, demolish."

The vision vanishes. But for days after, these words echo in the narrator: "I am not tired. I am not desperate. I need no rest. All I want is to rebuild."

In some of its language and ideas, there's a spooky correspondence between "A Strange Visitor" and a poem Robert McNamara has loved for sixty years: Rudyard Kipling's "The Palace." It, too, is about someone who wants only to build. It's about shafts running down, about work bedded on the structures of predecessors, about beautiful intentions gone bad, about messages that rise from the darkness. The refrain is, " *'After me cometh a Builder. Tell him, I too have known.'* "

Tran Van Tuyen wrote "A Strange Visitor" on October 30, 1965, but the story didn't appear within covers until the end of 1968. By then, a war minister in America was gone. By then, a public man in Vietnam was deep in other causes. In a few years he would be elected chairman of the opposition bloc in the South Vietnamese house of representatives, where he would raise his voice against government corruption, against intervention by tyrants.

"A Strange Visitor" got published as the title piece in a book of stories by Tran Van Tuyen. It was printed on thin manila pages with a soft binding and a green cover. In 1975, after the country fell, all family copies of this small book—along with photo albums, money, jewelry, and other personal items—were confiscated. But somehow the work traveled across oceans. One copy—maybe the only copy extant in America—is safe today in a blue slipcover in a Southeast Asian Studies library at Cornell University. The library let me take it out, bring it to an apartment-cocoon of displaced memory on the Richmond Highway in Alexandria, Virginia, where a fifth child and third son held the exquisitely fragile thing in his hands and said, "I read this story and I cry my tears."

G O N E   N O W was his closest aide. Behind him was the self-destruct of August 25. It was the fall of final torment, with an ill wife who had even less heart for it than he.

Always there had been his discipline. Always there had been his confidence. Always there had been the compulsion to try and rob time. And always there had been the numbers, the probity of the numbers. "I want to use some figures. Phil, do you have a pencil? Maybe I can write on the board here," he said during a Pentagon briefing, apparently his old self. It was September 7, 1967. It was something about the bombing of the north in percentile relation to total air operations, and it was 30,000 of these and 17,000 of those. The guys in the press room were propping up their eyes with toothpicks. When the chalk talk was done, the didact said, and you could look it up in the transcripts, "So it is fifteen percent of ten percent of thirteen-thirtieths that have been in dispute and it is to these that that committee addressed itself."

But mostly it was the sense of impending doom. It was as if Harpies grinned from trees. As the Washington *Daily News* wrote (on Halloween): "McNamara-watching has long been one of Washington's prime spectator sports, but under the awesome impact of Vietnam it now bids fair to replace Sunday with the Redskins as a recreation of the morbidly curious."

Behind him now too were ravages of a lesser kind—such as the nastiness he had had with Margaret Chase Smith on August 11. It happened two weeks before his bombing testimony. The lady from Maine, as her Senate colleagues called her, with her small defiant chin, accused him in public of being a liar. She was fed up with the years of truth-twisting. Several years before, after a crafty deception in which he had tried to use her name to bulwark his lie (it was about a shipyard closure in her state), he had come up to her office to apologize and smooth things over. She leveled him then with: "If I can't trust you on the little lies, sir, how will I ever believe you on the big ones?" Now, on the eve of the bombing testimony, Senator Smith (who sat on the Stennis committee and preparedness subcommittee) had released a statement saying he was a tragically dishonest man. He responded instantly with a confidential letter: "I cannot accept such a charge because it is not true." She wrote right back ("I am happy to respond to your letter of 11 August 1967 hand-delivered to my office at 12:09 p.m. today"), ticking off past lies. She closed the three-page letter: "Mr. Secretary, you have not only been less than forthright and accurate in your statements to me—you have been arrogant and derogatory in your attitude to me. . . . I note that you have sent a copy of your letter to the chairman of the senate armed services committee. This is to inform you that I am sending a copy of this letter not only to the chairman of the senate armed services committee but to the president as well." Whew.

Behind him now too was another indignity: having to slink about and make inquiries about returning to Michigan and Ford Motor Company. Earlier that summer he had run into Ford chief counsel William Gossett at a White House function. He had told Gossett (who had never really liked him) that he wished to give him a lift home from the party. Had something to discuss with him, he said. Gossett replied he already had a driver to take him to his hotel—could they talk tomorrow? But McNamara persisted, and late that evening, in the inkiness of a government car, he allowed he was thinking of leaving Washington, things hadn't worked out, the war was going bad—and did Gossett think Henry Ford might be interested in getting him back?

It didn't work out. (In *In Retrospect,* McNamara reported something I've not seen or heard of anywhere else: He had a Wall Street offer for $2.5 million.)

How close to cracking was Robert McNamara in the autumn of 1967? It's unknowable, but my interviews and research have led me to believe: quite close. Which I think speaks in its own way to the buried humanity rather than to the famous mechanicalness. The split man himself has always ridiculed speculation of a breakdown. He thinks of it as garbage, as garbagy as the idea he went to the World Bank for atonement, expiation. In *In Retrospect,* he wrote of his alleged cracking: "I was not getting answers to my questions; and I was tense as hell. But I was not under medical care, not taking drugs except for an occasional sleeping pill, and never contemplated suicide."

McNamara loyalists say such talk is just copy for the sensationalists. I remember the time I brought the subject up to Vernon Goodin, his oldest friend. No, no, Bob wasn't close to a breakdown, and Vernon knew it for a fact: He and his wife, Marion Sproul Goodin, had been with the McNamaras in Aspen, right after Bob left office. He was flying down the slopes. He was a tiger on the run they call "the slot." (Sure enough, I located an old AP story, written ten days after he was out, in March 1968, testifying to his ski brinkmanship. He was "bronzed by sun and wind after a week at his chalet in this mountain resort. . . .")

And yet. A White House aide, John Roche, dead now, told me, and told a number of other researchers too, that he had been with the president in the Oval Office on the summer afternoon when he put down the telephone and said, "Johnny, we can't have another Forrestal." LBJ had just spoken to Marg McNamara at Johns Hopkins Hospital. He had called to cheer her up following her stomach surgery, but somehow had grown alarmed at the thought of his secretary of defense hurling himself out of a window, which is what James Forrestal, Truman's defense secretary, did. Roche himself believed McNamara to be hanging on in 1967 by his fingernails.

In his 1991 book *The Triumph and Tragedy of Lyndon Johnson,* White House aide Joe Califano wrote that LBJ "frequently expressed to me grave concern about the secretary's mental and physical health." (Califano, who had once worked for McNamara, reiterated this to me in a 1995 interview.) On the same page of his memoir, Califano wrote that LBJ discussed McNamara's condition that fall with his aide Jim Jones, and that the specter of Forrestal was once more raised. And Neil Sheehan reported in his book that Johnson told George Christian, his press secretary, that McNamara had deteriorated into "an emotional basket case."

A decade ago, another ex–White House aide, Douglass Cater, deceased now, told me he could remember LBJ's telling him how McNamara came to him toward the last to say he couldn't sleep at night, he was afraid of breaking down. Johnson could have been lying for his own devices, Cater said, but he doubted it. And Cater's wife, Libby, told me she could remember coming home with her husband from a weekend at Camp David and writing in her journal about the president's anxieties over McNamara. They weren't calculated anxieties, felt Libby Cater. The president told her, "I'm just so worried about Bob. It's all on his shoulders. He's so stretched."

In his 1991 memoir, *Counsel to the President,* Clark Clifford wrote of the president's "[k]nowing McNamara was in a fragile emotional state, fearing even for his survival. . . ." When I interviewed Clifford a decade ago, he said a similar thing.

To McNamara, it's garbage.

On October 3, 1967, the secretary said in an auditorium at the State Department: "Good afternoon, ladies and gentlemen. Endurance is becoming a primary requirement in Washington these days. . . ." Two days later, the fifth, the secretary held a backgrounder at the Pentagon. In Boston the World Series had just opened between the Cards and the Red Sox. Bobby and Teddy Kennedy were photographed in a box at Fenway Park, flanking their wheelchaired father, who had to be taken out in a hurry and given oxygen. The next morning the New York *Times* would tell its readers that unofficial totals of killed and wounded, according to figures released in Saigon, were now 100,278. It broke down to this: 13,643 dead, 86,635 wounded.

In the press backgrounder of the fifth (no direct quotations permitted), reporters heard notes of self-pity and self-righteousness. The man fabled for memory said his memory wasn't that good. He said, ". . . can I predict the future? No. I have tried and failed, thank you."

> QUESTION: Today's news brings out the fact that we have just passed the 100,000 mark in casualties in Vietnam.
> SECRETARY McNAMARA: Well, first, it is not a new breakthrough.
> QUESTION: Well, it is over a certain mark.
> SECRETARY McNAMARA: It is not over a certain mark any more than yesterday it was over the day before. I think we want to be very careful how we talk about casualties because we can exaggerate.

That freighted word, stalemate, came up. He pointed to the large unit successes. Then, "There has been considerable argument on the question of: is there or is there not a military stalemate in the south? I do not know any qualified military observer, national or foreign, who believes that there is a military stalemate. I think the statements you are referring to, all of them from military observers, support my conclusion."

Seventeen years later, upon being handed this sticky quote on the stand at the Westmoreland/CBS libel trial, the witness studied the document, Exhibit 1803, then tried saying, in effect, why, look here, the words are printed in plain English right on the page: "military observer"—and of course he had been a civilian during the war. A technically astute try.

"Do you see that, sir?" the defense lawyer for CBS asked, bearing down.

> A. I do.
> Q. And in October of 1967 did this represent your views as to whether or not there was a military stalemate?
> A. It did not. That's not what I said. I didn't say there wasn't a military stalemate in my view. I said I don't know any qualified military observer who believes there's a military stalemate.

But that self-fragging was far up ahead. On the night of October 5, 1967, the McNamaras went to a party. A reporter for the *Post* was in the room and overheard him say he'd like to take Margy to the Orient "just as soon as I can get out of here." Instant copy for the a.m.

On October 21 came the sea snake across Memorial Bridge. On the thirty-first came the *Daily News* feature saying his ordeal was better spectator sport than the Sunday Redskins. Same day, at LBJ's regular Tuesday luncheon on Vietnam, he spoke bluntly and bravely against the war. The following day, he handed the president a seven-page memo, which I believe to be the third anchor point in terms of what got him out. Some people have spoken of this document as the "all-the-cards" memo. It came attached with a personal note on a small sheet ("Yesterday at lunch I stated my belief that continuation of our present course of action in Southeast Asia would be dangerous, costly in lives, and unsatisfactory to the American people") and was signed "Bob" under the typed name.

It was as lucid and strong a piece of work as the May 19 memo, but without the benefit of John McNaughton's phrasemaking. It urged a "policy of stabilization" in which there would be "no further increase in our forces in South Vietnam, and no expansion of our operations against North Vietnam." (One could study the paper psychologically just in terms of the word "no"—it's everywhere.) The secretary predicted how many total American deaths from the war the president could expect by the end of his current term on Inauguration Day in 1969: "somewhere between 24 and 30,000." (He was close: There would be 31,000 deaths.) The paper spoke of a people that "does not give the appearance of having the will to persist."

On the evening of the day he handed the president his all-the-cards memo, the Wise Men gathered in Washington. As Sheehan has written: ". . . it was a constellation of American statecraft and military experience that included Dean Acheson and Omar Bradley." At this meeting of tribal elders, McNamara said he was scared that everything he and Dean Rusk had done on the war since 1961 was a failure. The next morning, and into the afternoon, the Wise Men convened again, and the declassified notes of this session have since made it into many books. McNamara was at the table but appears to have spoken little. At points the president seems to enjoy sticking him in front of the others. From page 3 of the notes: "The president pointed out that the dramatic impact of the bombing traces to Secretary McNamara's testimony before

Senator Stuart Symington's committee. That generated both the hawks and the doves talking about bombing. The president said, 'I am like the steering wheel of a car without any control.' "

The group washed up for lunch, then commenced being wise again at 1:03 p.m. Clark Clifford brought up McNamara's comment of the evening before—that perhaps everything he had done on the war was worthless. Maybe that softened Johnson, because two pages over in the notes, he's saying, ". . . that no nation has been more enlightenly served than under secretaries Rusk and McNamara. He pointed out that these two are the highest type of manhood that this nation can produce."

The Wise Men, including George Ball, were in accord on the idea of getting out of Vietnam: Cannot be done. Unthinkable.

Perhaps as a precaution against the literary trash-pickers who would one day be rooting through his presidency, Johnson circulated McNamara's November 1 memo among his senior advisers. He asked for written comments. To some he gave it blind—but surely everybody could guess the identity of the palace apostate. The comments were overwhelmingly negative. Pay it no heed. Which is just what the president had been of a mind to do. In the words of war historian Stanley Karnow: "Typically, Johnson had sought a consensus in order to confirm his own inclination. . . ."

Five days after the Wise Men had disbanded and gone back to their investment-banking jobs or teaching posts or Supreme Court jobs, a man who was on his way out flew to Denver and gave a speech to the National Association of Broadcasters. It was his last formal address as secretary, and in the scheme of things a small potato. An oral recording of the speech exists in the National Archives, and on it there's choking and wheezing. He gets in all the numbers. He insists, as he did in Montreal, that international security must mean far more than hardware. At the close: "What we may lack is the willpower. If we do lack it, so be it. But let that be our conscious choice. Let us face the issues honestly, and admit to ourselves that we simply do not want to make the effort." Right after this speech, not that there was any direct correlation, the president called Treasury Secretary Henry Fowler and told him to get going hard on a nomination of McNamara to the World Bank.

And what is the truth of that murkiness? Well, one truth would be that LBJ slid him out because he was a liability—and an index of the sliding might be that he wasn't able to tell McNamara his name had been put in nomination to the bank's twenty directors and 106 governments. But trying to contain a secret like that was like trying to conduct a secret war.

The basic chronology: The previous April, McNamara had met with George D. Woods in Woods's private dining room at the bank. Woods's five-year term as president of the bank was due to expire in December 1967, and he told McNamara he wanted to recommend him as his successor. McNamara reported the conversation to the president, saying, "I will stay as long as you think necessary."

By September there were rumors in financial circles. McNamara had to have been aware of them.

In October, LBJ apparently asked McNamara if he was still interested in the bank. The answer was affirmative.

Weeks passed. The nomination got secretly made. The nominee wasn't told, though it's ludicrous to think he didn't know in a general sense what was happening. On Saturday, November 25, the AP got wind on the basis of a report filed by an Indian Nations Network affiliate in Oklahoma, station KRMG of Tulsa. (KRMG's Washington correspondent had gotten it from Congressional Majority Leader Carl Albert of Oklahoma.) The next day, Sunday, a Spanish paper in Miami had the tip. The next day, Monday, the twenty-seventh, the *Financial Times* of London had it. That broke it wide open. These various media had come by the story in the same way—contacts (mostly in foreign embassies).

Over that weekend, a career Pentagon employee named Henry Glass went to see McNamara. It was a Saturday and the secretary was in as usual, though not performing as usual. Glass remembers him sitting there, a man going down. Glass was a mid-echelon man who had drafted defense military "posture" statements as well as many other McNamara testimonies, and because of this he had unusual access. When I talked to Glass a decade ago, the moment was still fresh: "I'd spent a couple sleepless nights myself. I could see the guy was collapsing emotionally. . . . He kept saying we have to win the war in the south." Glass said he had no doubt in his mind McNamara was in danger of cracking that fall. "It was eating on him. He'd made such a mistake. . . . He could size and shape the forces, it was all theory, that sort of thing, and he was great at it, but the rest of it. . . ."

Late on Monday, November 27, 1967, with the press on both sides of the Atlantic all over the bank story, McNamara went to the White House and spoke with Johnson alone. He returned to his office and soon a presidential aspirant and strident war critic named Bobby Kennedy was in room 3E880 of the Pentagon. Now would be the perfect time for Bobby's great friend Bob to use his resignation to make a break with the war and LBJ, too. Deborah Shapley quotes McNamara as telling her, "Bobby would have been very happy to see me resign with a hell of a blast at Johnson, but I wasn't about to do anything that wasn't in my opinion in the national interest."

For two days the walls of Washington evasion and denial were thrown up. That's a lifetime. On Wednesday night, Bobby Kennedy had drinks with Arthur Schlesinger, Jr., and Pierre Salinger at the King Cole Bar in the St. Regis Hotel in New York City. Schlesinger afterward wrote in his diary: "Wouldn't any self-respecting man, I asked Bobby, have his resignation on the president's desk half an hour after he heard the London bulletin? . . . Why does he fall in with LBJ's plan to silence him and cover everything up? Bobby listened silently and a little gloomily. He said that he thought that was what would finally happen—that Bob would not take the World Bank job and would instead quietly resign from government."

Actually, by the time of the drinks at the King Cole, Bob had already stridden into the Pentagon's TV auditorium to take the World Bank job. The president released a statement that night as well. McNamara sat behind a desk and read a choppy statement, read it twice for the cameras. The statement revealed nothing of substance about why he was leaving, much less what he thought about the Vietnam War. He said he would be staying into the new year to help on the budget. He left the room and newsmen pursued him down the hall. It was a little after 8 p.m. on November 29, 1967. He was fifty-one years old. Seven years before, when he was the god from Michigan, it had been haste in. Now it was haste out (except he wouldn't actually be going for another ninety days). Seven years before, it had been glory in. Now it was insult out. In *In Retrospect,* McNamara got part of this wrong. He said the president announced the resignation the next day, but actually they had released their separate and wan statements at about the same hour that Wednesday night, the twenty-ninth.

IN THE *TAO TE CHING*, Chapter 68, it says: "A good soldier is not violent. A good fighter is not angry. A good winner is not vengeful. A good employer is humble. This is known as the Virtue of not striving." I showed that once to Tran Tu Thanh. He said, "Yes, it's about not hating your enemy."

I remember the time I brought to the apartment a magazine article about the poetry of Vietnam. There were beautiful pictures. One poem was titled "I Am Sad," and the picture beneath was of a peasant pedaling a bike on an iron bridge across a lotus pond. "I Am Sad" was discovered on the body of an ordinary soldier of the north, fighting with the Ninth Battalion of the 101st NVA. In the poem the soldier speaks to a comrade who has just died: "Your life runs out like a red silk banner. / Life is now too hard, dear brother. / So many dreams float in air."

Thanh read each word aloud. Dreams were floating in apartment air. "That poet was your enemy," I said. He said, "He's a human, a human being. They are my compatriots. My countrymen."

"But it was war, Thanh, you must have hated them."

"Ah, that's a problem. I hate them when I see them kill civilians. By that time, yes."

A short while after this: "Nobody knows in a war."

A short while after this, I brought out the most powerful photograph of the Vietnam War—the one in which General Nguyen Ngoc Loan, chief of South Vietnam's national police force, is executing a bound Vietcong at point-blank range. It was taken during the Tet offensive, February 1968, just as McNamara packed his things. The officer's arm is straight out; the barrel of his service pistol is almost in the bound man's ear. His head has just started to recoil.

"It was a war," Thanh said. "If you understand about him, you understand about me."

"You mean you could picture yourself doing that?"

"No. He couldn't contain himself. But no. I couldn't. On the other hand I understand what makes him pull the trigger."

Thanh knew General Loan in the war; in 1967 he worked under him at the province level. During Tet, while McNamara packed, Thanh was in a security office on the outskirts of Saigon, doing counterintelligence, conducting his own "interviews" with captured VC. These lifetimes later, Tran Tu Thanh has attended Vietnamese social functions in the Washington refugee community where he's sat on sofas beside Nguyen Ngoc Loan: an old, unhappy, and mostly reclusive escapee of the morally bad time.

Nobody knows in a war.

I remember the day Thanh and I drove to New Jersey and spent four or five hours eating and remembering with his two older sisters, Jackie and Pauline. Their Vietnamese names are Dam-Phuong and Lananh.

They have their own families, and their kids have matriculated at places named Harvard, Columbia, and Cornell, but the sadness that's in their brother is the sadness that's in them.

As it happened, Robert McNamara was on the literary hustings with *In Retrospect*. As it happened, Thanh was preparing a speech just then for delivery at the State Department on behalf of the Vietnamese community of Washington. (It was to mark the twentieth anniversary of the fall of Saigon.) On our way to Cherry Hill, he showed me an early draft. The speech had tough words for McNamara: "His mistake will be judged by the American people and history." Thanh talked of a "steward" who had been so "ignorant of the customs and aspirations of the Vietnamese people." But it wasn't hatred of the enemy I felt as I read the draft at a rest stop.

Back in the car, Thanh had a story about trying to sell Kirby vacuum cleaners door-to-door in Washington ghetto neighborhoods. "I have this sorrow, this experience to tell you," he said. "I must go into Maryland and northeast Washington. Yes, door-to-door. I knock on the door of this man. He was a homosexual. I said, 'I must demonstrate the Kirby machine.' He tried to caress me. I jumped back. I said, 'I am a former officer! I know kung fu!' " In his few years in America, the ex-officer with the law degree from the University of Saigon has mowed lawns, painted houses, buffed floors on a janitorial crew, done secretarial work—whatever would pay the rent. He got the Kirby job through an ad in the paper. It lasted four months. He had had only a shaky notion of the word "commission."

We arrived at Pauline's split-level on Black Latch Lane, and for the rest of the day I felt as if three dislocated Trans were showing me in oblique ways about the self-destructiveness of hating an enemy. A walled villa at No. 198 Hong Thap Tu kept curling from ruin. So too did the phrase, "What would Daddy think?" Jackie, second eldest, told me how those words have governed her life in diaspora. They all feel the weight of trying to live up to Daddy, she said. Jackie married into the family of a distinguished Korean diplomat and left Vietnam early. After the country fell, she worked hard to learn the whereabouts of her father and to get her siblings out of the country. Largely because of her stateside efforts, through work with amnesty organizations and congressional groups on Capitol Hill, all her siblings are free now. Jackie is a small, meticulous, precise, burning woman who's in computers for a *Fortune* 500 company. Her sister, Pauline, third oldest in the family, a long-ago Saigon literature major, fled Vietnam in 1979 as a boat person with her husband and four kids. They arrived in America with three duffel bags of clothing given to them by the Red Cross in the refugee camps of Malaysia. And now I was able to look around in Pauline's Cherry Hill home and see lacquered bureaus, tasteful side cases, painted Oriental figurines. I was being treated to such wonderful food. You can pave over a garden, confiscate books, burn albums, but some things—like breeding and the will to survive—will not so easily be destroyed. In the damnedest ways and places, like the capillary oozing of water, they will reroot, splinter the stone.

We talked of how wrongly the Americans did it. The word "lackey" was said again. I asked the two sisters, as I had asked their younger brother: Couldn't it be argued that if the Americans had never come with their bulldozing land war, the country would have fallen even faster and the Tran family would have suffered even more? There was silence. Jackie said, well, it would be a difficult thing to answer. Pauline said, well, her father had always just understood it to be wrong. Perhaps, she said, the native army could have somehow found the strength and character to stand up to the Communist forces—with the matériel support and financial backing of the U.S. It was the bullying and the pushing aside that had been so hurtful, Pauline said. "We lost our pride and sense of worth."

But I don't think any of us sitting at that table really thought the splintered and ineffectual and often corrupt ARVN forces could have stood up to the people on the other side, who were the heirs of a revolution and who had conquered the French at Dien Bien Phu.

On the way back to Washington, Thanh didn't talk much. At one point he said, "My son told me, 'I will get a good job and I will buy a house and you will live in it.' I thank him, but I told him I want to be independent."

I drove on. He began humming. I looked over. "It's 'Mockingbird Hill,' " I said. "Yes," he said. "Patti Page. That's a beautiful song. I sang it to myself many times in prison." He sang now: " 'When the sun in the morning creeps over the hill / And kisses the raindrops on my windowsill.' "

He hummed another. It was "Santa Lucia," an old Italian ballad. In his lightless tomb, the shackled man had composed new lyrics for the ancient tune. They were about a Vietnamese woman named Freedom, and he sang them softly for me in the darkness: "In my most beautiful dream I am waiting for your return / Understand that I am loving you to my last breath."

In a little while the fifth child and third son of a long-dead patriot dropped his head against the side glass and fell asleep. We were cruising on a big American interstate, safe, so far from his home.

IN *THE LIMITS OF INTERVENTION,* Townsend Hoopes wrote: "When all factors were duly weighed, one was left with the irreducible feeling that the most Byzantine of American presidents had given McNamara a fast shuffle, and had gauged his man's character, inner ambivalence, and fatigue well enough to be confident that he would go quietly and suffer the indignity in silence." In *A Bright Shining Lie,* Neil Sheehan wrote: "The high moral courage that Robert McNamara could summon up within the secrecy of the American state he could not summon up outside of it to denounce what the American state was doing. In all the years of the war that lay ahead he was never to speak publicly against it." In *In Retrospect,* Robert McNamara wrote: "Many friends, then and since, have told me I was wrong not to have resigned in protest over the president's policy. . . . I believe that would have been a violation of my responsibility to the president and my oath to uphold the constitution."

The last three days. It was almost as if he had to go through them before God would let him out—to go skiing in Aspen.

In the LBJ library in Texas, in box two of Set II of *Meeting Notes File,* there's a legal-size olive folder with a little adhesive tab at the top that says "February 27, 1968. Meeting of Advisers on Vietnam (President Did Not Attend)." Inside the folder are four pages of neat penmanship on a lined legal pad telling what went on, what got said, at that advisers' meeting and farewell luncheon. They're detailed notes, but in a sense they're the wrong notes, because they contain almost none of the emotional truth. For that you have to go to a different archive: somebody's head and heart.

What really happened that forenoon in an ornate little dining room at Dean Rusk's State Department is that a man with forty-eight hours left in his tenure rose and, without warning, began coming apart. It was the nakedness of the thing. One of those who saw it was Clark Clifford, his successor. The secretary of state was there. William Bundy was in the room. Another who left the meeting at one point—and so may or may not have been present at the moment of the coming-apart—was Nicholas Katzenbach. Another was Walt Rostow, and the final two were Joe Califano and Harry McPherson, who were over from the White House and were more junior than the others and thus perhaps a little more apt to be shocked at what happened. It was McPherson who kept the factual record in the neat hand that would one day get stored in the tabbed folder in the granite library beside the football stadium at the University of Texas.

I first learned of February 27, 1968, in Stanley Karnow's *Vietnam.* That immensely well researched book told of McPherson's sitting open-mouthed. McNamara's voice broke, and the tears welled up, "as he spoke of the futility, the crushing futility, of the air war." But none of this is in the meeting notes—what got put there was the paler record. I've since read greater or lesser descriptions of the moment in half a dozen other books (including McPherson's own memoir, where the treatment is pretty pale), and I've since talked about the luncheon with two others who were in the room: Clifford and Califano. (When I interviewed William Bundy, I inexplicably forgot to ask about it.) But it was Harry McPherson himself, eighteen years after it happened, in the spring of 1986, who brought the moment all the way up into the light for me. I spent a noontime walking on Connecticut Avenue with this old LBJ aide, and he opened up his head and heart. He did it generously, and by that I mean with a certain compassion and without particular judgment. We had already had a pretty long phone conversation, and had exchanged letters, and his reluctance to get into it was evident. I remember how he walked faster and faster in the warming April sun. "This is our Rialto," he said of Connecticut Avenue, stopping to wave to other prominent lawyers.

The moment: A number had already risen to speak. McPherson himself had spoken. To be sure, there was a general gloom in the room, it wasn't just McNamara. (When I talked to Califano about it, he stressed this point.) The meeting had been called in the first place as part of an ongoing discussion for a televised presidential speech on Vietnam. The original idea had been to come up with a major address that would reassure America on the Tet offensive, which had been going on for a month now and which was seeming to throw over everything about the war and America's perception of it. But the meeting at State took its own head and became a discussion on what the departing man referred to as Westmoreland's request for another 205,000 troops.

It was madness, he believed, putting another 205,000 in, it was all madness, out of control.

McPherson thinks it happened just before the stewards brought in lunch. Announcing he couldn't stay, McNamara, who hadn't been slumped in silence, who had been contributing to the discussion, got up—

> —and with such fury and passion and tears he's lashing out at the whole war, his voice rising and cracking and the room swelling with all of it: the goddamned bombing campaign, it's been worth nothing, it's done nothing, they've dropped more bombs than in all of Europe in all of World War Two and it hasn't done a fucking thing. . . . Just incredibly caught in the throat, like somebody in the third week of laryngitis. . . . I was shaken, riveted, the room looking down at its shoetops. The most emotional moment I've ever seen. I was riveted on McNamara. I was stunned. So was Joe. That's all we could talk about on the way back to the White House.

In the preserved notes in the acid-free box in Texas, there's a Harry McPherson sentence (it's in a parenthesis) that has Robert McNamara saying, "We are dropping ordnance at a higher rate than in last year of WWII in Europe. It has not stopped him." To get the rest, you have to search a different archive, go walking on the Rialtos of memory, some years after.

In his 1991 memoir, *Counsel to the President,* Clark Clifford told of "suppressed sobs" and the cracking of the "controlled exterior," and then wrote a sentence that I think explains everything: "We were all stunned, but, out of a shared pain and sense of embarrassment, we went on with the discussion as though nothing out of the ordinary had occurred."

The twenty-seventh was the first ordeal of his last three days. The day following, in the East Room, with the president in attendance, Robert McNamara choked out twenty-three words under the chandeliers. *Lies in my heart.*

And finally the twenty-ninth. A leap-year February. For some reason the Furies turned the mask comic. Someone at the White House typed a script for a tight noontime twelve-minute ceremony: "Indoor Scenario for McNamara Ceremony at Pentagon." There would be a presentation of another medal and a nineteen-gun salute and a fly-pass of the crack all-weather fighter, the F-11. But nobody counted on the hard rain, and the mangled PA system, and the umbrellas that kept whipping inside out, and the special elevator in the Pentagon garage that conked—wouldn't budge—between the second and third floors, leaving bloodless Bob McNamara pitched nose to nose in an overloaded box with his hot-as-a-chili-pepper commander in chief. In the LBJ library there's a hilarious memo about February 29, 1968 (the archivists know it as "the elevator memo"), written by a Johnson aide named Will Sparks, and I should say I'm indebted to it here.

The president motored over at 11:50 a.m. McNamara was waiting in the garage. Thirteen people got into elevator number thirteen—perhaps the first mistake. The box started up, stopped quietly. McNamara reached past the operator, a sergeant, saying, "Let me see if I can't get this to work."

Somebody said, "Isn't there an emergency switch?"

McNamara said, "You'd better use the telephone."

The sergeant opened the telephone box and spoke to a maintenance man. The maintenance man said, "Do you have a full load?" The sergeant said, "We sure do."

It was getting stuffy. Two aides pried the inside door slightly apart. A little air came in. Up above, the Secret Service wept like children.

Will Sparks was told to wedge the notebook containing the president's remarks between the two outer doors for more air. The rescuers finally came. Maybe ten or fifteen minutes had passed. The elevator was still suspended three feet below floor level, so someone procured a leather chair with wooden arms from a nearby general's office and put it inside the elevator so that Lyndon Johnson could climb out with his dignity intact.

Outside, the hard rain was falling, first rain in twenty-seven days, driest February on record. The fly-pass of the vaunted all-weather fighter was canceled. The loudspeakers weren't working, and the airliners lifting off from nearby National Airport tried to drown out the nineteen-gun salute. Somebody held an umbrella over the president and, theoretically, over McNamara too, but as LBJ said in the car afterward, "There was some kid holding an umbrella over my head which had a hole in it and the water was running down the shoulder of my coat. He was also holding it so that all the water fell on McNamara's glasses, who was standing at attention going blind. I told the kid to move the umbrella to the right and he moved it to the left, so that the only person who was protected then was him."

The honoree went back inside and his blue suit was soaked and his glasses were smeared and his shoes were covered with grass. At 5:25 that afternoon the president of the United States tried to reach his man Bob McNamara. But he had already left. A wire-service reporter wrote that the nine-foot desk was dinner-plate clean. The colossal reign of seven years and thirty-nine days was over. Except it would never be over.

Epilogue
BECAUSE OUR FATHERS LIED

*D*ying's the best
        Of all the arts men learn in a dead place.
I walked here once. I made my loud display,
Leaning for language on a dead man's voice.
Now sick of lies, I turn to face the past.
I add my easy grievance to the rest.

—*James Wright*

*M*y last things will be first things
        slipping from me.

—*Seamus Heaney*

F IRST THINGS: Back to that drizzly Friday night in 1972, that half minute of imploded anger in the dark of Vineyard Sound, when a short bearded man in tennis shoes and a murderous rage tried to hurl Robert McNamara off the Martha's Vineyard ferry. What took place there, I think, at an iron-grated railing, between a sixties artist and a figure of immense authority, call him parental authority, *was* and *is* the Vietnam War. That half minute seems to stand for it all.

The story, at least the bulk of it, was told to me in one sitting one autumn afternoon in 1985, which is to say thirteen years after it happened. When I first walked up to the artist, who didn't look murderous at all, he was standing in the doorway of the building on Martha's Vineyard where he has long done most of his painting and drawing. He had on tennis shoes and an old canvas shirt and a pair of khakis streaked with oil paint. He was bearded and looked to be in his early forties— maybe five feet six in height, maybe 130 pounds in weight. My first thought was that he was much too small to assault anyone. He made no move to invite me inside, just stood in the door with his arms crossed, working an aromatic pipe between thin pale lips. Five minutes earlier, I had spoken to him, for the first time in my life, from a pay phone 200 yards up the road. In the previous week I had made about two dozen calls to Martha's Vineyard and other places, trying to learn the artist's name and whereabouts. Then suddenly somebody was saying, yes, he knew right where the artist was, which turned out to be almost within earshot of where he had lived years before. I had flown up to Massachusetts and driven down to Woods Hole and bought a ticket on the ferry and ridden over to the island this day without any notion of whether I might find him home. I was afraid if I tried contacting him in advance, he would get skittish and tell me not to bother. So I decided to do it cold and on my luck.

"How do you know it was me?" he said from the doorway, chewing on the pipe, speaking softly. I just said, probably not very coherently, that I was writing a book about McNamara and that I couldn't really go on with this part unless he decided to help me. The artist didn't say anything, just kept studying me and working on the pipe. Behind him I could see canvases nailed to wooden frames, in various stages of completion.

"Sergeant Welch at Vineyard Haven remembered it was you," I tacked on.

The smallest edge came into his voice, and he came forward half an inch. "Well, maybe Sergeant Welch is wrong."

But in another moment I was let in and directed toward a lone chair. His studio was chilly and dimly lit but felt homey, too. A radio was tuned low to classical music. The artist stood across from me and with almost no prompting began telling the story. It seemed to fall out in a lump; all I had to do was scribble. His one stipulation was that I not identify him by name in anything I wrote. I hated hearing it but gave my word. About halfway through, he went over to a wood stove and knelt down and began building up a fire. It was as if the physical act of snapping pieces of kindling in two was helping him to remember small details. Parts of the story were enacted, and not just for my benefit, I suspect. When he got to the moment where the posing messenger turns wordlessly on the man behind him, the artist said, standing just above me, his movements in pantomime: "It was a pivot, you see, like this. One, two, three, then I've got him, he's in the air, he's going over."

That evening I rode back to the mainland thinking I had just rubbed the Rosetta stone of all the anger of the sixties.

A year later I went back to Martha's Vineyard and interviewed the artist again. I went for several reasons: to clarify some details of the incident, as he had described them; to ask if he would consider changing his mind and allow me to use his name in print; to inquire whether his reliving of the story for me the year before had seemed to alter anything in his life or work or maybe even in his feelings about the man he had attacked (inasmuch as my own feelings about the same man seemed capable of abrupt reversals). And, not least, to ask about the two friends who were traveling with him on the ferry that night. Because in the intervening year, as I found myself thinking and talking about this part of the book, I was told by several people that one of the two young men who had ridden down from Vermont with the artist in the pickup—who more or less supported what he did on the *M. V. Islander* that evening, if not exactly egged it on—was himself the son of a powerful American figure. A figure not involved in the war as such, but prominent in public life. In fact, several people who are frequenters of Martha's Vineyard told me they were almost positive it was this man's son, and not the artist (whom I was careful not to name), who had tried to hurl McNamara off. Even though I knew that not to be the case, there suddenly seemed another level of resonance to the story: pained sons assaulting important men who in a figurative sense could be their own fathers—well, if not assaulting, at least hanging in the vicinity while an assault goes on.

Indeed, I once had occasion, in the interval between the first time I talked with the artist and the day I went back to talk to him again, to bring up the incident to Robert McNamara's own son. I was on Craig's walnut farm in California, and the two of us had talked of many things that afternoon. Shaking his head slowly, wanting and not wanting me to go on with it, Craig, who was then in his mid-thirties, a father, a husband, a sensitive but most of all a peaceable man, said: "Whew, it almost could have been any of us out there that night." Then he had said, not looking up, his voice going low in exactly the way I have heard his father's go low, "Was Dad pretty shaken up, I guess?" Craig had heard of the incident before, although only in vague terms. He had never tried discussing it with his father, nor had he ever tried finding out anything about it on his own. For one thing, there were so many other bad things that had happened in and to his family back then, and none of those ever really got out into the open either.

When I spoke to the artist this time, he had just returned to the Vineyard from a week in New York, where an exhibition of his work was about to open at a private dealer's gallery in SoHo. He had sold a large number of paintings and drawings over the summer, he said. One went for $5,000. He said he was far from rich, but he wasn't starving anymore, either.

We talked on the phone the evening before. I was still in Woods Hole. A very young female voice had answered. "Daddy, it's for you," the voice said.

We met at 9:30 a.m., an October Saturday. The straw-yellow grasses one sees everywhere on the island were slashed with purples and golds; the wild asters were in bloom. The father of five children—two belonging to him; three being his stepchildren—probably would have liked sleeping in. But here was somebody stirring it up again.

"Yes, our talk last year brought the thing back up to a certain level of consciousness," he said. "Maybe some of it even got into my work, I wouldn't really know. To tell you the truth, I wonder if I'll ever be free of the damn thing, in one way or another."

"Yes," I said quickly, "in the same way the man you tried to throw into Vineyard Sound will probably never be free of Vietnam, in one way or another, even though you might say there's this whole other part of his life that's valid, more than valid."

He laughed, granting a point. It wasn't a very pleasant laugh. "I'll bet it wasn't even two weeks ago that somebody, a lady, brought it up to me—right in the spot where you parked your car a few minutes ago. By the way, I saw him again this summer. I was sitting in my car, waiting on my wife, who was in the grocery or something, and here he comes, walking down the sidewalk in Vineyard Haven, right at me, the big power walk, in khakis and some sport-shirt deal, eating up the street like he always does, just full of himself. I thought, Hell, what do I do, hop out and shake hands: 'Hello, Bob. Remember me?' I guess what I'm trying to say is I don't need it. I don't need that person coming up to me the other day and mentioning it. I don't really need you coming around again to remind me. I don't need to see McNamara when I'm in Vineyard Haven with my wife. I don't want sympathy out of the thing and I don't want to be hated for it, and I don't wish to be anybody's fantasy—or surrogate hero, either. I would just like to drop it. But it keeps coming back. You see, what got to me in the first place is here's this guy crossing Vineyard Sound on a ferry one Friday night whose very posture is telling you, 'My history is fine, and I can be slumped over a bar like this with my good friend . . . and you'll just have to lump it.' Well, I got him outside, just the two of us, and suddenly his history wasn't so fine, was it? Look, I'm a painter, I work in fairly immediate contexts. I responded to something. As I told you last time, I could have tried pasting him in the face with an obscenity in the lunchroom. I think it had a little more impact to make it a shot to the water."

I changed the subject. "Who were your two friends with you on the boat? I've heard one of them is the son of ———. In fact, some people believe he's the one who tried to throw McNamara over."

The anger subsided. "One of them, Michael, is dead now. I don't want to go into it. It was Michael who told me how bad McNamara looked when he came back into the lunchroom. Ripped up, Michael said. I've tried many times to imagine exactly what that looked like. The other friend of mine you're asking about—"

He stopped and stared at me. "Well, if I'm not going to allow you to use my name, and I guess I'm still not, how would it be fair for me to give you his?"

"I guess it isn't fair," I said, unable to keep the disappointment from my voice. But it seemed a kind of confirmation all the same; also a small edification.

I asked if his wife knew when she married him. "She knew about it before she met me. And she knew I was the one."

He went across the room and stood in front of a drawing pinned to the wall. The drawing was done in bold dark strokes and seemed to be presenting two not very attractive male heads positioned very close together, one staring out at the world, the other turning sideways, as if whispering a message to its companion. There was something freakish about the drawing, but the two male heads had power, all right. "You take these two heads, very quick strokes, they begin and they end, just two heads I drew one day with a lithograph block. Now I don't know where in hell these two heads came from. I mean, maybe I saw this nose in an alley one night when I was turning a corner. Maybe I saw this eye over in Chilmark. Maybe I saw . . . what I'm trying to say is that if you have something inside you you're itching to express, one way or another it's probably going to come out."

I was halfway down the path that leads away from his studio when he yelled, "Hey, thanks for coming back."

This was 1986, second time I went back. And what can I say of the artist in the years since, as we have sporadically stayed in touch? That he stands before canvases and does his work? That he still wishes the thing would go away, but it won't? That he and his wife aren't together, but that he and his daughters are even closer? That in a ravenous nineties economy he has had to find supplemental ways to earn his daily bread? That he still locates moments of extreme creative tension in fairly immediate contexts? That anger can still climb up inside his throat when he doesn't expect it? (I'm thinking of his reaction to the publication of *In Retrospect,* but specifically of his reaction when I had called to warn him that producers from *PrimeTime Live* were frantically looking for him, hoping to get him on shrouded camera for their big McNamara–Diane Sawyer interview.) That he's sorry about what he did on the inclement night of September 29, 1972—but that he isn't? That he still thinks it's better not to have his name put in print, even though enough people know he's the one? That having lived more than half his life, he finds himself more desirous than ever of trying to fit the pieces to the frame, including this piece, less than a minute out of his fifty-odd years?

The answer to all the above is yes.

LAST THINGS: What biographer David McCullough once said in a film documentary of Lyndon Johnson could be said of Robert McNamara: He rose up out of the 1960s as one of the central characters in a story of moral importance that ended in ruin. I think of Robert McNamara as a kind of postwar technocratic hubristic fable. He was an extraordinarily impressive person, almost a new Adam, who abused his trust, and knows he did, and has spent the rest of his life paying for it. As critic Edmund Wilson once said of Ernest Hemingway, another tragically split man with a public mask that was nothing like the private self: "He had a high sense of honor, which he was always violating; and this evidently gave him a permanent bad conscience." *Et tu,* McNamara. This above all, to thine own self be true. He wasn't. It was his greatest lie, really, trying to bifurcate, compartmentalize, who he was. You could say he had no sense of man's irrational side, even though he could be highly irrational himself. He was motivated to help create rational utopias, or something close to that idea, and the world disappointed him: Why weren't they more like he was? What he lacked, or lost, was intuition. For all his brains he couldn't fathom his own heart. Perhaps what seems saddest about him in the long view is the stone monument of his pride. He was not without American virtues and ideals. But he was terribly ambitious and he was terribly proud and he became, sooner than later, terribly arrogant. That is, until he fell. And then he became arrogant again. You could say with only slight exaggeration he had all the math down and none of the meaning. After he told a congressional committee how many tanks the Bulgarians had, Eugene McCarthy is supposed to have remarked, "Anybody who knows the answer to that has to be a bad guy." As novelist Walker Percy once said in another context: He was the kind of fellow who got all A's and flunked life.

There was a genuine warmth and humanity about him, which the world seldom saw. He had impulses for generosity and goodness: After JFK's death, when Jackie Kennedy said she had no place to live, he blurted he'd buy her a house. He could be very kind: After he found out a close associate from the World Bank years named Bill Clark had terminal cancer, he diverted from a trip-in-progress and flew to London to have breakfast with him. He told Clark he had three things to say: 1) Don't let them cut you up. 2) Don't let them experiment with you. 3) For God's sake, don't let them deny you painkillers, and if they're addictive, so what, because it's perfectly all right to be addicted in heaven. That was one Robert McNamara, but there were the others, including the person who couldn't stop himself from playing loose with the truth when the situation asked. "The more you dig, the more you find that this man just can't tell the truth," Senator John McClellan of Arkansas once said. He said it to George Wilson of the Washington *Post,* who covered McNamara during his entire Pentagon tenure. Wilson, a reporter of the old school, and by that I mean dogged and uncowed, has told me plenty of stories over the years of how he personally experienced—and in some cases got victimized by—the canny McNamara deception. I think it's hard for fine reporters like Wilson to see that the McNamara they wrote about daily had deep emotions, that he wasn't Hollow Man, not the Tin Man looking for a heart, no, it was just that the war minister condescending to them at the lectern was afraid of those emotions, afraid of their seeming womanliness, which has everything to do with his parental psychic history.

In a sense there was mendacity in the bloodstream—the first place a gifted son learned to fudge truth was at his mother's knee. (It was also the first place he learned what a remarkable person he was.) In so many ways the child was the father of the man. Those well-meaning and long-dead parents were such opposites: the all-devouring Nelle against the deep-channeled Rob, and their firstborn never quite having a chance, not for inner peace, anyway. This would be one way of understanding the whole story. I confess to being enchanted with the mysteries of 1036 Annerly Road in Oakland, California, in the twenties and thirties, and wish I could have devoted more of this account to his parents' lives, lives that the son has always wished to seal off. It wasn't startling to discover that in *In Retrospect,* a book of nearly 400 pages (counting notes), the author wrote two sentences about his mother and father—and neglected to give their names. (He also made a passing reference in one caption.)

As I was getting ready to write this epilogue, to compress into a handful of pages all the fleeing after-years, my eleven-year-old son— who was seven months old when I started this book—showed me something from a juvenile novel he was reading. One of the characters in the story was saying, "Each lie he told them made the secret bigger, and that meant even more lies. He didn't know how to stop."

The cost of the Vietnam War has been estimated at about $200 billion. America lost 58,000 lives, but the Vietnamese number is nearly beyond reckoning. In figures released in the spring of 1995, Vietnam said that 1.1 million soldiers who fought for the north or for the Vietcong died between 1954 and 1975 in wars against France, the United States, and South Vietnam. Two million civilians died during the same period. Estimates of the ARVN's casualties range from 185,000 to 225,000 killed, though the real figure is surely higher. The number of wounded or missing, both north and south, Communist and non-Communist, adds up to another 1.5 million, roughly speaking. So: something beyond three million dead in a wartime population of about 40 million, and maybe another million and a half of wounded or MIA.

Records show that defoliating herbicides were used in Vietnam beginning on an experimental basis in August 1961. The U.S. employed defoliants for nine years, covering 20 percent of the south's jungles and 36 percent of its forests.

And by late 1967, when Robert McNamara was leaving, America had dropped 1.6 million tons of armament on the north and south. As journalist Don Oberdorfer wrote in his 1971 narrative, *Tet!:* "The Vietnam avalanche came to twelve tons for every square mile of territory in both North and South Vietnam, and about a hundred pounds of explosive for every man, woman, and child, many of whom did not weigh a hundred pounds in flesh, blood, and bone." And it didn't work. And we didn't know how to stop.

By late 1967, when McNamara was getting out, 15,979 Americans had been lost. A year later, on December 31, 1968, the figure was 30,568. The balloon went up fast. In his final chapter, in a boxed chart, the author of *In Retrospect* made note of this statistic, as if to suggest: In the seven years of my watch, 16,000; but within a year, a doubling of the dead, for which I cannot and will not be blamed, for I'd gone elsewhere. But maybe I'm guilty of reading in, for the author wrote nothing like that in the book. Instead he wrote this sentence, at the opening of his concluding chapter, which had to do with lessons: "My involvement with Vietnam ended the day after I left the East Room." Perhaps it would have been closer to the spiritual truth of his life had he said his involvement with Vietnam *began* the day after he left the East Room.

Began at 5:10 p.m. on February 29, 1968. Which is when Robert McNamara was recorded as walking out of the Pentagon.

THAT IT WOULD NEVER BE OVER might have struck in a meaningful way on September 12, 1968, when Ward Just, in the Washington *Post,* said that "it is somehow indecent" that the man who bestrode the enlargement of the war for seven years and was now ensconced at the World Bank could cobble together a collection of his speeches and statements, call it a book, and barely mention Southeast Asia and what he had done there. Ward was a great war correspondent for the newspaper. McNamara had been out six months. The slender work offered up was called *The Essence of Security,* and it dealt largely with such issues as NATO, Soviet-American relations, first-strike capability. Establishment hands like Dean Acheson thought it nifty, noble even. Not Just, who said it was Robert McNamara's "literary Bay of Pigs." He said the book attempt was arrogant, it was badly conceived, and it was.

The man lived his life. He was in a new arena, the spotlight not constantly on, and it must have been so gratifying. But three years after he was gone, *The Pentagon Papers* came out, and there he was, spasming in the country's consciousness and conscience. This headline atop an op-ed piece in the New York *Times:* "McNamara as Speer." The writer of the piece, French journalist Sanche de Gramont, compared Hitler's minister of armaments to Lyndon Johnson's secretary of defense. Such men were not callous, he said. Speer had expressed growing doubts about Hitler and the war, as McNamara had been plagued and beset. But as managers and pure technicians, as "classless bright young men," they'd kept on. In Southeast Asia, a war kept on.

That was summer 1971. It was the following fall, September 1972, that a disaffected young man tried pitching an icon off a double-ended boat on a narrow walkway in choppy Massachusetts waters. (Twenty-three years later, this moment would not be discussed in *In Retrospect,* though other attacks and personal atrocities would.)

Two months before the ferry incident, on August 29, 1972, on the opposite coast, some frightening documents had first come to public light. These documents, written in blue ballpoint on thin parchment-like paper, with wavy lines and schematic box diagrams, had been found in a Berkeley garage amid a cache of explosives. To the authorities who had come upon them, they suggested a plot (and here I'll take up the language of California court papers) "to assassinate former Secretary McNamara and/or members of his family or to kidnap him and/or members of his family." From the internal evidence, the documents seem to have been written in 1969, a year after he was out. They consisted of drawings of the McNamara resort home in Colorado. They consisted of thumbnail descriptions of the McNamara family. They consisted of instructions on how the house might be approached and then entered. ("Balcony: runs along entire southwest side—no entrance onto it from outside. Can be climbed onto from front side corner.") At length, individuals associated with the name Symbionese Liberation Army, a radical terrorist group infamous for its involvement in the Patty Hearst kidnapping case, got connected with the papers. But who wrote them, and how that person or persons got inside the McNamara home to make the maps and write the descriptions—it's a mystery still.

(A decade ago, in the course of several long interviews, someone who's been a close friend of the family for more than half a century told me that McNamara once said he believed the person who wrote the documents and drew the maps was someone whom Craig McNamara had brought into the house unawares. In the documents themselves, on page 1, under "Family," this can be found: "son: Craig—19 years—long black hair & beard—wears wire specs, resembles father. . . . Excellent skier, mountaineer. quite strong & alert. about 5'11" tall. . . . Friendly, very open." I once brought up the documents to Craig. He answered he had never known anything about them, or their origins—the only thing he knew was how frightening they were. I believe that.)

There were moments of reprieve. In November 1973, the man not constantly in American light anymore took a walking trip in the Himalaya Mountains, accompanied by his spouse and two other couples. He was fifty-seven now. Some of the party got to 18,600 feet— these were McNamara and Willard Goodwin, fittest of the bunch. Some of the party got so sick they couldn't get out of a sleeping bag—this principally was Marg, who wished to go on for her husband, despite her hammering headaches. Two Nepalese police officers, one with a gun, one with a baton, followed the hikers as a kind of security detail. Porters lugged camp gear, and a tiny Sherpa sang out "Tea's ready" as he went from tent to tent in the early-morning hours with basins of fresh wash water. Someone got a photograph of McNamara picking up objectionable refuse, using two sticks as his tongs. (He deposited the poop in the bushes.) Mary Joe Goodwin, Willard's wife, known for her literary bone, wrote up the 150-mile walk in a thin, funny book entitled *A Mountain Reprieve.* The president of the World Bank contributed an epilogue, quoting T. S. Eliot: "We shall not cease from exploring / And the end of all our exploring / Will be to arrive where we started / And know the place for the first time." There were no untoward incidents at the rarefied altitudes.

Spring 1979: A developer of third-world economies is almost sixty-three. At the University of Chicago to pick up the Albert Pick, Jr., award, he's protested and burned in effigy by about 1,000 students. No matter, he makes a fine speech about hardware and security. (In the weeks before, he has instructed his ghost, Jack Maddux, to monitor developments, but that there's no question he'll go to Chicago for the speech.) The address reprises and expands on themes going back to 1966 in Montreal: "A society can reach a point at which additional military expenditure no longer provides additional security." James Reston, in the New York *Times,* is in thrall, and so are the pundits at *Time.* But David Halberstam—whose *The Best and the Brightest* is by now the touchstone of all Vietnam literary rage in America—cannot abide this unthinking adulation of a man whom he regards as a war monster, and so writes a letter to the editor: "James Reston's own life has been of such a single piece—values believed in, values lived—that it is a considerable shame that he uses his considerable talents and moral influence in an attempt to rehabilitate Robert McNamara, one of the most disturbingly flawed civil servants of this era. . . . In truth, McNamara lied and deceived the Senate and the press and the public. . . . He consistently lied to the nation about the levels of increment of troops. . . . But his greatest crime, like that of his colleague McGeorge Bundy, was the crime of silence." Other letters, pro and con, are printed, a McNamara boomlet on the *Times* editorial page. He has a way of flexing back, reminding us of all our national and personal failures and regrets.

In 1981, which is also the year he left the bank, after thirteen years, his wife died. How would a reined-in man tell this sadness? Well, for one thing he might swear a lot. What follows is the way Robert McNamara described Marg McNamara's death to me, in 1984, three years after the fact, when I was in the process of interviewing him over the course of several months for the Washington *Post.* He had a cough that day. The linear face was brown and a tinge sallow. It was the second time I had sat in front of him, and I was nervous. Poised before him was a white pad with rules, and now and then he would reach over and scrawl down a word. I remember his glasses, and how he removed them to polish the lenses. The spectacles seemed so delicate, so flimsy. They'd go perfectly on a Jesuit prefect of discipline, I kept thinking. When I'd entered the room, he'd said politely, "Take a seat right there, please." He was sitting in half-light behind an immense desk. He had just returned from Europe—had left America on a Tuesday, meeting in The Hague all day Wednesday, London that evening, flew home Thursday. Now it was Friday, and I was hearing of a woman's last year on earth:

"We were going to ski at Aspen. It was Washington's birthday, 1980. She went on a Monday and I was to come out the following Wednesday. After she got out there she called and said, 'Bob, I don't think I can ski.' I didn't know she had already talked to her doctor here and he had told her to come home immediately. She said, 'No way, Bob is coming out.' Anyway, she came on home, and one year later she was dead. It wasn't diagnosed as cancer right off. Jesus Christ, they took the whole goddamn lining out of her lung and six weeks from the day they did it, she was climbing a mountain with me. Thirteen thousand feet. She died on February 3, 1981. Three weeks earlier the president gave her the Medal of Freedom. She was national head of Reading Is Fundamental, you know. She started that goddamn thing all by herself in ghetto schools back in '66, and it went out all over the country. We heard about the medal on a Friday. It was the seventeenth of January. I had already taken her out of the hospital, because the goddamn hospitals are just awful on terminal-cancer patients. I set up a kind of hospital room on the second floor of our home, got nurses to come in twenty-four hours a day. It was wonderful to have her home. But Jesus Christ, was she in pain. I think she was on 200 milligrams of Demerol a day. I forget if that's right, I used to know. Anyway I said, 'Marg, you can't go to the White House.' And she said, 'Oh yes I can and oh yes I am.' Well, goddamn, she did lovely. I had this seven-passenger Caddy limousine and we got her into that thing, just rolled the damn wheelchair right up, and all of us piled in and went down there to Mr. Carter's White House. Of course, she looked like death's own self. She used to hallucinate from the medicine, and on the way down she said, 'Bob, what is that camel doing out there?' I said, 'Oh, honey, he's just out there.' Isn't that something? A goddamn camel."

That appeared in the eventual McNamara series in the Washington *Post.* Some while after the series, two members of the McNamara family—a son and a sister-in-law—let me know separately that *he'd* been the one trying to keep his wife *in* the hospital. He'd fought against bringing her home to die.

The one person in his life Robert McNamara seems to have loved without condition was Margaret McKinstry Craig McNamara. Maybe she alone ever understood him—not Nelle, not his children. Marg. She was sixty-five at her death. At the memorial service, a mourner got up and said, "Almost twenty years ago when I introduced Marg to my mother, my mother said: She must be very soft and loving to come home to." Mary Joe Goodwin, who knew her for four decades, told me: "They can't have sat around and discussed plasma physics. Evidently he didn't need or want that." Jim Wright, who knew her from the mid-forties onward, through the Ford Motor period and after, told me he could remember visiting Bob and Margy at their home in Washington after the war had overrun the family, and watching the ulcered wife getting up and gimping across the room to get some milk to go with her Scotch highball. Wright saw it and wondered, What's the point? McNamara's brother-in-law, Arthur Slaymaker, a very decent and nongossipy sort, once told me that toward the end of Marg's life the husband who so evidently adored her would take her out to play tennis and run her all over the court in the heat, then come back in and announce: "Wow, we just had a good game of tennis, and guess what, I beat her." It was just the astounding blindness to human things, showing itself even here.

Bank employees saw him at work on the day his wife died. He sent out telegrams to friends. Closed himself in his office and grieved. What was he going to do—lie in drink, quote from Irish poets? He went to the office. It was like keeping the squash date on the day John McNaughton died. It was like going on with the budget review at the Pentagon on November 22, 1963, after getting first word by phone of the rifle crack in Dallas. (From page 90 of *In Retrospect:* "Strange as it sounds, we did not disperse: we were in such shock that we simply did not know what to do. So, as best we could, we resumed our deliberations." Only when informed by the president's brother in a second call that the president was dead did the group adjourn in tears.)

At Marg McNamara's service at the Cathedral Church of Saint Peter and Saint Paul in Washington, on February 6, 1981, he sat numbed. Old friends from California and Michigan and other places came, a tribute not just to her. Afterward he and his children rented a small plane and flew to the Vineyard and walked the bare February sands. Craig McNamara made a brass urn and filled it with part of his mom's ashes, and later that summer McNamara, his second daughter, and Craig hiked up Snowmass Creek to Buckskin Pass. They spread her ashes at a spot where there's a lovely meadow with a creek flowing through and a blanket of wildflowers.

Robert McNamara dedicated *In Retrospect* to his wife: "In Memory of Marg, one of God's loveliest creatures. . . ." He wrote her into the book a good deal, at least compared with his children, about whom he made scattered mention. In 1986 and 1989 he also dedicated books to Marg. (The 1986 dedication of a nuclear essay, *Blundering into Disaster,* was shared by his children.) Perplexedly, a widower keeps dedicating books to a deceased wife, as he continues to hold his three children, much alive, at a certain remove. Anyone who knows the family, who's willing to speak the truth, will say this. In the period when I knew him well, McNamara's son said it to me, not bitterly so much as perplexedly.

In May 1982, Robert McNamara's only son got married in a less-is-more, do-it-yourself approach up at the walnut farm. Craig's father attended but decided to leave not long after the ceremony, as people were dancing and spreading themselves out onto the lawn, under the trees.

IT WAS AS IF the man were being pursued by furies; as if he'd been sentenced to ricochet continents; as if the idea of repose were unspeakably terrifying. He once went to see the World War II flick *A Bridge Too Far*—and bolted in the middle. It was the military blunders, he told his assistant at the bank, Bill Clark. Couldn't bear to be there in the dark watching them.

He once went to Puerto Rico, for a day. Once he went to Europe, on an overnight. Once (this was in 1986) he called up his college classmate Wally Haas and described what he intended to do that weekend: fly from Brazil to Los Angeles, attend a board meeting of the Bank of America (he and Haas were both board members), get back on the plane and fly right down to Rio again so he could finish up whatever it was he'd been doing down there in the first place. (Something on behalf of the Ford Foundation.) "Yeah, Wally, I mean, I must be crazy, I ought to have my head examined" is the way he put it, describing the forty-eight-hour plan, his laugh coughing through the phone wire. Those who loved him wished to see this condition sympathetically: It was the loss of Marg making him behave this way. To use his own phrase, he was filling up holes.

In 1983 his old friend from autoland, Jim Wright, was getting his hip replaced at George Washington University Hospital in Washington—and who comes in decked out in a jogging suit but Robert McNamara? Wright was gratified but found himself saying, "Bob, what in hell are you doing with all this running around?" McNamara said he didn't wish to be idle in his retirement.

How deeply it was bothering him in these years, "it" of course being the subject of Vietnam, no one seemed to know. Sometimes he could flatfloot you with his willingness to talk of it, or around it. Suddenly it was in the room, it was hydra-headed and heinous, the country's grievous error, his own. Old friends and associates, and not least his family, recognized that it was generally best to stay wide of it. "My conscience doesn't bother me at all!" he said one day at a Washington restaurant to Eric Sevareid of CBS News, shoving it from him like rotten food. That about ended lunch. Mostly he kept moving. The Portuguese have an expression: In the house of someone who's been hanged, one is not inclined to speak of rope.

Once he started right in talking about it. There he was in the exotic pages of Andy Warhol's *Interview* magazine. Yes. Robert McNamara and Vietnam amid spreads on Olivia Newton-John and Chevy Chase, amid double-truck ads for Calvin Klein underwear. This was November 1983. His good friend Ina Ginsburg got him to do it. She called him up and said she'd love to do a Q&A for Andy's magazine. No, no, he said, he didn't think so, but by the way, what the hell was *Interview*? She told him: sort of *People* magazine for the enlightened, very serious in its own way. She told him she did correspondency out of Washington for Andy. Well, I'd better not, Ina, he said. But in the end the conflicted man did it, anyway.

It was a very adroitly conducted interview, and at the top of the piece the magazine gave this little nod to vanity: "McNamara is equally energetic in his personal life. He is a most sought after man, having been widowed a little over a year ago. He now goes out with several women, but has a regular traveling companion when he goes abroad." Who was that?

There were Q&A's about nuclear issues and his development interests and so forth. He had declined a drink; they were having tea. The tape recorder was sitting on the coffee table between them. And now, halfway in, the questioner having slid it smoothly to the nightmare, the bolted box, this:

> IG: Were you under tremendous stress?
> RSM: Oh, surely. Of course. It was obvious early on that there was no military solution to the problem.
> IG: That was obvious early on?
> RSM: Surely. Early on. It was obvious as early as, oh, I'd say, mid-'65. Actually, I think it was obvious in—if not obvious, then many of us believed it was unlikely there was a military solution to it—as early as '63. And certainly by mid-'65 it was a more commonly held view. Therefore, the frustration of trying to move to a political track . . .
> IG: If it was so clear that there was no military solution, why did President Johnson continue to keep on adding and adding?

And then it's as if a man has come bolt upright out of his confessional dream.

> RSM: I don't want to discuss it. I have no comment.
> IG: I understand, but you were secretary of defense. You were in a position to tell him that it wouldn't work.
> RSM: I don't want to get into it. I've said all I'm going to say on Vietnam.

That same month and same year, November 1983, sixty-seven-year-old Robert McNamara appeared on a panel following an ABC television movie called *The Day After.* It was a drama about a town in Kansas after a nuclear attack. Of all the panelists—Henry Kissinger, Carl Sagan, Elie Wiesel—the man out of Vietnam memory seemed to me the most human and humble. I sat down and wrote him a letter, asking if I might interview him for the Washington *Post.*

The three pieces that appeared six months later, in May 1984, had him talking a little about Vietnam. In our first session the word had not even fluttered into the room. Like Banquo's ghost on Macbeth's stage, it had seemed to hover just beyond the automatic click of the inner-office door. Once he seemed as if he was going to say it, came right up to the lip of the word, then skittered off. This was the sentence: "It makes me goddamn furious when people say I went over to the World Bank to do penance for . . . Defense." There'd been only a half-beat delay. He was clicking a ballpoint on his desktop.

Those three *Post* pieces in the spring of '84 also put into print something gossipy that inner Washington had been talking of for almost two years: his curious romantic relationship, conducted more or less openly—or at least not in secret—with Joan Braden: career woman, hostess, confidante of power lovers, not to mention mother of eight and wife of syndicated columnist Tom Braden. When I'd first asked, at the end of a long second interview, about this relationship, the subject of the series turned toward the window, laughed, and said: "Oh, that. Well, I'm going to tell you two things. Number one: You write whatever you want to, whatever you have to. Just make damn sure you've got it right and that it's all factual. Number two: But obviously from my point of view, the less you say, the better." But it wasn't said threateningly.

A day or so after I had first brought it up, we spoke by phone. He said he wanted to illustrate what an open and understanding relationship the Braden thing was. He said he had gone out with her right after coming home from Europe the other day. Joanie, as she is sometimes known by her family and, sometimes, by the man who was going out with her, was about to leave for Spain with her husband. But she and McNamara wanted to be with each other that night. He took her to dinner and afterward they went by the Bradens' big yellow house in Chevy Chase. "Come on in," she said. "Tom's here and he'd like to see you. Susan's here, too." McNamara told me that Susan, one of the Braden daughters, went to Oxford and had a great interest in Central America. She loved going back and forth on intellectual matters with "Bobby Mac," as he was sometimes called by some of the kids in the family.

He related this by way of illustration and then said: "Look, I know the whole goddamn town's full of rumors, but the truth of the matter is there's only three people on earth who know what the hell is going on, and that's me, Joan, and Tom Braden. You talk to Tom. You talk to Joan. It's a very peculiar thing, I know. Look, she has eight children and she loves her husband very much, and she's not about to leave him for me or any other man, and beyond that I wouldn't marry her anyway, because I'm not a home wrecker. She occasionally travels with me, you know. We never travel as Mr. and Mrs. McNamara. We travel as Robert McNamara and Joan Braden. But she's a lovely girl. Beyond that, I enjoy her company." (A short time later, in a call to Braden, when I asked if the relationship was romantic, she said: "Yes, I will not say that it isn't." I reached her while she was in Europe with her husband, who was in the next room, drawing a bath.)

In the third of the three 1984 *Post* pieces, I quoted Robert McNamara's son, though not on Joan Braden. I had reached Craig one California noontime just before the pieces were due to run. He had just come in from the fields, and I pictured a man sitting at a wooden table with his flannel sleeves rolled. On the phone his voice sounded nothing like his dad's. It was soft, sibilant. I told him his father had given me the number the day before. I knew a little about Craig already—that he had protested the war at Stanford in the late sixties and early seventies and had been involved in some window-smashing and running in the streets; that he'd dropped out of college and had left the country and ridden a motorcycle 10,000 miles into Chile and later worked on a cooperative dairy farm on Easter Island; that he had gone to Mexico and worked in the sugar fields of Padre Ivan Illich; and that he was happily married to a woman named Julie and together they worked a 250-acre walnut operation set into the rim of the Coast Range, with his father as the co-owner and major backer of the enterprise. I didn't know at the time that Craig McNamara, one of the more sensitive and vulnerable people I've encountered in my journalistic life, had struggled for much of his adolescence with dyslexia and terrible ulcers.

"Nobody can get anywhere on Vietnam with my father, including me," Craig said in that first telephone conversation. "It's just not in his scope to communicate his deepest thoughts and feelings to me. I keep hoping for a change, a change in both of us. I tend to believe the truth should be out. I think he can stand the truth. He must want that, he must want everything, finally, to rinse and wash. I know I do. I don't want to hurt him, and I know that things hurt him, but I want the truth out, for all of us. I mean, I felt the contradictions of the Vietnam War. It was my father's war and I was his son. Our generation seeks that therapeutic response, my father's couldn't. I think we've always maintained a bottom line that I used to think every marriage had. We've always had a basic love and respect for one another, even when it was at its worst between us. I'm sure, for instance, it deeply hurt my mother and father when they came up to my room and saw me reading a copy of *The Best and the Brightest.* Or saw my American flag turned upside down on my wall. It's terribly hard sometimes to be his son. There is the deepest river of love between us, and it goes dry over Vietnam."

That was put in print. As it turned out, I didn't meet Craig for another full year, until his father had stopped speaking to me and I was well involved in this book. I remember what I felt the first time I saw the farm. Something so neat and soothing, off the grind of the interstate, set back in a little valley of California agriculture. There was a green yard and a white-frame house. Sprinklers were sheeting water at trees. Things seemed purposeful, lived-in, worked-on, sun-blessed. Inside were fine old wood pieces Craig and his wife had collected, and also flatware California pottery that had been fired in earthy colors. That first visit was in the late summer of 1985, and three months later I was back, and once again many stories were confided. Even if I had disliked the son—and I liked him a lot—I would still have been happy to go back. We would take long walks, I would take many notes. We would sit in his kitchen; once we went into town for lunch in the pickup. He talked, I wrote. Over the next three years we corresponded when we could. We would call each other on the phone, yak. He sent my son a red toy Ford tractor for Christmas. So far as I knew, Craig's father never tried to stop any of this, and again it was puzzling to me. I would return from the farm and say to my wife and friends that the best advertisement Robert McNamara could possibly have for himself was his third child, the one who hadn't scored straight A's, the one with the McNamarian looks but the mother's grace. So long as I could keep talking to the son, I knew I would be able to feel human things about the father.

The night following my second visit to the farm, in November 1985, I was lying on my bed in a cheap motel in San Francisco when I bolted up: There was Robert McNamara on Ted Koppel's *Nightline.* Some right-wing congressman was tearing into him. In truth, it was the attacker who seemed foolish. He said, "Now, I'd like to ask Mr. McNamara, the man who's come out of shameful and deserved obscurity, the man who gave us strategic hamlets, escalated response, gradualism—" which was when Koppel broke in. "Congressman Dornan, would you get to your—" which was when the right-winger interrupted: "—MIG sanctuaries, body counts, and free-fire zones—" which was when the host said: "Congressman Dornan, would you please be good enough to get to your question and let's limit the personal attacks!" It went right on: "All right. The man who gave us 58,022 dead in Vietnam, tells—"

The camera came close. You could see an Adam's apple bulging. Still, he didn't say anything. He sat there like those wretches in children's stories who produce a frog or a snake every time they try to open their mouths. There was a commercial break. Afterward the attacker tried again. Koppel cut him off. In moments like that, seeing him demolished, I could understand the running—indeed, have compassion for it. On a farm in Winters, California, bees might be hovering at flowers blue as flatware pottery. But Robert McNamara wouldn't be able to hear them. He would be riding an airplane across an ocean in the middle of the night.

I saw or talked on the phone or wrote to Robert McNamara's son in 1985, 1986, and 1987. Then there was a hiatus. In 1993 I called him. We hadn't been in close touch in a while, though we sent notes at holidays. I told him I had changed my thinking on the project and now I wanted to write about him as well as his father. I wished to make him a key figure in his own right. I said I would honor anything he had ever told me that was in confidence, but that the rest of it I wanted and intended to use, because we both knew that I had come to his farm first and last as a reporter, even if in the process I had ended up a friend. Two months passed and then, following two letters I had sent that didn't get answered, this note appeared in my mailbox, written on the familiar yellow stationery with "Sierra Orchards" at the top; written in the hand that I instantly recognized, a hand that for some reason always wants to make the first-person pronoun a lower-case "i."

Craig said: "In your letter dated 6.28.93 you state that you wish to refer to talks we had in 1985, 1986 and 1987. As you will recall neither you nor i recorded those conversations electronically or manually. Therefore i am not willing to give you permission to quote from them." He added that while he was "disinclined" to be interviewed further, he would consider answering written questions of a specific nature.

Craig McNamara and I have yet to bridge the space caused by that stilted and inaccurate note—though I keep hoping for a change.

But I am trying to tell a man's after-years more or less chronologically: Following the 1984 three-part McNamara series in the Washington *Post,* Craig's father and I continued to talk, fitfully, for about another six months (most of the conversations were on the phone, but once I sat fitfully in front of him), before lapsing into a circuitous half-light of communication, and then into almost no communication at all, except through his secretary. Almost all these after-talks coalesced around one thing: his involvement in the upcoming Westmoreland/ CBS libel trial, which, one way or another, he had managed to get himself locked into, first through a voluntary affidavit, then through an enforced deposition.

One week after the *Post* series, on May 16, 1984, I was seated in his office. He had ample dislike of the pieces, and I can remember being apprehensive on the five-block walk over to his office. He had just gotten in from Europe at 10:30 the night before. He turned his Harvard chair sideways. What he was focused on was the contentious pretrial maneuvering, and a subpoenaed deposition he had given, which the New York *Times* had gotten hold of and just written about, not flatteringly.

"I just feel bruised and battered," he said, but abruptly his tone changed. "Everybody's going to lose in this goddamn thing. The country, the media, Westmoreland. They kept asking me in their damn deposition if I was thinking what Rusk was thinking about the war. Hell, I don't know what Rusk was really thinking about the war, any more than he knew what I was really thinking. On the evening after the first day of the deposition, I went home and looked at some very private papers of mine to the president, which no one has ever seen, by the way, and reread them just to make damn sure what the hell I *had* told Johnson."

He made no offer to say what was in those papers. Instead he said, "Now to some people, and I know it, my public silence about Vietnam implies guilt. Maybe you think that. But let me tell you something: It isn't guilt at all. My reasons for not speaking out have as much to do with what's good for our country as much as with anything else. Yes, yes, I know that sounds Boy-Scoutish. But I think these kinds of public disputes are bad for our people. I really do. Now was I 'deceiving' the American people? Well, that's a very interesting question, but first you'd have to define for me what you mean by deception. I've said it a thousand times, we were trying to win the war in the field and achieve at the same time our diplomatic objective. One track was in the field, and the other track was through political channels. Is that deception? Is that being a liar? How would you define the word?"

He was leaning in very close, and before I could try to answer, he was onto something else. "It's just like that other word. That I'm 'unwise.' That's Halberstam's word. You take Lyndon Johnson. Was he unwise? He had a hell of a lot of weaknesses, God knows he did. He wasn't a student of history, he wasn't what you'd call a well-educated man, but let me tell you something: He knew people. It was absolutely intuitive with him. It was almost frightening, in fact. Now you take Dean Rusk—fine man, moral man, humble man. Was he unwise? You see, a wise man can make mistakes, that's exactly my point. You take those people in there now. Are they unwise? George Shultz—is he unwise? And by the way, none of these people I'm talking about 'led' us into Vietnam. The nation took itself into Vietnam." He tagged on, "Of course maybe you'd argue my definition of unwise." But of course he hadn't given one.

I spoke to him again that summer; the trial still hadn't started. When he'd first picked up the receiver (the secretary put me through), I asked, ritually, if I might come over to his office to speak to him in person. No, no, he was just leaving for New York, then on to Europe, back Thursday, board meeting at the Washington *Post* on Friday. "But we can chat now if you like for a few minutes," he said, pleasantly enough. But the bitterness quickly rose. "Every time I talk to the press, I put my foot in my mouth. I'm sick of it. I'm just too goddamn controversial." Still, he didn't hang up, didn't indicate that he wanted me to get off. Something almost wistful seemed to be entering his voice. "I just want you to know: I'd probably do everything all over again, you know, leave Michigan, give up the presidency of Ford Motor Company at half a million or whatever the hell it was to come down here and work for John F. Kennedy for $25,000 or whatever the hell it was. My family gained, I gained. Hell, yes, there were costs, unbelievable costs. But I'd do it all over again, too." The receiver was moving off from his ear. "Well, good luck to you," he said, as if he were leaving for Mars.

Summer of '84 went into fall. The trial began. Actually, the so-called "libel trial of the century"—a lawsuit over troop numbers and "order of battle" that no sane person could possibly understand—soon turned out to be just one more metaphor for the bottomless tragedy and disgrace it was supposed to have evoked. I attended whole long days, sitting glumly in the benches, waiting for some word of McNamara. Was he going to show? Every time a witness or an attorney or the presiding judge uttered "MACV," it seemed a sort of summons. I'd practically start from my seat: *Mac-Vee. McNamara.*

And then there he was one cold December morning. He came up the steps in an old trench coat, swinging a small brown overnight bag. His dark suit was cut tight and his white shirt was clean and pressed.

Two times in three weeks—or maybe it was three times in two weeks—
he had been across the Atlantic for meetings and conferences. He kept
moving past a battery of microphones and cameras, smiling broadly.
But in the cameras' unreal light the smile came off hard, almost garish.
I flashed on a poem by Thomas Merton: a blind man dazzled by fireflies
and his own nerve.

Six times in nearly six minutes he was asked in different ways by
his cross-examiner if he had believed one thing in his heart about Vietnam but had tried to pretend another to his country, and six times in
different ways the witness said: No, he had not. You could almost hear
a cock crow.

"I did not believe I expressed a different judgment to Congress than
the one I expressed to the president," he said.

"And is the same thing true with respect to your statements to the
public?" he was asked.

"I believe so," he answered. But in the huge room the words seemed
thin as the snapping of old bones.

They held him all day. Upstairs, during a recess, the cafeteria
became a free-fire zone on his psyche. The trial finally had passion. At
the table where I sat, half a dozen people—press and spectators alike—
were concentrating heavy fire on the bleached bones of the McNamara
reputation. "But at least he had the guts to show up here today, didn't
he?" I said to no one in particular, startled to hear myself saying it,
drawing queer looks.

Two days later, home, there was great weariness in his voice, but
great relief too. It was six on a Saturday evening, and a retired man was
hard at work at his office downtown. He picked up on the first ring, and
I fumbled for something to say, feeling funny, feeling invasive—though
not enough to hang up. I didn't know it, but this was to be the last time
in a long time I would have any direct contact with him. Our relationship was about to become a nonrelationship. Over the next several
years, I was to publish other McNamara articles in the Washington *Post,*
each a little more critical than the last. (I was growing far less naïve
about the lying, as declassified documents piled up in front of me.) I
didn't know it, but a kind of pattern was going to develop: I would
write and request interview time, suspecting the answer already, and
he would respond with one or two sentences, informing me that after
deliberation he had determined it would not be "productive" for us to
meet. He wrote such a reply on November 6, 1986, for instance, follow-

ing two impassioned letters I had written in the space of three weeks. Sometimes his reply wouldn't come typed by his secretary on the engraved stationery—he'd just return my own letter with a penciled note in the upper-right-hand corner: "To Mr. Hendrickson. I don't believe I can help you." He'd initial his name. I pictured him tossing the thing in the out-box.

But this was in our future. Two days after his December 6, 1984, Westmoreland trial appearance, in our last real conversation, I said on the phone to Robert McNamara: "I just wanted to say I felt funny for not attempting to come up to you at the trial and at least say hello." "Gee," he said, sounding guileless, "I didn't even realize you were there."

We chatted, to use the word he likes. Toward the end he said, "You see, the American public tends to believe Vietnam is a case of deception. The real history of Vietnam hasn't been written yet. Nobody's gotten it right. The historians and scholars have to do more work, and when that's finished, sure, I'll consider sitting down and talking to some people about it. Deception isn't the Vietnam problem at all. You see, the American people are not going to elect deceivers, and a president of the United States is not going to surround himself with liars. It just doesn't happen in the normal run of things. Deception isn't the problem. It happens to be a different problem entirely, one much more likely to occur, by the way, than deception." An old pattern in our fragmented talks seemed intact: He had informed me of what something is not instead of what it is.

AND HE RAN. It was nothing for him to land at Kennedy in New York, having just come back from Bangkok or perhaps a nuclear conference in Norway ("tremendous movement on that issue"), transfer airports, and go straight to the coast. Out there he might call his son from a pay booth at San Francisco International, starting right in: *Look, Craig, I've just landed, I'm grabbing a rental, I'll be up in two hours if that's okay, now look I don't want you or Julie going to any trouble, because I'm not staying over.* At the farm you could imagine him sitting on the sofa in the Sunday-afternoon light while the sprinklers wetted down the trees in the neat rows beyond the house. Then, a few hours later, against the pleadings of his son and daughter-in-law, you could imagine him back in the same rental car, back on the interstate, fuming as he finds himself stalled in the weekend traffic returning to the city. He might be staying that night in a monkish little room at the Pacific

Union Club on Nob Hill. Would sleep be a small death? Would he have a sudden desire to spend the rest of his life in a dark room with his face turned to the wall? It was not possible to know. For he was a man with the strangest moat around him.

In the fury of the moment he would go into a bookstore in a distant place and look up his name in the index of a new work on the war. In the fury of the moment he would agree to do a TV show. Once, he went on *Larry King Live*. This was 1986. He had just written a slim book about the nuclear age, and it was getting some good reviews, and deserved them—if you could blot out all the rest. King: "Our first guest tonight is the distinguished former secretary of defense and former head of the World Bank, Robert McNamara." Was he telling himself, *Bet it won't even come up*? He and the host chatted on his life in the auto business; they discussed how one must conduct himself as a public servant. "Always be honest," the host said. "Always be honest," echoed the guest. "And not always say everything," King said. "Well, no. I think at times it's perfectly permissible to withhold information, so long as one doesn't lie," the guest answered, finishing with: "But one should never mislead." It went on. King: "Something I must ask you. The other day I was at the Vietnam Veterans Memorial. And anybody in that administration then has to think about it. But we have subsequently learned that, of all the people in there, you were maybe the most dovish. Or certainly you had more questions to ask about it. Why didn't you quit?" The guest seemed to be going pale in living color. "Well, I had questions," he said thinly. "But when one is asked by a president to serve, and when one can continue to voice his concern privately, and when the president wishes to consider that, and weighed in a balance with other things, I think one has an obligation to continue. And I did." Eventually came the call-ins. A lot were flattering, bordering on obsequious. Host: "Camarillo, California, hello." A male voice: "Mr. McNamara, I'd like to know: If you're so concerned about the responsibility of public officials, why didn't you have the guts to speak up about the Vietnam War when you were secretary of defense? You led so many people to their deaths. Why didn't you have the guts to speak up, sir?" Even King seemed momentarily jolted. Later, he asked again, "Did you ever think of quitting?" The guard down, the mask off, the truth double-backing on itself: "Well, I could, uh, the answer is . . . yes."

The years passed. I did other things. I tracked him as I could. I'd hear stories he was going to write his own book. I discounted them.

Once in a while I would see him on the street, coming at breakneck, cutting crosswise through traffic, and it was always a bit unnerving, disconcerting. Damn, there he is, ghost of Washington, my own.

People would report having seen him eating his dinner alone in an Aspen cafeteria during a holiday.

In 1993 Deborah Shapley came out with her much-delayed McNamara biography, *Promise and Power,* and soon a scholarly reviewer in *The New York Times Book Review* was discoursing on how ". . . Mr. McNamara may simply be a liar; that he habitually told those he most wanted to impress what he thought they most wanted to hear. Having thereby satisfied his bosses at Ford, or the presidents for whom he worked, or the scholars who will ultimately determine his historical reputation, he then went on, [Shapley] suggests, to believe his own falsehoods, passionately and with utter conviction." Just a theory, among the possibles.

And then, fall 1993, the news he would do his own book. Within a year and a half the soul of an old machine had the damn thing out. "It isn't often you get to live long enough to acknowledge your mistakes," he told friends. He read his galleys, he skied to the tops of mountains, he prepared for the flooding light.

In Retrospect appeared during Easter Week 1995, when he was almost seventy-nine, when the dogwoods and redbuds and crab apple trees of Arlington National Cemetery seemed to be bleeding half the colors of the rainbow: roses into fuchsias into reds into deep, deep purples. That was one thought I had in the din that followed—so much seasonal birth in the presence of so many stirred feelings about death.

The memoir, billed as a mea culpa, inspired such instant rage in America, and really in the world, that it was hard not to think that some part of him wished it exactly that way—though surely the more conscious part of him had to be hoping, no, dying, for forgiveness. Still, something about the way he drew such lightning suggested a compelling half-conscious need. "This is the book I planned never to write," he said in the first sentence. There were some other good sentences: "I have heard it said about the difference between results and consequences that results are what we expect, consequences are what we get." And: "The beginnings of all things are small. . . ."

If anything, what *In Retrospect* proved, probably beyond any publisher's cash-register dreams, was that Vietnam hadn't gone away, it was only hiding, seething under the surface. As someone said, the Vietnam War was like malaria—awaiting a new moment. *In Retrospect* was the pin on the new grenade.

For the first moment or two of release, there was the sense that he might be forgiven. "VIETNAM: 'WE WERE WRONG.' EXCLUSIVE EXCERPTS FROM McNAMARA'S NEW BOOK," sang *Newsweek* on the cover, promoting its expensive buy. It was the stunning admission of it: *I was wrong.* What figure in government, past or present, had ever done this thing? And yet almost immediately the wheel turned. It was as if a body were rejecting its attempted transplant. A friend of mine said succinctly, "The sin is too large."

On the second day of publication, a veteran E-mailed to *USA Today:* "McNamara ranks with Hitler and Stalin as a perpetrator of crimes against humanity." On the third day, the lead editorial in the New York *Times* called him morally dead, spiritually bankrupt. To the *Times,* "Mr. McNamara must not escape the lasting moral condemnation of his countrymen. . . . His regret cannot be huge enough to balance the books for our dead soldiers. The ghosts of those unlived lives circle close around Mr. McNamara. Surely he must in every quiet and prosperous moment hear the ceaseless whispers of those poor boys in the infantry, dying in the tall grass, platoon by platoon, for no purpose. What he took from them cannot be repaid by prime-time apology and stale tears, three decades late." That editorial became a focus of much of the next month's flood-tide of ink and air talk about the war. Several weeks later, on book tour, when asked about the editorial by a reporter for my own newspaper, McNamara said, "Unbelievable." He shook his head briefly. He added, "That part I can live with. History is going to render judgment on that editorial." He'd wiped it from him.

On the fifth day of publication—Good Friday in America—an ex-Army nurse said on National Public Radio that she felt as though her husband had walked into the house to tell her he was having an affair, then described his affair, then told her he had a better idea: He'd write a book about it and make some jack. Thirty Good Fridays before, on April 16, 1965, *Life* magazine had hit newsstands in America, and in it were fourteen pages of photographs of a bony Marine and his helo mates and also a picture of a squalid box in a squalid line shed with "Valuables" stenciled on it. The president of the United States, with Lady Bird and Marg McNamara in the back, was squiring the sec/def around the ranch in his big white Caddy convertible. LBJ's man was about to wing to Hawaii, to up the troop ante and tell untruths about it.

He cried while sitting with Diane Sawyer. He said he never consciously deceived and that, yes, his children suffered horribly, but the better for it, the better for it. He seemed to be entering and exiting his mechanical robotic side within the same sentence.

An artist drew him with lizards and crocodiles slithering from his eyes. A reader wrote to *Time:* "Shame on McNamara for trying to assuage his guilty conscience by making us share his pain. He should have been man enough to carry his guilt in silence." A cartoonist for the Baltimore *Sun* had him madly scrubbing his blood-drenched hands with "Remorse—the soap for REALLY SORRY PEOPLE." On the letters page of the Washington *Post,* Bui Diem—an old dapper ex-ambassador living in Rockville, Maryland—said: "Robert McNamara's book is about Vietnam, yet after going twice through its 390 pages, I could not find a single instance in which he expressed any feeling for the Vietnamese people or their suffering."

He was on talk shows that got aired at two in the morning. "Just buy and read the book," he said.

If you did that, as I eventually did, *In Retrospect* began to seem considerably less than the "brutally honest" work it had been billed as being. Began to seem, as *The New Republic* said, "closer to a modified limited hang-out" confession. Began to seem sort of faux—an apology for the wrong things, geopolitical things, strategic things. It was as if a man had said to himself back there in his writing room, okay, I'll apologize to you on the first page—then spend the rest of the book refuting it. While I'm at it I'll yoke everybody else in for the blame. The closer you looked at the book, the more it seemed he was telling you all he did right.

The publicity tour had its defining moment on the night of April 25, 1995. He was at Harvard. A combat veteran and Boston area resident named John Hurley had read in the paper that McNamara would be appearing at the university. He showed up early, stood in line, found a place in the second balcony. Toward the end of the evening, when McNamara had gotten away with too much, Hurley rose to say that the book and his presence were "an obscenity." The veteran, who is a lawyer and a businessman, started in a calm voice, lost control. "My friend, my commander, Bert Bunting, died in Vietnam. McNally never saw Wyoming. Alan Perrault never saw Needham, Massachusetts, again. Sonny Davis didn't come home. They were torn to shreds, they were ripped apart. You ripped the soul out of the family of 58,191 families in this country, sir. And you remained silent. You said nothing. You let thirty years pass."

"So now your question," broke in the moderator.

"My question is, sir, why did Bert Bunting die when you knew the war was a mistake? Why did McNally die? Why did Kirkendall die, sir? Why did they sir, sir? Why did you remain silent . . . ?"

"You're going to have to read the book to get the answer. There's not time—"

"—Sir! Sir!"

McNamara: "Wait a minute. Shut up!" (On the audiotape at this point, you hear a woman in the audience gasping.)

Several minutes later a middle-aged woman came to the microphone. "Mr. McNamara, you don't know who I am." Her name was Maureen Dunn, and soon the details spilled out: Her husband, a Navy flier in Vietnam, was shot down over China in February 1968. Joe Dunn's ditched plane kept giving off distress signals. LBJ and his advisers gathered to discuss.

Joe Dunn's wife, on the other side of time, but not bereavement, had a document, standing at a mike at Harvard. "And you people sat there in that room for forty-five minutes, never addressing his name. He was always 'The China Incident.' He was twenty-five years old. So, you never had a face to see, or to know that he had a twenty-five-year-old wife and a baby, a one-year-old baby."

She wept. "This is very emotional for me. I didn't think I would be. But I'm that guy's wife. And you said . . . 'No rescue attempt should be made. Don't go after him. It's not worth it.' And all these years, Mr. McNamara, I've wanted someone from those ten people who were at that meeting to say to me, 'I am sorry.' And I'd like you to say that in front of all these people to me, 'I am sorry.' Please. I just want you to say, 'I am sorry.' "

"I have no recollection of the meeting and I can't—"

"It's right here."

"I understand what you have. But I haven't seen it and I'd like to see it. But let me just say this. If I said it, I'm not sorry, I'm horrified. I'm absolutely—"

"I'd like you to say to me, 'I'm sorry, Maureen.' "

"Well, I'll say I'm sorry, but that's not enough. I am absolutely horrified."

(For the record: The eyes-only document she held was declassified in 1990 and is available at the LBJ library in Texas. In the White House on February 14, 1968, the secretary of defense, who would be gone within two weeks, didn't say Joe Dunn's life wasn't worth it, not in those words. He said, on page 2 of "Notes of the President's Meeting on Violation of Chinese Air Space," that he recommended against trying to save the man "for the following reasons: There is a very high chance of losing three or four men in an effort to save one. The chances are better than 50-50, perhaps 60 to 40 that this would involve us in a conflict with the Chinese. . . . Because the risks are so high, I would recommend against this action.")

Not long after his night at Harvard, four Texas brothers, all decorated with Purple Hearts for wounds in Vietnam, announced they were suing Robert McNamara for $100 million.

And yet. In the midst of such emotion for a war that never went away were those with another point of view. The one I tried to listen to closest was a woman in the mountains of North Carolina. What I think Anne Morrison Welsh was telling me is that vengeance should be left to the vengeful. And that suffering and redemption—eventual redemption—are not incompatible ideas. On the contrary, each can give the other meaning, even comfort. Otherwise we're all locked in the triggering and embittering past. "I think McN. is undergoing *some* transformations, even this late in life. Unusual," Anne put in one letter as the summer drew near. In a note seven days earlier, she said, "I have experienced a lot of pain recently." *Lot* was underlined three times. It reminded me of a poem by Auden: "Musée des Beaux Arts."

> *About suffering they were never wrong,*
> *The Old Masters: how well they understood*
> *Its human position; how it takes place*
> *While someone else is eating or opening a window or just*
> *   walking dully along*

That summer, as most every summer, the man was on the Vineyard. If you were an habitué of that place, you'd have seen him some salt-air Saturday coming down the pavement in Vineyard Haven, the big power stride, in khakis and a sport-shirt deal, eating up the sidewalk. It would have been a mistake to conclude from such propellings-forward that he wasn't torn inside, ripped. Why, he was going to Hanoi in the fall, he told friends. To meet former foes.

ACKNOWLEDGMENTS

There is a real sense in which this book is only a record of those who believed in it. In the chapter notes I have tried to name as many individuals as I could who were instrumental in helping me gather the material for that section. In this space I would like to speak of those who were there with their belief and support over the very long haul.

My wife and my two sons—each lived the project in his or her own way, putting up with an author's moods and phobias when it wasn't going well. In the worst times, I knew I could always come home to Ceil, Matt, and John. Ceil, partner for life, was the quiet, reassuring force throughout.

My employers. In nineteen years at the Washington *Post,* I have been allowed four major book-writing leaves, more, probably, than even the finest university would tolerate, never mind any other newspaper. For this generosity of time and attitude stretching over almost two decades, I wish to pay respect to Ben Bradlee, Donald Graham, Leonard Downie, Robert Kaiser, Mary Hadar, Shelby Coffey (now heading the Los Angeles *Times*), and also the late Howard Simons; most recently, I owe thanks to David Von Drehle, Deborah Heard, and David DeNicolo. Two other *Post* people have to be named: Bobbye Pratt and Robin Groom; whenever I needed something dug out fast from the library or the photo file, they said yes. At the last, John Deiner of the *Post* did a close proof-reading.

Friends and colleagues. I guess I mean that very select number of good-hearted people who didn't fail to check on me at regular intervals as I sat in a small stuffy place and tried to do it: Render Denson, Butch Evans, Bill Gildea, Wil Haygood, Howard Kohn, Elaine Rubin, Mike Woyahn. Also my agent of a decade and a half, Edward J. Acton. I also feel a special indebtedness to James H. Silberman.

Mentors. Too many to name, so I'll just have to name the one who floats above all the rest: William Conrad Gibbons. There is no one outside my family and editor to whom I owe a larger debt. I met this historian and scholar in 1985, within six months or so after I had begun this project. He was then a foreign-affairs specialist at the congressional research service at the Library of Congress. His own work on Vietnam, which had already involved years of research, was just coming to public light. To date, Bill Gibbons has published, at Princeton University Press, four immensely respected volumes on the war, the latest of which brings the story of failed American policymaking up to January 1968. His current volume alone runs to nearly 1,000 pages of scholarship. Just to have the books would be a large aid for any author struggling with the war, but the truth is that, almost from the inception of our friendship, Bill has been willing to share whatever else he had, and I speak quite literally: He has given his time and advice; he has allowed me to see chapters-in-progress; he has given gratis hundreds of declassified documents from presidential libraries and other archives. It would have taken me years to acquire these documents on my own. Bill is semiretired now and lives in the folds of the Blue Ridge, and he and his wife, Pat, have taken on another amazing challenge, even as he goes on with the next volume in the series. I deeply miss our long walks around Capitol Hill.

Alfred A. Knopf. I am grateful to Sonny Mehta, Iris Weinstein, Carol Devine Carson, Ida Giragossian, Paul Bogaards, Bill Loverd, and Melvin Rosenthal, but above all to Jonathan Segal, my editor. Jon and I have been together one way or another for sixteen years and three books. He is nourishing and wise. He edits the old-fashioned way—with a pencil, going over the text page by page. Then he navigates it through the choppy waters of production. It was Jon, about four years ago, who nudged me toward the idea of trying the McNamara/Vietnam book again after I had put it aside. Not least of all the things he gave is the title. I had been coming up with dozens of titles, each of which I would start hating within a day or so of having thought it up. One day over steamed dumplings, Jon said in his offhanded way, "Really, I think the title has been sitting there all along in your epigraph." And so it was.

A WORD ABOUT INTERVIEWS

If declassified documents, oral histories, and newspaper articles are the ribbing of this narrative, the information I got from people—breathing sources—is its central nervous system. I talked to more than 500 people over a twelve-year period. Not all were "interviews" in the accepted sense of the word—sometimes just brief exchanges on the phone or in a letter, which turned out to yield a valuable piece of information or strip of texture. Other talks ran from the one-time, prearranged visit to the multiple, in-depth, sit-down, or walk-around session. For instance: Jim Farley. The second time I went to see him, in the fall of 1993, I stayed for three days, and we pretty much talked for all of it. Five times I have visited that pleasant hilltop manila-colored ranch house in Castro Valley, California. This doesn't take into account cross-country phone calls or letters, though in truth I'm the one who does the writing and calling. Farley, unlike some others in this story, is a terrible correspondent; if I get a postcard back, I feel lucky.

In the twelve years between the time I began this project in one guise and when I saw it published in another, there were large periods when there was no information-gathering at all; then, I had gone back to my salaried newspaper job or had taken up a different book.

Of the several hundred "real" interviews I did, down the tunnel of time, it is my relationship with the central character of the story that was—and in a way still is—the most equivocal; and it is that relationship, and the history of that relationship, that I feel a need to speak a little more of here, in that I think it is a part of the story itself.

As I related in the text, I first wrote to Robert McNamara in late 1983, asking to interview him for the Washington *Post,* after being moved by his appearance on a television panel. I'm sure he had never heard my name. Weeks went by. One morning early in 1984, he called our home on Capitol Hill before eight o'clock; I was in bed asleep. He was shooting out questions, and I was giving underwater answers. I kept trying to get myself off the wallpaper, keep the spaniel from yipping into the receiver. He said look here Mr. Hendrickson I'm not keen on the idea of any interview, you understand. He talked some more and then said he guessed I could come by for a chat, not that he was consenting to a piece, much less a "feature." He gave a date and time.

I must have passed the audition. (I remember boning up like a crazed person, and I also remember him saying at the end, as I was twitching to get away, "Well, I'll see you again.") Those McNamara encounters between February and May 1984 continue to form and inform my most visceral feelings about him. Never again have I been so physically close, though it's true I have sat in the first or second rows of auditoriums where he has spoken; and I once slipped a letter under his hotel-room door in Durham, North Carolina, where I thought I could hear him breathing just on the other side. (My four-page handwritten letter was an effort to convince him we should start meeting again.)

In the six months after the series about him appeared in the *Post,* McNamara and I talked five times—once in person, four times on the phone. All but one were substantive conversations, not as good as a face-to-face, but good enough. For instance, on October 23, 1984, he called me at 8:20 a.m. (I had tried him at his office the day before), and this time I wasn't in bed, and he was throaty and rapid-fire as ever. We talked about a number of things, though mainly about the Westmoreland/CBS libel trial, at which he was due to testify and loathing every thought of it. Near the beginning he said he had been hearing from some old high school and college friends in California and other places, and that they wanted to know whether to speak to me in connection with the book I had now formally undertaken about him. "I told them of course they should talk to you. That is, if they felt like it at all. I gave you my word I wouldn't try to stop anything you were doing, even if I personally wouldn't be able to help you out in any way." But of course he just *had* helped me out, once more, as he had been doing each time he had come on the phone in the last few months. For an instant I wondered, once more, if he somehow actually didn't know, or if he knew precisely—and was going on from there. Before I could think about it a second longer, he asked about my "timetable." I said I was just stumbling along. "Well, as I've told you, it's going to be pretty hard without me. Of course, I wish you wouldn't write a book at all." He laughed, and it sounded something like a cough.

The phone talk ceased, and in its place came an increasingly strained correspondence. Over the next several years, he was succinct and not uncourteous in rejecting my requests for interview time. Several times he answered through his secretary. In these same years I published some increasingly critical pieces about him in the Washington *Post.* Through the silence I could hear the rancor.

In the spring of 1994, after I was well into the project the second time round, and sensed it was working at last, and was by this time living on contracted book moneys instead of *Post* paychecks, I wrote again, asking if we might meet. I said: "We spoke fairly at length in 1984 for the three original Washington *Post* pieces, and then several times afterward, in person and on the phone. Then it ceased. This was your decision. I made other requests, and was turned down. So now, in another decade, I make the request again. Barring your participation in an interview format, I would nonetheless be willing to write out a list of questions. The list would be very, very long, I'd have to say. There are many, many things to ask. I want to give you a chance to respond to it all, have your say fully."

For the next few months we argued by mail about the possibility of a meeting, or something less. It was some contact, anyway. He said he feared I would seek to sensationalize his answers and his life. I said I would not. He said he would need to have the questions ahead of time. (". . . if you wish to send me the questions, I'll study them and then say whether I believe we should meet.") I cannot do that, I replied; much as I wish a meeting, you will have to make a commitment ahead of time to answer my sheets of questions. He answered, "I have never before agreed to an interview without knowing the type of questions I was to be asked." I responded that to submit hundreds of questions with no promise from him to answer them was nuts, the more so because we both knew he was in the process of completing his own book, which would beat mine to print by a year, if not more. It went on like this. My letters became scratchier; his had more composure.

But in the end I swallowed my pride and submitted three "sample" questions, no strings attached. I said he would be able to make up his mind from these three whether we should go forward. Two of the questions were more or less lob-jobs, though the third came high and inside with the evidence of a bald Vietnam lie. Several months later, on December 15, 1994, he replied to the three (the letter with the beautiful gray embossing ran onto a second sheet, an unheard-of thing), and then said that since I had shown that my approach was basically adversarial, he doubted whether further exchanges would be productive. And that is where it rests today. Except I would still like to talk to Robert McNamara.

Listed below are the names of the people I interviewed for one or more parts of this book, either in person or on the phone. I have noted with an asterisk the ones I talked to in person, and with a double asterisk those whom I interviewed more than once. (Sometimes the follow-ups were on the phone; whenever possible I went back to see my sources.) When two people were interviewed at once—usually a husband and wife—I have indicated it by listing the names together. All provided light in more than a decade of my McNamara/Vietnam wandering, and, sadly, some are no longer alive to judge the result. In most cases I worked with a notebook, not a tape recorder, believing, as I have believed for twenty-five years in journalism, that the exhausting and fierce tension required in trying to listen and write at the same time creates in the mind of the interviewer a vividness that tape can never give. You cannot get it all down with a pencil, no, but the reporter's ear manages to hear what is important, and it imprints itself. The great majority of the names below do not appear in the text, and at least one reason is because I was always bent on achieving narrative. But I am as grateful to all those unmentioned as I am to those who are named. For some reason I am in mind right now of an ancient shoe traveler in Salt Lake City named Mel Boley who described how Robert McNamara's father kept moist flakes of Bull Durham tobacco in a cloth sack in one watch pocket of his vest and a box of fine-grade papers in the other. In February 1986, I got off an airplane on my way to the West Coast to look up Boley, who had worked for R. J. McNamara and the wholesale firm of Buckingham & Hecht in the twenties and thirties. I couldn't get his name into the manuscript until now.

There is a small number of people I spoke with, in the years between 1984 and 1996, whose names do not appear below, and that is because each agreed to talk on the condition of anonymity.

The Notes on Sources that follow this list aren't meant to be exhaustive or all-inclusive line-by-line notes; rather, they are an effort to name the principal interviews for each section, to cite key published works, to give the date of a relevant article, to indicate in what archive or from what McNamara friend or foe I got a memo or some other kind of document. In the cases of the long chapter-portraits—of Farley, Morrison, Marlene Kramel, the Tran family, and the artist on the Vineyard ferry—all of whom represent the emotional core of this book, the reader should understand that *they* were the chief source of my information, which I then verified, double-checked, and supplemented in every way I could.

Sam Adams*, Sharon Stanley Alden, Howard Alderson, Robert Alexander, Susan Mary Alsop*, Ruth Amonette, Esther Angell*, Nguyet Anh*, Michael Ansara*, Pam Armstrong, David Ash*, Walter Baird, Patty Baker**, John Balaban*, Charles Baldwin*, George Ball**, Harry Barber**, James David Barber*, Betty Beale*, Leo C. Beebe*, Nguyen Ngoc Bich*, David Boies*, Rick Bolanos, Mel Boley*, Eugene Bordinat*, Lorraine Boudreau, William Boyer, Jr.**, Joan Braden**, Ron Bradley, Edward Braswell, Susan Brenner, William Bricca, Diane Brown*, Betty Ann Bryant, Lynda Van Devanter Buckley, Milton Bullock, Robert Bundt, William Bundy*, Russell Burrows**, Vicky Burrows*, Dan Calhoun*, Joseph Califano, Douglass Cater**, Jacqui Chagnon and Roger Rumpf*, Jean Wiest Chamberlin, Grant Chave*, John Chevier, William Clark*, Clark Clifford**, David Cole*, Chester Cooper*, Joseph Cooper**, Mary Beth Cooper*, Rosemary Cox*, Kay Craig**, Florence and Richard Crane, David Crippen**, Charles T. Cudlipp, Natalie Frank Currier, A. T. Troop Daignault*,

Malcolm Davisson*, Richard Deroche, Claudia DeWane, Alfred Dickinson*, Bui Diem*, J. C. Larry Doyle**, Muriel Drury*, Robert Dunham**, Harold Eddlestein, Dale Eddy, Robert Eggert, Sanford Elberg**, Daniel Ellsberg*, Elwood Engle, John Erichson*, Herbert Estes*, Norman Ewers*, Jim Farley**, Marilyn Farley*, T. J. Feaheny*, Dan Flynn, Michael Forrestal*, Barney Frank*, James Freeman*, Donald Frey*, Richard Fryklund*, J. William Fulbright*, Lynnette Fuller**, Virginia Gerrity, William Conrad Gibbons**, Roswell Gilpatric*, Ina Ginsburg, Henry Glass**, Alfred Goldberg**, Becky Goller*, Marion and Vernon Goodin**, Mary Joe and Willard Goodwin**, Anita Gordon, Chalmers Goyert**, Kenneth Green, Jerry Grenier*, Mr. and Mrs. Edward T. Grether*, Walter A. Haas, Jr.**, Robert Hagan, Gale Halderman*, James Halloran, Morton Halperin*, Harry L. Hansen**, Larry Harbeck*, Arthur Harris*, Harlan Hatcher*, Charles Havens*, Peter Havholm*, John Hax, Helen and Richard Hay*, Cordis Heard**, Diana Hellinger**, Jim Helmer and Fran Helmer Wollrab**, Bill Herrod*, Bill Hewitt**, Nguyen Hoa*, Richard Hodgson*, Townsend Hoopes**, Willard Y. Howell*, Ton-That Hung, Robert Hunter, John Hurley, Carol S. Hylton**, Paul Ignatius*, Alfreda Irwin*, Charles S. Johnson, Russell Johnson, Stanley Johnson*, Jim Jones**, Rex Jones*, Marty Kenner*, Ruth Kingman*, Chilton Knutsen, Mike Koll, Don Kopka, Glenn and Marlene Kramel**, Norman Krandall**, Dorothy Kriebel, William Kroger*, Victor Krulak, Jerry Kushins, Edmund Learned*, D. Jacqueline Lee**, Lyman Lemnitzer*, Harvey LeShur*, David L. Lewis**, Richard N. Lewis, Lawrence Lichty*, Anders Ljungh*, Nguyen Thanh Long**, Paul Lorenz*, Don Luce, Richard V. Lundquist, Myles Mace**, Jack Maddux**, Carson Magill**, Anna Lee Guest Mallory*, Bennie Mann, Henry May, Frank McBride, Stanley McCaffrey, David McChesney*, Paul W. McCracken*, Frank McCulloch*, Craig McNamara**, Robert S. McNamara**, Alexander McNaughton**, Harry McPherson**, Robert McVie**, Hubert Mee, Shirley Menard, Ben Mills*, Jean Booth Mitchell and Robert Mitchell**, Emily Morgan*, Sydney Morrell*, Thomas Morris*, Christina Morrison*, Ahmed Mustafa, Richard Neustadt*, William Newsome, Huan and Lananh Ngo*, Teresa Thanh Van Nguyen*, George Nickel, Christian Niemann*, Estelle O'Brien, Grace Barolet O'Brien**, Betsy O'Connell*, Laura Oliva, Howard Olsen, Marc O'Reilly*, Robin Orr, Tom Page*, Mark Patton, Celia Paul, Jean Peterson, Louis Peterson*, Rufus Phillips**, Le Thanh Phuong*, Philip Pierpont*, Jennifer Potter, Eugene Power, Ken Plusquellec, Mr. and Mrs. Richard Quigley**, Mike Radock, Louis Rasmussen, Don Reiman**, Lowell Rein*, Maxine Reith, Jonathan Rinehart, Agnes Robb*, John Roche**, Benson Roe, John Roemer*, Ruth Rosen, Hobart Rowen*, Thomas Sanders, Jr.*, Charles and Kitty Sawyer*, Leland Scott, Jr., Will Scott*, Fred Secrest*, Eric Sevareid*, Albert Shine, Derek Shows*, Sargent Shriver*, Dana Shuster, Tom Simonson, David Singer*, Arthur and Margaret Slaymaker**, Margaret Chase Smith**, Sharon Smith, Theodore

Sorensen*, Burnette and Neil Staebler*, Richard Steadman*, Fran Steckmest*, Helen Read Steele, John Stennis*, Mary Stout*, Edward Strong*, Elizabeth Cadman Stuart*, Richard Stubbing*, Marie Sweeney*, Virginia Teabay*, Nguyen Dinh Thang**, Walter L. Tommy Thomas*, James Thomson**, Andrew Thusen, Tran Tu Huyen*, Tran Tu Thanh**, Marietta Tree*, Henry Trewhitt*, Peter Vogel, Duy Vu*, Charles Wagner, Cynthia Lowell Wallace, Reverend Sumner Walters, Jr., Annie Mae Warner, Richard E. Warner, Paul Warnke*, C Gayle Warnock, George and Eleanor Webb*, Edward Weiss, Anne Morrison Welsh**, Emily Morrison Welsh*, Iris West, James West*, Walter Wiest, Charles Williams*, Brian Wilson*, George Wilson**, Carol Withington, Harris Wofford**, James O. Wright**, Adam Yarmolinsky*, T. O. Yntyma, Montague Yudelman*, Eugene Zuckert*.

NOTES ON SOURCES

Abbreviations

RSM	Robert Strange McNamara
NYT	New York *Times*
WP	Washington *Post*

PROLOGUE: A STORY OUT OF TIME

The experience of walking down an alley near a laundromat on Martha's Vineyard, toward a small intense man, who stood in the doorway of his studio, and who, after a rough minute, invited me in to tell his rough tale, is what led me to begin conceiving of a different kind of McNamara/Vietnam book. The ferry attack has popped up in print through the years—it's in James Reston, Jr.'s, *Sherman's March and Vietnam,* and it's in Anne Simon's *No Island Is an Island,* for instance—but the treatment has been shadowy and often enough in error. The reason for this, I believe, and so does the person who did the attacking, is that no one ever sat down, or was able to sit down, with the primary source. (Reading of the incident in Reston's book in 1985 is what sent me on a search for the artist.) An eight-paragraph AP wire story on October 12, 1972, was oddly helpful, and so was *The New Republic* of September 3, 1977. Simon's book aided on island culture and general background. Betty Ann Bryant, Kay Craig, Roswell Gilpatric, Marion Goodin, Anita Gordon, John Roche, Peg Slaymaker, Fran Wollrab, and certain Vineyarders told me what they knew or had heard about it through the years. It was the artist himself who proved to have it in the indelible and consistent way—in two tellings, a year apart. Barring RSM's voice, the artist's is the only one I remain willing to trust almost completely.

No reports or complaints filed: Anne Renaux of the state police at Middleboro, Massachusetts, checked records, both at regional and local barracks, and found that no record of the assault existed. Law-enforcement officials at Vineyard Haven reported the same, though there were officers there and in Falmouth, Massachusetts, who had the night in their heads if not their file cabinets. Diane Speers of the Woods Hole, Martha's Vineyard and Nantucket Steamship Authority did a search of the ship's log and found nothing relating to the incident. The corporate records of the Authority were also checked for personal-injury reports for the year 1972; nothing found. That night *was* closed out, on paper.

A postscript. A version very close to this one appeared in the *WP Sunday Magazine* on September 6, 1987. Several days after, I received this note from Jeanne Moore, RSM's secretary: "Mr. Hendrickson: As you may know, there are several inaccuracies in the article you published in Sunday's *Washington Post*. For example, the name of the man Mr. McNamara was speaking with before going to the wheelhouse to accept a call was not Ralph Meyer, but Talbot Rantoul, who was the President of the Rhode Island School of Design. You may wish to check with Mr. McNamara on the inaccuracies of your article if you decide to have it published again." I wrote back quickly and said that while I regretted an error of any kind in anything I wrote, I wished to point out that not only did the artist feel certain that the person RSM was standing with inside the lunchroom was a Vineyarder named Ralph Meyer—and that I had asked twice about it—but that another passenger thought so, too. I said that if, however, I was wrong in quoting the artist on this detail, I would be glad to make a correction or a deletion before the story appeared elsewhere. I then said that I was a little puzzled by her statement that I might "wish to check with Mr. McNamara," in that I had been trying for several years, as she was well aware, to arrange an interview with him. I said I would welcome any kind of contact to discuss almost any subject. I closed by saying I would be eager to know what other unspecified "inaccuracies" she was referring to, since I knew of none. I never received an answer to the letter.

As to who was standing beside RSM that night, Ralph Meyer or Talbot Rantoul, just before the artist led him out: I cannot say for sure. (Both men are dead, and their widows are uncertain.) So I have deleted reference to the name and put in an ellipsis.

PART ONE: AT THE OPEN NOON OF HIS PRIDE
In the Winter of 1955

The key interviews for understanding RSM in Michigan in the age of Auto Baroque were Chalmers Goyert, Eugene Bordinat, David Ash, Robert Dunham, David Lewis, Jim Wright, Harlan Hatcher, Norman Krandall, Ben Mills, Will

Scott, Fred Secrest, Charlie Baldwin, Leo Beebe, Bill Boyer, Donald Frey, Gale Halderman, Herb Estes, Charles and Kitty Sawyer, Neil and Burnette Staebler. The portrait could not have been done had not Darleen Flaherty at the Ford Industrial Archives so willingly opened her files; there I found RSM memos, expense reports, correspondence, speeches, employee-history questionnaires, dealer-visit notes (written in furious pencil on the back of envelopes). A smaller cache was found with the help of archivist and historian David Crippen at the Ford Research Center at the Henry Ford Museum in Dearborn. Also valuable were the Allan Nevins papers archived at Columbia University, especially the transcripts of interviews with RSM and the other Whiz Kids.

The most useful of the books I consulted: Allan Nevins and Frank Ernest Hill, *Ford;* Peter Collier and David Horowitz, *The Fords;* Robert Lacey, *Ford;* Booton Herndon, *Ford;* C Gayle Warnock, *The Edsel Affair;* David L. Lewis, Mike McCarville, Lorin Sorensen, *Ford, 1903 to 1984;* David Halberstam, *The Reckoning;* Deborah Shapley, *Promise and Power,* John A. Byrne, *The Whiz Kids.* A chapter, "World on Wheels," in John Gunther's *Inside U.S.A.* helped, and also a book of essays called *The Automobile and American Culture.* (For full book citations, see the bibliography.) The files of both the Detroit *News* and the Detroit *Free Press* (a former employer) were valuable. But no book or newspaper article helped or inspired in the way *The Best and the Brightest* did. Halberstam's portrait of RSM in autoland is one of the best short things he has done, in my view, and provided a line of thinking and feeling for this entire project, as should be evident. I stood on the shoulders of the giant, among giants; I still know sentences by heart.

All the following from Industrial Archives: cooling-system memo: February 1, 1955. Installation-of-radios *et al.* speech: September 25, 1954. Easy-closing doors memo: February 7, 1955. Statement and collateral details re accident with company car: November 23, 1953. Donald Riegel's letter: October 31, 1955; RSM's Harvard talk: September 5, 1958. Controllers Institute application: June 10, 1949. Mass-Producing Variety speech: June 15, 1956. Analysis of Hotel Bill: undated, but almost certainly from the mid-forties.

Both Chalmers Goyert and Robert Dunham told me about fainting. Deborah Shapley has reported on the bruxism and has quoted RSM himself. (See *Business Week,* December 17, 1960, following RSM's selection to JFK's cabinet, for a mention of how RSM "collapsed" once at Ford.) The teeth-grinding, and what it may have been sublimating in the other man, probably first came to public light in *Best and Brightest.* The Vietnam Muon Nam anecdote is in, among other places, Don Luce and John Sommer, *Vietnam: The Unheard Voices.* I found confirmation of RSM's election to the board of ruling elders at First Press in church minutes, January 27, 1955. The Hill Street incandescing quote is from Abe Peck, *Uncovering the Sixties.* The orange-juice-and-egg ritual goes back to college and is known by many RSM intimates. Descriptions of RSM's home were culled from family members and newspaper features and neighbors but also from my own tour of the house years afterward. (The University of California *Monthly,* June 1961, also described the interior.) The William Manchester quote re technological change is from his *The Glory and the Dream.*

Re the material that opens this chapter: his wife drinking milk: See the epilogue, and Jim Wright. Wigged-out woman: from family members, but it is also mentioned in *In Retrospect.* Nguyen Van Troi's capture was May 9, 1964, and was reported worldwide. Odd metaphors: See Parts Three and Part Five of this book. Pressed white shirts: Henry Glass interview; see Part Five. Reading Homer: family members; there's a passing reference in James C. Thomson, Jr.'s, "Getting Out and Speaking Out," *Foreign Policy,* winter 1973–1974. Ulcerated son: family members, and also Craig McNamara's own descriptions in his oral history in *From Camelot to Kent State.* Symbionese Liberation Army: See the epilogue for a fuller treatment. Pentagon briefing room: See Part Five. Tarmac at Andrews: See Part Three. In field fatigues leaving Saigon: See Part Four. Hit-them-in-the-nuts quote is from Arthur Schlesinger, Jr.'s, *Robert Kennedy and His Times.* Afraid of breaking down: See Part Five; Douglass Cater *et al.* Casualty figures: See Part Five. Dean Rusk's dining room: See Part Five for the full account.

In light of what he became, it was fascinating to find how little known RSM was in 1955—even within automotive circles. There had been scattered national references in the forties (*Steel* magazine, e.g.). *Look,* June 30, 1953, said: "The comptroller of the company, Bob McNamara, is only thirty-six [actually thirty-seven]—one of the ten 'whiz kids' who Henry Ford II garnered from the Air Force after the war." In the *Readers Guide to Periodical Literature,* there is one entry on him from March 1955 to February 1957, and it is just a squib from *Fortune.* From a Detroit *Times* feature June 9, 1957: "As politely as he could phrase it, McNamara, a slender six-footer, who is friendly but also reserved, said it did not particularly concern him that he is a virtual unknown outside of his company." Slim notices, about to change forever.

PART TWO: PHOTOGRAPH OF A LIFE, 1916–1960
A Cone of Light

The literature on RSM's California beginnings is distressingly thin. It is as if earlier biographers and journalists haven't thought his ancestry, parentage, and growing-up years very important; but it is also true, as God knows, that no one has ever gotten much help from the subject himself. To do this chapter, I talked with next-door neighbors on both sides, with high-school teachers, fraternity brothers, college officials; slowly, the dots filled in. Since so much of the early life, and the life of the parents, has long been concealed, the material that lay in census data, city directories, death certificates, probate records, funeral-parlor files, and West Coast shoe registries was invaluable. Even the Piedmont Council of the Boy Scouts of America turned out to have a full record of its former Eagle—including the date of every merit badge earned. A series of California books called The Great Register was very helpful.

The crucial interviews were with Vernon and Marion Goodin, Jim Helmer and Fran Wollrab, John Erichson, Fran Steckmest, Cynthia Lowell Wallace, Anna Lee Guest Mallory, Willard and Mary Joe Goodwin, Joe Cooper, Harry Barber, Bill Hewitt, Stan Johnson, Carson Magill, Phil Pierpont, Bill Bricca, Sanford Elberg, and Malcolm Davisson. The chapter would have been difficult to do had I not had long talks with two people which stretched over several years: Richard Quigley, intimate family friend, especially of the parents; and Peggy Slaymaker, RSM's only sibling. My greatest debt is to Peggy; every time I went to Santa Rosa, something else fell out. She brought forth (sometimes unwittingly) not just memories of her parents and brother but albums, rings, walking sticks, passenger manifests of sea crossings. In some sense I felt we were on a genealogical-cum-character voyage together. As I indicated in the text, she never knew of the domestic violence and subsequent divorce of her maternal grandparents, Elizabeth and William Miller Strange; the document was in court records in Yuba City, California, and discovering it was startling to us both. Quigley, too, gave me many images of Nelle and "Uncle Bob."

Others added still more family layers. Vern Goodin, for instance, RSM's oldest friend, told me of R. J. McNamara sitting down at the curb on the way home from work to get his breath. Christian Doc Niemann, ancient by the time I found him, got out the marbleized cardboard grading book from second-semester 1932 at Piedmont High in which he had marked down RSM's "Straight 1" in chemistry. Estelle O'Brien, a lifelong Oaklander, gave many insights and had even saved old letters from R.J. to Charley O'Brien, Estelle's father, who had sold shoes under R.J. The little girl who lived next to the McNamaras on the west side of 1036 Annerly in the twenties—her name is Cynthia Lowell Wallace now—described how her mother and Mrs. Mac would stand upstairs, on the second floor, their dust mops poised, talking through the two raised windows. When I pushed a little for something of Mr. Mac, she said, "Sourpuss, to tell you the truth."

Westering: Until this research, no living McNamara, I am certain, ever knew when the first-generation McNamaras departed the shoe benches of Massachusetts for greener Pacific dreams. Birth registries in New England and city-worker rolls in San Francisco proved it had to be between February 29 and October 1, 1868. After I had the California data, I worked backward to see the migration paths of both sides of the family: the McNamaras progressing from Ireland to Stoughton to the Bay; the Stranges from Fluvanna County, Virginia, to Carrollton, Missouri, to Yuba City. Only a fraction of what I found ended up in the text; so be it.

Sutter County *Farmer's* report of the divorce filing was May 28, 1897; RSM's little lie about rowing to the *WP* (liked the sport, but had to give it up as a soph) was June 18, 1961.

Among the books I consulted: Beth Bagwell, *Oakland;* R. A. Burchell, *The San Francisco Irish;* William Camp, *San Francisco;* Kevin Starr, *Inventing the Dream;* Tom Horton, *Superspan;* Charles Caldwell Dobie, *San Francisco;* Verne Stadtman, *The University of California;* Charles Wollenberg, *Golden Gate Metropolis;* Oscar Lewis, *Bay Window Bohemia;* Leonard Michaels, David Reid, and Raquel Scherr, eds., *West of the West;* George A. Pettitt, *Berkeley;* Henry Trewhitt, *McNamara;* Deborah Shapley, *Promise and Power.* (For full citations, see the bibliography.) An unpublished Cal memoir by Agnes Roddy Robb was useful, and so too Tom Albright's fine introductory essay in *Art in the San Francisco Bay Area, 1945–1980*; also, Brock Brower's RSM profile, in *Life,* May 10, 1968.

Lastly: In 1986, Professor Derek Shows of Duke University helped me immeasurably by making clear several fundamental Jungian concepts with which I then began to think in terms of an organizing principle for a narrative. Though I have long read Jung, I am in no way a schooled student of the work. And yet I will say here that Jung's small book-length essay, *Synchronicity: An Acausal Connecting Principle,* was a kind of crossing-over moment of understanding for me, as was a brief psychological essay by the great literary critic Malcolm Cowley. It's called "Hemingway: The Old Lion," and it's in Cowley's *A Second Flowering.* Perhaps the latter, which I read more than twenty years ago, was the real epiphany in terms of thinking and wondering about people who put on masks.

All Men Grow in Righteousness

The opening scene was built from news clips and photo albums (the bride's mainly), but mostly from the memories and memorabilia of those who were either dockside that night or involved in events leading up: Kay Craig, Peg Slaymaker, Vernon Goodin, Joe Cooper, Estelle O'Brien, Mr. and Mrs. Richard Quigley, Carson Magill, Jean Booth Mitchell, Phil Pierpont, Helen and Richie Hay. RSM himself filled in the wedding-invitation story in a letter to me, December 15, 1994.

My information on the Harvard years was drawn from many places; the key interviews were with Bill Hewitt, Wally Haas, Troop Daignault, Robert McVie, Alfred Dickinson, Richard Hodgson, Harry Hansen, Myles Mace, Edmund Learned, Charles Williams, Tom Sanders, Jr., Eugene Zuckert. Again, Peg Slaymaker was important. Some of these same—notably Mace, Hansen, and Learned—helped me grasp Stat Control at wartime Harvard.

Marilyn Reid, secretary to the B-School faculty, searched records to see that RSM didn't make assistant professor until July 1942.

The letters to Sproul and Deutsch were in the president's file at the university archives in Berkeley; I also found there the registrar's note to the provost re his grades.

His 3/5/38 student paper on gate receipts; his January 1941 questions drafted for the industrial accounting exam; the 1941–1942 course involving the Brettle Lane Cement case—these were at Baker Library's historical collection.

RSM's lifelong friend Harry Barber, with RSM's consent, provided portions of RSM's letters from Boston, and Bill Hewitt had details and photos of the summer of '38 cross-country trip, as did Willard Goodwin. In a drawer at the Albert Brown mortuary in Oakland, I found details relating to R. J. McNamara's funeral.

Failure to get honors: Learned and Hansen were the main faculty sources, but almost everyone I talked to from the class had a slice of the myth. The anecdote of Hosmer throwing down the pencil and saying, "The guy is arrogant," was told by Hansen, who, next to Myles Mace, had it all inside him re Harvard.

The summer of 1939 in prewar Europe: McVie, Dickinson, Hodgson, Williams, John Martin, Ron Bradley. (Most of those rode in the woody.) Bob McVie had extensive photos.

Joe Cooper showed me portions of his trout diary from 1940; Gene Zuckert had in his head the Sunday-night arrival at Soldiers Field, 9/15/40, the moon full and pearly. I checked; exactly so.

Again, Marg McNamara's honeymoon photo album with captions and other notations helped me describe that first faculty apartment. Hansen had pictures from Whitton Pond. Vern Goodin shared photos and memories from time spent visiting in Boston. A nearly full record of RSM's wartime service was at the National Personnel Records Center in St. Louis, though Mace's memories were crucial to the telling. Jim Wright, Ben Mills, and Henry Glass, cited earlier, helped me with Stat Control.

Re the final section of this chapter: When I began this book in 1984, I decided to research this moment exhaustively, thinking it might teach me things about the character of not just the man leaping from Ford but about the Kennedys, too. The two most important interviews, not always trustworthy for fact, were with the principals: Shriver and RSM. But Harris Wofford, Adam Yarmolinsky, Neil Staebler, Theodore Sorensen, Clark Clifford, and Richard Neustadt filled in certain details.

Re RSM's being caught totally off guard by Shriver's sudden visit to Dearborn: not exactly. Staebler, for one, who was chairman of the Democratic Party in Michigan as well as an Ann Arbor resident and friend of RSM's, had let him know that certain Kennedy people—among them Shriver—were making inquiries about his possible availability for a New Frontier post. It was not clear what the post was, or how high up. "Tell them to forget it, I'm full up here" was RSM's answer to Staebler, and passed back to Shriver. In 1985, when I inter-

viewed Staebler, he was certain he had spoken to RSM not long after the JFK
election to tell him of the Kennedys' general interest in him; and he thinks they
spoke about it again at least once closer to the end of November, as things were
heating up. Others in Michigan also verified that RSM had had at least a general awareness of inquiries being made. On the other hand, as I indicated in the
narrative, it is probably fair to say that RSM had no real clue on the morning of
December 7, as Shriver was preparing to take flight, as to *how* ravenous the
Kennedyites—including Jack himself—had become, and what they were about
to offer. That *was* a surprise. But the way RSM has long told it—no idea of any
interest on their part—is not truthful. In an April 1964 oral history with Arthur
M. Schlesinger, Jr. (it is at the JFK library in Boston), the interviewer asked:
"Was it a complete surprise to you?" RSM: "Oh, yes." Schlesinger: "This was
out of the blue?" RSM: "Completely out of the blue." Schlesinger: "You had no
intimations of any interest?" RSM: "None whatsoever." Later in that same interview, RSM told Schlesinger how "Finally, on the second meeting I accepted the
position." But of course he told members of the Detroit press that he had met
JFK three times before accepting. My own gut belief is that it was all over after
the first meeting: He was going to Camelot, getting out of cars.

On the point of the unconditionality of their offers, or at least the apparent
unconditionality: Both RSM and Shriver have talked of the flat-out nature of it.
(See, for instance, Shriver's speech at Southern Methodist University, March
29, 1984.) In January 1985, when I brought this up to Shriver, he said a little
defensively that, see, what I did not understand was that RSM's recommendations were so over-the-top, and how he had just reached the very pinnacle of
Ford. Shriver said he would go out there and do it all over again the same way.
He added that everything was being done with "Jack's knowledge, and subject
to his final approval," that Jack had reviewed every detail, and there was
always the "slim though real" possibility they might have to bail out on the
"candidate." Probably it *was* just like that, in JFK's mind, but the "candidate"
wasn't made to think so. He was being made to think he was being proffered the
moon. As RSM said to Eric Sevareid in a CBS-TV interview: "Sarge . . . had
been instructed to accept an answer of yes, but not to accept an answer of no,
and that in the event my answer was no, that I was to be asked to see the president himself." In the 1964 oral history with Schlesinger, he said that Shriver
had been "authorized to accept a favorable reply, but in the event the reply was
unfavorable, he had been instructed to ask that I meet with the president to discuss the matter in person." Which is to say the meeting in Washington was
employed as a wedge, not presented as a contingency or condition. Wild and
risky business.

As if to prove it, Bobby Kennedy said in *his* oral history for the JFK library
(February 1964) that Shriver got on a plane and flew out and "offered him the
job of secretary of the treasury or secretary of defense." Interviewer: "Had the
president known him?" RFK: "No, he had never met him." Then you practi-

cally hear Bobby's gears grinding: "Oh, he didn't *offer* him the job, he asked him if he might be interested *if* the president offered him the job."

Where are those talent-search files, in which RSM got checked out to a fare-thee-well? Nobody seems to know, including Will Johnson, chief archivist at the JFK library. They've never surfaced. I don't doubt that rushed calls were made and many memos written. But where's the paper trail? Does it not exist?

Published works and archival sources for this chapter were plentiful. For the B-School years, Melvin Copeland, *And Mark an Era,* was good, if authorized, reading, and so too Malcolm P. McNair, editor, *The Case Method at the Harvard Business School.* At Baker Library I found notebooks, memos, correspondence, essays relating to the Stat School on campus, and the years after. (See, for example, Dan Throop Smith, "Putting Bombing on a Business Basis.") In archives at Bolling Air Force Base in Washington were correspondence, essays, programs, memos relating to Thornton's Stat Control. (See especially USAF Historical Studies Nos. 57 and 99.) Again, the Nevins interviews at Columbia University with the Whiz Kids were valuable; also Byrne, *The Whiz Kids.* (For full book citations, see the bibliography.)

Getting him: A batch of published works by JFK intimates have discussed the overwrought talent hunt, and to cite three: Schlesinger, *A Thousand Days;* Theodore C. Sorensen, *Kennedy;* Harris Wofford, *Of Kennedys and Kings.* Halberstam's *Brightest* was crucial to my thinking in terms of how much of it—as regards RSM, anyway—was glitz and rush instead of painful examination. Shapley in *Promise* had certain key details. Elie Abel, in "The Thinking Man's Business Executive" in *The Kennedy Circle,* supplied a good chronology. But my best sources were newspapers, with which I plotted it all out, day by day, almost hour by hour.

The closing anecdote, re oxcart, is from William Conrad Gibbons, *The U.S. Government and the Vietnam War, Part II.*

Finally: It is of no small irony—to me, at least—that in 1937–1938, just as a scientific rationalist and pragmatic liberal from the Pacific Coast was, you might say, being hydroponically re-created in Boston, and also just when FDR's New Deal recovery had begun to stall badly (somewhere between 7 and 10 million Americans out of work, and the stock market falling sharply), that the social prophet James Burnham was struggling to conceptualize a book called *The Managerial Revolution.* He believed capitalism was doomed and socialism would take its place, and that the manager class would constitute the new world order. When it appeared, reviewers thought it not altogether believable.

PART THREE: DIED SOME, PRO PATRIA, 1965 IN AMERICA
Another Ride with Yankee Papa 13

The wheel that made it turn was Farley; I still feel uncommonly fortunate to have found, then engaged in so much talk, the flesh-and-blood man out of the black-and-white, thirty-year-old photograph I had seen as a seminarian. But a dozen other interviews were vital to the telling, and I have named or quoted or referred to most in the text: Norman Ewers, John Hax, Bennie Mann, Peter Vogel, Dale Eddy, Marilyn Farley, Jerry Grenier (his half brother), Jean Peterson, George Ball, Chester Cooper, J. William Fulbright. The son of the late Larry Burrows, Russell Burrows, provided not only hours of talk and gave his father's unpublished notes of 3165 but also helped with photographic materials, some of which were not published in the original *Life* story. Hax made available not only his own fine unpublished war memoir, *Life of Pops,* but lent other papers and documents. The squadron's yearbook (it's called the *Cruise Book*) was a pot of gold in terms of my getting down the small and large details of the unit's history. At the Marine Corps Historical Center in Washington, Fred Graboske helped dig out the relevant command chronologies, casualty reports, and after-action reports. Farley himself brought forth a trunkful of letters and souvenirs relating to that day and all that flowed from it.

To construct the account of what was going on in Washington while he was figuratively and literally against his box, I used the Gravel edition of *The Pentagon Papers,* but also the raw declassified documents themselves. Newsreels and newspapers were important, as was Episode Four ("LBJ Goes to War, 1964–1965") of the PBS series *Vietnam: A Television History.* The public statements of RSM, on file at the Pentagon, were indispensable, as were audiotapes of same at the National Archives. William Conrad Gibbons, *The U.S. Government and the Vietnam War, Part III, January–July 1965,* was easily the most complete and authoritative source, and I have already stated my unpayable debt to this historian and friend in terms of what he personally taught and gave. The opening chapter ("The Decision to Intervene") in Herbert Y. Schandler, *The Unmaking of a President,* helped guide my thinking, as did these works: Larry Berman, *Planning a Tragedy;* Brian VanDeMark, *Into the Quagmire;* George Ball, *The Past Has Another Pattern;* Chester Cooper, *The Lost Crusade;* and Stanley Karnow, *Vietnam.* Additionally, these were important: Halberstam, *Brightest;* Shapley, *Promise;* Doris Kearns, *Lyndon Johnson & the American Dream;* Neil Sheehan, *A Bright Shining Lie;* Townsend Hoopes, *The Limits of Intervention;* U.S.G. Sharp, *Strategy for Defeat;* George McT. Kahin, *Intervention;* Gabriel Kolko, *Anatomy of a War;* George C. Herring, *LBJ and Vietnam;* Jack Shulimson and Charles M. Johnson, *U.S. Marines in Vietnam;* Lyndon Johnson, *The Vantage Point;* William Westmoreland, *A Soldier Reports;* Maxwell Taylor, *Swords and Plowshares;* and, of course, RSM's *In Retrospect.* (For full book citations, see the bibliography.)

Henry Graff's *NYT Sunday Magazine* piece was published July 4, 1965. The statistic of 43 million Americans losing someone in Vietnam, and the statistic of 100,000 veterans dying prematurely, are both from the Friends of the

Vietnam Veterans Memorial. The Kearns bombs-to-troops quote is from her *Lyndon Johnson.* The Hemingway quote re Caporetto is from his *A Farewell to Arms.* The ten-year *People* magazine feature on Farley was March 18, 1985. The Turner Catledge memo re the seance with LBJ was in the Arthur Krock papers at Princeton. The *Life* update on Farley was October 1979.

I feel obliged to note to the reader that Brian VanDeMark was RSM's collaborator on *In Retrospect,* a book whose reporting and agenda I do not admire. Yet VanDeMark's own 1991 *Into the Quagmire* is a first-rate source, I feel, and I decided to use it to tell the escalation story. In the spring of 1995, when RSM's book was being condemned, an apparently taken-aback VanDeMark was quoted as saying to a Manhattan tabloid columnist, "I kept his feet to the fire." I cannot possibly see how that is so.

Lastly: That day, Jim Farley tried to save two Marines—Lieutenants Eddy and Magel—from a stricken sister ship, YP-3. A third Marine from YP-3, Sergeant Owens, was gotten to safety in Farley's copter. But there was a fourth man riding in YP-3, and in the *Life* story—as well as my own narrative—he didn't get a mention. His name was Sergeant Cecil Garner, and he was from rural Arkansas, and in the chaos of the attack he had managed to dismantle his machine gun and wage his own private war in the weeds until he was rescued by another crew from the squadron. He sustained wounds and was later transferred. What I'm trying to say is that there were almost too many heroes on 3165, or too many to write of between the covers of one book. If there were time and justice, they'd all be sung, and not in the backnotes.

Lyrics for a Bunker

Works consulted: Philip Bagenal, *The Illustrated Atlas of the World's Great Buildings;* Jack Raymond, *Power at the Pentagon;* Perry M. Smith, *Assignment: Pentagon;* E. A. Rogner, *The Pentagon;* Nita Scoggan, *Pentagon Tidbits.* (For full book citations, see the bibliography.) Robert Scheer's fine essay in *Ramparts* ("The Winner's War"), December 1965, helped me see it as a building, and so too an essay in Roger R. Trask, *The Secretaries of Defense.* But the best source on the Pentagon as a symbolic American place was Alfred Goldberg, historian for the Office of the Secretary of Defense and author of *The Pentagon.* I found Goldberg himself to be a scratchy, authoritative witness. I asked if he was fond of the place he's worked in for decades. "This is too big to love," he snapped. "It's the vastness inside." And I thought of RSM.

Among those I interviewed for stories about the building, and RSM in it: Paul Warnke (the unmarked door off the hall); Jack Maddux (Tos the barber); Paul Ignatius (the sec/def's clock).

I spent a week taking the public tour, on which I found my own queasiness. It was always so good to get out into real air.

The Burning of Norman R. Morrison

The original piece I did for the *WP* on this family was published December 2, 1985. The date of RSM's Westmoreland/CBS trial appearance was December 6, 1984, and is also discussed in other chapters of this book. The letter from the woman in Troy, New York, appeared in the Baltimore *Sun* after the act. The letter from Marian E. Manly was published in *I. F. Stone's Weekly,* November 15, 1965. The issue of the *Weekly* Norman saw on the day he died was dated November 1, 1965. The Charlotte *Observer* piece on the Quaker cell in the city's midst was October 26, 1959. Hobart Rowen's column in the *WP* re talk of RSM as assistant president was November 21, 1965. M.F.K. Fisher's quote is from her *Stay Me, Oh Comfort Me.* The Pentagon Papers commentary re RSM's public optimism on the war (as opposed to his private pessimism) is in the Gravel edition, volume 4. Harry McPherson's comment re RSM's giving the president an enormous amount of optimistic information long after he'd grown disillusioned is from the *U.S. News & World Report* Special Report on Vietnam, October 29, 1990. The January 6, 1966, dinner at Arthur Schlesinger's home in which RSM said he didn't regard a military solution as possible is told in the author's *Robert Kennedy and His Times.* Victor Krulak's seventeen-page memo, "A Strategic Appraisal, Vietnam," was with his papers at the Marine Corps Historical Center. RSM's essay in *Newsweek,* "On Avoiding the Draft," was August 3, 1992. The Emily Dickinson line that opens this chapter is from a letter to Mrs. J. G. Holland, mid-December 1882.

Like the previous, this chapter is almost entirely the product of my own reporting and interviewing. But, again, the telling depended crucially on the original willingness of the three surviving Morrisons, but most especially on Anne Morrison Welsh, whose cautious good faith in my direction now travels back more than a decade. Without Anne, Norman Morrison would have remained dead in my imagination, a strange, sad footnote to a strange, sad war.

Yet others, as I subsequently found, held the man close, and I've tried to mention or quote as many as I could in the text. Of these, Don Reiman was primary; he loaned a yellowed folder full of newspaper and magazine clippings as well as much correspondence; then he told me almost everything he knew about the friendship. Another important source, not named in this chapter: Walter Wiest, a retired Pittsburgh seminary professor who had taught him ethics and theology. When I asked, as I have asked many, if he was shocked to hear the news of November 2, 1965, he said: "I never would have predicted that Norman or anyone else I knew would have done a thing like that. . . . On the other hand, after I'd absorbed it a little, I could see how it seemed to fit the pattern that his life had suggested to me." To understand that pattern, I traveled to Norman places: Erie, Chautauqua, Wooster, Pittsburgh, Baltimore, and the spot at the Pentagon where he lit the fire.

These works helped me on Quakerism: Jessamyn West, *Quaker Reader;* Douglas V. Steere, editor, *Quaker Spirituality;* Daisy Newman, *A Procession of Friends;* Marice Creasey, *Bearings;* Steere, *On Being Present Where You Are;* Steere, *On Speaking Out of the Silence.* For the story of Abraham and Isaac, I read, not without difficulty, Kierkegaard's *Fear and Trembling.* (For full book citations, see the bibliography.)

To construct what was happening on the policy side of the parable, I relied fundamentally on six sources: *The Pentagon Papers;* the declassified documents themselves; the public statements of RSM as they exist in transcript at the Pentagon, on microfilm at the Library of Congress, and on audiotapes at the National Archives; Gibbons, *The U.S. Government and the Vietnam War, Part IV;* newspaper articles of the time; and *In Retrospect.* For interviews, Chester Cooper, Daniel Ellsberg, George Ball, Townsend Hoopes, and, most especially, Bill Gibbons shaped my thinking. Many of the Vietnam works cited in the Farley chapter were relevant in this one, but I should specially name Sheehan, *Lie;* Cooper, *The Lost Crusade;* Karnow, *Vietnam;* and Shapley, *Promise.* But above all: Harold G. Moore and Joseph L. Galloway, *We Were Soldiers Once . . . And Young.* It is the definitive work on the human pain of the Ia Drang, and it is possible to see the evolution of the book through Galloway's fine *U.S. News* cover story, October 29, 1990. A 1994 ABC News documentary on the Ia Drang, *They Were Young and Brave,* also aided me.

Historians, scholars, and journalists who reported the war will long debate: What was it exactly that caused the principal architect to turn? My own belief, as I have sought to show, is that it was two events, working in concert. Almost a decade and a half ago, Karnow, in *Vietnam,* wrote: "Until late November 1965, McNamara had believed firmly in the American crusade in Vietnam. But his attitude altered perceptibly during his quick trip to Saigon at this juncture . . . he was shaken by the evidence that North Vietnamese infiltration into the south had risen so dramatically . . . [he] returned to Washington to offer Johnson a bleak set of options." It was with interest that I saw on page 222 of *In Retrospect* RSM's apparent concurrence, indeed RSM's seeming flat taking of another's prose: "Westy's talk [of adding 400,000 more troops by the end of '66, and maybe 200,000 more in '67] . . . shook me and altered my attitude perceptibly. . . . I returned to Washington to offer the president a bleak choice between but two options. . . ."

What Karnow and other fine chroniclers of Vietnam have not heretofore seen, in my judgment, is the catalytic influence of a faithed man who went silently with a child to a raised garden three and a half weeks before that perception-altering trip to Vietnam. It was the two moments—Norman and the aftermath of the Ia Drang—that effected the private turn, or so I believe, if I cannot prove it. The first brought a human response in RSM, the second a numerical. Which to me only restates the theme and the moral: tragically split man, trying to deny, or at least keep down, the perceived weak underside. Which is really where so much of his strength had lain all along, if he had only known.

Two additional points. In the late 1960s a bitterly anti-American film called *Far from Vietnam* was released in art theaters and on university campuses. The collage of sequences, produced by a team of French directors, showed footage of American bombing runs on the north as a narrator announced in dead-flat tones: "A country with 200 million inhabitants spends more on wrapping paper than 500 million people in India spend on food." Toward the close of the documentary, the viewer is taken to the diminished family of Norman Morrison in Baltimore. It can't be long after the act. Anne is in a sleeveless print dress and speaks in soft cadences and yet with staunchness, too. She's lanky and attractive and has her long dark hair pulled in a ponytail. Her three children are playing about her and in the backyard, where one sees a door leading to a storm cellar, a bike on its side, an overturned trash can, an inquisitive-looking dog. The whole, soft, heartbreaking sequence doesn't amount to more than three or four minutes out of the bitter ninety-minute film; but for me it was like coming upon a preserved eight-millimeter home movie shot in the chaotic and yet somehow accepting aftermath.

Finally: In November 1995, thirty Thanksgivings after a burning, in a piece called "Remembering Norman Morrison," Anne Morrison Welsh wrote in Friends *Journal:* "A great weight came down upon us, creating a Before and an After in our lives. Over the ensuing years we have suffered greatly, and still suffer to this day. However, as we are now more fully able to face this tragedy with honest emotions and sharing, we are gradually becoming healed." Amen.

PART FOUR: SHADOWS, AND THE FACE OF MERCY: 1966 IN AMERICA
The Way It Comes to Us in Dreams

The texts of the Montreal and Chatham speeches are from the OSD (Office of the Secretary of Defense) historian's office. The portrait of the women of Chatham College, class of '66, is drawn essentially from the graduates themselves, and many of those I interviewed are identified in the narrative. The June 17, 1966, content analysis of RSM's speeches came from the OSD historian's office. James J. Kilpatrick's column was published June 5, 1966. Richard L. Strout's piece was June 10, 1966. The *Time* magazine piece on RSM's underestimating the war's spiritual and actual costs was July 5, 1971. Carl Jung's quote on the persona is from *The Basic Writings of C. G. Jung.* Isak Dinesen on sorrows being borne is from her *Out of Africa.* The quote re RSM's being likened to Hitler is from the Austin (Texas) *American-Statesman,* April 30, 1995. Laverne Ransbottom's quote is from the same paper, May 2, 1995.

Nurse data. In the narrative, I said "something like" 11,000 women served in the military in Vietnam, and "maybe 7,500" were nurses. The ironic truth is that in the high-tech McNamarian body-count logarithm war, no one ever computed the exact number of nurses. Were they not thought important enough? (It should be said here that not all nurses were female, as is sometimes forgotten; nor were all nurses Army nurses. The Navy and Air Force brought caregivers to the war, though in far smaller contingents.) Somehow it is easier to find the nursing figures from World War II than from Vietnam. Both the Vietnam Women's Memorial Project and the historian's office for the Army Nurse Corps at the U.S. Army Center of Military History gave me much help in the research for this chapter, but they could not supply the hard McNamarian numbers on nurses. (Diana Hellinger, at the Women's Memorial Project, was especially generous with her time.) According to Major Connie Moore, current historian of the Army Nurse Corps, the reason for the inexactness has something to do with the nature of an undeclared—and unpopular—war. "No one sat and played bean counter," she told me. But for all the softness about data and numbers, there is by now a significant body of Vietnam nursing literature, ranging from oral histories to poetry to autobiography to serious academic studies. In the narrative, I mentioned three popular works, but there are easily a dozen more where women are speaking their feelings in powerful ways—and that is all I was after, anyway. Dan Freedman, *Nurses in Vietnam;* Keith Walker, *A Piece of My Heart;* and Kathryn Marshall, *In the Combat Zone,* were all first-rate in helping me think about the kind of nurse I wanted to write about. An essay by Iris J. West, "The Women of the Army Nurse Corps During the Vietnam War," which was published in the commemorative book for the dedication of the women's memorial in November 1993, provided a very good nursing overview. Sherwin B. Nuland, *The Face of Mercy,* has a fine section on trauma medicine in Vietnam. The 1986 first in-depth study of women and war stress that I referred to in the narrative was done as a dissertation by Jenny A. Schnaier: *Women Vietnam Veterans and Their Mental Health Adjustment;* and while other important studies have since been done, the psychological picture of what the war did to "non-combatant" females is still a subject of debate. The Louis Harris survey I referred to in the narrative is taken from an article on women vets in *Newsweek,* November 12, 1984. (For full book citations, see the bibliography.)

To tell the other side of the chapter—the animus side—I again relied on *The Pentagon Papers;* on the ten-page declassified document of October 14; on RSM's public statements; on Gibbons, *Vietnam War, Part IV;* on newspapers of the day; and on *In Retrospect.* Gibbons has a detailed account of the LBJ/RSM 1966 budget deceptions, though I need also mention Halberstam's *Brightest* and Shapley's *Promise.* Again, Karnow, *Vietnam,* was important to my general understanding of the narrative thread of 1966. My talks with Jack Maddux were very important. For the November incident at Harvard, my interviews with Barney Frank, John Balaban, Michael Ansara, Mark Dyer, Richard Neustadt, and Adam Yarmolinsky were valuable. Neustadt told me of the dinner with faculty that evening, after the fracas, in which RSM was asked why he had given his moving speech at Montreal the previous May, and his answer: It was childish, shouldn't have given it.

The two epigraph quotes leading off the chapter are from, respectively, "Religion in Values in Public Life," fall 1994, Harvard Divinity School Forum; and Nuland, *The Face of Mercy.*

Patty Baker, '66 alum of Chatham College, who is connected now to a divinity school at Northwestern University, wrote several years ago of the deceptively serene alma mater where an animus dipped down and gave a surprising speech: "The city spread around our hilltop. . . . Even the sun, shining red through the smoke of the distant mills, seemed to reinforce that we were set apart in splendid isolation." That was in a piece about her old art prof, Frank Hayes, who put a gun to his head on Yom Kippur the year after she and her classmates had left the manicured hilltop. Things are almost never what they seem on the outside.

Lastly: I once asked Marlene Kramel about how she kept from vomiting and running out of rooms where people were screaming and bleeding to death. It was the adrenaline and the fear, she said. She told me of a fragment-memory of a night (or was it day?) when she was the only RN on duty: just a corpsman and herself. It must have been at the old 85th Evac, not the new 67th, where she later worked in Qui Nhon. Yes, the 85th, because she could see the big, open tents, the corrugated roofs, the Quonsets, the ash cans up on skids. CASUALTY RECEIVING it said in neat stenciling over the door, as if to mock the chaos washing up her insides.

"There were twenty-five malaria patients in there. They had high fevers, they were vomiting. That's who I was supposed to be taking care of." But then the choppers and the doctors running.

"Every one of the doctors is yelling for me. Just me and the corpsman. I didn't know what to do next. Start this. Do that. Everybody's yelling at me. I couldn't do enough. I felt like I hadn't performed adequately."

I said, "Are they screaming?" I didn't mean the doctors, I meant the faces she couldn't see.

"I can't remember. I can't remember blood, even. I can only remember, 'What am I going to do?' And the doctors moving at tremendous speed. And I'm there. And I'm not able to move fast enough. I can't remember anything else. That's all I remember. I don't remember. I remember frantically getting on the phone and saying, 'I've got to have help. It's just me and the corpsman here.' " She blew out a breath. "But obviously it ended."

PART FIVE: WOUND LIKE A WHEEL,
1967–1968 IN AMERICA
In the Shattering

Opening scene: It was built from newspaper accounts and film clips (NBC-TV had the most complete footage); then I layered in what I knew from many sources: my own interviews, archival material, oral histories, other works on the war. For instance, Craig McNamara's pay-phone call to his dad from St. Paul's School is taken from his own account in a series of published sixties oral histories called *From Camelot to Kent State.* Shapley, in *Promise,* has reported in several places in her text on the weekly Wednesday visits to the Boston psychiatrist. Both the note from the White House apparatchik and the typed script for the ceremony were found in the President's Appointment File at the LBJ library. The LBJ "King Lear" quote is from Kearns, *Lyndon Johnson.* Henry Glass, who was at the ceremony, remembered the president coming over and putting his arm around RSM, though the film showed it otherwise.

Bookending set of numbers: The figure of 1,335 dead and 6,131 wounded is from the U.S. Army Center of Military History. Two years after that number had been reached, on October 6, 1967 (it was a Friday in America, and the previous night Carl Yastrzemski had hit a homer in the fourth in the World Series), the *NYT,* page 1, column 1, published this subhead: "AMERICAN CASUALTIES IN WAR NOW EXCEED 100,000." Unofficial totals announced in Saigon put the killed at 13,643, the wounded at 86,635, for a total of 100,278, while the Pentagon's figures were 100,269 killed or wounded through the previous Saturday.

Reston's column in *NYT* on art of resigning: March 9, 1969. Gloria Emerson's comment re chaining them all to the wall is from *Newsweek,* April 15, 1985. Op-ed piece in *NYT* on Tran Van Tuyen as Solzhenitsyn of Vietnam Gulag: September 17, 1976. Tom Wicker's *NYT* column, June 4, 1967, cited the figure of 2,929 casualties in one week. *Newsweek* piece on RSM emplaning for the front was July 17, 1967. The Reuters wire was July 9, 1967. McNaughton's comment re the administration being out of its head was in a memo to RSM, May 8, 1967. Martin Luther King, Jr.'s, comment re America as too arrogant was made April 30, 1967 (from the pulpit of the Ebenezer Baptist Church in Atlanta, with Stokely Carmichael in the congregation). LBJ's humiliation of RSM ("You know so goddamned much about it") is from Gibbons, *Vietnam War, Part III.*

Margaret Chase Smith dust-up of August 11: Many years later, in her hometown of Skowhegan, I found Smith perched like an exotic bird in a sunroom overlooking a wide, curling river named the Kennebec: the memory perfect. She was eighty-eight. She had on a strand of pearls. There was a linen hanky tucked into the band of her silvery wristwatch. "Well, I wouldn't take lies, no, I wouldn't let them lie to me, no matter how big they thought they were," she told me in her plain, measured, Mainer's speech as we sidled onto the topic of RSM.

RSM making secret inquiries to go back to Ford: this story is told in detail in both Peter Collier and David Horowitz, *The Fords;* and in Byrne, *Whiz Kids;* the authors of both books talked to Gossett. I also sought to do my own confirming, but by then Gossett was too aged and ill to come to the phone. Karnow's quote about LBJ and consensus is from his *Vietnam.* Date of RSM's speech to broadcasters: November 7, 1967. Re the newsbreak of his leaving: *Newsweek,* December 11, 1967, in its Periscope section, wrote an excellent account of how it happened. For years it has been the accepted version that the *Financial Times* had the tip first; not exactly. Arthur Schlesinger, Jr.'s, diary comments re RSM's silence are quoted in his *Robert Kennedy and His Times.*

Tran family. Since I've never been anywhere close to Vietnam, and had only bare knowledge of the culture and history of the Vietnamese, the portrait depended crucially, as with all the other portraits in this narrative, on the cooperation of the Tran family itself. Not only did the Trans—but especially Tran Tu Thanh—give themselves over to hours of talk, but they loaned whatever supporting documents and articles they managed to bring with them into diaspora. For example, a small news feature that Thanh's sister Jackie had on the relationship of Giap and Tuyen from the Korea *Herald,* September 27, 1972, was helpful. In terms of interviews: In addition to the family members, the key people who helped me either with the Trans or with Vietnamese culture in general were Bui Diem, Nguyen Dinh Thang, Nguyen Ngoc Bich, James Freeman, Bill Herrod, Nguyen Hoa, and Nguyen Thanh Long. (Of the last two: The former is a Southeast Asian specialist at the Library of Congress; the latter is a refugee Catholic priest in Maryland who ministers to a Vietnamese parish; neither knew the family.) Among books I consulted for background: Joseph Buttinger, *Vietnam: A Dragon Embattled;* Frances FitzGerald, *Fire in the Lake;* Bui Diem, *In the Jaws of History;* James Freeman, *Hearts of Sorrow;* Karnow, *Vietnam;* Bernard Fall, *Street Without Joy* and *Hell in a Very Small Place.* Robert Kaiser's Vietnam series, May 15–16, 1994, the *WP,* influenced me. Mostly, though, it was my trips to Thanh's apartment, to eat that exotic food, to hear that unsentimental sadness, that gave me the slivers of understanding.

The other side. Again, I depended primarily on these: the narrations and analyses of *The Pentagon Papers;* the raw declassified documents themselves (most especially for the May 19 and November 1 memos; and for the meetings of August 18 and November 2); the public statements of RSM; Gibbons, *Vietnam War, Part IV;* transcripts of the CBS/Westmoreland trial; transcripts of RSM's testimony before Congress on 8/25/67; the White House daily diaries that are at the LBJ library; and newspaper and magazine articles of the day. In addition to histories cited in previous chapters, or those named in this chapter, Larry Berman, *Lyndon Johnson's War,* was especially helpful. Phil Goulding, *Confirm or Deny,* was useful in its own silly way as an apologia for RSM, his former boss. Two books that helped me see the story of intervention from *their* side, the Vietnamese side, were Bui Diem, *Jaws,* and Kahin, *Intervention.* My interviews with Morton Halperin, Townsend Hoopes, Paul Warnke, Jack Maddux, Henry Glass, Harry McPherson, John Roche, Clark Clifford, and Douglass Cater all provided slants of light on 1967. John McNaughton's son, Alex, helped me much with his dad, even allowing me to look at desk diaries.

A lot of the chapter, indeed the book, has to do with the tangled questions of loyalty and obedience to authority and the problem of "dirty hands in America." This last is the title of an essay by Michael Walzer ("Political Action: The Problem of Dirty Hands") in *Philosophy and Public Affairs 2* (winter 1973). In addition to a book quoted in the text (*Resignation in Protest*), I also found the following helpful: Sissela Bok, *Lying;* Albert Hirshman, *Exit, Voice, and Loyalty;* Paul Ekman, *Telling Lies.* A June 15, 1968, piece by John Osborne in *The New Republic* was valuable. But by far the two most meaningful pieces for me were by James Thomson: "Getting Out and Speaking Out," *Foreign Policy,* winter 1973; and the now-classic "How Could Vietnam Happen? An Autopsy," *The Atlantic,* April 1968. I got as much from this last as I got from Halberstam describing RSM in autoland in *Brightest,* and my own talks years ago with Jim Thomson in Boston were a major source of early inspiration. (For full book citations, see the bibliography.)

Epilogue: Because Our Fathers Lied

The reprise of the night on the ferry is taken from my *Post Magazine* piece, September 6, 1987; it's as previously published, save for minor updating and stylistic changes. Tanks the Bulgarians had: At a Vietnam symposium at Hampden-Sydney College, September 1993, I heard McCarthy tell an extended version of the story, and it brought down the house. Re buying Jackie a house: It was said at Bethesda Naval Hospital on the night JFK's body was brought back from Dallas; the story is detailed in William Manchester, *The Death of a President.* (What he said to her was that he would buy her back the one she and JFK used to live in in Georgetown.) Diverting to London: William Clark interview. Senator John McClellan's remark was most recently quoted in a George Wilson column, *Navy Times,* May 1, 1995. Costs of war: Nobody really knows, but the $200 billion is an accepted figure. In April 1995, North Vietnam released numbers on dead and missing, military and civilian. The defoliant statistics are from Gabriel Kolko, *Century of War.* The RSM-as-Speer column in *NYT* was July 1, 1971. The SLA papers were found in the court archives of Alameda County, California. The friend of the family I referred to re RSM's once believing that Craig McNamara may have unwittingly brought that person or persons into the McNamara home: This person told me the story on the condition of anonymity. Details of the Himalayan trip are from Mary Joe Goodwin interview and her *A Mountain Reprieve.* Halberstam's letter to the *NYT* was June 10,

1979, and some other details are from Jack Maddux. My RSM series in the *WP* was published May 8–10, 1984, and the Marg quote was in the opening piece. The mourner speaking at her memorial was Lydia P. S. Katzenbach. A wife taking milk with her Scotch: In addition to Jim Wright's memory on this, I asked Marg's late sister, Kay Craig, about it, and she recalled it was so. Leaving Craig's wedding early: Peg Slaymaker and Kay Craig interviews, among others. "A Bridge Too Far" story: William Clark interview. Rio-to-L.A. story: Wally Haas interview. The Jim Wright hospital story: Wright interview. Eric Sevareid story: Sevareid interview. Background of *Interview* magazine piece: Ina Ginsburg interview. *Nightline* attack occurred November 21, 1985, and the quotes are from transcripts. The Larry King appearance was November 24, 1986, and the quotes are from transcripts. *NYT Sunday Book Review*'s assessment of Shapley's *Promise* was January 17, 1993. *USA Today* letter re *In Retrospect* was April 11, 1995, and *NYT* editorial was April 12. *Time* letter was May 15, 1995, and *Sun* cartoon was April 19. Bui Diem's letter in *WP* was May 11, 1995. Two weeks before, on April 27, 1995, also in the *WP,* Townsend Hoopes—who had worked under RSM—wrote a letter to the editor about the "sad, unwitting contradiction of purposes" of "this curious undertaking." He said: "Nor can he articulate practical lessons to be learned, for he is still unable to acknowledge the primary lesson—that a man who is a principal architect of a war policy, but who has come in mid-war to believe that the policy is carrying the country over a precipice, has an obligation to resign and go public with his doubts." RSM's night at Harvard is from audiotapes and transcripts, and also from my interview of a *WP* correspondent who was in the audience. I called John Hurley at his home in Massachusetts.

On May 15, 1995, the four Bolanos brothers, natives of El Paso, all veterans of the war, all recipients of the Purple Heart, filed suit in U.S. District Court for $100 million against Robert McNamara. Their hope was twofold: to force McNamara to come into court and defend himself; and to get an order barring him from reaping profits from his book. "What he has done is the epitome of repugnancy," the youngest of the brothers, Rick Bolanos, said. By sending soldiers into battles that he knew they could not win, McNamara violated his oath of office. Rick Bolanos is a teacher and high-school football coach, and when I spoke to him almost a year after the suit had been announced, he told me that he and his brothers had tried to represent themselves, knowing the odds against it. He said that he and his brothers—Louis, Ben, and Bill—had received thousands of phone calls, letters, and telegrams of support from fellow veterans and others. The suit was eventually dismissed for failure to follow proper legal procedure. (One thing they didn't do was serve notice on McNamara of the suit.) And yet a high-school football coach in west Texas said that legal efforts to make McNamara accountable are going forward, *whatever* the odds.

SELECTED BIBLIOGRAPHY

Albright, Tom. *Art in the San Francisco Bay Area, 1945–1980.* Berkeley: University of California Press; 1980.

Bagenal, Philip. *The Illustrated Atlas of the World's Great Buildings: A History of World Architecture from the Classical Perfection of the Parthenon to the Breathtaking Grandeur of the Skyscraper.* New York: Galahad; 1982.

Bagwell, Beth. *Oakland, Story of a City.* Novato, Calif.: Presidio; 1982.

Balaban, John. *Remembering Heaven's Face: A Moral Witness in Vietnam.* New York: Poseidon Press; 1991.

Ball, George. *The Past Has Another Pattern.* New York: W. W. Norton; 1982.

Berman, Larry. *Lyndon Johnson's War.* New York: W. W. Norton; 1989.

———. *Planning a Tragedy: The Americanization of the War in Vietnam.* New York: W. W. Norton; 1982.

Bok, Sissela. *Lying: Moral Choice in Public and Private Life.* New York: Pantheon; 1978.

Bolen, Jean Shinoda. *The Tao of Psychology: Synchronicity and the Self.* New York: Harper & Row; 1982.

Bowman, John S., ed. *The Vietnam War: An Almanac.* New York: World Almanac Publications; 1985.

Bui Diem, with David Chanoff. *In the Jaws of History.* Boston: Houghton Mifflin; 1987.

Burchell, R. A. *The San Francisco Irish, 1848–1880.* Berkeley: University of California Press; 1980.

Burnham, James. *The Managerial Revolution.* New York: John Day; 1941.

Buttinger, Joseph. *Vietnam: A Dragon Embattled.* Vol. 2, *Vietnam at War.* New York: Praeger; 1967.

Byrne, John A. *The Whiz Kids.* New York: Currency Doubleday; 1993.

Camp, William Martin. *San Francisco.* Garden City, N.Y.: Doubleday; 1947.

Caro, Robert A. *The Years of Lyndon Johnson: The Path to Power.* New York: Alfred A. Knopf; 1982.

――――. *The Years of Lyndon Johnson: Means of Ascent.* New York: Alfred A. Knopf; 1990.

Charlton, Michael, and Anthony Moncrieff. *Many Reasons Why: The American Involvement in Vietnam.* New York: Hill and Wang; 1976.

Collier, Peter, and David Horowitz. *The Fords: An American Epic.* New York: Summit; 1987.

Cooper, Chester L. *The Lost Crusade: America in Vietnam.* New York: Dodd, Mead; 1970.

Copeland, Melvin. *And Mark an Era: The Story of the Harvard Business School.* Boston: Little, Brown; 1958.

Cormier, Frank. *LBJ: The Way He Was. A Personal Memoir of the Man and His Presidency.* Garden City, N.Y.: Doubleday; 1977.

Cowley, Malcolm. *A Second Flowering: Works and Days of the Lost Generation.* New York: Viking; 1973.

Creasey, Maurice. *Bearings.* (Swarthmore lecture.) London: Friends Home Service Committee; 1969.

Cruikshank, Jeffrey L. *A Delicate Experiment: The Harvard Business School 1908–1945.* Boston: Harvard Business School Press; 1987.

Dobie, Charles Caldwell. *San Francisco, A Pageant.* New York: D. Appleton-Century; 1934.

Ekman, Paul. *Telling Lies: Clues to Deceit in the Marketplace, Politics, and Marriage.* New York: W. W. Norton; 1985.

Emerson, Gloria. *Winners & Losers: Battles, Retreats, Gains, Losses & Ruins from a Long War.* New York: Random House; 1976.

Fall, Bernard. *Hell in a Very Small Place: The Siege of Dien Bien Phu.* Philadelphia: J. B. Lippincott; 1966.

――――. *Street Without Joy: Insurgency in Indochina 1946–1963.* Harrisburg, Pa.: Stackpole Books; 1961.

FitzGerald, Frances. *Fire in the Lake: The Vietnamese and the Americans in Vietnam.* Boston: Little, Brown; 1972.

Freedman, Dan, and Jacqueline Navarra Rhoads: *Nurses in Vietnam: The Forgotten Veterans.* Austin: Texas Monthly Press; 1987.

Freeman, James. *Hearts of Sorrow: Vietnamese American Lives.* Stanford, Calif.: Stanford University Press; 1989.

Gettleman, Marvin E. *Viet Nam: History, Documents, and Opinions on a Major World Crisis.* New York: Fawcett; 1965.

Gibbons, William Conrad. *The U.S. Government and the Vietnam War. Parts I, II, III, IV.* Princeton, N.J.: Princeton University Press; 1986; 1989; 1995.

Goldberg, Alfred. *The Pentagon: The First Fifty Years.* Washington, D.C.: Historical Office, Office of the Secretary of Defense; 1992.

Goulding, Phil. *Confirm or Deny: Informing the People on National Security.* New York: Harper & Row; 1970.

Greene, Graham. *The Quiet American.* London: William Heinemann; 1955.

Halberstam, David. *The Best and the Brightest.* New York: Random House; 1972.

———. *The Fifties.* New York: Villard; 1993.

———. *The Powers That Be.* New York: Alfred A. Knopf; 1979.

———. *The Reckoning.* New York: William Morrow; 1986.

Hayes, Walter. *Henry: A Life of Henry Ford II.* New York: Grove Weidenfeld; 1990.

Herndon, Booton. *Ford: An Unconventional Biography of the Men and Their Times.* New York: Weybright and Talley; 1969.

Herring, George C. *LBJ and Vietnam: A Different Kind of War.* Austin: University of Texas Press; 1994.

Hirschman, Albert O. *Exit, Voice, and Loyalty: Response to Decline in Firms, Organizations, and States.* Cambridge, Mass.: Harvard University Press; 1970.

Hoopes, Townsend. *The Limits of Intervention (an inside account of how the Johnson policy of escalation in Vietnam was reversed).* New York: David McKay; 1969.

Horton, Tom. *Superspan.* San Francisco: Chronicle Books; 1983.

Iacocca, Lee. *Iacocca.* New York: Bantam; 1984.

Isaacson, Walter, and Evan Thomas. *The Wise Men: Six Friends and the World They Made: Acheson, Bohlen, Harriman, Kennan, Lovett, McCloy.* New York: Simon & Schuster; 1986.

Johnson, Lady Bird. *A White House Diary.* New York: Holt, Rinehart and Winston; 1970.

Johnson, Lyndon Baines. *The Vantage Point: Perspectives of the Presidency, 1963–1969.* New York: Holt, Rinehart and Winston; 1971.

Johnson, U. Alexis. *The Right Hand of Power.* Englewood Cliffs, N.J.: Prentice-Hall; 1984.

Jung, C. G. *The Basic Writings of C. G. Jung.* New York: Modern Library; 1959.

———. *Synchronicity: An Acausal Connecting Principle.* Princeton, N.J.: Princeton University Press; 1969.

Kahin, George McT. *Intervention: How America Became Involved in Vietnam.* New York: Alfred A. Knopf; 1986.

Karnow, Stanley. *Vietnam: A History.* New York: Viking; 1983.

Kearns, Doris. *Lyndon Johnson & the American Dream.* New York: Harper & Row; 1976.

Kesaris, Paul, ed. *Public Statements by the Secretaries of Defense.* Part 3. The Kennedy and Johnson Administrations 1961–1969. Frederick, Md.: University Publications of America; 1983.

Kierkegaard, Søren. *Fear and Trembling: A Dialectical Lyric.* Princeton, N.J.: Princeton University Press; 1945.

Kolko, Gabriel. *Anatomy of a War: Vietnam, the United States, and the Modern Historical Experience.* New York: Pantheon; 1985.

———. *Century of War: Politics, Conflict, and Society Since 1914.* New York: The New Press; 1994.

Krulak, Victor. *First to Fight: An Inside View of the U.S. Marine Corps.* Annapolis, Md.: Naval Institute Press; 1984.

Lacey, Robert. *Ford: The Men and the Machine.* Boston: Little, Brown; 1986.

Lewis, David L., and Laurence Goldstein, eds. *The Automobile and American Culture.* Ann Arbor: University of Michigan Press; 1983.

———. Mike McCarville, and Lorin Sorensen. *Ford, 1903 to 1984.* New York: Beekman House; 1983.

———. *The Public Image of Henry Ford.* Detroit: Wayne State Press; 1976.

Lewis, Oscar. *Bay Window Bohemia.* Oakland: Yosemite-Dimaggio; 1956.

Luce, Don, and John Sommer. *Vietnam: The Unheard Voices.* Ithaca, N.Y.: Cornell University Press; 1969.

Manchester, William. *The Death of a President: November 20–November 25, 1963.* New York: Harper & Row; 1967.

———. *The Glory and the Dream: A Narrative History of America, 1932–1972.* Boston: Little, Brown; 1974.

Marshall, Kathryn. *In the Combat Zone: An Oral History of American Women in Vietnam.* Boston: Little, Brown; 1987.

McNair, Malcolm P., ed. *The Case Method at the Harvard Business School.* New York: McGraw-Hill; 1954.

McNamara, Robert S. *In Retrospect: The Tragedy and Lessons of Vietnam.* New York: Times Books; 1995.

Michaels, Leonard, David Reid, and Raquel Scherr, eds. *West of the West: Imagining California.* San Francisco: North Point Press; 1989.

Moore, Harold G., and Joseph L. Galloway. *We Were Soldiers Once . . . And Young.* New York: Random House; 1992.

Morris, Charles R. *A Time of Passion: America, 1960–1980.* New York: Harper & Row; 1984.

Morrison, Joan, and Robert K. Morrison. *From Camelot to Kent State.* New York: Times Books; 1987.

Nevins, Allan, and Frank Ernest Hill. *Ford: Decline and Rebirth, 1933–1962.* New York: Charles Scribner's Sons; 1963.

Newman, Daisy. *A Procession of Friends.* New York: Doubleday; 1972.

Newman, John M. *JFK and Vietnam: Deception, Intrigue, and the Struggle for Power.* New York: Warner Books; 1992.

Norman, Elizabeth M. *Women at War: The Story of Fifty Military Nurses Who Served in Vietnam.* Philadelphia: University of Pennsylvania Press; 1990.

Nuland, Sherwin B. *The Face of Mercy: A Photographic History of Medicine at War.* New York: Random House; 1993.

Oberdorfer, Don. *Tet! The Turning Point in the Vietnam War.* Garden City, N.Y.: Doubleday; 1971.

Olson, James S., and Randy Roberts. *Where the Domino Fell: America and Vietnam, 1945–1990.* New York: St. Martin's Press; 1991.

Palmer, Bruce, Jr. *The 25-Year War: America's Military Role in Vietnam.* Lexington, Ky.: University Press of Kentucky; 1984.

Parton, James. *"Air Force Spoken Here": General Ira Eaker and the Command of the Air.* Bethesda, Md.: Adler & Adler; 1986.

Peck, Abe. *Uncovering the Sixties: The Life and Times of the Underground Press.* New York: Pantheon; 1985.

Pettitt, George A. *Berkeley: The Town and Gown of It.* Berkeley: North-Howell; 1973.

Raymond, Jack. *Power at the Pentagon.* New York: Harper & Row; 1964.

Reedy, George. *Lyndon B. Johnson.* New York: Andrews & McMeel; 1982.

Reeves, Richard. *President Kennedy: Profile of Power.* New York: Simon & Schuster; 1993.

Reston, James, Jr. *Sherman's March and Vietnam.* New York: Macmillan; 1984.

Riesenberg, Felix. *Golden Gate: The Story of San Francisco Harbor.* New York: Alfred A. Knopf; 1940.

Rogner, E. A. *The Pentagon: "A National Institution."* Alexandria, Va.: D'Or Press; 1984.

Schandler, Herbert Y. *The Unmaking of a President: Lyndon Johnson and Vietnam.* Princeton, N.J.: Princeton University Press; 1977.

Schlesinger, Arthur M., Jr. *Robert Kennedy and His Times.* Boston: Houghton Mifflin; 1978.

―――. *A Thousand Days: John F. Kennedy in the White House.* Boston: Houghton Mifflin; 1965.

Schnaier, Jenny A. *Women Vietnam Veterans and Their Mental Health Adjustment: A Study of Their Experiences and Post-Traumatic Stress.* Ph.D. dissertation. In vol. 2 of *Trauma and Its Wake,* ed. Charles Figley. New York: Brunner & Mazel; 1986.

Scoggan, Nita. *Pentagon Tidbits.* Manassas, Va.: Royalty Publishing; 1992.

Senator Gravel Edition. *Pentagon Papers: The Defense Department History of United States Decisionmaking in Vietnam,* vols. 1, 2, 3, 4, 5. Boston: Beacon Press; 1971; 1972.

Shapley, Deborah. *Promise and Power: The Life and Times of Robert McNamara.* Boston: Little, Brown; 1993.

Sharp, Ulysses S. G. *Strategy for Defeat: Vietnam in Retrospect.* Novato, Calif.: Presidio Press; 1978.

Sheehan, Neil. *A Bright Shining Lie: John Paul Vann and America in Vietnam.* New York: Random House; 1988.

Shulimson, Jack, and Charles M. Johnson. *U.S. Marines in Vietnam: The Landing and the Buildup, 1965.* Washington, D.C.: History and Museums Division, Headquarters, U.S. Marine Corps; 1978.

Simon, Anne. *No Island Is an Island.* Garden City, N.Y.: Doubleday; 1973.

Singer, June. *Boundaries of the Soul: The Practice of Jung's Psychology.* Garden City, N.Y.: Doubleday; 1972.

Smith, Margaret Chase. *Declaration of Conscience.* Garden City, N.Y.: Doubleday; 1972.

Smith, Perry M. *Assignment: Pentagon. The Insider's Guide to the Potomac Puzzle Palace.* Washington, D.C.: Brassey's (U.S.); 1993.

Sobel, Robert. *Car Wars.* New York: E. P. Dutton; 1984.

Sorensen, Theodore C. *Kennedy.* New York: Harper & Row; 1965.

Stadtman, Verne. *The University of California, 1868–1968.* New York: McGraw-Hill; 1970.

Starr, Kevin. *Inventing the Dream: California Through the Progressive Era.* New York: Oxford University Press; 1985.

Steere, Douglas V., ed. *Quaker Spirituality: Selected Writings.* New York: Paulist Press; 1984.

Stockdale, Jim and Sybil. *In Love & War: The Story of a Family's Ordeal and Sacrifice During the Vietnam Years.* New York: Harper & Row; 1984.

Stone, I. F. *In a Time of Torment, 1961–1967.* Boston: Little, Brown; 1989.

Tanzer, Lester, ed. *The Kennedy Circle.* Washington, D.C.: Luce; 1961.

Taylor, Maxwell D. *Swords and Plowshares.* New York: W. W. Norton; 1972.

Trask, Roger R. *The Secretaries of Defense: A Brief History, 1947–1985.* Washington, D.C.: Historical Office, Office of the Secretary of Defense; 1985.

VanDeMark, Brian. *Into the Quagmire: Lyndon Johnson and the Escalation of the Vietnam War.* New York: Oxford University Press; 1991.

Van Devanter, Lynda. *Home Before Morning: The Story of an Army Nurse in Vietnam.* New York: Beaufort Books; 1983.

———, and Joan A. Furey, eds. *Visions of War, Dreams of Peace: Writings of Women in the Vietnam War.* New York: Warner Books; 1991.

Walker, Keith. *A Piece of My Heart: Stories of Twenty-Six American Women Who Served in Vietnam.* Novato, Calif.: Presidio Press; 1986.

Warnock, C Gayle. *The Edsel Affair.* Paradise Valley, Arizona: Pro West; 1980.

Weisband, Edward, and Thomas M. Franck. *Resignation in Protest: Political and Ethical Choices Between Loyalty to Team and Loyalty to Conscience in American Public Life.* New York: Grossman; 1975.

West, Jessamyn. *Quaker Reader.* New York: Viking; 1962.

Westmoreland, Gen. William C. *A Soldier Reports.* New York: Doubleday; 1976.

Wofford, Harris. *Of Kennedys and Kings.* New York: Farrar, Straus and Giroux; 1980.

Wollenberg, Charles. *Golden Gate Metropolis: Perspectives on Bay Area History.* Berkeley: University of California Press; 1985.

INDEX

CREDITS FOR ILLUSTRATIONS

A NOTE ABOUT THE AUTHOR

Paul Hendrickson has been a feature writer for the Washington *Post* since 1977. He was born in California but grew up in the Midwest and in a Catholic seminary in the South, where he studied seven years for the missionary priesthood. Two decades later this became the subject of his first book, *Seminary: A Search*. He has won a number of journalism awards, including three from the Penney-Missouri feature-writing competition, and has held writing and research fellowships at the Alicia Patterson and Lyndhurst foundations. His previous book, *Looking for the Light: The Hidden Life and Art of Marion Post Wolcott,* was a finalist for the 1992 National Book Critics Circle award. He lives with his wife, Ceil, and their two sons, Matt and John, in Takoma Park, Maryland.

A NOTE ON THE TYPE

The text of this book was composed in Melior, a typeface
designed by Hermann Zapf and issued in 1952. Born in
Nuremberg, Germany, in 1918, Zapf has been a strong
influence in printing since 1939. Melior, like Times Roman
(another popular twentieth-century typeface), was created
specifically for use in newspaper composition. With this
functional end in mind, Zapf nonetheless chose to base the
proportions of his letter forms on those of the golden
section. The result is a typeface of unusual
strength and surpassing subtlety.

Composed by North Market Street Graphics,
Lancaster, Pennsylvania

Printed by Quebecor Printing,
Martinsburg, West Virginia

Designed by Iris Weinstein